ECHOES 30: THREE DECADES OF PULP FANDOM'S GREATEST MA

Table of Contents

ALL ARTICLES WRITTEN BY TOM JOHNSON UNLESS OTHERWISE NOTED

EDITORIAL	3
THE BLOODY SEVEN	4
BY GINGER JOHNSON	
FANTASTIC FIGHTING MEN OF FICTION	26
SOME ORIGINAL PULP HEROES	43
CONTAINING "ALIAS MR. DEATH," "THE ANGEL," "THE AVENGER," "THE BLACK BAT," "THE CRIMSON MASK," "DAN FOWLER—AN ODD ENTRY," "DOCTOR DEATH," "THE EAGLE," "THE GREEN LAMA," "G-X: THE PHANTOM FED," "MARK HAZZARD," "JOHNSTON McCULLEY CHARACTERS," "KI-GOR," "THE MAN IN PURPLE," "THE MASKED DETECTIVE," "THE MASKED WOMAN," "THE MOON MAN & BRONZE SHADOWS," "MR. JONES," "THE PURPLE SCAR," "RED FINGER," "RED MASK," AND "SECRET AGENT 'X'"	
SECRET SERVICE AURELIUS SMITH	87
THE SHADOW'S LADIES	90
AN ESSAY OF NEW PULP HEROES	95
THE COMING OF THE BLACK POLICE	117
CAPTAIN SATAN	128
THE BELMONT SHADOWS	142
THE GREEN GHOST	171
THE BLACK HOOD	200
THE MISSING RED FINGER	207
PULP LADIES	210
THE LONE WOLF DETECTIVE	217
THE CARETAKERS FROM HELL	222
YESTERDAY'S MAN OF TOMORROW	229
BY WILL MURRAY	
THE HOUSE NAME THAT FELL OFF	234
BY WILL MURRAY	
THE MYSTERIOUS DR. ZENG	237
BY WILL MURRAY	
REPRINTS	240
THE GREEN GHOST	241
BY JOHNSTON McCULLEY	
THE RED SWORD	252
BY JOHN DRUMMOND	
DORUS NOEL	280
THE BLACK SHADOW	281
A LOOK BACK	297
BY GINGER JOHNSON	

This package © 2012 Altus Press and Ginger & Tom Johnson. "Yesterday's Man of Tomorrow," "The House Name That Fell Off," and "The Mysterious Dr. Zeng © 2012 Will Murray. All other new articles © Ginger & Tom Johnson. "The Bloody Seven" was originally published in Echoes, Special Issue, June 1982. "Fantastic Fighting Men of Fiction" was originally published in Xenophile #22, 1976. "Alias Mr. Death" was originally published in Altus Press reprint book in 2009. "The Angel" was originally published online in 2011. "The Avenger" was originally published in Nemesis #15, Spring, 1983. "The Black Bat" was originally published in Altus Press reprint volume in 2010. "The Crimson Mask" was originally published in Altus Press reprint volume in 2010. "Dan Fowler—An Odd Entry" was originally published in Echoes #69, February 1992, as "Crimson Crusade." "Doctor Death" was originally published in Altus Press reprint volume in 2008. "The Eagle" was originally published in Altus Press reprint volume in 2012. "The Green Lama" was originally written for Altus Press Green Lama Introduction, but not used. "G-X: The Phantom Fed" was originally published Pulp, Winter, 1978. "Mark Hazzard" was originally published online. "Johnston McCulley Characters" was originally published in Pulp Detectives, 2010. "Ki-Gor" was originally published in Altus Press reprint volume, 2009. "The Man in Purple" was originally published online. "The Masked Detective" is an original article. "The Masked Woman" is an original article. "The Moon Man & Bronze Shadows" was originally published in Echoes #37, June 1988. "Mr. Jones" is an original article. "The Purple Scar" was originally published online. "Red Finger" was originally published in Altus Press reprint volume, 2010. "Red Mask" is an original article. "Secret Agent 'X'" was originally published in Altus Press reprint volume, 2008. "Secret Service Aurelius Smith" is an original article. "The Shadow's Ladies" was originally submitted in Nemesis #16, December 1983. "An Essay of New Pulp Heroes" was originally submitted to Pro Se for inclusion in volume titled Turning The Page, but book was never published, and appears here for the first time. "The Coming of the Black Police" was originally published in Echoes #50, August 1990, as "The Armageddon Syndrome." "Captain Satan" was originally published in James Van Hise' Pulp Masters, 1996, as "The Ambassador From Hell." "The Belmont Shadows" was originally published in Age of The Unicorn #8, 1980, as "From Shadow to Superman." "The Green Ghost" was originally published in the booklet, The Green Ghost, in 1991. "The Black Hood" was originally published in Echoes #52, February 1991. "The Missing Red Finger" is an original article. "Pulp Ladies" was originally published in Golden Perils #8, March 1987, as "Oh, Those Beautiful Ladies." "The Lone Wolf Detective" was originally published in Echoes #58, December 1991 and #67, Feb 1993. "The Caretakers From Hell" was originally published in Echoes #60, April 1992. "Yesterday's Man of Tomorrow" was originally published in the Comico Buyers' Guide, November 11, 1983. "The House Name That Fell Off" is an original article. "The Mysterious Dr. Zeng" is an original article. "The Green Ghost" was originally published in Thrilling Detective, March 1933. "The Red Sword" was originally published in Popular Detective, February 1945. "The Black Shadow" is an original story. "A Look Back" is an original article.

Now Available:
RIDING THE PULP TRAIL

by **Paul S. Powers**
edited by **Laurie Powers**

Here for the first time are twelve Paul Powers stories written in the years after *Wild West Weekly* stopped publication. Six of these stories were published in magazines such as *Exciting Western, Thrilling Western, The Rio Kid Western* and *Thrilling Ranch Stories*. The other six are brand new stories—never before published—that were discovered in 2009. Altogether they make for an outstanding collection of western stories that represent the glory years of the Western short story and the best of Powers' prolific pulp Western career.

340 pages ♦ $24.95

Also Available:

Alias The Whirlwind
BY JOHNSTON McCULLEY

The Complete Adventures of Senorita Scorpion, Volume 1
BY LES SAVAGE, JR.

THIS COLLECTION CONTAINS **6 NEW STORIES** PLUS 6 CLASSIC PAUL POWERS TALES

ALTUS PRESS • THE NAME IN PULP PUBLICATIONS
Available at AltusPress.com, Amazon.com and Mike Chomko Books

Editorial

Ten years ago, when we published *Echoes Revisited*, I never thought there would be a 30th Anniversary issue of *Echoes*. But here we are, ten years later, and thirty years since the first issue of *Echoes* was published in June 1982. We remember the beginning as if it was yesterday, however. And recall the joy of seeing each issue in print. The magazine was a work of love. That it lasted for 100 issues as a magazine can be attributed to that love. From the very beginning, we tried to emulate *Bronze Shadows*, the fanzine that influenced us. To be sure, we were a fanzine, and *Echoes* was strictly amateur in production and appearance. The typos were ours. The writers and artists were the best and most knowledgeable in pulp fandom.

There have been a lot of changes in pulp fandom since those long-ago days. There is still a fascination with the old magazines, and especially the heroic characters that populated them. In those prehistoric years, there was little in the way of reprints, except for Doc Savage and the occasional lesser hero. Fans photocopied issues of *The Shadow*, *The Spider*, and others, and swapped them for photocopies of other pulps with other collectors. Some collectors even sold their photocopies for $5.00 each. It was the only way we could obtain some of the missing stories. Today, reprints abound. Collections are being published of the most rare of the stories, and new readers are discovering them for the first time.

Even new stories are being written featuring the old characters. Some great, some not so great, and some that are pure crap. But the enthusiasm for the old characters is phenomenal. Where the pulp heroes influenced the comic books in their early days, the comic book writers today are turning comic books into pulp stories. This has led me to create the title of Culp Era to replace the old standby, Pulp Era. Everything from cartoons to fairy tales are being called pulp, until now it's indistinguishable from any other medium.

© Tom Johnson

True pulp fandom does still exist, as there are many faithful fans out there keeping the old heroes and pulp magazines alive for future generations. But the new stuff may eventually overwhelm the old. With the Internet, there is no longer need for fanzines like *Echoes* or *Bronze Shadows*. But we had our day, and perhaps it's time to pass the baton to a new generation—the Culp Era fan.

Such is the state of pulp fandom today.

Tom Johnson
January 2012

The Bloody Seven

By Ginger Johnson

In 1979, Mike Cook, publisher of *The Unicorn*, wrote my husband suggesting an article on a group of individuals calling themselves Pulpsters, Inc. (Since changed to Pulpsters, Ltd.) But Tom felt that under the circumstances it wasn't appropriate for him to compose anything on these Brothers, of which he was a member. He thought it might be something for me to look into. For a long time I believed a story was there, just waiting to be told. After months of deliberation and consultation, the following… a biography if you will… is the final result. I would like to dedicate this to the man who first considered these seven men a worthwhile subject—Mike Cook. (Mike's young life was tragically cut short due to a massive heart attack, but Greenwood Press published his research in two large volumes, *Monthly Murders* and *Mystery, Detective, And Espionage Magazines*. Plus, with Stephen T. Miller, Mike coauthored *Mystery, Detective, and Espionage Fiction: A Checklist of Fiction in U.S. Pulp Magazines, 1913—1974*, in two volumes; also from Greenwood Press.)

Characters like The Shadow, The Spider, The Phantom Detective, were a few of the pulp heroes dedicated to protecting mankind from those insidious villains who trod the pages of the magazines each and every issue from 1931 through the early 1950s. One used a mocking laugh; one used a flaming red seal; one used a domino mask—all means of identity.

This article is about another group of men, each dedicated to preserving those fantastic pulps. Their collecting, etc., is not just a hobby to any of these men. It's more a love; a love for the old fiction, and an intense desire for those heroes of yesterday they knew so well, to remain alive for other people; to get others interested so the pulps will live on for future generations.

I am referring to Pulpsters, Ltd.; seven men who have, over the years, written articles and illustrated same, and spent many hours over notes and research in order to breathe life into, and revive the adventures of Doc Savage, Operator #5, Secret Agent "X," and countless others from the pulps. Asking no monetary gain, they are pleased to pass along that feeling of enjoyment which always lingers when they call up The Black Bat, The Green Lama, The Whisperer—and many, many others. You have seen their names, now read about them. I am sure you will agree with me in knowing that they are truly in their own right—The Magnificent Seven.

Here, I would like to pause and give space for the Founder of Pulpsters, Ltd; Wooda (Nick) Carr:

"The Magnificent Seven, The Brothers, The Brotherhood, all terms of respect when I refer to Pulpsters, Inc. We are a small group of men, all pulp magazine collectors and historians who have one goal: To perpetuate the fascinating mystique of the old magazines, not for any monetary gain, but for our love of them. To preserve said magazines for future generations. There has been one change, however: Pulpsters Inc.

From PulpCon in 1977. Pictured from left, going around the table clockwise: Norman Saunders, Harry Steeger, Jack Deveny, Walter Gibson, Earl Kussman, Bob Sampson (partially obscured), Tom Johnson, Nick Carr. This shot was supposed to represent The Shadow cover for "The Lone Tiger," where The Shadow sat at the table with his agents.

is now known as Pulpsters, Ltd. The reason behind this change is simple; there are no more active memberships available to anyone. With the final disposition of all the small golden skulls, symbolic of Pulpster membership, said roles are therefore irrevocably closed. The "Honorary Membership" category is strictly reserved for those who made the original Pulps what they are. We of the seven wish only to now perpetuate the fascinating mystique of the old magazine, not for any monetary gain, but for our love of them. Actually the title 'Honorary' symbolizes a higher degree of commendation than that of the regulars. We are merely followers. At the present time the seven active members who vote are as follows: Earl Kussman, Nick Carr, Jack Deveny, Franklyn Hamilton, Don Hutchison, Tom Johnson, and Robert Sampson. The "Honorary Members" were Harry Steeger, Ryerson Johnson, Alden H. Norton, and Walter B. Gibson. "Honorary Artists" were Norman Saunders and Walter M. Baumhofer, Harold F. Cruickshank, and Frederick C. Davis. All are deceased now. Admitted into "Sisterhood of Pulpsters" were Helen Deveny and Virginia (Ginger) Johnson.

Wooda Nicholas Carr II

On August 7, 1975, Nick Carr and his lovely wife, Eunice, graced our home in Emerado, North Dakota with a visit. They could only stay for a few hours, but during that time I was very impressed by this couple, and I felt very close to both of them. Nick is very knowledgeable on the pulps, and totally dedicated to the revival of interest in the magazines. Eunice and I had a long conversation about many common interests while Nick and Tom retired to the den to pour over Tom's small and meager collection. They were like children, with beams on their faces, as they went from shelf to shelf commenting on cover art and stories.

All too soon the visit had to come to an end. Their schedule called for further stops in North Dakota, to visit relatives before their return trip home. Tom and I enjoyed their visit immensely and are looking forward to many future visits with these fascinating people.

Nick was raised in Jamestown, ND, at the home of his parents, at the State Hospital for the Insane. His father held the position of Superintendent. His mother was on the medical staff. He learned the 'abnormal' side of life before the normal, in a sense, growing up with mental patients.

The family moved briefly to Scottsbluff, Nebraska, then to Santa Cruz, California, where Wooda attended high school. Then his father joined the Civilian Conservation Corps as a physician at Springerville, AZ. There, Nick finished high school. The next move was to Phoenix, AZ, where his father was employed as a psychiatrist, at the Phoenix State Hospital. During the time he lived in Phoenix, Nick worked part-time for Gorimshaw Mortuary and did night duty at the state hospital as a Night Ward Attendant. While attending Phoenix Junior College he majored in English, with particular attention to writing short stories and radio scripts. Following his induction into the Army, because of his medical background, he was assigned to the Medical Department. His interest in writing, which had begun many years before, served him well, in that during his tours of duty at various military hospitals, he wrote newspaper columns and scripted two radio shows for the Armed Forces Bedside Network at Walter Reed Army Hospital, Washington, DC. One was "Tails of the west," and the other was "Radio Workshop." He also wrote for the Medical Technicians Bulletin. This writing interest continued throughout his military career. Now, one might say that it started to blossom when he wrote the Senior Class Play titled "The Old Post Office Stove."

Following military retirement he renewed his association with the old pulp magazines once read in North Dakota as a youngster. He began collecting not only the pulps but recordings of such programs as *The Lone Ranger*, *The Green Hornet*, *The Shadow* and

Wooda Nick Carr Facts:

Pen Names: Nick Carr and Dickson Thorpe.
Age: Born 2 December 1923 in Jamestown, ND.
Marital Status: Married to Eunice Elizabeth Meyer, 30 May 1955 in Fort Wayne, Indiana, Previous marriage to Pearl Prentice. She passed away 13 December 1954 from cancer. Both are R.N.s.
Physical Description: Height: 5'9." Weight: 160 lbs. Hair: white. Eyes: brown, wears glasses and has scar on upper lip due to childhood accident.
Parents: Dr. John D. Carr, M.D., Dr. Agnes Thorpe Carr, M.D. Both deceased.
Sister: Carlotta Carr Brown. Younger than her brother.
Education: Graduated Springerville, AZ, Round Valley High School, May 1941. Attended two years Phoenix Junior College, Phoenix, AZ prior to his induction into the military service.
Military Service: Entered the Army on 28 October 1942. Tours of duty include Europe and the Far East, and within the United States. Served with the First Cavalry Division in Korea as a Chief Psychiatric Technician. Made a career of the military. Retired on 1 May 1966, with the permanent rank of E-7.
Sports: Swimming.

Little Orphan Annie.

This led to his writing for many different pulp-oriented magazine They include: *Bronze Shadows, Pulp Era; The Mystery Readers Newsletter, The Mystery Fancier, Stan's Weekly Express, Pulp, The Good Old Days, Penny Dreadful, Xenophile, Fantasy Mongers, Bakka Magazine, The Doc Savage Club Reader* and *The Unicorn*. One short story, "The Bird" was penned for *Skullduggery Magazine*. Two books: *America's Secret Service Ace*, and *G-8, The Flying Spy* were published under the Pulp Press banner. His newspaper articles include those found in the Jamestown *Sun* and *The Lacy Leader*, Lacy, Washington. He contributed an article for *Unmasked Heroes of the Pulps*, by James Hanos, published in Greece. He assisted in writing segments of articles on Operator #5 and G-8 for *Captain George's Whizzbang*. One single article appeared under his by-line for this same publication titled "The Scarecrow."

He says, "If there is any literary blood flowing in my veins it is probably due to the fact that I am related to the poet Robert Burns and my cousin is the noted mystery writer, John Dickson Carr."

His writing remains strictly a hobby and his dedication to the preservation of the old pulp magazines is beyond question. His influence on my husband and myself, as with many others, will remain a lifetime. The respect that we hold for this fine human being can never die.

The following interview took place in 1982.

Ginger: Who is your favorite pulp character?
Nick: Operator #5, with G-8 second, then The Spider.
Ginger: Why is Operator #5 your favorite?
Nick: Because of his patriotism, love of country, and dedication to duty. This is also very true of The Spider and G-8, and it ran as one underlying theme in all of the novels. During my youth in the thirties that word 'patriotism' had meaning, and one growing up became acutely aware of his flag and country. I find this is sadly lacking today.

Ginger: Do you have a favorite novel?
Nick: No, but the early Frederick C. Davis' Operator #5 stories do stand out in my mind today, There is also one particular novel of the Purple Invasion series titled "The Bloody Forty-Five Days," that has always remained buried within my subconscious. It was this story in fact that really awoke my interest in the bloody pulps once again. Apparently it was a feeling that had remained dormant since childhood. I located the epic in a used bookstore one day and asked the owner if he could get more of them. Also the revival of Doc Savage in paperback was another catalyst.

Ginger: Do you have a favorite pulp author?
Nick: No. In my mind all of those who penned the hero pulps were rather unique in their own right. In growing up, I never dreamed the names of Curtis Steele, Maxwell Grant and Kenneth Robeson were not real people. Among my greatest thrills were meeting Walter Gibson, Ken Crossen, Ryerson Johnson and Mrs. Lester Dent.

Ginger: Since you write articles, was there anyone who influenced you to write, or what to write?
Nick: When it comes to doing Pulp oriented articles, I probably owe much to Fred Cook and his wonderful publication *Bronze Shadows*. Fred gave me a free hand to pen what I chose, with little editorial comeback. In looking back over some of those early articles I wonder how on Earth Cook ever put up with some of them. I was free to say whatever crossed my mind and had a tendency then to write my own fiction version of what might have happened to certain pulp characters. Since then, I resolved to stick to the facts, ma'am, as they were recorded by the original authors and have seldom ventured from that pathway. In my book *G-8, The Flying Spy*, for example, I did this in commenting how G-8 just might have been one of the pilots who shot down Kong from atop the Empire State Building. This is conjecture. I think now the writers should stay with the facts. Like Tom Johnson, I admire the work of Robert Sampson. This man is a fine writer and I have yet to come across anyone who can touch his style. Sometimes I have a tendency to go wondering off in various directions when doing an

article. Sampson has reminded me of this a few times and as a result my work now (I think) remains on the straight and narrow with little ventures into the side avenues.

Ginger: What issue of *The Spider* did your letter appear in?

Nick: "The Spider and the Flame King," December 1942. I never saw the letter until just a few years ago when someone called my attention to it. I think that man was Alan Grossman. Probably the reason I missed it was because in October of 1942, I left Phoenix, AZ, going into the military service. I had literally no time for much reading at that time.

Ginger: When did you get the idea for Pulpsters, Ltd.?

Nick: You won't believe this, but I can't pinpoint the exact date. It was a few years ago now however. At the time I never thought it would go beyond the simple comradeship of the original group.

John R. Deveny

On July 1, 1975, Tom, Kevin and I were on our way to Texas for a vacation from North Dakota and the military. We decided to detour into Minnesota for a visit with some friends that we had never met. We had known them from our correspondence, as many people in collecting meet.

"Captain Jack" Deveny and his lovely, gracious wife Helen came out to meet us and we were thrilled to finally meet this couple face to face. We went inside their beautiful home and set down to a long awaited talk. Jack has a den in his house with a sign above the door stating "Captain's Quarters." Inside, the first thing that caught my attention was a painting in oil of Doc Savage, by Frank and Brian Hamilton. It was fantastic!

We then got involved in looking at Jack's complete collection of G-8, and a selection of other hero pulps such as *Secret Agent "X," The Shadow, Doc Savage* and an issue of *Amazing Stories* featuring the first appearance of Buck Rogers, plus many, many other items. In addition to all this, Helen has a collection of Big

Jack Deveny at PulpCon in 1977.

Little Books—which included the three issues of The Shadow.

The friendly hospitality that we received from this fine family is common among collectors today. We felt that we had met life-long friends. As with all good things, the visit was over too soon. We had to be on our way. We took with us the hope of a future visit with these fine people.

Northwest Airlines hired Jack as an aircraft groomer in 1940. He served in the Navy during WWII. During the war, he married Helen Harrington, his Minnesota sweetheart, in New York City. After the war, Jack returned to Northwest where he continued his career until his retirement as a Boeing 727 Captain in 1981.

Jack was born the youngest of five children. "The early years were difficult during the depression," he says, "but I can't really realize the difficulty of those times as we always had food and a place to live. As Moss Hart said in his book, *Act One*, "You really cannot realize poverty if you are surrounded by it and it is only at some later date you realize the world is somewhat unequally divided between the rich and the poor!"

Jack recalls Saturday mornings in Sioux Falls where he would make his trek up and down the alleys checking the trash cans for aluminum pots and pans, copper wire, zinc jar covers… anything to sell to the junkman… a successful morning would probably realize from 10 to 15 cents. This would be enough for a double feature along with a cartoon and one chapter of some on-going serial at the Western or Capital Theaters. Buck Jones, Ken Maynard, Bob Steele, Tim McCoy, Hoot Gibson and Tom Tyler all come to mind. Five cents was the admission, which would leave enough for a hamburger or Coney Island.

In about the seventh grade, Jack says he managed to acquire a job selling *Liberty Magazine*. Newspaper routes were impossible to obtain, as most kids passed the route on to their brothers. *Libertys* sold for five cents from which he made 1½¢. Fifty magazines was a spectacular week. He used to pick up his weekly supply of *Libertys* at the Dakota News Agency in the alley behind the Cataract Hotel—they were also the distributors of the other magazines, including the pulps. He says, "That smell of pulps is still with me, and I can see the stacks of pulps: *The Spider, The Shadow, Doc Savage, Dare-Devil Aces* and of course *G-8 and His Battle Aces."* His first pulp was *G-8* and he was hooked on that series permanently.

His family moved from Sioux Falls to the Minneapolis-St. Paul area in 1935, to a farm where they raised chickens and garden vegetables. Every Saturday there was a trip into town to sell chickens, eggs and vegetables. The treat of the trip was a double feature at The Bijou (still 5¢, and a chance to buy some coverless pulps at the used magazine and bookstore. *G-8s* were 2 for 5¢… same for other comparable pulps. G-8 is still one of his favorites, although he has diversified a lot over the years.

Jack was always engaged in sports through school and on the sandlots. Although he was involved with hockey, basketball, track and football, his favorite was baseball, and in 1939 he was signed to a contract by the St. Louis Cardinals organization. In the spring of 1940 he reported to their minor league training camp at Springfield, Missouri. He played only a couple of weeks in the Class B Western Association when he injured his throwing arm sliding into third base.

He then went back to Minnesota driving a truck for an excavating company and playing semi-pro baseball later that summer. Driving a truck at 85¢ an hour was good money in 1940, but there was not any

---

Jack Deveny Facts:

Age: Born 23 March 1921, on a small farm near Artesian, South Dakota.
Marital Status: Married Helen Louise Harrington in July 1944, in New York City, New York.
Education: Attended grade schools through the seventh grade in Wessington Springs and Sioux Falls, South Dakota. The family moved to Minneapolis, Minn in 1935 and he graduated from Bloomington (Minneapolis suburb) High School in 1939. In addition would be several service aviation courses, University of Minnesota Extension Courses, many technical courses and classes, various airlines comprehensive and specialized classes and a correspondence course in electronics.
Children: Four; Michael, Kathleen, Leigh and Deborah.
Grandchildren. Five: Michael, Patrick, Ryan, Dawson and Hillary.
2012 Postscript: Deveny, Captain (ret.) John R. "Captain Jack" age 85, of Cape Coral, FL, formerly of Edina, passed on, December 30, 2006. He is survived by Helen, his wife of 62 years; children, Michael (Theresa), Kathleen (Mark), Leigh (Gregory), and Deborah (Douglas).

future there, so he applied for a job at Northwest Airlines and was hired as a ship cleaner in December 1940 at 28¢ an hour… pay was poor but the future appeared bright.

A year later he started his apprenticeship as a mechanic. Initially he worked in the propeller shop, and then, line service. On Navy Day in 1942, in Kansas City, Kansas, he joined the Navy. After boot camp at the Great Lakes Naval Training Station, Jack was assigned to Naval Air Transport Squadron 3 at Fairfax Airport, Kansas City, Kansas, as an Aviation Machinists Mate 2c. Three months later he was upgraded to AMM1c and a year later to aviation Chief Machinist Mate. Over the next 39 months he served with the Naval Air Transport Squadron's 2, 3, 4, 10, 12 and 13… in Kansas City, New York, Alameda, Hawaii, Kwajalein, Guam and Leyte.

Incidentally, he declined to return to the St. Louis Cardinals organization after obtaining the job at Northwest Airlines. A professional ball player who was a close friend was responsible for some excellent advise in this regard… During the war he played with various service teams and after the war, with semi-pro teams on weekends.

Jack was discharged from the service in January of 1946 and returned to the airline, obtained his Aircraft and Powerplant licenses and advanced to Master Mechanic and in 1948, to Crew Chief. Late in 1948, he became a Flight Mechanic on the DC-4s and in September of 1949, a Flight Engineer on the Boeing 377 Stratocruiser. In 1957, Jack and five other Flight Engineers purchased a 1946 Cessna 140 and started their pilot training. Five of the six eventually became Captains with Northwest Airlines. One passed away from a heart attack before completion of his pilot training. 1963 was Jack's first year as co-pilot and in 1968 he checked out as a Captain. The aircraft he flew were the Douglas DC-6 and DC-7, Lockheed L-188 Electra, Boeing 707 and 727. Over the years as a flight crewmember, he accumulated 25,000 hours.

He is officially on a medical retirement now until his scheduled retirement date of March 23, 1981. (Jack has since retired, of course.)

Jack's wife, Helen, (Sisterhood of Pulpsters) was born in Minneapolis, MN and has lived in or near the city all her life, except for 1944 and 1945 while Jack was at the Naval Air Station in Brooklyn, N.Y.

Helen attended St. Olaf College in Minnesota before her marriage. She says, "I like to think my art training there has made my life more interesting and helped me appreciate the talent of a true artist such as Frank Hamilton."

Helen's interests have always been in fields related to art, whether it be gardening, and flower arranging, painting or carving, needlework and sewing, interior decorating or cooking. She enjoys them all.

Helen enjoys the artwork of the pulps most of all, although she also reads what takes her fancy. She has a great respect for Edgar Rice Burroughs' contribution to the pulps, among others.

Interview conducted in 1982.

Ginger: I know from our visit to your home that you and Helen have many collections. Can you name a few of them?

Jack: We collect boy's books, pulps/radio premium memorabilia, 16mm movies of first runs such as some of the best Bogarts and other favorites from that great era of movies; Northwest Airlines and Milwaukee Railroad souvenirs. Big Little Books. Old radio shows. Big Band Music (especially remote broadcasts from the '30s and '40s). Some original art. Miscellaneous jazz. Certain Sunday comic pages…

Ginger: What are your favorite pulps and stories?

Jack: I'll pick just a few: "The Living Shadow" and "Gangdom's Doom" by Maxwell Grant; "The Blizzard Staffel" and "Fangs of the Serpent" from *G-8* by Robert Hogan; miscellaneous others… *Unknown, Bluebook, Argosy, Famous Fantastic Mysteries* and *Fantastic Novels*; "The Blind Spot" and other stories by Homer Eon Flint and Austin Hall; many by A. Merritt such as "The Moon Pool;" Dr. Syn series by Russell Thorndike; Fu Manchu series

Jim Steranko, Walter Gibson and Frank Hamilton.

by Sax Rohmer; Alexander Botts series by Wm. Hazlett Upson (a hilarious series with Botts as a bumbling Earthworm Tractor salesman); Tarzan and other series by Edgar Rice Burroughs; Thornton W. Burgess Nature and Animal stories; Horatio Alger and Horatio Alger Jr. stories which had a profound effect on my life.

Ginger: Who is your favorite artist?

Jack: Frank Hamilton, who, like wine, improves with age. A multi-talented and fine man. In my estimation his work can be compared with the best of Hal Foster, Alex Raymond, J. Allen St. John, Virgil Finlay and others....

Franklyn Hamilton

Neither Tom nor I have ever met this very talented man face to face. We both feel that we know him and have for years. We have corresponded by mail for years and talked at great length over the telephone. Although the phone calls and letters are most welcome, I feel that I know him best by his art-works. Frank has done so many things over the years for articles by Tom, Nick, Bob and so many others that choosing a favorite is an almost impossible task. I know my favorite was the tribute he did to John Wayne that Mike Cook put in the October 1979 issue of *The Unicorn*. As John Wayne has always been my favorite, and his death was a great loss, I wrote to Frank and praised his interpretation of John's feeling to his country. Frank, in turn, sent me something that I shall treasure for all my days; an autographed copy of this great work by this genius. The tribute is a personal favorite because Frank and I share this loss, and the tribute says how John Wayne felt about this great Country of ours. I'm sure that John would have liked it as much as I do. Well… almost. Thanks again, Frank.

Tom and I are eagerly looking forward to meeting this man someday. We already know that he is one of the best.

Shortly before WWII, Frank and Dolores married. He gave all his copies of *The Shadow* and *Doc Savage* pulps to his boyhood chum, Charles T. Barner, who also had a considerable number of *Shadows*. The years passed and memories of the pulps faded, as did his interest in art. When Bantam re-issued Doc Savage in 1964 a spark of nostalgia struck, but these paperbacks were all that Frank could find to revitalize his feelings for the pulps.

Frank remembers telling Brian, when he was 14 years old, about The Shadow, The Spider and the others, and stressing vehemently that Bama's Savage was an imposter, and wishing that he still had the Baumhofer poster so he could show Brian the Real Doc Savage!

In 1968 Charles Barner found about 38 *Shadows* that had escaped the paper drives of the war, and gave them to Frank. Most were coverless, but they were more than enough to get him into his own little, private, one-man fandom… or so he thought. He dug the old paint box out and started copying the covers that were there. He soon developed an appetite for more pulps as his paintings turned out well, considering the years he had been away from it. The artwork he considers most natural for him is black and white stippling. He is very apprehensive about doing oils, but I think he does a fantastic job with any style.

Frank gradually bought a number of *Doc Savage* pulps, but really wanted only those with Baumhofer covers. By the time he found out Baumhofer had done none after 1936, he had bought, through the mail, quite a few that he didn't really want. He now has all the Baumhofers from issue 1 to his last in 1936.

Frank was also buying *Shadows,* through the mail, from all over the country until he only needed three to have the complete run of 325. He finally managed to achieve number one, "The Living Shadow." Later on he would receive as a gift from Jack Deveny the two remaining *Shadows* that completed his set.

In 1970 or 1971, Frank was introduced to the fanzine *Pulp,* by Bobby Van, who he met in a book store in New York. He subscribed and found names and addresses of fellow collectors… fans, like himself. He would never be the only pulp collector again! In fact, *Pulp* was where he made his 'fanzine' debut. In the fourth issue he had published, anonymously, a small sketch of Captain Fury, followed by another of Doc Savage in the fifth issue.

Bob Weinberg then asked to use one of his Shadow drawings on the cover of Frank Eisgruber's *Gangland's Doom.* Frank sent Winberg two drawings which were well accepted. They also brought a letter, a phone call and an autographed copy of *Gangland's Doom* from Walter B. Gibson; who he later met in New York in 1975 and again at Frank's own home in 1976.

Frank Hamilton Facts:

Born: June 10, 1919, in Gloucester, Mass. **Died—**Jan. 28, 2008.
Marital Status: Married Dolores on September 1, 1940, in Gloucester, Mass. Delores Hamilton, Frank's wife passed away January 13, 2002.
Parents: Esther Abbis (Wilkie) and Frank Howard Hamilton; both deceased. **Brothers/Sisters:** Had a half-brother, William Earnest Hamilton, who died many years ago, and Frank says, "He could make a piano sit up and roll over when he played it."
Children: Three: two sons and one daughter. Bruce is a fine police officer, married with two children; Brian is a very talented artist, perpetrator of the Lamont Award, and single; Bonnie is a good wife and mother of two.
Grandchildren: Four: Shawn, Heather, Craig & Paula.
Education: Graduated from Gloucester High School in 1936.
Associated with, but not in, the military before and during WWII.

In 1974 Earl Kussman wrote to Bob Weinberg praising the covers. Bob sent the letter to Frank. They became fast friends, via the mail, and Earl was responsible for Frank meeting and joining (again by mail) the group known amongst themselves as Pulpsters, Ltd. He continues his art to the pleasure of everyone who sees it.

Some time back he collaborated with Mike Avallone on a series of illustrations and articles on the pulp heroes of yesterday. This combined work from these very talented men were printed in the *Mike Shayne Mystery Magazine.*

Not enough can be said about either of these men's contributions and talent in writing and art work. Each man's contributions to the history of the pulp magazines are highly acclaimed, but by combining their talents they have reached a high degree of expertise in bringing beauty and knowledge to those not familiar with the 'Bloody Pulps', which is what Pulpsters, Ltd., is all about. Bravo, Gentlemen!

Don Hutchison

Although I have not met Don either, we know him from his letters and his articles in different periodicals. He is a very dedicated and informative writer. The love he has for the pulps comes through in his writing. Anyone reading his articles wants more of them to appear.

His interests are varied. He admits to having a teenager in his brain who still loves Doc Savage, the world of Oz, Chandu the Magician, John Carter and Dejah Thoris.

Richard Wentworth and his Nita, King Kong, Captain Nemo, Tom Sawyer, Sheena, Sherlock Holmes, Tarzan, Fu Manchu, Rudolph Rassendyll, G-8 the Master Spy, Randolph Scott, dinosaurs, She-Who-Must-Be-Obeyed, the Park Avenue Hunt Club, Mad Carew, La of Opar, King Arthur, Buck Rogers, Phineas Fogg, Robin Hood, John Wayne, Karloff and Lugosi, Captain Midnight and his Secret Squadron, The Phantom Detective, The Green Lantern, The Shadow, the Daredevils of the Red Circle, Spy Smasher and many, many others.

Tom and I are looking forward to, one day, getting together with Don and his family and talking aver the common interests between us.

The pulps were not Don's only entry into the land of imagination. Before he reached school age, he says he remembers his mother reading the 'funnies' to him: Brick Bradford, Little Orphan Annie, Boots and her Buddies, etc. At the age of four, he lived for the sound of the daily newspaper hitting the front porch. By the time kindergarten rolled around, he was able to read, and was hopelessly hooked on fantasy. His mother never learned to read for enjoyment, but she was able to instill, a love of reading and of fantasy to him through her daily chore of reading the funnies to her one and only son.

Later, Don graduated to the early four-color comic books; he says he had them all. *Action Comics* #1, the first *Batman, More Fun, Nickel Comics, Whiz* #1, and more. He kept them all in a large cardboard box. At the age of ten he contracted Scarlet Fever. After recovery, the doctor calmly suggested to Don's mother that she burn everything burnable that he had come in contact with. Out went the comic collection. It was a loss he never got over. And little did his mother suspect that someday those same comics would be worth far more than the house they lived in.

Somewhere during that time, Don discovered the public library and became an inveterate reader; not

---

Don Hutchison Facts:

Born: April 21, 1931, in Toronto, Ontario.
Marital Status: Married to a wonderful lady named Jean.
Education: Graduated from Northern Secondary School in 1958.
Description: Height 5'9," Weight 155 lbs, eyes brown, hair brown, sports a short, trimmed beard that is brown (he says it's turning white, like snow dropping to the bottom).

From left: Bob Sampson, Helen Deveny, Jack Deveny, Diane Sampson, Don Hutchison, Earl Kussman, Frank Hamilton and Nick Carr.

strange for an only Child—about par for the course, you might say.

Don's father was not an educated man. He was the son of a farmer who married young, and migrated to the big city just in time for the Great Depression. He never lacked for a job, but he did back-breaking work for as little as six dollars a week. By the time Don started growing, his father had worked his way from truck driver to fuel oil dispatcher, and things started looking up.

A friend of Don's father first introduced him to the pulp magazines. He passed on a pile of old *Shadows*. Don had been acquainted with The Shadow from the radio melodramas and the Street & Smith comic, of course, but there was something about the pulp Shadow that seemed special. It may have been the covers. Or it may have been that Don was outgrowing comic books as a source of literary inspiration. Probably, a combination of both.

Later, Don discovered a stack of issues of *The Spider* at a local used magazine shop. They cost him a nickel each and he sneaked them into the house two at a time under his sweater. It was a case of love at first sight. The fact that he felt impelled to sneak the *Spiders* into their house was part of the fascination: Those beautiful, half-clothed women, the grotesque madmen waving blow-torches, chains and whips, or pouring molten metal from bubbling cauldrons. And those titles! "Hordes of the Red Butcher," "Death Reign of the Vampire King," "Laboratory of the Damned," "The City That Dared Not Eat." The comics, and even The Shadow, began to pale into insignificance.

Don searched out other pulps and came up with *G-8 and His Battle Aces.* While it doesn't do a thing for him now, alas, he still remembers his first reading of G-8's December 1938 adventure, "The Bloody Wings of the Vampire." Don told me, "It scared the pants off me. I was hopelessly hooked on the pulps and their preposterous, flamboyant, larger-than-life heroes. Time has not diminished the memory of that first enthusiasm. As we grow older we cannot always relive those early enthusiasms, so we collect the artifacts that once stirred such excitement in "the boy with tennis shoes, the high fevers, the multitudinous joys, and the terrible nightmares."

As a young man Don spent most of his summer vacations on his grandparents farm about 40 miles North of Toronto, thus enjoying the best of both worlds. As an only child, he read everywhere he went, country and city. And attended all the movies it was possible to see, mostly the Saturday matinees.

After graduation, he promptly got a job working for IBM. Although he hated the work at IBM, he stayed for nine years, until desperation forced him into making a giant leap. His love of movies, combined with an interest in acting, writing and photography, led him to send a brochure from Brooks Institute's Motion Picture Production Course in Santa Barbara, California. They sent him the information and he decided to make a wild career leap at 27 years of age. Since then he has been actively engaged in the motion picture industry; as a film editor, then editor/cameraman, and now as a full time Director of Photography, mostly on television documentaries. In the 22 years his work has taken him all over North America, and into such disparate parts of the world as West Africa, the Caribbean and the high Arctic. This coming summer he may be filming a major series

In Egypt, Israel, Turkey and Jordan for the Encyclopedia Britannica PBS. Or he may not. One thing about his line of work—it's never predictable.

Like his friend Nick Carr, Don's interest in the old pulps picked up somewhere around the time that Fred Cook began publishing *Bronze Shadows.* He met Fred and Rusty Havelin at the 1967 Science Fiction Worldcon in New York and began collecting the pulps again about that time.

Don never did write anything for Fred's magazine, but began doing articles on the pulp heroes for a local magazine, *Captain George's Whizzbang,* and later for such other periodicals as *Xenophile, The Monster Times, Penny Dreadful, Bakka Magazine, Black Box, Rocket's Blast and Comic Collector,* and *Collector's Dream.* In 1974, *The Globe and Mail,* Canada's national newspaper, paid him 20¢ a word to do a lead article on Doc Savage for their entertainment section—an assignment he says he would have gladly handled for free if they had only known. In the course of researching the article, he conducted a telephone interview with producer George Pal on the set of his Doc Savage movie in Hollywood. Mr. Pal was a real gentleman and they talked about Doc and the pulps for more than half an hour, during which time Mr. Pal assured Don that he was playing the character absolutely straight for the movie; a promise that he was not allowed to keep. A few years ago Don appeared a number of times on *The Great Canadian Time Machine,* a weekly television series on such nostalgic subjects as old movies, comics and the pulps. Needless to say, they covered the pulp era pretty thoroughly. Later, Don was interviewed on a radio program along with Walter Gibson, but never did get to hear the finished results.

Don has been a science fiction fan since the 1940s when he first discovered H.G. Wells' *Time Machine,* and such SF pulps as *Planet Stories, Famous Fantastic Mysteries, Captain Future,* et al. While still in high school, he was on the committee for the Torcon, Canada's first World SF Convention, and had the same honor more than two decades later when this city hosted its second World Con. Both conventions featured Robert Bloch as Guest-of-Honor.

In answer to my question of his favorite pulp

character, Don related, "My favorite hero pulp magazine remains *The Spider*. To this day there is something in me that responds to Norvell Page's frenzied, apocalyptic visions of a super hero who is not infallible. Richard Wentworth makes mistakes and people die because of them. The Spider's war on criminality is long and bloody; he is a victim as well as victor in the battles waged. But because Wentworth has that inner spark that fanaticism if you will, that pushes him farther than the others could probably stand to go, he triumphs. It is a pulp vision clothed in flesh and blood. It is an epic series of encounters, perhaps the only true epic in the history of the hero pulps, and the differences in Page's own belief in the character he writes about. It was the character of Richard Wentworth that made the magazine so popular. In all the pulp field, Wentworth stood alone as… the Master of Men."

Thomas E. Johnson

Tom is the hardest of all these men for me to write about. We met in 1958, and married in 1961.

Tom introduced me to pulps when he started re-collecting them, for which I am deeply grateful, for they hold a fascination for anyone.

Tom has a knack for reading deeper into a story and coming up with articles on little known or recognized facts or characters. As with Nick Carr, Don Hutchison, Bob Sampson and countless other people, Tom loves the pulps and this carries through in the articles he writes.

Pulp, Doc Savage Club Reader, The Unicorn, Xenophile and *Megavore* are some of the publications that Tom has written for. He enjoys writing up these articles that will keep the interest in the pulps alive for all, and he does this very well. He wrote several articles for *Unmasked Heroes of the Pulps*, published in Greece by Dimitri (Jim) Hanos, and has contributed one book for Bob Weinberg's Pulp Classic series; *Secret Agent X-A History*, with Will Murray.

Tom was the youngest of three children. He delighted in making life miserable for his two older sisters by catching snakes, lizards and various insects and threatening to put them on the girls. Born of poor parents, Tom lived in the country with his family, where they ate whatever his father could trap or grow.

Before the World War II, Tom's father had been in the Army—assigned to the Cavalry Division, but when the war broke out, he enlisted in the Navy. After the war, and return to civilian life, he found no work in Seymour, so he packed up his family and moved to Wichita Falls, Texas.

In a small apartment above a cafe, and overlooking the street of 'skid-row' and the train depot, Tom got his first taste of big city life. His only playground was the streets and sidewalks, which he shared with the drunks and winos of the 'badlands.' At night, the streets were often filled with menacing drunks, the denizens of his area, when fights (fists, knives and guns) broke out in the beer dives and shooting galleries along the street. But he learned to dodge those menacing, reaching hands that seemed to threaten little boys. It was the mornings that he feared the most, as it was his duty to go after the fresh milk and bread for breakfast, and the bottom of the narrow stairwell usually contained a victim of the previous

Tom Johnson Facts:

Pen Names: John Edwards and Eddy Thomas.

Born: July 26, 1940, in Seymour, Texas.

Marital Status: Married Virginia Elaine (Martin) on 12 January 1961, in Wichita Falls, Texas.

Children: One: Kevin Edward, born 17 July 1966.

Parents: Frederick William Johnson (deceased) and Myrtle May (Hill) deceased. Sisters: Two: Dorothy Place and Wanda McDowell (deceased).

Favorite Sport: Boxing/Judo/Karate.

Military: Spent 20 years in the Army as a Military Policeman, from 24 November 1958 to 1 February 1979. Retired as a non-commissioned officer (E-6).

night—a drunk, passed out from too much booze, or beaten up and left there by others.

To help make money for his parents, Tom sold newspapers at night, along this strip of bars and shooting galleries. He learned to 'hit' the bars early, before the drinkers became too drunk, and while they still had money. This way he received some big tips. But eventually the 'boss' of the newsboys found out about the big tips and started shaking the boys down at night for their tips.

But there were also some good memories of the 'badlands'; Tom would go over to the train depot when the trains came in, and listened to the returning soldiers talk about the 'big war', and their adventures. On the corner of the street was a drug store, where Tom would spend hours looking through the comics, and thrilling to the covers on those beautiful pulp magazines which made him daydream of the action depicted in those scenes. Around the corner, and down the street from the drug store (but still a section of the badlands) was the Gem Theater—a movie house that played adult shows in the evening, but every Saturday morning had the films that thrilled every kid; for nine cents Tom could see those fantastic B westerns (double features every Saturday), the Bowery Boys or Bud & Lou. Plus those wonderful 15 minute serials. An added thrill was always the previews of the adult movies that were playing that evening. ("It was here that I learned about girls," he says, jokingly.)

The 'badlands' had a policeman who walked the beat, and Tom learned to respect and admire these men who put their lives on the line every night. He learned that the policeman was his friend, and he could depend on the cop on the beat. (In the 1960s a terrible tragedy struck, which touched Tom considerably; the Gem Theater was gutted by fire, and as three police officers remained on duty outside, the outer wall collapsed, falling on those policemen, crushing them beneath its massive weight.)

In 1950, after having lived in the 'badlands' for

Leigh Brackett and Tom Johnson, 1977.

over three years, Tom's father got a job at the Air Force Base, and they could finally move to a better location. His father bought a small mobile home, and set it up behind a lumberyard only half a block from the Boy's Club. One block away was a park with playgrounds. But it was the Boy's Club where Tom spent every free minute he had. He was taught boxing and spent many hours in the ring, until girls and 'Rock-N-Roll' music drew him away from the Boy's Club around 1955.

It was during this time that Tom's father was hurt on the job, and they moved from Wichita Falls, back to a farm near Seymour. Here Tom entered high school and went out for football— "But the sport liked to have killed me," he said, "so I eventually switched to the wrestling team." But now farm work took all his extra time, and there was little time for self-enjoyment. There was school during the day, and farm work in the evenings and on weekends.

1958 found Tom fulfilling two life-long dreams with one action. He joined the Army as an M.P. (Military Policeman). Tom spent 20 years in the military service as a military cop. The adventures he had in the service rivaled those tales he had heard from the soldiers in the train depot many years previously. He served over-seas in France, Turkey, Guam, Vietnam, and twice in Korea, plus visited other lands and met many peoples.

In 1961 Tom married his hometown girlfriend, Virginia, who was only 15 years old at the time of their wedding. "I married her young," he says, "so that I could raise her right. But it went wrong somewhere, because she still doesn't listen to me."

Tom grew up as a hero worshipper. He looked up to people who performed deeds of heroism—from the cop on the beat, to Roy Rogers in the cinema. He thrilled to the many radio heroes of the '40s and '50s. The comics, too, were filled with his kind of adventure, and introduced him to the many heroes of this media. He remembered the pulp magazines he had looked through as a kid—at the corner drug store—but had never read. It was in 1964 that he read his first pulp hero, Doc Savage, in the Bantam reprints. But it wasn't until later that year when he found some of the Belmont Shadow series, did he become 'hooked' for life on the pulp heroes. It wasn't until 1970, after Vietnam, and an assignment to California, that Tom was given a chance to relive the past and the pulp magazines. A fellow serviceman, and Doc Savage fan, had once subscribed to a fan magazine called *Bronze Shadows*. He let Tom read his set, and Tom became acquainted with names like Nick Carr, Lynn Hickman, Fred Cook and others.

In 1971 he drove into Los Angeles and visited Hollywood Blvd. where he searched the many bookstores. In the basement of one store he found what he was looking for—*Doc Savage* and *Shadow* pulps. With $33 in his pocket, he bought 11 pulps—ten issues of *The Shadow* & one issue of *Doc Savage*. Also in this year, Tom made contact with Bob Sampson through correspondence. Bob introduced him to Lester Belcher, Earl Kussman and Nils Hardin, and they all assisted him in his search for pulp magazines. The friendship of these four men helped him on his way to becoming a pulp collector. Other names soon followed—Don Hutchison and Randy Cox.

In 1973, Tom was reassigned to North Dakota. Upon arriving at his new duty station another letter was awaiting him. This time from a man Tom had admired since *Bronze Shadows*—Wooda N. Carr. Tom had written several newspaper articles, and through the insistence of Nick Carr, he submitted an article to Nils Hardin for his publication of *Xenophile*, then several more to Robert Weinberg, for his fanzine *Pulp*.

To bring Tom full circle, he answered an ad in a magazine placed by Jack Deveny. Then he was put into contact with Frank Hamilton, artist extraordinaire, to complete the circle. Shortly thereafter Tom was contacted by Nick Carr, and advised that he had been selected as a member within "Pulpsters, Ltd.," a group founded by Nick.

In July 1977, Tom attended PulpCon VI in Akron, Ohio. He finally got to meet some of the people he knew from letters: Bob Sampson, Les Belcher, Nils Hardin, Bob Weinberg, Fred Cook, Randy Cox, Walter Gibson, Leigh Brackett, Harry Steeger, Norman Saunders, etc., as well as renew his acquaintance with Nick Carr, Jack Deveny and Earl Kussman.

Ginger: Who is your favorite pulp character?
Tom: I would have to say The Shadow, with Doc Savage a close second, then Secret Agent "X," The Phantom Detective, and the rest following.
Ginger: Why is the Shadow your favorite?
Tom: I think it is the fascinating character of The Shadow, fighting hidden masterminds, in a style superhuman to us. Reading the newspaper headlines of today, we could use the likes of The Shadow again.
Ginger: Do you have a favorite issue?
Tom: Not really, unless it would be "Zemba." Actually I

like all of the stories written by Walter Gibson. But only a few written by the others.

Ginger: That would probably answer my next question. Who is your favorite author? If Gibson, who else would you include?

Tom: Certainly Gibson, then maybe Lester Dent, G.T. Fleming-Roberts, & others. But Gibson would be first.

Ginger: Since you write articles, was there anyone who influenced you to write, or what to write?

Tom: I think that Nick Carr influenced me most. I enjoyed his articles about Operator #5, along with his many other articles. But particularly liked the way he reported on Operator #5 in *Bronze Shadows,* and wanted to turn out articles like those. Bob Sampson's reporting and writing style has also influenced me greatly, but few can write in Bob's style as it's unique in its own right. Actually the more simple style suits my own writing the best. Both Bob and Nick are very good writers, and deserve credit as being an influence on my own writing.

Ginger: You do a lot of writing under the heading of 'Fading Shadows'. Is this taken from *Bronze Shadows?* Or reference to Gibson's Shadow?

Tom: Actually neither, but then, maybe both. Fading Shadows is what I would like to think the Brotherhood is all about. It's nostalgia; something that once was (pulps) but now only cast a shadow on the wall, and with the changing light that shadow seems to fade from sight. The Brotherhood is trying to bring that shadow back into the light, by writing about what it (pulps) once was. We want the new generation to be able to see that shadow. I started writing newspaper articles under this heading, and it has stuck with my magazine articles.

Since the above interview took place in 1982, Tom has gone on to publish *Echoes*, the pulp hobby magazine, under the Fading Shadows imprint, plus we started a line of fiction magazines, covering several genres, also under the imprint. Tom also continued some of the pulp characters in short story format, such as The Black Bat, Phantom Detective, Secret Agent "X," The Lone Eagle, and created two neo pulp characters of his own; The Black Ghost and The Masked Avenger. He is currently writing a series of jungle stories in the tradition of Edgar Rice Burroughs: three have been published; *Jur: A Story of Pre-dawn Earth, Savage Land of Jur,* and *Lost Land of Jur*. A fourth, *Queen of Jur* is in the hands of his agent. In the mean time, Tom also published several additional studies of pulp characters: *Dan Fowler: Ace of the G-Men, The Original Masked Marvel* (Phantom Detective), *The History of the Purple Wars* (Operator #5), *The Black Hood, The Green Ghost, The Black Bat,* and "The Dennis Lynds Shadow" in *From Shadow to Superman.*

Also under the Fading Shadows imprint, five other unrelated books were published: Bill Thom's *Hero Pulp Reprint Index*, Rick Lai's *The Bronze Age: An Alternate Doc Savage Chronology*, and Rick Lai's *Chronology of Shadows,* Gary Lovisi's *The Winged Men,* and Imogene Stewart's *I Was a Minonite Lady,* the last two being fiction novels.

Earl J. Kussman

On 26 July 1975 we were finishing up our trip to Texas and had decided to detour over to St. Louis on our return to North Dakota. We wanted to meet and visit with a man that had helped Tom a great deal in his quest to read as many of *The Shadows* as he could, because we could not then afford to buy them. Earl Kussman had sent Tom his own *Shadows* for us to read and return. This man trusted Tom with these treasures even though they had never met.

Earl, his lovely wife, Helen, and two of his three sons welcomed us into their home. We were honored with a view of Earl's collection of pulps and also a view of their son Steven's plants. Steven has a green thumb that I envy. He took us around and showed us all his treasures and named them all. The lovely plants seemed to flourish for him. His eyes lit up each time he talked of any of them. He is clearly very proud, and rightly so, of his garden of beauty. Thank you, Steven, for allowing us to admire your treasures.

Jack Deveny, Earl Kussman, Robert Weinberg and Robert Sampson.

Earl does not write articles, although his knowledge on them is extensive. His letters are always warm and friendly. We read each one with great enthusiasm. And we are all eagerly looking forward to meeting this nice family again at some future date.

Earl started reading pulps after a Christmas gift of *Tarzan the Terrible* and *Tarzan the Untamed* in 1933. "Burroughs was the culprit that hooked me for life on adventure stories," he said.

These books were hardbacks and one dollar each. Most of the series were easy to find in the hardback editions except some John Carter and David Innes. It took him years to find these until Ace pocket novels started Burroughs' works in the early 1960s.

Earl supplemented his Tarzan cravings by finding the 5¢ Chicago tabloids drawn by Hal Foster. Also in 1934, Flash Gordon started in the St. Louis *Post Dispatch*... this led to lots of comic books but only with art that appealed to him.

During this time Earl found *The Shadow, Doc Savage* and *Operator #5* with large doses of *Amazing, Fantastic, Air Trails* and *Flying Aces*. He read many others too, but not with the supreme anticipation of *The Shadow, Doc Savage* and *Operator #5*.

"Then I picked up a copy of *Famous Fantastic Mysteries* with 'Dwellers of the Mirage' by A. Merritt which led me into a world of fantasy. Strangely, I never read *Weird Tales*, and I attribute this to the lurid covers. Mothers didn't go along with girlie cover art and it would have entailed—problems," Earl wrote.

Earl found used bookstores and for a few cents, back issues could be bought. Every extra dime went for new or used pulps. He saved 10¢ each day from his 15¢ lunch money and did all kinds of odd jobs to get an extra dime or quarter to feed this addiction.

Earl saved a lot of these magazines in an old trunk

and boxes. During the war, his mother gave a part of these to the local war drive on paper and metal. He has had water destroy others, but he still has a few hundred.

He didn't know that other people collected pulps until he met Ed Kessell, through a newspaper ad. They traded some pulps and later found a garage and a small shack filled with pulps for sale. The collector had died and his widow had about 5,000 to sell. They met Nils (Tony) Hardin through this sale.

Ed mentioned Bob Sampson and Nick Carr, and supplied addresses, so a letter correspondence and trades were started between them. Earl met Bob at PulpCon I and Nick at a later one in Akron Ohio. Earl was introduced to Tom Johnson by mail, then in person at his home in St. Louis and again at PulpCon VI in Akron, Ohio.

When Bob Weinberg published, *Gangland's Doom*, Earl wrote him a letter stating that a certain Frank Hamilton's art was great. Bob sent this letter to Frank and that was the start of another friendship through the mail as these two had never met up to that time.

Earl writes, "In my opinion, there is no other artist that has captured the style and flavor of the original pulp artists. Frank has surpassed all black/white line artists and that includes Cartier. I have a color cover of 'The Man of Bronze,' but with color changes, and it is a thing of beauty. The real Doc Savage and not the short-haired Bama version."

"In closing, how can I thank all the great people that I have met through this common interest? Jack Deveny and Helen, Will Murray, Fred Cook and so many others; how can a man have such friends? God bless you for touching my life."

Earl, all of these people and so many more, are blessed, as you are their friend in return.

Robert Dale Sampson

What can one say of a man as talented as Bob Sampson? I have never met him, but Tom has. Tom describes Bob as being "a friendly, quiet man who listens to those around him, and absorbs every piece of information that he hears." I know him from his letters and articles.

His articles are many and very informative. His sense of humor is a delight. When he sent me some notes for this article, he wrote, "Surely you don't want to know the truth of that business up in Calagary 12 years ago. And, frankly, if I have my way, the real story of the Seamstress of Marburg will never be told."

His letters are always open, friendly and honest. My impression of his writing is best described by the following quote taken from Stan Blair's interview with Frank Hamilton. "Bob Sampson coins superb phrases that the mind delights in rolling over its tongue before swallowing, as one does with an excellent old brandy."

Bob's father was a sales representative, freight division, of the New York Central Railroad, which kept moving the family from place to place. They moved about once every 18 months.

Bob taught himself to read early in life. His parents supplied him with those big 7"x9" hardback collections of Tarzan and Orphan Annie strips. As soon as he discovered the library, he worked through Dr. Doolittle and everything that Thornton Burgess ever wrote about rabbits, toads and beavers. He would

---

Earl Kussman Facts:

Age: Born 17 January 1924 in St. Louis, Mo. Earl Kussman died January 15, 1992.
Education: Up to three years college at St. Louis University.
Military: U.S. Marine Corps. for three years.
Marital Status: Married Helen Maender on 26 April 1947.
Children: Three; Mark 3-10-48, Steven 10-20-50, Tom 11-19-54.
Employment: U.S. Post Office (21 years-letter carrier, 15 years-supervisor.)
Retirement: July 1979 with 36 years.

Bob and Diane Sampson.

check out 5 books in the morning and have them back by afternoon—checking out some more.

In Florida, Bob discovered Tom Swift; in Nitro, W. Va., Jules Verne; in Charleston, W. Va., Sherlock Holmes, Ellery Queen and H. Rider Haggard.

In junior high school, in 1939 or 1940, Bob met pulp magazines. Dozens of pulps were on the shelves at the drug store. He read *The Shadow, G-8, Doc Savage, The Spider, Amazing Stories* and others. He started buying *The Shadow, Doc Savage* and *Unknown* every month plus every second-hand issue that the Used This And That stores had. These were paid for by selling empty coke bottles at 2¢ each, to the local grocery store.

They moved to Tulsa, Oklahoma. This was Bob's third high school. He graduated, and joined the Army Specialized Training Reserve Program, a wing of which was based at the Louisiana State University. He took pre-engineering training. He was there for a year, then he enlisted in the Army. He was in Infantry training for 18 weeks, and then was shipped off to Europe. Fortunately, the war in Europe ended while his transport was still crossing the Atlantic.

He served out his tour in Marburg, Germany, working in the Locator Section of the Replacement Depot, then returned to Columbus, Ohio, to which his parents had moved.

Bob then enrolled in Ohio State to begin a career in Chemical Engineering. He says, "This lasted two years and terminated because even those most favorably disposed to me could find no trace of mathematical ability in my nature."

He entered the College of Education to train as a teacher. He was sustained through this by having two splendid teachers and the campus humor magazine, *The Sundial*. It was in *The Sundial* that he first saw his own words printed.

After graduation, Bob was accepted at the Alliance (Ohio) High School, where he taught English to the tenth and eleventh grades. He was there for a year, but was not satisfied. He gave it up and returned to Columbus, where he was taken on as a continuity writer at station WCOL to write ads.

This was a glorious, wonderful, pleasing job, with charming people, in a no-future, no-pay position. He put in an application for editor at Wright-Patterson Air Force Base in Dayton, OH. He was hired at double his teaching salary… $7,200 a year… a fortune in 1950. From Dayton, the Air Force transferred him to Middletown, PA to a new publications office. Diane and he married, and moved to Middletown. Was there for eight years.

The Air Force, in its infinite wisdom, decided that among others, this base was no longer necessary. They closed it down, opened a new office up, fired part of the people, and reduced others in grade. Bob was among the later, at lower pay in an administrative directives unit.

At this time, however, the U.S. Army, in Huntsville, Ala., was hiring for the Saturn Heavy Launch Vehicle program. He was taken on there, again in publications, transferred to NASA, when that new agency took over the vehicle development program from the Army.

In 1968, some undisclosed person sent him a copy of *Bibby's Fantasy Trader*. In this adzine, he learned that pulps were still available. He bought a 12/15/37 *Shadow* for $1.25. He told me, "This began it. Before I quite realized what I was doing, I was re-collecting those long-lost *Shadows* and *Docs* and *Phantom Detectives*. And *Famous Fantastic Mysteries* and *Fantastic Novels* and *Astounding*. And *Nick Carter*, and in they flowed, to my wife's awful horror, package after package. For the first time in years, I sat down to write something about these, publishing a few pieces in the *Mystery Reader's Newsletter*. Back in 1952, while still in Dayton, I had spent some evenings trying to write fiction and was accidentally published in *Planet Stories* (one story titled "Feline Red") and *Science Fiction Adventures* (one story titled "The Rocket Pistol"). *Blue Book* had returned a detective story with the suggestion that I improve and resubmit it, which never happened, since I got married and moved to Pennsylvania, and dropped everything to do with writing for some years. But now in Huntsville, I started working the machine again. Somehow I had been in touch with Bob Weinberg and worked up a Shadow piece for him, and so gradually go back into work."

We are so glad that you did get back to work, Bob, as there are a lot of your fans out here. We really enjoy your writing.

Interview conducted in 1982.

Ginger: Who is your favorite pulp character?

Bob: As far as a favorite pulp character, favorite magazines, and such preferences—well, my taste changes by the day. 1931 *Black Mask* suits fine this week, Next week, it's 1915 *Blue Book* or 1947 *Doc Savage*. I keep returning, however, to *The Shadow* and *Doc Savage*.

Ginger: Who is your favorite author?

Bob: I have no favorite pulp author, although I think very highly, indeed, of Lester Dent and Walter Gibson. And also T.L. Stribling, H. Rider Haggard, Nick Carter, G.T. Fleming-Roberts, Fred Nebel, H.C. Bailey and Robert Turner.

Ginger: Who influenced your writing?

Bob: Most of my writing influences have been quite outside pulp circles—Chandler and Dent, most certainly. But most accurately, Algernon Blackwood, E.B. White, Walter Tilden Clark and Scott Fitzgerald.

Now you have read about these great men, each of whom have contributed so very much to the rediscovered era of the pulps. My interest in the pulps is the same as all the men in this group; undying. All these men discovered pulps when they were in their teen-years, so in their mind's eye, they are still like children when they have a pulp in their hands.

Except now, they realize that these old magazines are irreplaceable in our history, so they handle them as one would an infant. The pulps are fragile, and to a great many people, they are a very important part of our lives. We don't want any damage to come to these great pearls of yesterday. We want them all to stay and stay and stay and be shared by all, of all ages. The reading enjoyment that lies between all those beautiful covers cannot be forgotten. The authors and artists of those days probably never dreamed of there ever being an interest in collecting or researching their works fifty years after the date of publication. The publishers considered the life of a pulp magazine approximately one month!

The time and money that these seven men have put into their collections was sometimes misunderstood, even by their wives. I know that I thought Tom was a little crazy at first. The money he spent (which never in any way put us into a bind) could have been

---

Bob Sampson Facts:

Age: Born 19 April 1927, in Cleveland, Ohio. Robert Sampson died October 30, 1992.

Marital Status: Married Diane Lee (Hamilton) on 14 December 1952, in Columbus, Ohio.

Children: Three; Cynthia Carol (now Mrs. Rod Lindsey, with three children of her own), Robert John (with one son), and Sarah Anne (still unmarried, but in Radiographic Technology, at a local hospital, expecting to graduate next year).

used to get an 8"x10" portrait done of our cat, or a second hair-dryer for the family, as I didn't like for the guys to use mine. But I could not really complain, as this hobby did not go down the drain, as drinking alcohol would; nor was it something that took him away from me, family and home.

I began to understand though, after I started reading the pulps, the letters from other collectors, the fanzines, the articles written by the collectors and seeing the wonderful art works by Frank Hamilton. This all opened up, for me, a whole new world. A world has become a classroom, with me an avid student, willing… no… yearning to learn more; then to teach others the joy of this world of pulps. I understand Nick's idea of founding the group of "Pulpsters, Ltd." And I hope this article will explain the dedication of these men.

But, remember, you stand beside them. These men are not the only ones in this field. I cannot name all of you as space must be limited. But you all know the names of authors, artists, collectors, researchers, writers of articles and publishers of fanzines. We all stand together with the same goal; that of renewing the interest in the old pulp magazines for us former generations and future generations.

Updates

Wooda "Nick" Carr Moved from Mesa, Arizona to Fort Wayne, Indiana.

Has written six books, all pulp related as follows:
- *America's Secret Service Ace* (two printings)
- *The Flying Spy* (two printings)
- *The Western Pulp Hero*
- *The Other Pulp Detectives*
- *The Saddleback Gladiator* (saga of the Rio Kid)
- *The Pulp Hero*

Wrote the Introduction to *The Spider* by Robert Sampson.

Contributed segments to the following books:
- *Mystery and Detective and Espionage Fiction*, by Cook.
- *The Amazing Pulp Heroes* by Hullar-Hamilton.
- *History of the Purple Wars* by Tom Johnson.

His name is mentioned in a book by Lee Server, *Danger is My Business*.

His name is mentioned in the following books as a character in the story:
- The Avenger, *The Black Chariot* by Goulart.
- *The Six-Gun Apostle* by Lee Davis Willoughby.
- The Destroyer by Warren Murphy.

Wrote the introduction for a Spider reprint: "City of Dreadful Night."

Has written articles for "The Good Old Days" and "Reminisce."

Has written for numerous magazines including *Echoes, The Doc Savage Quarterly, Unicorn, Megavore, The Mystery Fancier, The Doc Savage Club Reader, Nemesis, Pulp Vault, Golden Peril*.

Don Hutchison has had eleven books published in the U.S. and Canada from 1988 to the present. His pulp-related titles are: *The Super Feds* (Starmont House, 1988), *It's Raining Corpses in Chinatown* (Starmont House, 1990), *The Great Pulp Heroes* (Mosaic Press, 1996), *Scarlet Riders* (Mosaic Press, 1998), and *It's Raining More Corpses in Chinatown* (Adventure House, 2001). *The Great Pulp Heroes* has gone into three printings since its original publication and is soon to be translated into Portuguese for Brazil.

In 1992 Don created and began to edit a series of best-selling horror anthologies titled *Northern Frights*. The books consisted of new stories written in the *Weird Tales* tradition, but set in his home country of Canada. Authors included Hugh B. Cave, Robert Sampson, Robert Bloch, Rich Hautala and Charles Grant. The series went on to win numerous awards and award nominations and was often cited as one of the best dark fantasy series of the 1990s. It was terminated in 2001 with a volume titled *Wild Things Live There—The Best of Northern Frights*.

Don continues to extol his love of the pulps with frequent appearances on television and various convention panels. He is still happily married and, at this

© Tom Johnson

From the left, Earl Kussman, Diane Sampson, Helen & Jack Deveny, Frank Hamilton, Don Hutchison, Bob Sampson, and Nick Carr.

writing, continues to enjoy good health. The fact that he and The Shadow share the same birth month and year (both born April 1931) must have something to do with Don's life-long attraction to that wonderful era when the pulps routinely entertained millions of readers with their unique brand of entertainment.
Tom Johnson & Ginger have retired all publications on December 1, 2004. We have continued in the printing field, however, as Tom is still writing and I edit his works. ♦

Fantastic Fighting Men of Fiction

By Tom Johnson

In any series of books containing a single character or hero, there is at least one characteristic that brings the reader back for the sequels. The Mike Hammer series of the early 1950s was a good example of this; for Mickey Spillane made his character of Mike Hammer in a mold that was fairly new to the reading public. Hammer was a rough, and mean clear through and through, private detective. Spillane even added a little sex to give his novels a racy touch. His format worked, as each and every novel sold millions of copies. One of the attractions in any series that pulls me back for more, are the fantastic fighters and their fighting techniques. The weak hero never held much of an attraction for me, and this includes the later issues of *Doc Savage* (1944-1949), which only have the comic antics of Monk and Ham going for it. The tougher the character was, the better. I didn't care if my hero fell into a trap in the story, as I knew he would always win his way out of it… and probably knock the dickens out of somebody when he did get out: And if martial arts are thrown into the story, then I am hooked for life. One such story was the novelization of the premiere *Kung Fu* television series, *The Way of the Tiger, The Sign of the Dragon* (1973) by Howard Lee:

> It was the year of 1871 when he walked out of the desert. Tall, slim, wearing denim pants and a loose-sleeved shirt, a thin hat pulled down over his head shading his eyes from the harsh California sun. He at first appeared to be Caucasian, but on a second look you could detect the Oriental heritage of his background. He knew the building, with its swinging doors, for what it was; a drinking place, where men with dry throats could quench their thirst. A few men were gathered at the counter, while others were grouped around tables, talking or playing poker. He asked the man behind the counter for a glass of water and could feel the tension in the air, and could sense the many eyes starring at him.
>
> Town toughs. Local bullies. They can always be found in any community no matter how small. Men who derive pleasure by inflicting pain on weaker men, or people of other nationalities. The man that attacked the stranger from the desert was like that. He possessed a hatred of all Chinamen. Large and powerful, it was probably not the first time he had harassed the Chinese of this small town. But this time he was to learn a lesson, that all men cannot be pushed around nor mistreated. He would not obtain enjoyment from this encounter, but instead… defeat.
>
> "My name is Fuller," he said to the stranger. "Maybe you've heard of me. Everybody hears of me eventually. I've got a nose for Chinamen, friend, and you smell a little yellow to me." As Fuller moved forward, the stranger brought his stein of water up in a light gesture, so delicate that it might have been accidental, except that the stein now rested against Fuller's shirt, stopping his advance. Fuller slapped at the glass, but with one fluid motion the stranger moved the glass away and brought his elbow sharply into Fuller's shoulder, sending him reeling back

toward the poker table. Fuller recovered, grasped a chair and raised it over his head. As he started to swing the chair, the man from the desert grabbed it by its bottom rung and simultaneously lashed out with his foot, once again sending Fuller crashing back into the poker table. Fuller became maddened by his cohorts' laughter… at his expense, and pulled a hunting knife from its sheath. Fuller lunged forward, the knife held at gut level. The Oriental's foot flashed out again, striking Fuller's knife hand and sent the knife flying through the air, upward, coming to rest in the ceiling of the saloon.

The movie and the television series featured David Carradine in the part of Cain, the Kung Fu hero, but perhaps we should thank the late Bruce Lee, the "King of the Martial Arts," for introducing the American people to the art of Kung Fu. His films are praised today as the ultimate of the fight scene. He was great, undoubtedly, but I cannot help but think that it may have started many years before Kung Fu became a household word. Perhaps we can even go back as far as the pulp era, where the pulp heroes were often described as being able to fell a man—or an ox, with a single blow of a powerful hand, And wasn't it true? How often we thrilled to their exploits, whether they used fist, feet or sword. They were always the master of the fight scene. No matter what the situation called for: boxing tactics, la savate, ju-jitsu, knowledge of pressure points and nerve centers, swords, or merely strength and speed, they could supply it, giving us action and adventure in every story.

The rapier was never more efficient as it was in the hands of our pulp heroes. When this thin blade saw service in the hands of Richard Wentworth (The Spider), we knew that it would draw first blood:

> Their swords slithered and rang as they clashed against each other. Twice the Masked Man's point flicked Wentworth's guard, to be brushed aside at the last moment. It was a dangerous game Wentworth was

The Spider, August 1943.

playing. He must build up the man's confidence by exposing himself to the other's sword: The Masked Man stretched out in a low, viciously aimed thrust. Wentworth leaped back a yard. He made his riposte very slow, and it was brushed aside so that he was forced once more to jump away from an attack. His rapier met the slashing attack of the Masked Man and turned it aside. With a sudden feint, the Masked Man hurled himself forward in an enormous long, low thrust. He braced himself with his left hand on the floor and the rapier drove straight for the Spider's stomach. The Spider leaped high in the air, and, diving downward above the thrust of the rapier, he drove his own sword its full length into the body of the Masked Man: The blade went in through the collarbone, went diagonally down through his entire body. The force of The Spider's lunge, driving downward, hammered the Masked Man to the floor. The Spider crouched over him, then flipped him over on his back. The Masked Man

FANTASTIC FIGHTING MEN OF FICTION   27

was already dead. With a simple gesture, The Spider pressed his seal upon the man's forehead; ("The Spider and the Crimson Horde," Auguat 1943).

But The Spider didn't always kill with his rapier, as we can see in this encounter:

"On guard Spider:" His rapier sang against Wentworth's steel. "I'm going to kill you!" Wentworth smiled. He feinted for the left breast, tapped Holland's blade hard, circled... and lunged like lightning for the right breast. But his adversary's parry was swift and sure, and a riposte missed Wentworth's throat only because his recovery was of a speed that had never been surpassed on the mat of any Salle D'Arms of the world. The blades rang harshly as Holland began a fiery attack. Wentworth stood firm, steely wrist turning thrust and lunge into a bewildering sequence. Wentworth's right forearm had been scratched; Holland had felt the sting of the point upon his cheek. It was The Spider who broke the deadlock. He had never been a conventional swordsman. He knew the French and Italian schools of fence, the tricks of a score of masters. Without a preliminary flourish, he broke the half-instinctive rhythm, he broke the thrust and parry, lunge and riposte. Instead of parrying, Wentworth swayed his body aside at the hips and his rapier licked out for the breast of Charles Holland. The maneuver was perfectly executed. Holland's point ripped through Wentworth's coat, but missed flesh. Wentworth's sword pierced... and then he did a queer thing... a mad thing. Instead of driving his point home with a stiffened arm and shoulder, he threw his hand up, as if he had driven a harmless foil button, against an opponent's plastion in a friendly assault. He had spared Holland's life ("Green Globes of Death," March 1936).

Richard Wentworth did not include the rapier as part of his armament when he took the guise of The Spider. However, another individual did. He was America's Secret Service Ace, Jimmy Christopher, Operator #5. Around his waist was wrapped a leather

© Argosy Communications

The Spider, March 1936.

belt, which hid a thin arm of steel... a rapier. With a quick twist of his wrist this deadly length of steel would be unsheathed and the fight that followed would usually be swift and deadly... for Jimmy's opponent:

The masked man turned. "Operator #5, you are an honored graduate of the famed Salle D'Arms of the great Scherevesky, who is peerless master of the epees. I, in turn, also trained with him. Let us match our skill with rapiers!"

The foils clashed in the light through the ritual, which brought them to guard. The foils clinked. Christopher's swift Degrassi lunge was adroitly parried. He followed with an instant recovery. Operator #5's steel blended into invisibility. Its darting moves became faster than the eye could follow. The man in the mask retreated frantically, slashing wildly to avoid the onslaught of deadly steel. He pressed desperately to restrain the forced attack… and went back. A swift lunge: A quick recovery on the part of Operator #5.

Two men standing motionless. Above the heart of the man in the mask shone a small spot of red. He stood erect, his arms dropping. From his loosened fingers the magnificent foil fell… ("Master of Broken Men," September 1934).

The supple blade struck sparks from the moonlight as he whipped it downward and leaped. Grifo screamed. Singing torture seized his gun-hand. The razor edged blade flicked at his wrist and drew red. The keen needle-point pierced the nerves, brought paralysis to the finger that Grifo tried madly to tighten on the trigger.

Metal clashed with metal, and as if by magic power, the flexing blade snatched the heavy weapon from Grifo's fingers and whirled it away through the pouring smoke. Operator #5 stepped forward, the point of his epee poised stingingly against the flesh over Grifo's heart ("Legions of Starvation," December 1934).

When it came to the fencing foils, Jimmy's swordsmanship was probably the greatest, though the Spider's skill was close, if not equal. However, I tend to lean toward Jimmy Christopher's swift, but violent bouts with the rapier. His moves were coldly executed, violently performed and deathly serious to his opponents. The villains who faced Jimmy usually learned of this mistake too late, as can be seen in the action from "Siege of the Thousand Patriots," (February 1937):

Operator #5, December 1934.

The cold air crashed with sparks from the two blades. Goetz's sabre clashed against Jimmy's as he slashed downward with relentless blow after blow to break down Jimmy's guard. Goetz slashed downward powerfully at Jimmy's shoulder. The blow would have sliced Jimmy's arm off had he not parried it skillfully in seconds. Then he twisted sharply, and executed a swift lunge. Goetz had been carried slightly forward by his slashing blow, and Jimmy's recovery after the parry had been so spectacularly swift that the Colonel had no time to defend himself. Christopher's sabre reached its mark unerringly, piercing Goetz's throat. Blood spurted in a livid stream as Jimmy's sabre went through the man's neck. Goetz's eyes opened wide in terror, and a gurgling scream died in his throat.

While on the subject of "fantastic swordsmen,"

FANTASTIC FIGHTING MEN OF FICTION   29

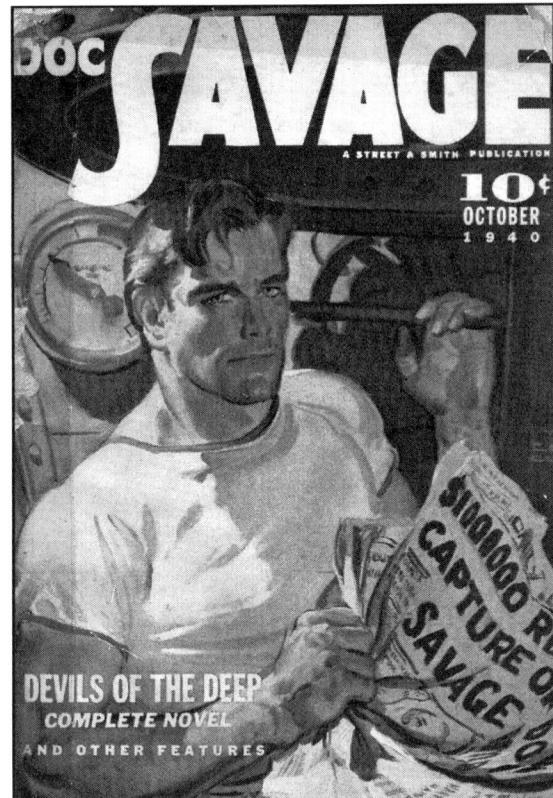

Doc Savage, October 1940.

we must not forget the noted lawyer and aide of Doc Savage, Brigadier General Theodore Marley "Ham" Brooks. Ham was seldom without his slim, black cane, which, when given a gentle twist to the handle, out came a slender blade of steel. The point of Ham's rapier was always coated with a mild anesthetic that, when the point flicked an opponent's body, it quickly put him to sleep. In the October 1940 issue of *Doc Savage,* "Devils of the Deep," we find this encounter:

> His arms started up. One of those arms held his-sword-cane. The sheath dropped off that cane as Ham pressed a button. The point of the sword flicked out twice with lightning speed. The tall gunman tried to pull the trigger of his automatic. He couldn't. The point of Ham's sword had barely flicked the gunman's wrist, but that had been enough. The point was covered with a fast-acting anesthetic.

Though Ham Brooks was no Jimmy Christopher or Richard Wentworth, when it came to the epees, there was one other which I feel deserves mention; Don Diego Vega… Zorro, an excellent swordsman, schooled in Spain by a master. In Don Diego's roll of Zorro he dueled with many opponents, always marking them with a "Z" carved on their cheek or forehead… the "Mark of Zorro." In the November 1944 issue of *West,* which contains the story "Zorro strikes Again," we find this encounter between Zorro and Captain Ortega:

> The blades touched, rang. Light flashed from them as they sang of a song of combat. Feet shuffled on the floor of packed earth. Captain Ortega was noted for skill with a blade. But after he had felt out his adversary for a moment, he knew he had met his equal, if not his master. He redoubled caution and set to work seriously. Ortega pressed the fighting and Zorro gave ground. The masked man worked along the wall to get the flickering of the tapers out of his eyes. Then he, in turn, pressed the fighting. Zorro's blade seemed like a live thing as it darted. Ortega felt himself being driven backward. The perspiration stood out on his face. Zorro was playing with him, he knew. He drove Ortega back against the wall again. Zorro's blade darted in, he gave a quick twist of his wrist, and Ortega reeled aside, and almost collapsed against the wall, dropping his blade.
> "Now, you bear my mark on your cheek, senor," Zorro told him.

So, now, who says that the pen is mightier than the sword? Some of our heroes just might disagree with that.

The sword was, indeed, a part of our heroes fighting techniques. Even The Shadow mentioned that he preferred the epee in the novel "Death About Town," July 15, 1942. But The Shadow had other talents and used them most in his exploits, seldom using an epee. The Shadow's ability was that of a ju-jitsu master. Often the fight scene would describe the gangsters as flying through the air, or bounding back from The Shadow as if they were nothing but rubber balls. Possibly he is best noted for his swift entrance into an affray, or combat with the killers of scum-land, as is depicted in "Death About Town":

> That blackness gave an announcement of its approach in the form of a fierce, challenging laugh that impaled the men who heard it to swing in its direction. The sweeping mass materialized. It came like a living cloudburst, in the person of The Shadow! A cloudburst that delivered hail in the form of metal. Its lightning was the spurt of guns, its thunder their echoes. Sweeping in from the side passage, The Shadow was raking the lobby with bullets, and masked men were diving to escape his fury. Their own guns answering frantically were too hurried even to annoy the intrepid fighter, whose attack had all the power and motion of a cyclone.

The Shadow was at his best when he fought with gangs of crooks. It left no doubt with anyone, that he was the master of the encounter. When The Shadow fought with a lone individual, the fight was usually quick, but efficient. He often employed ju-jitsu tactics to great advantage:

> A hand whisked toward the Shadow stabbing a long blade of bronze. The knife point missed for the creature that drove it was flying through the air, whipped like a thing of rope under The Shadow's lashing strength ("The Invincible Shiwan Khan," March 1, 1940).

> That hand took Laverock's wrist with a vice-like twist that doubled it. Laverock's arms and body followed, spinning in midair, to be stopped by The Shadow's up-thrust knee. Rolling sideward as The Shadow released him, Laverock reached the floor. His fall was broken, but his head took something of a thump as it fell back against the filing cabinet. No wonder Laverock was dazed. His

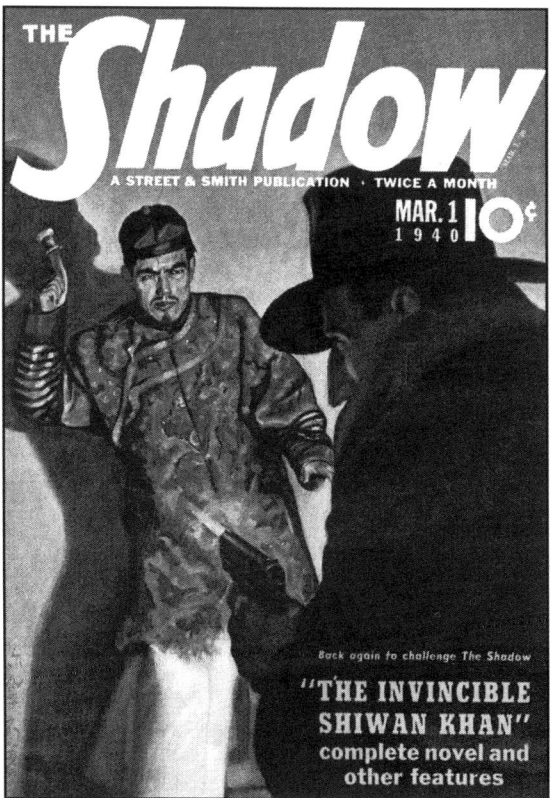

The Shadow, March 1, 1940.

whirl had included a somersault, which left him staring back at the desk across which he had come ("Death About Town"). The Shadow was a superman: His battles with gangland, during the 1930's and 1940's, are classics to be remembered. His agents, through their association with the cloaked avenger, were also intrepid fighters and should also receive mention. Their many fights with the scum of the underworld, their many penetrations into the badlands, made their lives very dangerous. But somehow they survived, possibly due to their abilities as fighting men.

Men who were fearless and obeyed their invisible chief without question. Harry Vincent was probably The Shadow's right hand man and he served this master of darkness from the very beginning until the last, often wearing his master's black attire to protect The Shadow's cover as Lamont Cranston. A gym coach in "Death About Town" recognizes Harry's ability and comments that Harry

FANTASTIC FIGHTING MEN OF FICTION   31

could become a great boxer:

> Rydal took a stance, and Harry immediately responded with instinctive footwork, that brought another nod of approval from Rydal: Jericho Druke was another of the Shadows agents who was a fantastic fighter. Jericho was a giant African with bulging muscles and giant, enormous strength. Many a time his powerful muscles and large fist intervened in time to save The Shadow or another agent from impending doom: Coming like a sledge hammer, Jericho's big fist met the Mongol's ugly face. The blow struck with a sickening crunch as it hooked up beneath the Mongol's huge jaw. It took the killer's feet from under him, carried him across the back of the truck, where he balanced limply, then pitched headfirst to the curb. There was another crack as the Mongol's skull met the cement ("The Invincible Shawan Khan").

The Shadow and his agents were undoubtedly the best, when it came to fighting underworld thugs. As mentioned before, The Shadow used ju-jitsu tactics in his fights, so now lets look upon another agent who used both judo and karate tactics.

He has no name that is known, so we must refer to him as Secret Agent "X." He was mysterious, lived constantly in disguise and had his own share of battles with the underworld, and the masterminds that controlled them. He was also well trained in the martial arts. In the novel "Brand of the Metal Maiden" (January 1936), we see three incidents where the Agent is at his best:

• Sam Rubens made the mistake of attacking X from the rear. He sprang upon the Agent's back where he remained for an incalculable fraction of a second before a ju-jitsu grip dashed him across the room to fall across the unconscious bodyguard.

• Ordinarily, X could have laid the batman out with a blow to any of the important nerve centers of the body.

• Hell hung in the balance of that blow as his right fist steamed into Zero's biceps with such force that the nerves in the man's arms were paralyzed.

Doc Savage, March 1943.

Zero's fingers straightened. X followed the telling blow with another straight to a point just below Zero's heart. It was a blow capable of killing that X had mastered long ago. But he had reined it in just enough so that its effect was merely paralyzing.

Secret Agent "X" refrained from killing, preferring that the criminals be sent to jail for their crimes. The case just mentioned is a good example of this. However, many of the master-criminals he fought were accidentally killed in these novels of high adventure and excitement.

The Secret Agent had knowledge of the pressure points, which is taught to the true karate-trained men and women. Before becoming a black belt, the karate student must learn of these pressure points. This brings to mind a certain doctor who was familiar with and used this technique to subdue the many villains he fought. He was, of course, the "great Man of Bronze," Doc Savage: mental marvel and physical giant. Trained from childhood to fight for the right and punish evildoers, traveling from one corner of the world to the next, in pursuit of his profession! In the novel "The Awful Dynasty" (November 1940) we see a good example of his talents in the knowledge of nerve centers:

FANTASTIC FIGHTING MEN OF FICTION

> The Bronze man's left hand whipped out, took hold of the powerful fellow and held him rigid. Doc used a neck hold that rendered the man incapable of movement. He was the same as paralyzed.

Perhaps one of Doc's best fighters was his aide, Lieutenant Colonel Andrew Blodgett "Monk" Mayfair. Monk was an expert in the rough and tumble technique of fighting, but often amazed us when he performed stunts which even most karate black belts do not care to attempt. Take, for instance, the fight scene in "The Black, Black Witch" (March 1943):

> Monk staged a rebellion, assisted by Ham. Monk began with the unusual gymnastic feat of jumping into the air and kicking two men in the face simultaneously. What his feet did to the two faces was one of his pleasant memories.

A feat indeed. Try it sometime. And then who can forget one of Monk's most fantastic fights. The one which is recorded in the novel "The Talking Devil" (May 1943), when Monk fought Butch, a mild mannered, weak appearing bookkeeper who not only was a crook but a teacher of ju-jitsu! Monk tackled him, thinking that it was really a waste of his time, only to become helplessly entangled in a fight he could not possibly hope to win. If it hadn't been for Renny, Monk might still be helplessly tied in knots. But Renny did come to Monk's rescue… only after yelling for Ham to come and see Monk in such a position, then knocking Butch unconscious with one of his massive fists.

Probably G-8, the Master Spy, had little knowledge in the martial arts, as he seldom used this technique. Though pulpster Nick Carr says that he was indeed trained in this fighting technique. But usually G-8 did away with his foes by smashing a blow from a hard right hand, to the unfortunate's face, or else a sledging automatic would send his opponent to the Promised Land. But if G-8 did not use these fighting techniques, at least a few of his enemies did… on him! In the novel "Aces of the Damned" (August 1938), we read of this encounter (G-8 is confronted by a giant Oriental):

> Now, as he was spun around, the automatic was snatched from him. With some strange power of Oriental wrestling, powerful fingers gouged into his flesh at strategic points. G-8 became suddenly paralyzed, helpless.

Perhaps the real fighter of Hogan's heroes was football star Bull Martin. A giant of a man, in both size and strength, he won many a day for the Battle Aces. In the July 1940 issue, "The Damned Will Fly Again," we find Bull at his fighting best when pitted against "The Brute":

> He made a wild lunge at Bakko. The brute-man went down before his attack, losing his whip. With a yell of rage, Bakko rose to his feet. Bull was waiting; Bakko came at Bull with flailing arms. Bull met him with a well-aimed left and then a right that drove Bakko against the wall. Bakko was wobbling. Bakko's head was only an inch or so from the wall. Bull doubled him with a left in the solar plexus and brought up a right. Bakko's head snapped back. His skull struck the rock wall with a crunching, cracking sound.

Later, in the same novel, Bull is pitted against the terrible "Herr Grun," but this fight is short and sweet:

> Instantly, the big fellow jerked the stocky, animal-like body around. Snatching him in a sudden ju-jitsu hold, he rose up and flipped Herr Grun backward over his knee.

Jimmy Christopher, alias Operator #5, was the man most skilled in the martial arts (with the possible exception of Secret Agent "X"). His training was very impressive, and we regret that he did not perform these deadly arts more often. His fights were against some capable adversaries, and they would have been classic fight scenes if, instead of picking up rapier or gun, he would have continued the fight with flying feet and slashing hands. In the premiere story of Operator #5, "The Masked Invasion" (April 1934), we learn of Jimmy's training when confronted by Loo Kong, Oriental mastermind:

> "You were once for a period of three months the private sparring partner of Gene Tunney, who was at that time heavyweight champion of the world. He was of the opinion that if you had chosen to do so you might have become a world champion yourself in a lighter class.
>
> "If I am not mistaken, you are an honored graduate of the world famous Salle D'Arms of Scherevesky, who is a master without peer of the fencing foils. Some years ago you trained intensively in the science of ju-jitsu under Kashawatska Hoia in Tokio, who personally instructs the Heavenly Protectors, or bodyguards, of his Imperial Highness, the Emperor of Japan, Son of the Sun."

Just how intensive this training was we can judge from his encounters on page 10 of "Masked Invasion":

> The masked young man's fingers seized his wrist. Swift movements followed. The other man's arm dropped, paralyzed. Swift sure pressure on a major nerve had rendered it powerless. The masked man's hand darted to the other's neck. A muscle snapped as the man opened his mouth to shout, but no sound came. His vocal cords were no longer working. A painless ju-jitsu touch had accomplished that. The surprising visitor thrust stiff fingertips against the other man's temples, deftly, suddenly twisting. The victim's eyeballs rolled as he slid to the carpet.

In "The Green Death Mists" (November 1934), we again see Jimmy in great action:

> The flash of the gunmetal in the light was a signal that sent Jengis Dhak upon Operator #5 with a ferocious leap. A ju-jitsu blow had robbed him of his automatic…

Operator #5, April 1934.

now he replied in kind. He seized Jimmy Christopher's wrist, leaned swiftly, twisting until the bones of the wrist crunched and gritted. He whirled away as Jimmy Christopher stood frozen by the intense pain that seized him. Against the blue of the sky the Mongol whirled. He faced Operator #5 with his long-nailed hands rising. Jimmy Christopher stepped slowly closer, while wind soured past them, while hoarse cries echoed from below. They confronted each other with steady eyes… Jengis Dhak's black and glittering, while Operator #5's midnight-dark, shining with a deep light. The Mongol's lean, powerful body tensed for a spring as his claws flexed to reach for Jimmy Christopher's throat. "The blight you have put upon the world, Jengis Dhak," Jimmy Christopher grated, "can be wiped away by one agency alone… death:" Operator #5's left hand darted toward the buckle of his belt. A sharp click sounded. A swift jerk drew the narrow leather sheath from the belt-loop, flung it into the air, baring the supple blade of Toledo steel. It whipped like lightning, needle pointed, razor sharp…

As the Mongol leaped, a shrill scream tore from Jengis Dhak's colorless lips… his claws slashed desperately at Operator #5's throat… dropped. Stepping back quickly, Jimmy Christopher held his rapier poised… a blade now darkened with blood. Across the crimson of Jengis Dhak's robe a fresh redness flowed… the color of doom.

Operator #5 even trained Diane Elliot in some of the finer points of ju-jitsu it seems. In the March 1939 issue, we find this encounter:

Diane tensed, watched him coming toward her with what he intended to be disarming unconcern. Every nerve a-tingle, every muscle flexed… and then she darted at him, desperately trusting again to the ju-jitsu that seemed to be her only weapon. Her hands secured their hold, tightened in one of the surest grips Jimmy Christopher had taught her… only to have it broken, to have her arms twisted until it seemed that they must pop from their shoulder sockets. Helplessly her face turned up to Kasuga Tosa's. "One of the finest grips taught by the master, Kashawatska Hoia," he admitted, his face almost against hers, "but unfortunately it seems you do not know its counter grip."

In mentioning the female martial-artist, one cannot forget the small, dainty, and lovely Miss Nellie Gray, whose expertise with judo surprised many men and foes. Introduced in the second issue of The Avenger, "The Yellow Hoard" (October 1939), we find this encounter:

At one moment Carp had a none-too-close paw on the girls arm. At the next he seemed to have leaped into the air in an-attempt at a backward flying somersault. An attempt that didn't come off very well, because he lit on his back and shoulders with a grunt.

Pat Savage, pretty bronzed-haired cousin to Doc Savage, was also a lady to beware of, as we can see in the novel "Men of Fear" (February 1942):

He met Pat's fist, which landed expertly against his windpipe. That brought his head back. Pat's other hand landed against a spot where nerve centers were most exposed. The man dropped as senseless as if he had been shot. "Ju-jitsu, " Pat said proudly, "I've been practicing."

The Phantom Detective, too, was a very skilled fighter and had learned the French fighting method of "la savate." In "The Crime Castle" (December 1934), we read this encounter:

Dick Van Loan's supple body was moving in a swift, coordinated motion. He bent low at the hips, swerved his body out of the arc of the descending knife blade. Almost in the same motion, he pivoted on the ball of his left foot and his right foot whipped upward. His toe cracked against the knife-man's wrist. The knife flew out of the thug's grasp, struck the wall and clanked to the floor. The Phantom had disarmed the thug by "la savate," a measure of defense he had learned from a French apache.

La savate wasn't the only fighting tactics Van used, as we can see from the novel "Grim Shadow of Hate" (June 1941). This time Van is pitted against a very large, fat woman, who seems to be able to fight like a man:

His quick Oriental hold on a nerve caused the poisoned feather to drop… Van shot his fingers toward the nerve ganglia at the base of the woman's jaw. Her eyes partly glazed, but she was strong, and tried to fight him off.

The Phantom Detective was a very skilled fighter and could have, if he had wanted, been the heavy-

The Masked Detective, Summer 1942.

weight champion of the world. But when it came to the use of "la savate" there was at least one hero who was without peer. That man is none other than Rex Parker, alias The Masked Detective, or more commonly referred to as "The Mask." He was an expert in the French form of fighting and practiced this technique constantly. In the novel, "Alias The Masked Detective" (Fall 1940), we find him in practice with a life size dummy model. The dummy is constructed with a rounded base, whereas it could be knocked over, then bounce back into an upright position:

> Rex stepped close to the dummy. His right foot came up in a flash, which the eye could hardly follow. The dummy went careening to one side. As it bounced back, Rex's foot moved again. This time his toe caught the dummy full in the face and sent it rocketing backward.

As it rebounded, his foot caught the dummy's head in a lightning blow.

The Mask usually subdued his opponents very quickly with this fighting technique; a mixture of English style boxing and fencing movement, only with the hands and feet both being used. In the novel, "The Canal Zone Murders" (Summer 1941), we read of this encounter between The Mask and a German spy:

> The German gave a wild shout and lunged toward the gun. At the same moment the Masked Detective moved in fast. The spy managed to wrap fingers around the weapon and with an exultant cry started to raise the gun. To his amazement the Masked Detective stopped short and made no move to deter him. The spy's hand swept upward. Then he was aware of a sudden movement on the part of the Masked Detective. The mysterious man's right foot flashed up, like that of a graceful dancer. The toe caught the spy squarely on the point of the jaw. Bone cracked. The gun dropped to the floor and the spy crashed down heavily several feet away. He didn't get up again.

Unfortunately, by the end of the series, Rex Parker drops the use of a mask, as well as la savate, becoming merely a newspaper reporter. As well as a highly successful private detective. However, this doesn't stop his girlfriend, Winnie Bligh; she does have certain skills as a fighter. ("Monarchs of Murder," *Thrilling Mystery*, Fall 1944):

> Winnie's smile faded. "Look here Miss Fairfield. I don't like that. And if you want to get tough, I can get tough, too. Now put that gun away before I take it away from you."
>
> "Stand back!" Cynthia snapped.
>
> Winnie laughed. Her hand shot out with the skill that Rex Parker had taught her. She knocked the gun aside, seized Cynthia's wrist, squeezing the muscles.

FANTASTIC FIGHTING MEN OF FICTION

> Cynthia looked surprised as the gun dropped to the floor.

But if Rex Parker drops the use of la savate, it seems that another of our heroes, Tony Quinn, alias the Black Bat, takes up the technique about this time. Of course, it might be noted at this time that the author who created the Masked Detective was Norman Daniels, who also wrote the Black Bat stories, and many of the Phantom Detective novels. It's possible he also introduced la savate to the stories.

In "Murder on the Loose" (*Black Book Detective*, Summer 1945), a Black Bat story, Tony's aide big Butch O'Leary has a strange encounter with Jacques, a huge fat man, who seems to be merely testing the ex-boxer:

> Butch's arms opened wide and he moved forward, fast for a man of his bulk. He started closing those arms to encircle the fat man and jar him back against the wall. But inexplicably the ceiling took the place of the floor. The four walls spun like a merry-go-round gone wild and then Butch crashed down on his face.
>
> "Judo," the fat man said. "Attack me again, my friend. This time I will show you how to disable a man efficiently."
>
> Another rush carried him to the fat man, and then Butch was jarred clear his insteps. The fat man had thrust out his right hand, palm upraised, and Butch had run full tilt into it.
>
> "You see," the fat man explained, "it is done only with the heel of the hand. But there is much preparation first. The hand must be developed until it is like steel. You start when very young, methodically striking the hand against the edge of a board until you can crack the board with one blow."

Okay, Jacques is good, probably an expert in karate as well as judo. At least a black belt degree. His name being French, you can well imagine that he is also an expert at la savate. But when he tackles the Black Bat, we find just how powerful our black-clad nemesis of crime is. Later in the novel, we read the following:

> As Jacques bent to seize the intruder's throat, the Black Bat kicked him neatly under the chin. Jacques went reeling back, squealing with pain. But he came on again, in a wild charge. Jacques knew how to fight, and he possessed tremendous energy. He lacked only one thing—restraint. He forgot to keep a cool head, and the Black Bat didn't.
>
> Jacques ducked under the Black Bat's swing and seized a wrist with both hands. He arched himself to throw the Black Bat against the wall with a judo twist. Instead, the side of the Black Bat's hand came down against Jacques' neck—a crippling blow against nerve centers that sent Jacques to his knees.
>
> The Black Bat stepped back and waited. He wanted Jacques to absorb more punishment than this….

Perhaps one of the most memorable fight scenes of all involved the Spider's mate. Nita van Sloan, in the novel, "Master of the Death-Madness." August 1935. The Spider lies gravely wounded in a hospital, recovering from several bullet wounds, which he had suffered at the hands of the police. Nita dons the guise of The Spider and sets out on her own campaign against crimedom. She, as The Spider, has been captured by Jackson Grant, the priest of Anubis, and taken to the Egyptienne, Nephtasu. Nita is searched and disarmed by the Egyptienne's two servants. But, later, Nita turns the tables and takes a gun away from Jackson Grant, crashes the butt of the weapon against his head and mortally wounds the two fellasheen. But before she can deal with Naphtasu, the Egyptienne attacks her and the fight that follows is certainly one to remember in the annuls of the pulp magazines:

> Such lithe, swift movement from the woman was so unexpected that Nita was driven back to the wall from the force of the attack. The two fellasheen were kicking

• NITA VAN SLOAN •

out their lives upon the floor; Jackson Grant was unconscious at her feet, but Naphtasu…! Her two hands closed cleverly on Nita's gun wrist; violent pain stabbed the arm. Nita dropped the revolver, struck with her left hand. Not with a clenched fist—her weight and the strength of the wrist could not stand that—but with the first two fingers of her hand forked and stiff—straight at Napthtasu's eyes!

The Egyptienne dodged back, losing her hold. The gun lay on the floor between them and the two women stood gazing at each other, panting a little—Nita with her woman's grace that had betrayed her despite the grotesque garb of The Spider; Naphtasu superb in one of those heavy silken gowns in which she delighted; a dress without decoration, simple of line so that her exquisite figure might show to its greatest advantage. The gown was a pale, apple green and her hair piled above it, was a pillar of twisted fire.

It was Nita who advanced, lightly, alertly on the balls of her feet, her right arm slowly regaining sensation after the application of the paralyzing ju-jitsu hold. Nita was adept at that art, too, for Wentworth had insisted on her learning it, just as he had the rudiments of fencing. Nephtasu awaited her coming with her pale lips still mocking, but with hatred in her eyes. "I shall break you before I kill you, fool:" she called slurringly.

Nita sprang forward, feinting for a wrist grip, a hammerlock. She saw from the deft shifting of Tasu's muscles what her counter would be and struck swiftly for the chin with the heel of her hand. If it had landed, the blow would have jolted the Egyptienne's head backward on her shoulders and a swift slash with the edge of the other hand would have paralyzed the larynx, made her an easy prey. Instead. Nephtasu snatched Nita's wrist, flung her backward toward the floor, drawing her knees upward. She intended to jam those feet against Nita's body, whirl her with the momentum and leverage of the fall and smash her down, broken and helpless, perhaps dead. Only one defense against that. Nita must go with the fall, but work it to her own advantage. She balled, held to Nephtasu's wrists just long enough, and, catching the impetus of the thrust of the Egyptienne's feet, she turned an easy somersault in the air, landed on her feet, rolled once and came up alertly.

Nephtasu was rising lazily from the floor, sure of her conquest, and Nita's rush took her by surprise. She reeled backward from a forthright, unscientific thrust of both hands and pitched backward into the shallow tinkling fountain, which formed the room's center. The Egyptienne, sitting in the fountain's basin, in what should have been a ludicrous position, was in the act of throwing a knife. Nita ducked under the flying blade, but was compelled to whirl to face a new attack as Nephtasu sprang forward.

Nita let her eyes go wide with terror as the hating face of the Egyptienne neared her. Her head began to jerk frantically from side to side as if she sought escape. As Nephtasu, exultant, sprang toward her, Nita dodged aside, caught one of the woman's outstretching hands and spun on her heel. It was a cleaver throw, and perfectly executed. Nita's hands held for a moment, then slipped loose. Nephtasu, propelled by the force of her rush, was whirled about off-balance, tripped over Nita's dragging foot and flung spread-eagled, face down toward the floor.

Nita knew what must be done and she acted without hesitation. Completing her whirl upon her heel as Nephtasu struck with a muffled scream, she sprang bodily upon the Egyptienne's back and struck twice, violently with the hard edge of her hand upon the back of her victim's neck. Then Nita reeled panting to her feet and Nephtasu lay where she had fallen, a bedraggled, half-nude woman in a well-torn dress, still lovely with the pile of her glorious hair streaming about her....

Yes, our heroes were fighting men... brave, patriotic and intelligent, and their women fought right beside them through every exploit, hardship and danger. From as early as the late 1800s, Nick Carter... Detective... was swinging his fist to right wrongs and punish evildoers. His action took us to the 1930s, the 1940s and into the early 1950s, where the hero carried us through page after page of the pulps, with fighting action and adventure. But gone now are our heroes, pure of heart, and enter into the realm of the anti-hero. Heroes that can be good, or bad, whichever mood fits him. No longer are they "pure of heart," but sometimes cruel, violent and nasty characters full through. In the fifties, with the demise of the pulp hero, we were given another detective named Mike Hammer who taught us that good guys weren't always good. Then came a series, which is considered to be classics of karate fight scenes: The Earl Norman Thrill Books. There were nine titles in this series from the late 1950s and early 1960s. These novels were crammed pack-full of action, with page after page of karate fights:

Kill Me in Roppongi
Kill Me in Yokohama
Kill Me in Yoshiwara
Kill Me in Yokosuka
Kill Me in Tokyo
Kill Me on the Ginza
Kill Me in Shinjuku
Kill Me in Shimbashi
Kill Me in Atami

The titles alone were suggestive of the action within the pages of Thrill Books.

The hero was Burns Bannion, an American soldier who had decided to remain in Japan after his Army hitch was up... for the purpose of studying the art of karate. To make a living Bannion took on jobs as a private investigator. His weapon was... his body: And he gave us page after page of deadly karate fights:

Scarface was watching my every move. His eyes were glued on my right hand. He should have kept them there, but he shifted his eyes quickly as I drew back my left arm into a rigid position. A quick jab with my left, a jab so fast his eyes had trouble following it. This threw him off balance and caused him to lean towards me. This was what I wanted him to do. My right hand, with fingers spread apart in a "nukite" position, shot out and upward past the bridge of his nose, into his eye sockets... and that was the end of Old Scarface. *(Kill Me in Shimbashi)*

Kunio's hands shot around the back of Fentriss' neck. With a snap he drew Fentriss' face downwards in one quick motion. At the same instant that Fentriss' face came down, Kunio's right knee came up like a sledgehammer. This action made a mash of what had once been a face. Fentriss, with the strength of a dying man, straightened and flung-out his hands, although he now had no eyes left to see with. An erect, Fentriss gave Kunion a chance for the last needed blow. His right hand went high in the air and came crashing down with a "shuto" blow on Fentriss' neck. This bare hand blow landed the calloused lower edge of his right hand smack along the side of the neck below the ear and smashed the lower half of Fentriss' neck bone back into his skull. *(Kill Me in Yoshiwara)*

Gently I lifted Kim until he was standing erect, his back against the chimney. He looked me straight in the eye as if he were thanking me for saving his life. The look went out of his eyes when I slammed the heel of my right hand against his chin. The power and angle of the blow drove his teeth together with a loud grinding crunch. His lips were flecked with blood and a steady flow of the crimson began to dribble over his bruised and battered chin. He sputtered, "Why you hurt?"...

"I'll hurt you like you have never been hurt if you don't tell me who sent you to kill me," I said.

"If I promise to tell you, you shake hands like in America?"

Nodding my head, I relaxed the arm that held him against the chimney. He stuck out his right hand. I clasped

it in the good old American custom of friendship. I had an idea what was coming and hoped I was ready for it....
(Kill Me on the Ginza)

The series was credited to Earl Norman, but the author was Norman Thompson (born in 1915), a radio, stage, and film actor who got his start in radio with Orson Welles' Mercury Theater. In fact, he claimed to be part of the famous production of *War of the Worlds*. He went into movies later, appearing in about 23 films. Because of his likeness to John Wayne, he eventually became a stunt double for the famous actor. He was an Army Ranger in the military, but after WWII, he worked thirty years for the Department of Defense in Japan, as entertainment supervisor for U.S. bases throughout the Far East, bringing entertainment to the military clubs for U.S. servicemen. An expert in karate, he wrote the nine Bannion stories while in Japan. He later transferred to Hong Kong, where he set a final story, *Hang Me In Hong Kong*, but dropped Bannion for a new character named Rick Shaw. After retiring, he moved to California, where he died on February 3rd, 2000. Sadly, I've never read this final novel.

Burns Bannion opened the way from then on. On to the karate fighters, the Kung Fu fighters, the Judo experts and even a few that employed the fighting techniques of "la savate." New titles like The Executioner, The Destroyer, The Revenger, The Black Samurai, and of course, *Kung Fu*. Not only the paperbacks, but the comics, too, have taken up the theme with such comic books as *Yang, Iron Fist, Deadly Hands of Kung Fu, Master of Kung Fu*, and *Kung Fu Fighter*. Some great, others not so good, but they are there... fighting heroes and anti-heroes... slashing with hands and kicking with feet.

In 1968 and 1969, Michael Avallone, author of the popular Ed Noon series wrote two novelizations for the television series *Hawaii Five-O*. Now Ed Noon was no slouch either when it came to beating up the bad guys, but in the second novel of the *Hawaii Five-O* series from Signet, Michael Avallone does a tremendous job with a la savate fight scenes between Steve McGarrett and a French assassin:

> The Frenchman suddenly halted on a dime, reversed his body and his large left leg shot upward and outward in a murderous kick. McGarrett didn't get out of the way completely. A booted heel, heavy and hard cannonaded against his shoulder and more pain joined the bruised muscles in his arm. He bobbed left and right, measuring Tornier, rapidly pistoning his good arm in a series of short powerful jabs. But Tornier, determined to use la savate, the killing French art of foot fighting, was not to be reached with a fist.... (*Terror in the Sun*, p. 66)

And, just as the pulp fictioneers influenced young men and women of the early 1900s with patriotism and the unconquerable hero, so does the writer of today. Across the country spreads the influence of the martial arts under one name or anther. And each new actor wishing to become the next Bruce Lee of film and legend. And our fictional heroes march on through the pages of the great American fiction media... books. Whatever characteristic it is that brings you back for more, you will find it in your favorite series of fictional paperbacks. And the aura was there in the pulps, also. It brought the G-8 fans back month after month; The Spider, The Shadow, Doc Savage and Secret Agent X... all had their own personal appeal for the readers back in the days of the pulp magazines. As for me, it was always those fantastic fighting men of fiction that brought me back for more! ♦

Some Original Pulp Heroes

By Tom Johnson

Alias Mr. Death

Believe it or not, there was a time when we didn't have a Doc Savage, Spider, Operator #5, or Secret Agent "X." There was an odd void between 1931 and 1933, between Walter Gibson's "The Living Shadow" and Kenneth Robeson's "The Man of Bronze." The publishers were undoubtedly hard at work trying to come up with a character magazine to rival the Shadow Magazine over at Street & Smith.

It was during this setting that D.L. Champion, writing as G. Wayman Jones, wrote the ideal pulp heroic character story in 1932. That novel was *Alias Mr. Death*. What the novel did for the upcoming character pulps, at least for the Thrilling Group, was to set a formula they would use and follow for the next twenty years. Whoever was responsible for recognizing the potential of the novel is not known, unless it was publisher Ned Pines, or senior editor Leo Margulies, but that is immaterial at this late date. However, it would become the formula for their tremendously popular hero, the Phantom Detective that debuted in February 1933. It may well have influenced The Spider, Master of Men, which appeared from Popular Publications in October 1933, as many of the same elements appear in the early stories.

Alias Mr. Death is about a young millionaire man-about-town named James Quincy Gilmore, Jr., who eventually takes on the guise of a phantom killer called Mr. Death to avenge his father's murder. In

Interior illustration from the "Alias Mr. Death" series.

what would become a typical Phantom Detective plot, Jimmy uncovers evidence against the Murder Club, discovering that nine wealthy men of the city are involved in high crimes. He identifies each of these men in nine segments, published in *Thrilling Detective* from February through October 1932. In each novelette, he kills one member of the Murder Club, leaving a small white card with the words, "Alias Mr. Death" in black letters. This calling card device would transfer to a crimson spider seal in The Spider, and a bat in flight for the Black Bat. I don't recall The Shadow ever leaving such a clue at the scene of one of his kills.

Like the Phantom Detective to come, he became a nemesis and feared by the underworld. The leader of The Murder Club would remain a mystery until

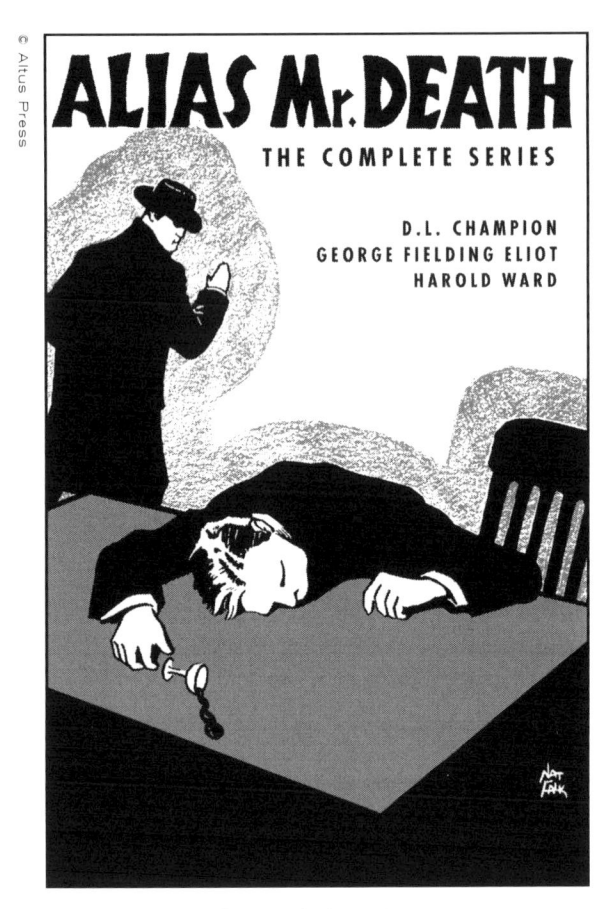

Alias Mr. Death: The Complete Series, 2009.

the last chapter, and the story would end in a fiery climax. It had all the thrills and action the reader wanted in their pulp fare.

Following the lead of *The Shadow*, which debuted in 1931, Mr. Death dons a terrifying hood and robe to disguise his true identity, as well as inspire fear in the hearts of evildoers. Zorro and The Shadow were already sporting weird costumes, so this new vigilante appeared to be following a trend that was about to explode in the pulp world. However, it was to be the Phantom Detective that carried on Jimmy Gilmore's battles. Perhaps the hood and robe were too close to The Shadow to suit Street & Smith, for when the Phantom appears on the scene, he merely wears a domino mask to hide his identity. The hood and robe have been tossed aside.

Many elements in this story ended up in dozens of plots outside of the Phantom Detective, but it is that series Mr. Death resembles the most. In just a few months after the last segment of *Alias Mr. Death*, the first issue of The World's Greatest Detective would be on the stands, and Street & Smith would cry foul, saying the Phantom Detective was a knock-off of their character, The Shadow. However, before they could bat an eye, the stands were filled with similar costumed crime fighters. The dye had been cast, and the hero pulps were flooding the market, thanks in part to D.L. Champion and *Alias Mr. Death*.

After the nine-segment novel in 1932, Mr. Death returned in two more novelettes seven years later: "Death Takes the Wheel" (*Thrilling Detective*, April 1939), and "Decks of Death" (*Thrilling Detective*, May 1939). Whether or not these later two entries were by D.L. Champion, I don't know. They were better written, but I understand Champion had honed his writing skills by then, so who knows?

Newkirk City, the town of the action in *Alias Mr. Death*, played a part in the Dan Fowler story, "King of Crime" (March 1936), an entry probably written by D.L. Champion.

Champion wasn't a particularly strong writer in 1932, at least in his novel-length work. But his novelettes were better written. So the formatting of *Alias Mr. Death* as nine novelettes read somewhat better than his early Phantom Detectives.

Alias Mr. Death appeared just as pulp publishers were looking for masked vigilantes to compete with The Shadow, and good or bad, Champion's story fit the formula they wanted. True, today that formula may appear dated, but in 1932 the readers loved it. And so did the publishers.

That's how legends are born.

The Angel

"Corridors of Doom" by Anthony Field (AKA Anatole Feldman) from *New Detective*, July 1935, features The Angel. "The Whole Hospital Became a

Lurking Place of Horror and Cunning Death" Six-feet-two, 180 pounds of "lean bronzed manhood, Steve Oakes, who lived by taking chances," was down to his last ten dollars, so he went to friend and "ally in certain extra-legal transactions that had baffled the police of the city" Jack Quinn on what to do with it. Steve wonders if he should put it on gambling to get more money or go down to headquarters "and see if we can muscle into something that might give us more action for our money." Quinn's suggestion of ten bottles of bootleg gin was out.

As they talk under the street light near the hospital, an ambulance tore out of the driveway, weaved, and headed straight for them. Jack Quinn pushes Steve out of the way as the ambulance pinned his left leg to the lamppost. It continued on before striking a fire hydrant and brick wall. Going to see the driver he tells Quinn, "That wasn't a madman driving that ambulance… it was a dying man! Not only a dying man, but a murdered one! Stabbed a dozen times if he was stabbed once."

Quinn's broken leg is operated on and he is given a room. Steve notes that the nurse that came into the room was nervous while taking vitals, especially when told a dead driver caused his injuries.

Steve Oakes knew that his work was just beginning. He left the room. On the opposite side, further down to his left, stood an open door of a capacious linen closet… slipping inside and closed the door after him.

"Thoughtfully he took the handkerchief from his pocket, tied it around his neck, tucked the white folds beneath his vest. He worried the lob of his ear a moment, then came a sudden decision. With deft fingers he yanked up the handkerchief and adjusted it across the lower part of his face, and by this simple device he changed his identity from that of the brother of Inspector John Oakes to that of—The Angel." This appears to merely be a disguise until he does become The Angel at the end of the story.

It had been months since that name and mysterious character had first startled the New York police and underworld alike. The Angel! Suddenly appearing out of nowhere, materializing and vanishing like a veritable winged ghost, he had been the amazing mystery of the year. And nemesis of crime and criminals!

No one had noticed that the birth of "The Angel" had been coincidental with the murder of Martin Oakes, the grand old man of the police force. Not even Inspector John Oakes, Steve's brother and Martin Oakes' son, had ever seen the connection.

Old Martin Oakes, however, had bequeathed the heritage of a born man-hunter to both of his stalwart sons. John Oakes, following close in his father's footsteps, had succeeded him as Inspector of Detectives. But young Steve, turbulent, reckless and restless, back

New Detective Magazine, July 1935.

SOME ORIGINAL PULP HEROES   45

home after years of buccaneering around the world, had small liking for the discipline of the force.

His father had been murdered, but instead of tracking down his slayer in the blue harness of a copper, Steve had preferred to play a lone and more dangerous hand. With only Jack Quinn, faithful comrade of a hundred adventures, to share the secret, he plunged into the vortex of the underworld as a self appointed avenger.

He had succeeded—his father had been avenged. But once in the reckless game, he had found that he couldn't get out—didn't want to get out. Perilously skirting beyond the borders of the law, he too had dedicated himself to the tradition of his father. Only, after his own fashion… It was that very spice of double danger that set sparks dancing in his eyes now It was thus that The Angel was born….

Such an extra-legal, irregular operator as The Angel, however, had no place in the regulated community, as Inspector John Oakes saw it. Preying only on the underworld though The Angel was, he constituted, in Inspector Oakes' mind, a menace to society. Twice the Inspector encountered him face to face in his operations' and both times the Inspector had been worsted. Furious, he had himself placed a reward on The Angel's head… He thought of his younger brother, Steve, as he had once seen him with Jack Quinn—two lazy, reckless, oil-stained ne'er-do-wells, better satisfied to earn a precarious living by doubling for Hollywood movie stars in dangerous stunts than by any regular steady job.

The Angel figured to start at the morgue but heard a strange noise behind a door. His hand went out to the knob… turned it so slowly that his muscles ached. It was the kitchen area and Quinn's nurse was on the floor dropping something down the floor drain. He re-entered the room noisily and asked her name and about the body of the ambulance driver. Nurse Mary Moore, at mention of this, choked back a cry, "You're a detective?"

"No Madam, you're wrong; but every detective in

© Two Books

CORRIDORS OF DOOM

A New "Angel" Novel By

ANTHONY FIELD

The Whole Hospital Became a Lurking Place of Horror and Cunning Death

New Detective, July 1935.

the city is looking for me… I am the Angel!"

She heard a patients call bell and her duty took over. She pushed past him and left the room. He closed the door and opened the floor drain, digs out a blood red stained scalpel with its tip broken. He frowns, pulls meditatively at the lob of his ear. He put it in his pocket and whistling "a gay little melody" continues looking for the morgue. Steve finds it and from his pocket he slipped a key of peculiar design. It had been cunningly fashioned by a master locksmith and unlocks the door, a la The Phantom Detective! To be fair though, all the pulp heroes went to the same locksmith to get one! All except Doc Savage who must have made his own. No locked door was safe in the city with all of them around.

Whistling again, he searches the dead body finding

an unfired gun and five thousand dollars (pay-off money, but for what?). Strange that no one had searched the body before this, and the body has been in the morgue for quite a while by now.

With gun in hand, Inspector John Oakes enters the room saying, "What the Devil! Who are you?" This is strange as earlier in the story it states that they have met twice before and the Inspector even has money on The Angels head!

"Not the Devil… I am The Angel" The Phantom Detective also stated, "Not the Devil… I am The Phantom!" Again, the handkerchief may not be his 'normal' disguise so John Oakes did not recognize him after meeting him twice before.

The Angel quips with the Inspector (his brother) much like The Saint by Leslie Charteris or many of McCulley's characters (Avenging Twins, Crimson Clown, Mongoose) when caught in a deadly trap. Steve asks who the dead man is and the Inspector, rocking back and forth on his heels, says "Sid Moyer of the underworld. This time I've got you where I want you. Angel, huh? Swell! Let's see you spread your wings and fly out of this little spot."

"Why not? I've done it before. All I have to do is clap my hands. Watch!" He claps his hands and at the same time kicks a stool through the air into John's stomach. The other two detectives fire guns but the bullets only tear his jacket sleeve. Steve's gun, a Luger, was now on his brother and he told the others to stop firing. He tells a doctor to study the ambulance driver, finds that he has been stabbed nine times by a scalpel. Before he left the phone rang and he answers it. He told his brother that the Superintendent of the hospital, Dr. Gaynor, wanted to see him in his office right away. He then leaves amidst "bullets hammering a savage tattoo against the wood."

Steve lurks outside the fire escape of Dr. Gaynor's office. Five people are present: Gaynor, Nurse Mary Moore, another nurse, Gay Peronne, Dr. Carpenter, millionaire Silas Brent, patient of the hospital and who founded and endowed it. Nurse Gay looks as if someone has taken unfair advantage of her—and that she didn't like it. When Inspector Oakes arrives he is informed that five grams of Radium has been stolen valued at two hundred and fifty thousand dollars. The two nurses and Dr. Carpenter were on the same floor when the radium was stolen from a locked narcotics cabinet. Carpenter found the radium missing and a large bloodstain on the floor. The Inspector learns that Silas Brent had recommended that murdered driver Sid Moyer be hired. The Angel enters through the window, Luger in hand, and asked who owned the scalpel he takes from his pocket and tosses to his brother. None answer, but he spies a nervous Dr. Carpenter. "I didn't want a feminine response this time, I wanted a masculine one—and I got it." Then he leaves through the window.

Steve explains to Quinn the facts up to that point, gives him an automatic and leaves to continue investigating. He finds Nurse Gay Peronne in the narcotics room prying open the cabinet, takes an item, and then meets a blond, mustached patient, Notorious London Ned, the slickest and most daring of international thieves! In Ned's room he finds a letter from Gay: "Dear Ned, I couldn't get away last week. Better come to the hospital yourself, as a patient. It's here to get. Your loving, Gay." A bottle of chloroform was also found under his mattress.

Millionaire Brent enters the room, saying he saw Gay and Ned down the hall, heard a noise in the room and came to investigate. London Ned enters next with a gun and tells Steve to get rid of his. He tosses it on the bed and when a scream is heard down the hall regains his gun, knocks Ned to the floor and leaves. In another room he finds that Mary Moore had screamed when hit on the head and knocked out. Steve, unmasked at the time, asked her if the person who hit her got the radium. In surprise she says, "How did you know?" Then she refused to answer anything else and she leaves. In the hall, Steve finds a nurses pin with torn cloth on the floor.

Again he informs Quinn of the goings on, then:

From his pocket, he proceeded to bring forth a number of small but decidedly interesting objects—relics of the days when he had risked his life almost daily as a daredevil movie double. He applied them now with sure and practiced fingers. With the aide of a small pocket mirror, his face was swiftly transformed—the Phantom Detective again.

It was with ironic humor that had originally suggested the disguise. And now under his expert fingers, his clean-cut, bronzed face was subtly transformed into an innocent, wide-eyed, innocuous one. It could have been the face of a soda-jerker, a ribbon clerk, or a bookkeeper. A wad of cotton in his cheeks accounted for the round face.

But it was the notorious face of the avenger—sometimes the Angel of Death. And by that token, Quinn knew that the action was swiftly reaching a climax. This is probably the true disguise of The Angel—Feldman mentions a couple of times later about the "innocent face" (as with an Angel).

In the hall, near the elevator, two blows meant to kill, knock Steve out. Still Death stalked those corridors of doom. He awoke in a darkened storage room in the basement with dead Gay Peronne's body on top of him, the smell of chloroform about her. He found her shirt torn where her nurse's pin should have been. There's a big problem with this part of the story as if a whole chapter has been left out—if Steve is in disguise and no one knows him, just waiting innocently by the elevator, why was he knocked out and left for dead? Had Mary Moore originally stolen the radium to be attacked by Gay? Steve decided to check London Ned's room as Gay was seen there last. Leaving as not to disturb the smudged footprints in the dust.

It comes out that Mary had scared off who originally opened the radium cabinet and then had taken it herself to give to Dr. Carpenter. Carpenter turns out to be honest and wasn't about to steal it, although why did he say he found it missing when Mary really did?. While The Angel listens from one room he notes that Millionaire Brent is listening from London Ned's room.

Mary and Carpenter go to Ned's room to talk to Gay, thinking she is there. The Angel then enters also and tells Brent to come from the closet. "Who are you?"

"Nemesis! I am The Angel—an accusing Angel. Accusing you of killing the crook ambulance driver you got into the hospital to help you steal the radium. You stabbed him when he tried to snatch the radium from you and run! But your tussle had caused a noise, brought Miss Moore—and she had found the radium where you had dropped it to stab that driver. You watched her—and when Gay Peronne attacked her and stole it, you followed Gay Peronne, you murdered her—your second murder, Brent—and left her in the storeroom of the basement. But you didn't find the radium on her—she had already hidden it. So you came up here to where she must have hidden it…"

The footprints in the basement are from his slippers, not shoes. The Angel searches his bathrobe and finds the radium in Mary's thermometer.

The Angel and Brent fight briefly, then London Ned enters with a gun. He tells The Angel to get rid of his gun and Steve slides it on the floor behind Brent. The Angel asks doesn't Ned want to say goodbye to Gay, then tells him that Brent killed her. In animal rage Ned turns to face Brent and in that moment of distraction The Angel throws his fist and knocks him out cold. This gives Brent a chance to grab Steve's Luger and as he faces them from the hallway door is shot from behind in the shoulder by Quinn. "The end of the last round and I got in just before the final gong. Just the same I'm getting sick of saving—."

"Stow it!" orders Steve. He had almost disclosed their relationship together—had almost betrayed the identity of The Angel.

In Quinn's room Steve removes The Angel's disguise as he hears of the arrest in the other room. In the hall he asked his Inspector brother about it and he's told millionaire Brent had went broke on the market and thought of stealing the radium and he should take Quinn in for packing a rod without a license… "But he did the department a little service tonight, so I'm going to let him get away with it. But get him out of here before I change my mind."

We're told to, "Watch For More Stories of The Angel and Jerry Quinn in Future Issues of *New Detective Magazine*, the Detective-Mystery Magazine for Intelligent Readers." So, it must have been planned to continue the series by Feldman and the editors.

The Avenger

In the roaring heart of the crucible, steel is made. In the raging flame of personal tragedy, men are sometimes forged into something more than human.

It was so with Dick Benson. He had been a man. After the dread loss inflicted on him by an inhuman crime ring, he became a machine of vengeance dedicated to the extermination of all other crime rings.

He turned into the person we know now: a figure of ice and steel, more pitiless than both; a mechanism of whipcord and flame; a symbol of destruction to crooks and killers; a terrible, almost impersonal Force, masking chill genius and supernormal power behind a face as white and dead as a mask from the grave. Only his eyes, like ice in a polar dawn, hint at the deadliness of the scourge the underworld heedlessly invoked against itself when crime's greed turned the retired adventurer, Richard Henry Benson, into—The Avenger ("Justice, Inc.," September 1939).

During the 1930s the name of Kenneth Robeson was like magic to the readers of the pulp magazines. Kenneth Robeson was the 'house name' used by Street & Smith for their very popular series of Doc Savage, which had begun in 1933 following the success of The Shadow. The editors at Street & Smith decided to capitalize on the magic name, so they created another series, which also used the Robeson house name, and advertised the new series as being written

The Avenger, September 1939.

by the creator of Doc Savage. The new magazine appeared on the stands, with the first issue dated September 1939, in a novel titled "Justice, Inc.," and featured… as its hero… a character called The Avenger. Where Doc Savage had been known as "The Man of Bronze," The Avenger is billed as 'The Man of Steel.' Another difference was in the authorship of the two series; Lester Dent had made famous the character of Doc Savage, while Paul Ernst scripted the new adventures of The Avenger, both using the Kenneth Robeson house name.

This new series was a carbon copy of the Doc Savage adventures; the same type of mystery, excitement, adventure and characters. The exploits of The Avenger were so close to that of Doc Savage that the readers were unaware of the difference in authors, and read both series with equal enthusiasm. It is the

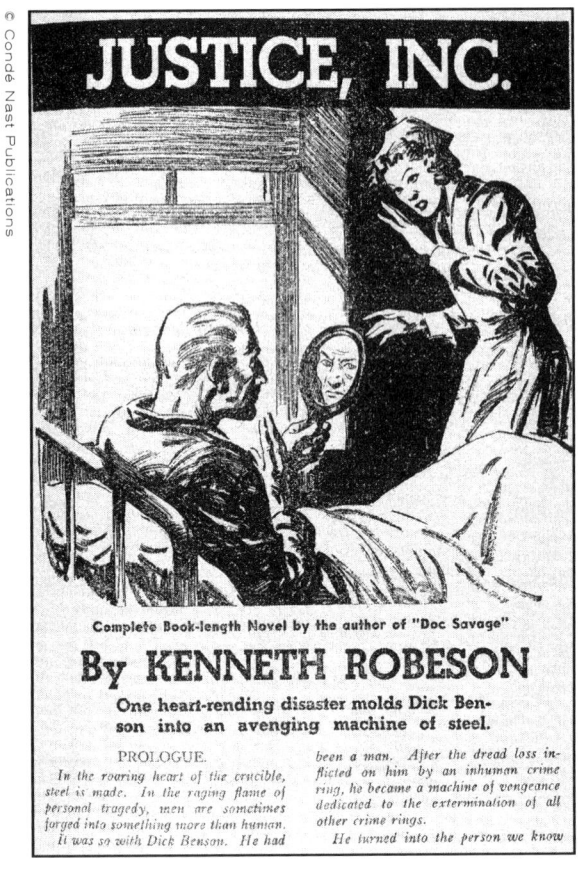

The Avenger, September 1939.

above Lake Ontario. The plane's crew and passengers tell Benson that he had boarded the plane alone. The shock of his double loss turns Benson's hair white and leaves his face paralyzed and a colorless horror.

Benson becomes The Avenger, and begins his own campaign to search for the answer to the tragic disappearance of his family. Benson solves the mystery by the end of the story, but vows to continue his campaign against crime… as The Avenger. He wasn't a big man, just average in size. He stood five feet eight inches tall, and weighed no more than a hundred and sixty pounds. But ounce for ounce, his sinew and muscle are packed with force beyond any scientific explanation:

> Benson's right hand lashed out. There was less than a ten-inch swing behind it, but his fist hit the jaw of the nearest man like a knob of iron on the end of an iron lance. The man fell back as if he had been shot. One-handed, Benson twisted the arm he held, and the second man moaned, then screamed and slumped in the seat—passed out from the pain. The third man kicked frantically at Benson's head.
>
> That was a mistake, for Benson's slim and terrible right hand went out… steely-white fingers caught the calf of the vicious leg… and squeezed. The third man yelled, for up his body, from vital nerve points streamed pain too great to be borne. ("Justice, Inc.")

considered opinion of many researchers that "Justice, Inc." is too superior of a novel to have appeared in a pulp magazine. It was certainly above average for the novels then appearing in the pulps. In my own opinion it has at least more plot, if not characterization, than any Doc Savage story, though many Doc Savage fans may not agree with me.

In the opening chapter of "Justice, Inc.," we are introduced to Richard Henry Benson, his wife, Alicia, and their little daughter, Alice. They board a plane for Montreal, as it is readying for take-off from the Buffalo airport. While on board the plane Benson leaves his lovely wife and daughter to go to the plane's lavatory. He was never to see them again, because while he was in the lavatory his wife and little Alice were dropped through a trap door of the plane, high

Benson refrains from killing, but carries two weapons Mike and Ike. The man with the still, white face took two things from a mass of wrappings. One was a knife, the other a gun. But they were like no knife or gun the dour Scot had ever seen before. Ike, the knife, was about eight inches long over all, and had practically no handle. The blade was double-edged, with a reinforcing spine down the middle. When Benson tilted the weapon a bit, MacMurdie saw that the handle was a light, hollow tube. Benson had designed the knife himself. Mike, the gun, was a caliber .22, but that was the only thing standard about it. The barrel was almost as long as the barrel of a target pistol. The cylinder, to streamline the gun, was small and held only four cartridges. The butt slanted so that it was almost in a straight line with the barrel. Altogether, it was almost like a straight piece of blued steel tubing with a little bulge for a cylinder and a slight bend for a handle. There was a silencer on it. Benson rolled his trousers legs up to the knee. To the inside of the left calf he strapped a slim sheath, and in it he slid the razor-sharp knife. To the inside of the right calf, so that it conformed to the bulge of steely muscle there, he strapped an almost-as-slim holster into which he slipped the tiny gun. ("Justice, Inc."). Benson had acquired his knife-throwing skills when he was a world traveler. With Mike he can hit a dime at fifty paces… or crease a man's skull, rendering him unconscious without killing him.

During his travels Benson had amassed many fortunes, and other skills as well. But, to compete with Doc Savage, Benson and his crew uncover a wealth of Aztec gold ("The Yellow Hoard," October 1939), which enables him to fight crime in the style of Doc Savage.

The Avenger acquired several aides during the series, each being introduced through the plot they were involved in. Their characters were explored and built up, plus Paul Ernst even employed Dent's own use of "tags" for his characterization of the people involved in the stories. Two aids were introduced in the first story, "Justice, Inc.," they were Fergus Mac-Murdie, the Scot, and Algernon Heathcote Smith, the giant. Or Mac and Smitty as they were commonly referred to.

Fergus MacMurdie stood over six feet, and had coarse red hair and bitter blue eyes. His hands doubled into fists like bone clubs. His feet were the biggest Benson had ever seen, and they made the bony legs above them look even bonier. He was a knobby figure of a man with ears that stuck out like sails on each side of a thick-skinned red neck. He was a Scot, and preferred to be called Mac. He had completed three years of medical school, but too poor to finish. He was a licensed pharmacist, and had several pharmacies before crooks destroyed his businesses and killed his family.

Algernon Heathcote Smith has a huge face, moonlike and placid, with peaceable and not-too-intelligent-looking china blue eyes. His voice was rather high for his vast bulk. For he was a giant; standing six feet nine inches, and weighed two hundred and eighty-five pounds. He was fifty-three inches around the chest, and wore size-nineteen collar. His arms were bigger around than most men's thighs, and his legs were pillars fit for building-foundation purposes. Under his arms, among the barrel of his chest, the slabs and knots of muscle were so ponderous that his arms couldn't hang straight down—they crooked out so that they looked stubby, though actually they were almost of gorilla length. Smitty was an electrical engineer—one of the best, and a graduate of Massachusetts Tech.

Mac and Smitty were The Avenger's answer to Monk Mayfair and Ham Brooks of the Doc Savage adventures. No other aids could have been introduced in the first novel, as it was already too thick in plot and action. Instead they would be added in future stories, to add to the next plot, the next action, and the next adventure.

Miss Nellie Gray was introduced in the second novel, "The Yellow Hoard." She was the daughter of an archaeologist, and had yellow-bronze hair and gray eyes, and the finest pink-white skin you'd ever care to see. She looked like a dish of peaches going somewhere to be eaten with cream. She looked as little and delicate as something made of porcelain. But her appearance was deceiving—for during her college days, instead of going out for tennis or basketball, like most sports-minded young girls, she had studied ju-jitsu, boxing and wrestling. After graduating from school she had taken advanced training, thus becoming an expert in the fighting technique of ju-jitsu:

> At one moment Carp had a none-too-clean paw on the girl's arm. At the next he seemed to have leaped into the air in an attempt at a backward flying somersault. An attempt that didn't come off very well, because he lit on his back and shoulders with a grunt. ("The Yellow Hoard")

Josh and Rosabel Newton were introduced in the third novel, "The Sky Walker" (November 1939). There was a close bond between these two—man and wife. Graduates both, of Tuskegee Institute, Josh was a most amazing fellow; A tall and gangling Negro, he looked sleepy and dull-witted. But Josh was a highly educated and singularly intelligent man. He appeared thin and spindling, and stood six feet two inches tall. Rosabel was slenderly rounded, pretty. They were a black couple, making them unique in the annals of the hero pulp magazines. Highly intelligent, they became quick aides to The Avenger. Being black was an asset to this group of crime-fighters, as they could easily infiltrate an area, through a job, and not be under suspicion of the criminals. However, the Avenger novels portrayed them as intelligent, serious, and without fear; completely disregarding the black stereotype of the radio and theater of the 1940s. The parts they played in the Avenger novels would be equal to that of the other aides in the series.

Cole Wilson was introduced in the middle of the series, in a story titled "Murder on Wheels," November 1940. He was to be the last aid of The Avenger. He was a young fellow, and rather striking-looking. In fact he was considered handsome, with straight brown hair, high off his forehead, and with alert black eyes and a heavy jaw. Cole Wilson's reason for being introduced into the series is something of a mystery. At times he struck me as a young Lamont Cranston or Secret Agent "X," and he was certainly a crime-fighter of ability. He even appeared as an equal to The Avenger (at least in "Murder on Wheels"), with some differences. His character was ideal as a possible spin-off series; and his description is the same as most young pulp heroes of that era.

Another change in this novel is the return of Benson's facial muscles and re-birth of his hair… which completely changes our hero, something not common for a pulp character. Though still called The Avenger, he was lacking that character's description of dead face and white hair, which the readers had come to know as The Avenger. Now he only has the appearance of Richard Benson. If the readership was not already declining, then it must have done so with this change. Who decided on the change (either Ernst or the editors) is unknown. But it was a mistake. Benson loses that 'fictional' reality of a pulp hero and, at the same time, Cole Wilson is introduced into the series. And Cole Wilson was good enough as a pulp hero to have been given a secret identity… and his own magazine. Strange! What was going on? I don't know, but there was a decline in The Avenger's popularity. Maybe they were looking for a new character in case the Avenger magazine failed… and Cole Wilson would have been a good choice to carry on in his own magazine.

The series was well written, and probably enjoyed the same readership as that of the Doc Savage adventures. But, unfortunately, it was to suffer the same fate as all late entries into the pulps did… and die a shorter death than the earlier entries. The Avenger only lasted for twenty-four issues in his own magazine; then, in 1942, he was assigned to the back pages of *Clues Detective,* another magazine published by Street & Smith, where he appeared in short stories for five more exploits. With this change also came a change in authorship—as Emile C. Tepperman is now writing the stories as Kenneth Robeson. In the August 1944 issue of *The Shadow Magazine,* the last appearance of The Avenger was presented—again written by Tepperman.

Paperback Library began reprinting The Avenger novels in 1972. They used cover artist George Gross for their new series, and his covers caught the eyes of a new generation of readers. George Gross had contributed cover art to the pulps—at least for *Jungle Stories*, and his new covers for Paperback Library were of a higher quality than those first Avenger covers for the magazine. The series was a sell-out, and Paperback Library reprinted the twenty-four novels by Paul Ernst. They decided against reprinting the short stories of The Avenger from *Clues Detective* and *The Shadow Magazine*. Instead, they hired pulp fan Ron Goulart to write new stories about The Avenger, but keeping the action in the 1940s. Ron Goulart turned out 12 new stories, each with a fantastic title. But something was missing, and even the beautiful covers of George Gross could not save the series past the 12 new entries. At the present time there are no plans to bring back the character of The Avenger. However, Robert Weinberg reprinted the five short stories from *Clues Detective* in his fanzine, *Pulp*. Only the one short story from *The Shadow Magazine* has not been reprinted.

Hidden gold of the Aztecs. A man walking in the sky. Invisible planes. Messages traced in blood. A plague of death. Fine-white powder-like snow. Ancient Egyptian ring. Six hundred year old curse. Millions in missing securities. Indian rain gods. Paul Ernst. Misty clouds. Deadly lightning bolts. Mac-Murdie. Howling dogs. Secret weapons. Tiny man. Green smiling dogs; Lost civilizations. Smitty. Ancient manuscripts. Robots. Dying man exhaling fire. Nellie Gray, A murderous gunman. White hair. A dentist's forceps. Emile Tepperman. Three gold crowns. Gold medallions. A twisted dwarf. Josh and Rosabel. Power failures. Saboteurs. Strange disease. Rubber factories. Stolen art. Ape-like creatures. The black orchid of death. Stolen formulas. Cole Wilson. Superhuman killers. Fiendish laugh. Wholesale murder. Secret military devices. Secret inventions, Cryptic messages. Bloody killings. Werewolves. Ron Goulart. Horror films. Dead actors. Spy rings. Time travel. Devils. Masks. The Prince of Darkness. Disc-like objects. UFOs. Comic books? Wonderman?

The Avenger, November 1940.

Suicides. Machine of death. Mike and Ike. Gestapo. Vampire killings. Part flesh, part metal. Invisible man. Fog-shrouded haunted islands. Ghosts. Action. Thrills. Adventure. Death. Fights. Escapee.

It was a fascinating series; about a man driven towards vengeance by the terrible murder of his family—a tragedy that accidentally destroys his facial muscles and turns his hair white. The stories were filled with action, adventure and excitement in the tradition of Doc Savage. The series was well written, and the character of The Avenger was well thought out by pulpsmith Paul Ernst. Benson was a superman, with superhuman strength… a fighter, escape artist, and top-notch crime-fighter. The series should have lasted. It didn't. The war may have been responsible, but there could have been other reasons. Whatever the case, the exploits of The Avenger were much too

SOME ORIGINAL PULP HEROES 53

short. Yet it deserves a place in pulp history; and *The Avenger Magazine* should be placed on the collector's shelf… right next to the *Doc Savage Magazine,* the cousin of The Avenger!

The Black Bat

The Thrilling Group kicked off their second round of pulp hero heavyweights in 1939 with a new story featuring Alias Mr. Death, then in June the Candid Camera Kid popped up in *Detective Novels* and in July we found the Black Bat in the pages of *Black Book Detective.* More heroes would follow in 1940 and '41. Standard's wordsmith, Norman Daniels, created many of the new series.

Daniels' original idea was for Tony Quinn to fight crime as The Tiger. Blinded in the courtroom by acid, the damage left scars around his eyes, giving him the moniker. The story was accepted, but Leo Margulies, head editor for Standard at the time, wanted something that would coincide with a magazine they'd recently picked up, *Black Book Detective.* A short story series that ran in a previous title, The Bat, in Popular Detective, may have influenced their final decision. The Tiger was changed to The Black Bat, and became one of the most popular of the late edition heroes for Ned Pines' Thrilling Group. It was merely coincidence that The Black Bat and Batman started during the same period.

Standard slapped their house name, G. Wayman Jones on the stories to let Norman know the character belonged to them, but he became the main author for the series throughout its long run. He told me that Leo wanted the character to have the feel of The Shadow, and that every time Walter Gibson got a raise, so did he. In "Markets of Treason" (Winter 1944), the Black Bat does drop the ribbed cape, and now merely wears black to blend into the shadows. The stories continued to be top notch. However, the bat regalia was now missed by most readers.

The July 1940 entry, "The Black Bat's Flame Trail" is the first unknown author assigned to the series.

Black Book Detective, July 1939.

Will Murray believes this author is Whit Ellsworth, but I lean more towards Prentice Winchell (most familiar to readers under his pen name, Stewart Sterling). Two more stories, "The Black Bat's Dragon Trail" (January 1941) and "The Black Bat's Summons" (July 1941) are also unknowns. Perhaps the three are by the same author. I suspect at least two of them are.

There is no question on the next ghost author. Laurence Donovan wrote three non-Daniels entries, "The Murder Prophet" (September 1942), "Millions for a Murderer" (March 1943), and "Without Blood They Die" (Summer 1943). The rest of the stories are by Norman Daniels until the end of the series. Daniels told me that a new editor had been assigned to the series, replacing long-time editorial head, Leo Margulies. Who this new editor was, he couldn't remem-

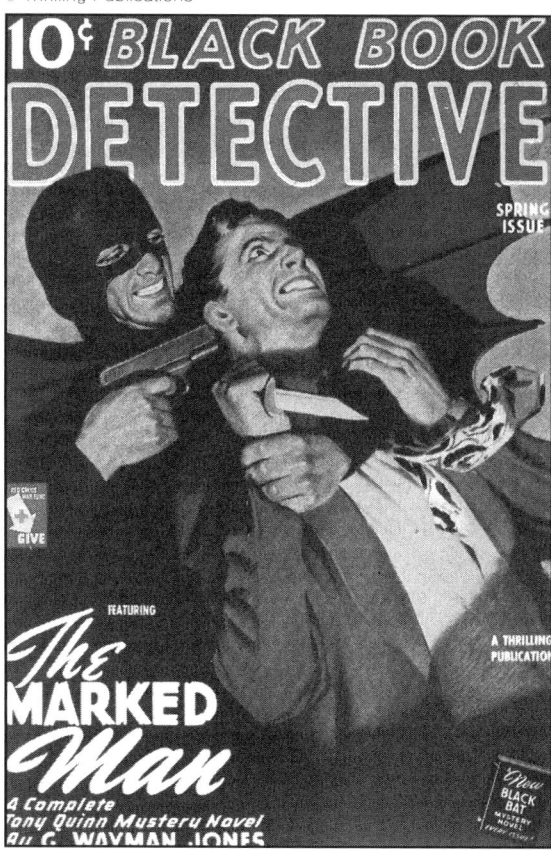

Black Book Detective, Spring 1945.

ber, but said it was a woman, and she wanted more adult content to the stories. Norman didn't feel comfortable writing sex scenes, so she brought in another author. "The Eyes of Murder" was promised for Spring 1952, but didn't appear. Instead, the next novel to appear is Prentice Winchell's "Hot, Willing, and Deadly" (Winter 1953). A little research does turn up an old novel titled, "The Eyes of Death" by Stewart Sterling. It was a Dan Fowler story published in November 1941, and involved Nazis. My guess is that Sterling planned on rewriting the Fowler story into a Black Bat entry, but it didn't happen. "The Eyes of Murder" more likely was rewritten as "The Staring Killer" a Phantom Detective novel. The Black Bat series appeared to have came to an end. However, a year later it was resurrected and Sterling/Winchell is back with another story. "Hot, Willing, and Deadly," which was probably more in keeping with what the editor wanted. Another story is promised, "The Lady of Death" by Prentice Winchell. It doesn't appear. The series does end this time. Winchell/Sterling rewrote "The Lady of Death" as "The Lady's Out for Blood," and sold it to *Triple Detective* (Spring 1953); Tony Quinn had been replaced. Norman Daniels had written an unpublished Black Bat story, "The Celebrity Murders," but it never appeared (in the pulps, at least). Daniels would rewrite the story as a "paperback original" in 1960.

Stewart Sterling was a good writer, and had worked in the pulps for many years. I'm sure he was writing Phantom Detectives, early Dan Fowlers, and probably those early Black Bats. I wish we could find his records, as I'm sure we would uncover some interesting facts, as well as possibly some unpublished manuscripts. But those final Black Bat stories were an incredible jump from a good series, to mediocre stories. The sex and rough language the editor wanted just didn't work well on Norman Daniels' 1939 creation. Personally, I think they should have left it alone.

As with all of the single character pulps, the early stories were the best in the series. So it was with the Black Bat. At least up through the end of the World War, we had some exciting stories of Nazis and sabotage, and even some super criminals. After the war years, the stories tended to tone down, becoming more simple crimes, especially the "long ago crimes," where something happens years before that now surfaces into some new crime. Until the end, when we are given drug or juvenile gang-related criminal activity. Or, as with Prentice Winchell, prostitution and crimes of passion. Good stories perhaps, but I missed the super criminals and foreign agents bent on the destruction of America.

I often wonder how the series would have fared had it began in the early Thirties, as a companion to The Phantom Detective. There is a possibility it would have been more popular, and even outlasted the great Phantom. Unfortunately, it would have been created by someone else, and ended up with an even more chaotic authorship. Perhaps it's best the series waited until 1939 after all.

The Crimson Mask

The Crimson Mask was another of those late creations from Ned Pines' Standard titles, appearing in *Detective Novels* (Better Publications) beginning in August 1940. Bylined Frank Johnson, the stories were initially written by pulp scribe Norman Daniels before being handed off to Leo Margulies' stable of writers.

Pre-dating the Purple Scar by a year, Doc Clarke would be something of a chalkboard for plastic surgeon, Doc Murdock, whose police officer brother was murdered by gangsters. When Murdock's brother washed ashore, his face was bloated and discolored. The plastic surgeon made a hideous mask that resembled his dead brother's face, which he wore to frighten criminals. Doc Clarke's father, also a police officer, had also been murdered; shot in the back of the head. The result caused a strange crimson discoloration around his eyes. A pharmacist by trade, Robert Clarke dons a black suit and crimson mask to battle gangsters. Another similarity in the Purple Scar and Crimson Mask, both had offices in a poor neighborhood, where they helped the downtrodden and were well thought of by the community. Doc Murdock was active with his plastic surgery clinic, while Doc Clarke was a pharmacist at the corner drugstore on Carmody Street.

There's little doubt that both series were created by Leo Margulies through editorial committee.

The novelettes were typical formula, and so too were the characters. Sandra Gray, a nurse at the local hospital was Doc Clarke's love interest. He was also aided by David Small, a friend and former college classmate. And the ever-present police official, in this case former Police Commissioner, Theodore Warrick. Naturally, the Crimson Mask would step in when a case surfaced that was too baffling for the police.

Oddly, for a pharmacist, Doc Clarke is a scientific criminologist as well as a ballistic expert and make-up artist. He can crack a safe, use ventriloquism, and has knowledge of the nerve centers in the human body. No science escaped his study in the pursuit of criminals. I might add that these traits were part of the make up of all of the masked crime fighters. And there's also little doubt that the same authors who were churning out the Phantom Detective and Dan Fowler were also involved in the Crimson Mask's adventures, as well as Standard's other lead stories.

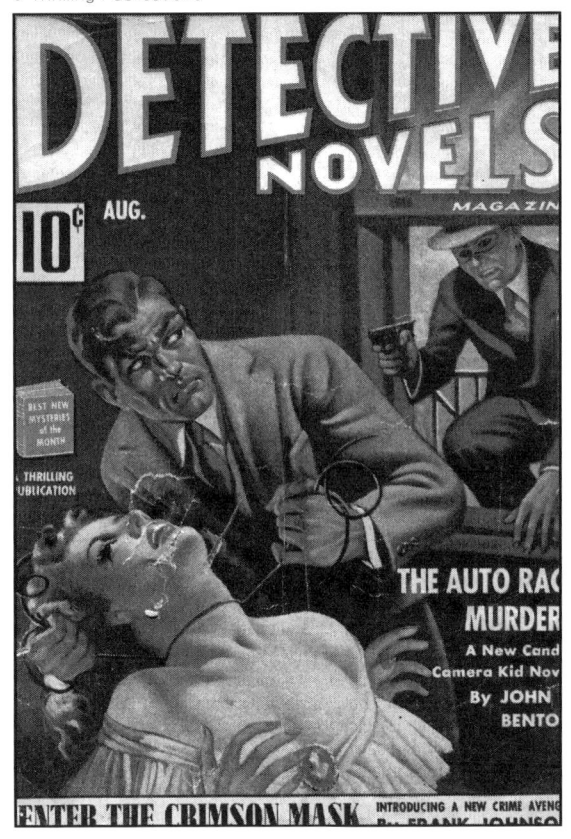

Detective Novels Magazine, August 1940.

That the series lasted for 16 stories is proof that it was successful. The Purple Scar only made it for four adventures, and the Masked Detective ended after 13 stories. But this success might be attributed to the magazine title, *Detective Novels,* which was running numerous short story characters at the time, including the very popular Jerry Wade—the Candid

Camera Kid.

Unfortunately, very few of the late pulp entries had a successful run beyond a few years. The war in Europe, coupled with the paper shortage in America, and many of Standard's stable of writers heading off to the war effort forced a shortage in the pulp industry. Not to mention the poor economy at the time. And with the price of the magazines jumping from a dime to fifteen cents by the mid 1940s, readers were undoubtedly being more selective with their change; Standard would end up dropping most of the latecomers, relying instead on the original titles that had brought them this far. The Phantom Detective and Dan Fowler (from *G-Men Detective*) would continue until the end. Only one of the 1940s title would make it, and that was the Black Bat in *Black Book Detective*.

All in all, it was a shame, though. Characters like the Crimson Mask were a lot of fun, and added much color to otherwise formulaic detective stories. They deserved to have their day. Too bad, it was so short lived.

Dan Fowler—An Odd Entry

Secret Agent "X" was a "Lone Wolf" crime-fighter, published by Ace Magazine Group. And though he basically operated alone, there were a number of individuals who aided him in his adventures: Betty Dale, the petite, blond-haired, blue-eyed, love interest throughout most of the early stories; Jim Hobart, head of the Hobart Detective Agency, often used by "X" in his investigations (the Agency was actually owned by Secret Agent "X"); Harvey Bates, the head of another investigative organization that was also created by Secret Agent "X;" K-9, identified in the later novels as Ronald Holme, was the head of a secret government agency, and was the actual boss of the Agent X. Though other names appeared and disappeared throughout the run, the characters listed here were the main aides to the hero.

There was also a similar line-up for many of the other pulp heroes. Let's look at a few of these series:

The Black Bat *(Black Book Detective):* Carol Baldwin was the pretty blond-haired, blue-eyed, love interest for the Black Bat; Silk Kirby was the Black Bat's personal aide; big Butch O'Leary aided the Black Bat in his investigations; Police Commissioner Jerome Warner (early stories); McGrath went from a detective-sergeant to lieutenant, to captain of detectives, and finally inspector by the end of the series.

The Phantom Detective: lovely, dark-haired Muriel Havens was the love interest of the Phantom Detective; Steve Huston, crime-reporter and aide to the Phantom; Chip Dorlan was his young protégé; Frank Havens was the newspaper publisher and confidante to the Phantom.

The (Green) Ghost: Merry White was a petite, dark-haired, green-eyed vamp and love interest of the Green Ghost; Glenn Saunders was the hero's double; Tiny Tim Terry is aide and friend to the Green Ghost; Joe Harper is a friend and hanger-on; Edward Standish is the Commissioner of Police.

Dan Fowler *(G-Men Detective):* Sally Vane is the pretty, blond-haired, blue-eyed, love interest of Dan Fowler; Agent Larry Kendal is Dan's partner in most cases; Agent Klein will assist in most cases; the Director of the FBI (Dan's only boss), J. Edgar Hoover, of course.

The point to all this is that each of these characters was interchangeable within most of the main pulp character series. Sometimes Muriel Havens might end up with blond instead of dark hair. Even Merry White's green eyes turned blue at least once! And G.T. Fleming-Roberts wrote all of the stories about the Green Ghost, and created the character of Merry White. It was very easy for one author writing one series, to write one of the other series. Just change the names of the characters and presto! Norman Daniels once commented that he kept a file card on all of the main characters for which he was writing. That way he could pull up the file cards for data about any of the characters. It could easily become a mess if the authors didn't do so. The three main writers of *The Spider* were Norvell Page, Emile C. Tepperman and Wayne Rogers; the three main authors of *Operator #5* series were Fred Davis, Emile C. Tepperman, and Wayne Rogers. Emile C. Tepperman wrote several of the Secret Agent "X" stories, and probably several of the adventures of the Phantom Detective and Dan Fowler. The market was wide open.

There is a question in the early research, that G.T. Fleming-Roberts might have written three unpublished Secret Agent "X" stories. Looking over the previous paragraphs, we can see that it would have been very easy for Fleming-Roberts to make a few changes in characters, and these unpublished Secret Agent "X" stories could have been turned into another series character. We can eliminate The Spider and Operator #5, as Robert Weinberg uncovered the identities behind the authors of those stories. We know all about Doc Savage, The Shadow, The Avenger, and most of the others from the Street & Smith and Popular Publications houses. To be honest, the main area of our investigations should be aimed towards the Standard Magazine Group, concentrating most of our attention on the Phantom Detective and Dan Fowler.

Regardless, at this time there has been no serious investigation into the authorship of these two popular pulp series and the actual authors may never be known except in a few cases. I would imagine that about 90 percent of Norman Daniels' work in both Dan Fowler and the Phantom Detective is known. And his other work, as well.

However, back to the Secret Agent "X" series. As most readers are already aware, this series was started by Paul Chadwick (probably through editorial suggestions), with a few of the early stories being written by Emile C. Tepperman. With the June 1935 issue, G.T. Fleming-Roberts began writing the stories, eventually making it his own series. He would write 21 of the published stories and possibly three more that were not published as Secret Agent "X" stories,

G-Men Detective, April 1939.

though they were written as such. The last Secret Agent "X" entry, "Yoke of the Crimson Coterie," was published in March 1939, so it is at this point that any suspicious novels should start to appear.

The Secret Agent "X" title actually went through a number of changes of its own. At first, the sub-title of the magazine was "The Man of a Thousand Faces." This sub-title lasted until the November 1935 issue, when it suddenly changed to "Detective Mysteries." With the December 1936 issue, it became "G-Men Action Adventures," or sometimes "G-Men Action Mysteries," and returning to "Detective Mysteries" with the February 1938 issue.

Personally, I feel that G.T. Fleming-Roberts' best stories appeared during the 1935-36 period. After the February 1937 story, "Death's Frozen Formula," and with the change in sub-title to "G-Men Action

Adventures," the character takes on more of a G-man persona; plus, Secret Agent "X" becomes more hard-boiled and uses wise cracks when speaking. This is totally unlike the early characteristics of the Agent. He begins traveling to more distant locales, finally leaving the confines of New York behind him. All of the main characters are eventually dropped, with the exception of the Agent's boss, K-9, who actually makes a couple of appearances now: "Claws of the Corpse Cult" (April 1938), and "Corpse Contraband, (December 1938).

Similar to the Fleming-Roberts' later Green Ghost story, "The Case of the Walking Skeletal" (Spring 1941), the Dan Fowler story that appeared in *G-Men Detective* one month after the Secret Agent "X" magazine folded sounds a lot like an Agent X adventure, and the plot smacked of G.T. Fleming-Roberts. The story in question is "Crimson Crusade," from April 1939. The final Secret Agent "X" issue was "Yoke of the Crimson Coterie" (March 1939). Even the titles are similar!

Two mysteries occurred six years previously; the famous kidnapping of the young baby of our national hero, Major-General Robert M. Vanderlaugh, and the ransom of five hundred thousand dollars that was paid for the return of young Bobby Vanderlaugh. But the child was never seen again, nor was the money. Shortly after the kidnapping, six men left for an expedition into the Jungle of South America. These six men, Winston Holt, G.W. Yardley, Warren Breen, Alfred Burg, Joseph Welch, and Monte Maroni eventually returned to America—without Warren Breen, who had supposedly been killed during the expedition by local headhunters. Maroni, Borg, and Welch were known criminals, and the leading suspects in the Vanderlaugh kidnapping. They were picked up and questioned by the police. However, they could not be proven guilty in the kidnapping case, but were convicted on lesser crimes. The kidnapping was never solved.

Maroni had been released early, but Borg and Welch had received life sentences. But now someone has rescued the other two from prison, and they are immediately identified in bank robberies. However, one by one, Maroni, Borg, and Welch appear to get killed, ending up with their hands chopped off! Their faces are also disfigured beyond recognition. Our hero is ordered onto the case and he decides to start with the mysterious expedition to the Amazon region, interviewing the remaining members. Winston Holt appears to be dying from some unknown jungle fever, six years after the expedition. He had been the scientist/archeologist for the trip. G.W. Yardley had been the actual "great white hunter" who had led the expedition into South America. Supposedly, Maroni, Welch, Borg and Breen had financed the expedition.

The story that our hero hears is that the expedition had discovered a temple in the jungle containing a great treasure. However, when Breen removed the jeweled eyes from the temple statue, the local natives got very upset. The expedition runs for their lives but Breen is caught and "supposedly" killed by the local headhunters. But he yells a promise of vengeance against his partners who have left him to die.

Our hero believes that the expedition had something to do with the kidnapping. But he can't understand why the members are losing their hands. Our hero is with Winston Holt when he "dies" from the mysterious fever. But crooks enter the house and escape with the body! Our hero wonders, For his hands, maybe? During the removal of Holt's body, one of the gang is shot in the hand. When our hero locates the remaining member, G.W. Yardley, his hand is bandaged. He claims that he purposely burned his hand to keep Breen from killing him for the secret he holds. For he believes that Breen is still alive, that he had escaped from the headhunters.

Now, more of the story unfolds. The six men had each drew the portion of a secret map on each of their hands, so no one person would be able to find the temple again without the help of the others. This map supposedly shows the way to the hidden temple and the great treasures. And somebody wanted this map and was killing the members of the ill-fated expedition for their hands.

But now our hero understands all. The hidden temple is merely a red herring, and he knows who the killer is. What had really happened was that the crooks had taken the Vanderlaugh baby to the Amazon jungle, along with the ransom money. The money was now hidden in the temple. The supposed treasure was merely a blind for the innocent dupes accompanying the expedition. The killer needed the hands in order to return to the area of the temple for that fortune. Our hero sets a trap and captures the killer who turns out to be….

The natives had kept the baby and were raising him as one of their own. Our hero notifies the appropriate authorities and the South American officials rescue the child to be returned to his parents, and the old kidnapping case is finally solved.

Doesn't this plot sound familiar? It should. G.T. Fleming-Roberts, among others, used it over and over again. Now, let's go back to Secret Agent "X," where we left off a few paragraphs ago. When the sub-title changed to "G-Men Action Adventures," our hero started sounding more like a G-man. From mid 1937 to the end of the series, our hero could have been impersonating Dan Fowler of *G-Men Detective*. Or, more likely, Dan Fowler was impersonating Secret Agent "X" in the last of his series. However you look at it, Secret Agent "X" starts talking and acting like Dan Fowler in those last novels. And his mysterious boss, K-9, becomes active in the cases. In fact, K-9 starts acting more and more like Dan Fowler's "Director" of the FBI

I did read all the Dan Fowler stories, and tried to identify the authors of each story. I've tentatively identified many of them. There are still many suspects, and a few unknowns, some of which we may never identify. Even a possible Norman Daniels not previously credited to him (but who knows?). And there are many stories that could have been by just about anybody. Even G.T. Fleming-Roberts. Though I can't positively identify any of the 1935 to 1938 novels as his, I have some suspicions. For instance, in "Crossroads of Crime," March 1939 is a story that takes place in Hawaii. A young FBI agent is already present, but is killed just prior to Fowler's arrival. Sally Vane arrives to look after the agent's sister after the killing. A few months earlier, Secret Agent "X" also had a case in Hawaii, in "Claws of the Corpse Cult," April 1938, in which an agent-in-place is killed about the time of Secret Agent X's arrival. He and K-9 take care of the agent's wife while they investigate the case. The Secret Agent "X" story is superior to the Dan Fowler story, but Fleming-Roberts could have written both. But, again, there is no proof the Fowler story was written by Fleming-Roberts. It's just a curious similarity.

Oddly, the very next Dan Fowler story is "Crimson Crusade," April 1939, one month after the last published Secret Agent "X" adventure from Ace, and this one, I'm sure makes me think of G.T. Fleming-Roberts, and it is the story this article is about. I believe that "Crimson Crusade" is the 42nd Secret Agent "X" story, though it was not published as such. There are a couple of strong indications that the story had been re-written. First, Fowler again wears a disguise! He was a G-man and proud of it. He often worked undercover, but a disguise was not necessary. Not normally. But in the story, "Crimson Crusade," he not only takes over the identity of one of the suspects (something more common with "X"), but he is in perfect disguise! But here's the real clincher is this scene:

> A pain like a bayonet driving into his side hurled him to his knees.

Remember the scar in X's side, received as a wound on the battlefield in France. This was the scar that gave "X" his identification. Often this wound caused him great pain in moments of stress and danger.

Secret Agent "X," December 1937.

When Fleming-Roberts rewrote the story, he kept the pain scene, just making it appear as an injury for Fowler. There is also a scene with Fowler flying a plane, something that was not normal for the G-man during this period. But Agent X did have several planes! Now, I must also admit that Steve Payne, who is very familiar with Fleming-Roberts' writing style, says this is not his writing style. Remember, I only said I was almost certain—though not 100%—so there is that question still lingering.

I certainly believe that the Green Ghost story, "The Case of the Walking Skeleton," was a plot from an old Agent X entry, whether or not it was one of the missing "X" stories would be hard to tell. "Skeleton" may have been a re-working of the plot from "Crimson Crusade," or even some earlier story. Fleming-Roberts did re-use plots more than once.

As for one character being turned into another, this was probably very common in the pulps. For instance, the May 1938 Dan Fowler story had to have originally been written as a Phantom Detective story. That story, "T.N.T." also had another oddity: Dan Fowler has Doc Savage's muscles! (Donovan, maybe?) And the October 1938 Phantom Detective story, "Graduates of Murder," reads like a Dan Fowler entry! It's not the Phantom you see as you read the story, but Dan Fowler, a G-man.

Will Murray is responsible for identifying the second Captain Hazzard story that was never published, as the September 1938 Secret Agent "X" story, "Curse of the Crimson Horde." Will also identified a Black Bat story, "The Murder Prophet," as a story originally written as a Whisperer novel. Within the pulps, nothing was impossible. And for Agent X, the master of disguise, it was no problem for him to turn into… Dan Fowler!

Doctor Death

Edward P. Norris is almost as much of an enigma as Doctor Death. He first appears in the May 1933 issue of *Rapid Fire Detective,* in a story titled "The Death Gambler," and features Nibs Holloway, the star field man for the Jewelry King, Joseph Calweiner, a dealer in rare jewels. Nibs has a pale, expressionless face with blue eyes, and smokes cigars and cigarettes, while drinking his whiskey straight. He carries an armpit shoulder holster, is lightning fast on the draw, and shoots straight. He is also a master of disguise. Norris doesn't appear again until August 1934 in *All Detective,* in a story titled, "Doctor Death."

Doctor Death is a sinister, unknown figure whose deathlike mask and cold-blooded deeds have branded him with an evil reputation throughout Europe as a powerful, infamous international criminal. He is described as having a ghastly face and deathly eyes, silvery white hair, and wearing a long black gown. No name is given to him, though he books passage on a ship under a Russian's name, and is said to be as strong as three men.

In a final confrontation between Nibs and Death, a gun discharges, blowing Death's face off, and he's deader than a doorknob. In fact, the story ends with the evil genius being put in cold storage on the ship and waiting transportation back to New York.

This ended Doctor Death. Or did it?

Following is a list of the short stories found under the Edward P. Norris's name:
- "The Death Gambler," *Rapid Fire Detective* (May 1933)
- "Doctor Death," *All Detective* (July 1934)
- "A Deal in Phonies," *All Detective* (August 1934)
- "Cargo of Death," *All Detective* (September 1934)
- "Death's I.O.U.," *All Detective* (October 1934)
- "Thirteen Pearls," *All Detective* (January 1935)
- "In Step With Death," *Secret Agent "X"* (July 1935)
- "G-Man Ghost," *Ten Detective Aces* (October 1935)
- "High Seas Homicide," *Ten Detective Aces* (December 1935)
- "Red Devil," *Clues Detective* (February 1936)
- "Murder Rides the Tandem," *Thrilling Detective* (January 1938)
- "Farm Kid" (April 1940) *Popular Detective*

Now, there's nothing to say that this list is complete. And Norris may have written under a few pseudonyms. I don't know. But from this listing, it appears that his writing is somewhat erratic. I haven't read "A Deal in Phonies," or "The Death Gambler," but have heard they were both Nibs Holloway stories, sans Doctor Death. I'm guessing that Norris only planned the one story with Doctor Death, but the character was so popular the editor asked Norris to bring him back, so by the third story he is mysteriously resurrected.

In "Cargo of Death" we are told that the ship on which Doctor Death had been put on ice mysteriously caught fire and sunk, Nibs escaping on a lifeboat

All Detective Magazine, July 1934.

and the body of Doctor Death going down with the ship. In this second story, Doctor Death leaps from a sixth story window, crashing to the cement below, breaking every bone in his body as his life is crushed from him. But he will appear again, trust me!

At least two more times.

However, after the fourth short story, "Thirteen Pearls," Norris is replaced, and the character is given his own magazine, *Doctor Death*. This time, three stories appear, written by Harold Ward under the Zorro pseudonym. And Death finally gets a name: Dr. Rance Mandarin. Nibs Holloway is also replaced by Jimmy Holm, and a love interest, Nina Ferrera is brought in to lengthen the yarns.
- "Twelve Must Die" (February 1935)
- "The Gray Creatures" (March 1935)
- "The Shriveling Murders" (April 1935)

A fourth story was promised, "Murder Music," but was not published. However, at least two other stories were written, "Waves of Madness" and "The Red Mist of Death," the first title likely being the original "Murder Music."

So what happened? Why was Norris replaced on the Doctor Death series? And why did he write so few stories in his career? He started out strong, with five stories in six months, then only six more stories over the next five years. Something was going on. Either he was writing under pseudonyms or a job interfered with his writing. When I was researching the Secret Agent "X" authorship, I wanted to list Norris as a suspect for some of the early stories that were most likely touched up by Chadwick (if, indeed, someone else was involved with the series), but that just didn't make sense. If Norris was writing novels, surely he would have been brought in for the Doctor Death novels. Plus, the time line just wasn't right for the Secret Agent "X" stories. As I think about it, he would have been perfect as a Phantom Detective scribe! There were many Phantom stories during this period that are suspicious as to authorship. My next thought was that maybe he was working as an editor, but that didn't ring true, either. As an editor, you would think he would be writing for the magazine he was editing. But Norris was writing for several different pulp houses during this period.

Nope, Norris remains an enigma to me. Maybe somebody else has information on the man, not me. Hell, I don't even believe Doctor Death is dead!

The Eagle

In Fall 1939, the same year that *Secret Agent "X"* and *Operator #5* ceased their long runs at Ace and Popular Publications, Ned Pines' Standard magazines launched *Thrilling Spy Stories*, which featured a new character called The Eagle. Written by Norman Daniels, under the house name of Capt. Kerry McRoberts, the hero is Jeff Shannon, America's top secret agent. It is also the year that Leo Margulies, the head editor for the

Thrilling Spy Stories, Fall 1939.

Thrilling line appears to be trying to revive their floundering titles. It is also the year that Superman appeared in comic books, so this might have had some influence on all the new pulp characters. But it's hard to say. From 1939 to 1941, several new characters would appear in a burst of creative juices that had to come from editorial committee: The Black Bat in *Black Book Detective,* the Crimson Mask and Candid Camera Kid in *Detective Novels,* the Purple Scar in *Exciting Detective,* The Ghost and Masked Detective in their own magazines, and The Eagle in *Thrilling Spy Stories.*

Whether their main titles were slipping in sales, or the publisher was just looking for a way to increase sales with new characters is hard to tell. But the influx of new characters came at a bad time. The war in Europe and the Pacific was about to cause havoc in the pulp publishing industry with a paper shortage.

SOME ORIGINAL PULP HEROES 63

This new burst of energy was short lived, and very few of the new characters survived past a few years. The Eagle only lasted for five stories and disappeared without a mummer. But it was an interesting series.

Like Secret Agent "X," the Eagle was a Lone Wolf secret agent, though his main foe is the Nazis, not American gangsters. He is tall, maybe 28 or 29 years of age, neatly dressed in a blue suit, and described thusly: the collar of his white shirt was immaculate, the tie just the right color. He has brown hair and friendly blue eyes; as The Eagle, he is known the world over, from Tokyo to Berlin—known and feared! In the first story it appeared that he was going to be given a love interest, but the editors must have changed their minds. After all, a secret agent should operate alone, especially if his assignments are going to take him to foreign locales and dangerous intrigue.

Norman Daniels would eventually become a pretty good writer of spy thrillers, as his 1960s Man From A.P.E. and Baron of Hong Kong paperback series show, but in the 1930s and '40s, he was more at home dealing with American gangsters, and the occasional Nazi saboteurs. The Eagle was a fun series, but Mr. Daniels wanted to write the stories as he would typical gangster novels, and at times they may have missed the mark as spy thrillers. The series might have fared better at the hands of G.T. Fleming-Roberts. One thing they sorely missed were the femme fatales that Fleming-Roberts introduced so easily to his spy stories, and Daniels would later bring into his own spy stories, but not yet.

Still, for whatever its failings, Norman Daniels was a top-notch writer, and his stories are always fun to read, and so too are the adventures of The Eagle.

We know that Leo Margulies always had several stories on hand when he released a new title, or at least had a call for submissions among his stable of writers. Although the series was eventually given to Mr. Daniels, there were undoubtedly stories submitted by other authors. One such title was very likely, "The Black Dragon" by Capt. Kerry McRoberts (Will Murray thinks the author is actually E. Hoffmann Price), which appeared in the February 1940 issue of *Popular Detective*. The story involved Japanese interests in the Philippines. G-2 is not mentioned, and the name of the agent is changed from Jeff Shannon, but we are told he was called to the Philippines recently. Unfortunately, for some reason the story was not included in the series, and was a stand-alone spy adventure.

When the Eagle series ended, Norman Daniels had a few plots left over. One story, "The Last Train to Freedom," was very likely the sixth entry in the Eagle series. Published in the October 1943 (it was submitted in October 1942) issue of *Detective Novels*, the story actually takes place in 1941, prior to America entering the war, but after Germany has occupied France. The character of The Eagle is changed to an Embassy clerk (sometimes called an agent) from somewhere, who penetrates occupied Paris to warn Americans to get out. But he is too late, the Gestapo has already arrested the Americans, and are holding them for exchange of German prisoners elsewhere. From there, the story becomes a simple murder mystery, with a touch of intrigue.

Undoubtedly, there are more unused stories out there, masquerading as something else. We may never know the full history of the pulp houses and their main characters, but after all these passing years since the demise of the magazines, we are still learning some of their secrets.

The Green Lama

Kendell Foster Crossen, writing as Richard Foster wrote the pulp adventures of the Green Lama, an American who studied in the Orient to become a Buddhist Priest. His real name is Jethro Dumont, but usually takes the name of Charles Pali. Although in his comic book counterpart, the Green Lama could fly, the pulp version was more typical heroic crime fighter, like the rest of the masked crusaders. He didn't actually wear a mask, although he was a master of disguise; his costume consisted of a monk's robe with hood. It was a golden-yellow with a green border. He didn't use a gun, but was proficient with a whip-like dark scarf that he wore around his neck. A master of jiu jitsu, he knew the human anatomy and could render a foe senseless or immobile with a touch. He would also swallow a mixture of radioactive salts, which would give him an electrical charge at his mere fingertips. Being a mystic, he could call upon strange powers at times.

There were only 14 novels in the series, and each story can be read separately, but they were written in chronological order, and each adventure begins where the last one left off, making the complete run one long novel. To my knowledge, this is the only pulp series to ever do this.

Another oddity was the numerous characters that appeared in the stories. Geshe Tsa-rong was his Mongol servant and friend. John Caraway was the police official. Several people appear for a few issues, then disappear, but one of the most interesting was a mysterious woman named Magga, who apparently has similar abilities to his own, and saves his life every so often, only to vanish as mysteriously as she had appeared.

The Green Lama didn't have his own magazine, appearing instead as the lead novel in *Double Detective*, from April 1940 to March 1943. Many of the titles were later reprinted in *A Vulcan Mystery*, a digest magazine in 1945.

I'm not familiar with all of Crossen's pseudonyms, but there are not a lot of stories found under his name, or that of Richard Foster and Ken Crossen, so it's possible he was writing short stories under other aliases at the time. Besides the Green Lama, he also wrote the last Dan Fowler story for *G-Men Detective*. As far as I know, he didn't write any Phantom Detective stories. After the pulps died, he became a successful paperback novelist; his most popular was the Milo March series under the name M.E. Chaber. He also wrote numerous radio scripts and television dramas.

Double Detective, April 1940.

But it's the Green Lama series he's better known for in the pulps, and it's probably for the character, not his writing. Though that surely played a part. However, I think the comic book persona has kept the Green Lama alive all these years. Regardless, the series was both interesting and a lot of fun. And it was the author, Kendell Foster Crossen who made the characters come to life.

G-X: The Phantom Fed

Popular Publications' very popular *Ace G-Man Stories* contained some very fantastic heroes, such as Emile C. Tepperman's "Suicide Squad," William Cox's "Phil Towne" series, "The Ghost" by Wyatt Blassingame, and many others: all brave operatives of the FBI men who worked alone, "lone wolves" of the crime fight-

SOME ORIGINAL PULP HEROES   65

ers. But perhaps the strangest of all of them was that famous agent known only as G-X.

G-X lived among the hobos, residing in their "jungles," and ate at their campfires. He was known by the denizens of the Hobo Jungle simply as "Hobo Jerry." He had light grey eyes, and kept a quirk of humor on the corners of his wide mouth. He had broad shoulders and the well-poised body of a middleweight boxer. He was the top ace of the FBI, and had devised a secret code which only three men in Washington could decipher. No one knew what G-X looked like, not even his fellow operatives, and no one lived after seeing his face and connecting the mysterious G-X with him. Crooks feared him, almost to the point of superstitious fear. It was as if he traveled among their own circles; to come from nowhere and bring death to the big shots and their aides as well. The crooks would mumble to their kingpins that "… you name that guy, you look on his face, and then you're… dead."

It wasn't hard to figure out his ways, as the denizens of the hobo jungle were men of crime who had chosen this life to hide their faces from the law, and among this group, G-X had met and built up the friendship of a little crook known as "the Sidney Gimp." The Gimp had a vicious, thin, wizened face. A crime-steeped little gargoyle, he tailed at the heels of G-X as the jackal follows the lion. Long ago, the underworld had placed a ten grand bounty on the head of G-X, and this little killer of the Hobo Jungle would have gladly collected the booty had he but known that his "pal" was in reality the dreaded FBI agent. However, he never discovered this secret, and remained the constant companion of G-X in all of his adventures.

The stories were well written, though contained much too much plot for a short story. Many stories contained plots and counter-plots with twisting angles and deeply laid plans: enough to fill a full-length novel.

G-X fought espionage agents as well as the un-

Ace G-Man Stories, April 1942.

derworld masters of crime. The big bosses never failed to connect Hobo Jerry with G-X, and invariably, most of the characters were killed off by the end of the story, except, of course, for The Sidney Gimp, who was never the wiser as he was usually unconscious by the shattering conclusions.

The complicated plot in the story titled "G-X and the Slaughter Machine" *(Ace G-Man Stories* for November/December 1939) could have filled an entire full-length novel instead of an 18-page short story, as this one was. An FBI agent is killed while investigating the theft of missiles. Another agent mysteriously vanishes after being assigned to the case. Then G-X, the Phantom Fed, takes up the chase.

He learns from the Sidney Gimp that the killer is a character known to the underworld as "The Chiller." The victims have been found stabbed to death by a knife stroke into the hollow of the collar bone, penetrating to the heart, Sidney Gimp informs G-X (Hobo Jerry) that this killer had once been involved in smuggling Chinese illegally into the United States, then killing them with the same knife stroke, keeping the money he was paid to fly them over.

G-X takes to the trail of a Chinaman, following him onto a train. The man is killed by a Japanese with a knife, who then attacks G-X. The FBI agent is saved by a lovely Chinese girl.

The story winds up on a ship, which The Chiller is using to transport the stolen munitions to a Japanese ship. But even The Chiller is not aware that his Japanese partner is planning to blow the ship up, with everyone on board, as it comes into the midst of the American fleet which is anchored off the coast.

There is a fight between the Japanese and the Chinese agent. The Phantom Fed escapes, taking the unconscious Sidney Gimp with him. The ship travels far away from the American fleet before it is blown to bits by the Chinese, killing all aboard. The lovely Chinese girl and all of her compatriots, who were trying to keep the munitions out of the hands of their enemies, were also killed in the explosion on the ship.

In the story titled "G-X and the Gorilla Girl" in the August 1940 issue of *Ace G-Man Stories*, the Phantom Fed, with the aid of The Sidney Gimp, is attempting to join the gang led by "The Cobra." This villain is having his men set up rich people for extortion. However, now his men are being killed by a giant gorilla—or so it seems. One of his men is found crushed and mangled, clutching what appears to be the hairs from a gorilla. Then another of his men is slain in the same manner as the first. This man had a camera and when the film was developed the last frame shows a giant gorilla attacking towards the lens of the camera.

G-X, through an exciting adventure, locates the gorilla and finds that the creature is actually controlled by a lovely girl—but he does not believe that she is killing the gangster. Eventually G-X makes contact with The Cobra, and finds that it is the evil villain, himself, who is killing his own men by dropping them down an elevator shaft, which crushes and mangles their bodies. He has taken the picture of the gorilla with the camera found on his murdered assistant. G-X also discovers that The Cobra was killing his own men for the money, which was their share of the extortion racket. The reason The Cobra was framing the murders on the gorilla was to blackmail its owner, thus forcing the girl to marry him—she was the daughter of the owner of the beast.

In this story, everyone is not killed for a change, except, of course, for those unfortunate individuals who found out that Hobo Jerry was G-X, the Phantom Fed. The Sidney Gimp was knocked out by the Cobra before the action comes to an end, and luckily before the Cobra can identify G-X to anyone, let alone the little killer at G-X's side.

G-X was a tough hombre to face in any situation—if you happen to be a criminal. From the story titled "G-X and the Submarine Pirates" (April 1940), we find this scene:

> …Then the Strangler lurched toward Jerry, hands outspread, thick lips distorted in the hellish grin of a maddened Simian.
>
> Jerry speared him with a left. The right that followed wiped the grin into a smear, and set the Strangler back on his vertebrae.
>
> "That one was for the girl, you swab! Now get up and I'll give you one on my own account!"
>
> That quick knockdown had cooled the Strangler's rage. He came to his feet slowly, coolly vicious, alert to another surprise. Jerry felt an icy wave of uncertainty. Here was no ordinary stumblebum facing him, but a crafty, bone-breaking grappler with the strength of a gorilla, and murder in his little brown-flecked eyes. Let the Strangler once grip him with those great, crushing paws…

G-X could certainly handle himself in any situa-

Frederick C. Davis.

tion, and this made for some good reading in my estimation. He had all of the qualities needed for a super pulp hero; only the basic theme of the series was what made it a strange storyline. As a youth I think most of us were fascinated with the concept of a hobo's life. I know that I was, anyway. But this series gave us another picture of that way of life—the side of crime.

Harry Lee Fellings was the author of this series and his stories are among the best that appeared in *Ace G-Man Stories*. G-X would have made a good character hero in his own magazine. The background and history of the Phantom Fed were left a mystery, as was his true name. Due to his life among the hobos, he was not associated with a girlfriend in the series, though there was always a lovely young girl in the stories.

Perhaps that beautiful young Chinese girl, Lotus Flower, should have been allowed to escape the explosion in "G-X and the Slaughter Machine." And, if not become his romantic interest, at least she could have been a recurring character in the series. Oh well, that is the way of the pulps….

Mark Hazzard

Frederick C. Davis was a prolific short story writer. Though most pulp enthusiasts remember him as the author of the first twenty Operator #5 stories over at Popular Publications, perhaps his best known creation was the Moon Man for *Ten Detective Aces;* the Moon Man was actually Stephen Thatcher, a detective-sergeant on the police force, who donned a type of fish bowl helmet and black robe to fight crime. He was considered a criminal, and there was a standing order for the police to shoot the Moon Man on sight. The stories were pretty standard pulp fare that worked from a formula. Sue McEwen was the love interest, and she was the daughter of Detective Gil McEwen, who was constantly trying to catch the Moon Man. Ned Dargan also assisted the Moon Man.

In 1935, Fred Davis introduced fighting D.A., Mark Hazzard to the back pages of the Secret Agent "X" magazine, running simultaneously with his Moon Man stories over at *Ten Detective Aces*. An easy enough task because the Mark Hazzard and Moon Man stories were carbon copies of each other, except Hazzard didn't wear any kind of costume. Hazzard wasn't his real name, either. Falsely convicted of a crime he didn't commit, young Dennis Grant had changed his name and took on a new identity. The fighting D.A. was always looking over his shoulder as a hunted criminal. Even the supporting characters from the two series were almost identical, and one story could have been switched to either character as the need arose—or recycled with minor touches of the typewriter.

There were 38 Moon Man adventures, from June 1933 through January 1937. Unfortunately, Mark

Hazzard didn't do as well, ending after only six stories in six months. Davis must have tired of the Hazzard/Moon Man formula, or someone at Ace wanted him to do something different. Just a few months after the Hazzard series ended, Frederick C. Davis had a brand new series in the back of *Secret Agent "X."* Ravenwood was completely different from either Hazzard or the Moon Man, and would have actually made a nice full length novel adventure series. However, it only lasted for five issues during 1936, then also ended. Sadly, the Moon Man would cease in only a few months too.

Regardless of its short run, the Mark Hazzard stories were quality writing and good story telling. It may have suffered from the fact that the hero didn't have a gimmick like Ravenwood, or wear a neat costume like the Moon Man. Personally I've always felt that the series should have been added to any Moon Man collection because of its similarity to that character, but for some reason it has been overlooked over the years, and publishers have missed a golden opportunity.

Johnston McCulley Characters

Johnston McCulley almost single-handedly created the costumed hero all by himself! Although many of his characters wore strange costumes: The Man in Purple, The Crimson Clown, The Green Ghost (early series), Thunderbolt, The Mongoose, etc., his most famous creation was that of Zorro, the masked avenger who rode the west righting wrongs and punishing evildoers. Wearing all black, he was an expert with both whip and sword.

"The Curse of Capistrano" was a five-part serial, running in *All-Story Weekly* from August 9th, 1919 through September 6th, 1919. Other titles soon followed: "The Further Adventures of Zorro," a six-part serial, "Zorro Rides Again," a four-part serial, "The Sign of Zorro," a five-part serial, and a two-part serial, "Mysterious Don Miguel." But most of the adventures were various length short stories, which appeared in *West* from 1944 through 1951.

At least half a dozen Saturday Matinee serials were produced for the theaters, from Clayton Moore's *Ghost of Zorro,* to Linda Stirling's portrayal of a female Zorro in *Zorro's Black Whip,* my all-time favorite. In all of the matinees, Zorro was dressed in the familiar black regalia, complete with whip and guns, some times a flashing sword for excitement. In addition, several top-notch, movies were released. Television produced two excellent Zorro series, which remained true to the character, and were highly popular during their time.

As the movies proved, Zorro was a visual success, more so than the printed text of the short stories and serials from *Argosy*. Comic book publishers loved the character, as Zorro was the ideal hero for the comic reader. Let's face it, without Zorro there would not have been a Lash LaRue or Durango Kid. To take this a step further, The Lone Ranger, the Green Hornet, and all of the masked rider cowboys of the silver screen owe their influence to Johnston McCulley's famous hero.

But if Zorro was an influence to one media, he was an influence to all. The pulps, called such because of the cheap wood pulp the magazines were printed on, was preparing for the Roaring Twenties when Zorro appeared in 1919 as the five part serial. In the 1920s, the pulps were publishing a lot of crime fiction and adventure stories, and characters like the costumed hero had to wait until the 1930s for their appearance. In fact, there was only one new Zorro in the 1920s, and that was the six-part serial in 1922.

After the Wall Street crash of 1929, the readers were looking for heroes. They were tired of the criminal element in their life and the media. Johnston McCulley, under his own name, and a number of house names, gave the reader the heroes they needed. Characters started appearing with names like the Green Ghost, The Mongoose, The Crimson Clown, The Man in Purple, and others, all by Zorro creator, Johnston McCulley. Another early series, The Bat, as written by "C.K.M. Scanlon" (a house name), was a costumed hero that researchers say had to be by McCulley, as well. And I agree. Foreshadowing masked female vigilantes like the Domino Lady, in 1921, McCulley wrote "The Masked Lady." He didn't miss any bets. With the beginning of the costumed hero, other greats began to appear: The Shadow, The Spider, The Phantom Detective, The Ghost! Green Ghost (later series), Masked Detective, the Crimson Mask, The Scar, and many others. All owe their success to Zorro creator, McCulley.

With the short run of The Bat series in *Popular Detective* for 1934, this costumed hero crossed two mediums, the pulps and comic books. In 1939, Standard Magazines came out with The Black Bat, about the same time as the comics brought out Bat Man. Since Standard published both The Bat and The Black Bat, it's easy to see the influence for The Black Bat. From "The Bat Strikes," November 1934, the character of Dawson Clade is contemplating what identity he might assume to bring terror to the underworld, when suddenly a bat flies into the open window, startling him. With the terror of the bat also came the identity for his alter ego, The Bat. This same scene, or one very similar, occurs as Bruce Wayne is seated in his study, contemplating the idea of bringing terror to the underworld, when a bat suddenly flies through his open window. The Batman was instantly born.

When I decided to create my own continuing series for our magazines, I drew from Johnston McCulley in structuring my characters of The Masked Avenger and The Black Ghost. Both characters wear black and go about masked, bringing fear to the underworld. Modern day Zorros, dressed all in black, with guns blazing, a weird, mocking laugh, and evildoers cringing in fear as retribution steps from the shadows to bring downfall upon the minions of evil. Regardless of their choice of weapons, the heroes owe their very existence to Johnston McCulley and Zorro.

From the very beginning Johnston McCulley brought the reader exciting stories of masked and costumed heroes. But of all his creations, the one most endearing—and long-lived—was that of Zorro.

Over 80 years, since 1919, the character is still very popular in all medias. Only rivaled by the character of The Shadow, Zorro proves to be ever ready to ride the trail again. And though we may forget The Shadow, Zorro is never far from our thoughts. The rider in black, a fast stead, a whistling whip, and a sharp sword, beware evildoers, the time has come for his vengeance!

Although the costumed hero didn't appear

to catch on until The Shadow in 1931, and then the pulps came out with dozens of costumed heroes over the next ten years: The Phantom Detective, The Spider, The Ghost/Green Ghost (second series), Masked Detective, Crimson Mask, The Red Mask/Red Hood, The Black Hood, etc. They lasted for a period of twenty-two years, and then disappeared, The Shadow in 1949 and the Phantom Detective in 1953.

The pulp hero began in 1931 with the publication of The Shadow from Street & Smith. In 1933, the floodgates were opened with dozens of heroes from Doc Savage, also from Street & Smith, to G-8 and The Spider from Popular Publications, and The Phantom Detective from Standard. In 1934 there was another round of releases, Operator #5 from Popular Publications, Secret Agent "X" from Ace, and then minor heroes appeared in 1935 & 1936 from most publishing houses, with a final push in 1939 & 1940 with the last batch of costumed heroes. But the war effort caused a shortage in paper, and the pulps and comic books suffered because of the paper drives.

By the 1950s, with the war over, the readers were looking for something new. The paperback novels were replacing the pulps, and comic books were doing a booming business once more, while television was grabbing the attention of book readers. The pulp hero died in 1953 when the last hold out, The Phantom Detective ceased publication, though a few western and science fiction pulps continued for a while, most stories were merely reprints from years past.

Condé Nast bought out Street & Smith, and has kept up the copyrights on Doc Savage and The Shadow, while Popular Publications—sold to Argosy Communications—have done the same. Although Ace still exists as a paperback publisher, they did not renew their copyrights on their pulps, and thus let them lapse into the public domain. The same can be said for the Standard line of pulps, which eventually became Popular Library, a paperback house.

Although Doc Savage and The Shadow are under copyright, there have been a number of fan fiction novels written for both series, with the hopes that eventually a paperback company will obtain permission to publish both series again, with some new novels [note: this has now happened]. There are at least eleven Doc Savage novels waiting, as well as one Shadow novel. In the meantime, a number of parodies of Doc Savage have been written: Doc Wilde, Doc Terror, and Doc Atlas, among others. Publishers are even publishing new stories on many of the characters that are in public domain, and have brought in new writers to write new stories featuring such characters as Captain Hazzard, The Moon Man, Secret Agent "X," The Black Bat, The Phantom Detective, and others. And we can credit Johnston McCulley for his early vision that would spark a trend lasting a hundred years!

Ki-Gor

In 1963 I was stationed in France, with the 202nd MP Company, and working patrol for a black NCO named Foster (I think that was his name). When I stopped by the station for a cup of coffee, I found Sgt. Foster reading a Tarzan paperback by Edgar Rice Burroughs. This was during my hardboiled detective period, when I was reading Mickey Spillane and Shell Scott. I remembered the old Tarzan movies with Johnny Weismuller, and asked Foster if the stories weren't a little racially demeaning, and he told me they weren't. After we discussed the Burroughs' Tarzan for a while, he convinced me to read one of the stories. That was my introduction to jungle adventures, and I have been a fan ever since.

I haunted the Stars & Stripes bookstore on base, until the lady that ran the establishment got to know me like a son. Whenever I would walk into the store, she would grab me by the arm and say, "Look what just came in!" And take me to a paperback with a jungle scene or dinosaur on the cover. This was how I discovered Doc Savage in 1964, when she led me to *The Thousand-Headed Man*, which had Doc fight-

Jungle Stories, Winter 1938.

ing with a giant snake while a witch doctor looked on. So by then I was hooked on Edgar Rice Burroughs and Kenneth Robeson. I probably shouldn't tell this story, but in 1964, during the Cypress Crisis, I was among a group of Army soldiers sent to an Air Base in Turkey for a NATO exercise, in case we had to deploy to Cypress. Well, being Army on an Air Force base wasn't conducive to good treatment. We were stuck away from the more civilized air force personnel, and didn't get much sent our way. Being Army, we quickly learned our way around though, and one of the first places I discovered was where the special services stored books that was to be distributed to the air force personnel. A few nightly raids, and our Army unit had reading material. Of course, I had first choice of any Edgar Rice Burroughs paperbacks! Or anything with a jungle scene or dinosaur on the cover.

Tarzan, of course, was the inspiration for many imitations in the pulps. I think that over the years I have found any and everything that remotely resembles the original Jungle Lord. One of those imitators appeared in *Jungle Stories,* a Fiction House publication, beginning with the Winter 1939 issue, and running until Spring 1954, amassing 59 issues (although some titles were repeats). The hero was Ki-Gor, a bronzed-skin muscular giant, wearing a loincloth with a knife in a sheath at his side, and bow and quiver of arrows over his broad shoulders. Standing six foot tall, he has blue eyes, and shoulder-length hair bleached white by the sun. Unfortunately, the novels were very uneven. His blue eyes would often turn gray, and his white hair would become yellow in some stories.

However, it was the adventures that counted. Fantastic jungle stories of lost lands, lost civilizations, prehistoric monsters, giant snakes, elephants running amok, and talking gorillas. Everything a good jungle adventure should be. Ki-Gor was in reality the surviving son of a missionary named Robert Kilgour, who lived among the beast of the jungle after his father was killed. He eventually met—and married—Helene Vaughn. She is quite competent, but is constantly being captured. Two other aides are in all the stories. Timbu George, who was once George Spelvin, an American Pullman porter and ship's cook, and who eventually became a Masai chief; And little N'Geeso, chief of the Kamazila Pygmy tribe.

As with most pulp fiction of the period, the Ki-Gor stories were formula at best, but highly imaginative, and were probably the most successful and popular of the Tarzan imitators. The titles alone were enough to whet the appetite of young readers perusing the newsstands: "The Empire of Doom," "The Cannibal Horde," "Caravan of Terror," and "Where Man-Beasts Prowl." And those are the milder titles! The action within the pages of *Jungle Stories* brought us the adventure we craved. Ki-Gor, the White Jungle Lord deserves his niche on the shelf beside Tarzan The Ape Man. The jungle belonged to them!

I can still see that old lady from the Stars & Stripes grabbing my arm once more, and saying, "Look what just came in!"

The Man in Purple

Richard Staegal and Betty Hayler were both individually wealthy and were planning to be married, but each had an adventurous soul, and it was decided that before they wed, they should seek out danger and excitement. Staegal adopts the guise of The Man in Purple. With his fiancé and chauffeur, he calls his team the Three Rogues.

Richard Staegal is a tall, slender man. Like Zorro's Diego, "Dick" pretends to be something of a wimp:

> Taking a handkerchief from his pocket, Richard dabbed it to his forehead a couple of times, then: "Yes, indeed, Detective, and I say, I wish you would leave honest working men alone and catch that purple scoundrel that is causing all this fuss! My fiancée is so frightened, she insists that we depart immediately, and I can't say I blame the dear!"
>
> "Uh huh," Troman growled. "Well, if I may make a suggestion, I think everyone in the airport should duck your heads, there is going to be an explosion in about two minutes, and we don't know how powerful it will be!"
>
> "Oh, dear heavens," Staegal whimpered. "Please do as he says, my dear."

Miss Betty Hayler is betrothed to Richard Staegal, and is the daughter of a family of wealth and social position. She has dark hair and dark eyes.

Broph was barely five foot, two inches tall, diminutive and weighed in at 106 pounds. He could have been a jockey, but had ended up pulling petty crimes. Although now employed as a chauffeur, he had once been a petty crook.

> Staegal opened his coat and took from around his

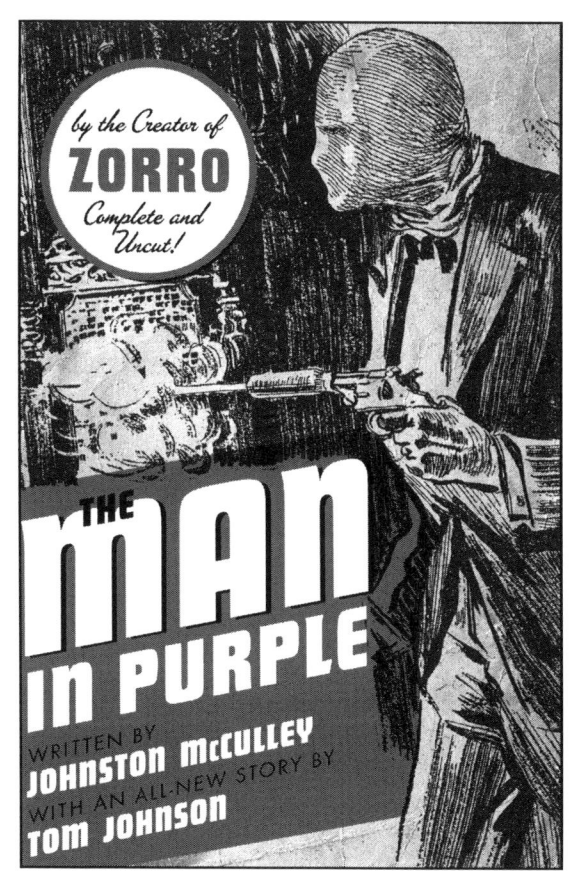

The Man in Purple, 2010.

> body a peculiar, thin, purple suit consisting of trousers and coveralls, which he slipped on over his clothes. He put on the big hood and adjusted the mask, donned gloves, then made sure the electric torch and automatic pistol were ready. He destroys every suit after each use by pouring acid over the material from a small bottle. He is sort of altruistic crook. He robbed from swindling financiers and crooked rich men and gave the proceeds to the poor.
>
> Detective Troman appeared to have one job on the Force—capture the Man in Purple! ("The Man in Purple")

As the beautiful socialite left the office of the mayor, all eyes watched her departure. There was silence in the room for several minutes after she was gone, then:

"What a gorgeous creature!" Mayor Tompkins sighed.

"Be careful of your thoughts, Mayor," Detective Troman warned. "Richard Staegal once whipped three hoodlums without breaking a sweat. I dare say, if the Man in Purple does meet up with that fellow, I would like to be around to see the fists fly!"

"Who do you think would win, Detective?" District Attorney Flemings asked.

"It would be a toss of the coin. The Man in Purple has the strength of three men, at least. The other night, I was dropped through a trapdoor, and would have most likely broken my neck, but the rogue caught me by the shoulders as if I was no more than a paperweight. I am a big man, as you gentlemen can see, and I probably have a hundred pounds on the thief. I hate to admit it, but he probably saved my life!"

The Masked Detective

Rex Parker was one of those late arrival masked crime fighters from Ned Pines' Standard pulp house, beginning in Fall 1940 with his own magazine, *The Masked Detective*, under the byline of C.K.M. Scanlon. This was the period when someone at Standard, probably Leo Margulies, the man in charge of the single character line for Pines at the time, was trying to revive their super hero pulps. The Phantom Detective and Dan Fowler (over at *G-Men Detective*) were also suddenly seeing some changes. Perhaps there was a slump somewhere. Sales may have been dropping, and Pines ordered Leo to look for possibly some new characters. Whatever the situation, suddenly the Black Bat appeared in *Black Book Detective* in July 1939 and The Ghost popped up in January 1940. The Crimson Mask showed up in *Detective Novels* in August 1940, The Eagle appeared in *Thrilling Spy Stories* in Fall 1939, and the Purple Scar appeared in Fall 1941.

All of the new characters seemed a little off the beaten path, except for maybe the Black Bat and The Eagle. The Crimson Mask was a pharmacist by day, and crime fighter by night. The Ghost was a magician

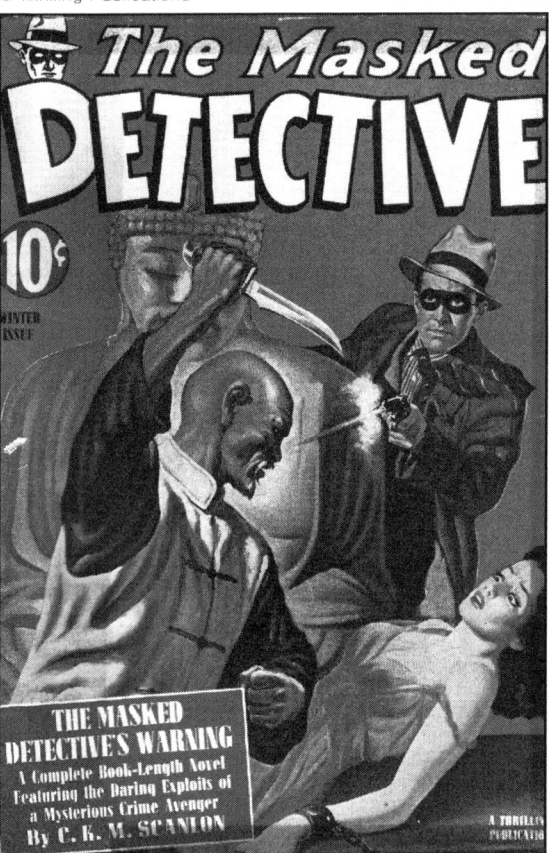

The Masked Detective, Winter 1941.

turned crime fighter, and the Purple Scar of all things, was a plastic surgeon that turns to fighting crime after his brother is brutally murdered. The Masked Detective, more commonly referred to as the Mask, is uncommon in the fact that he isn't a young millionaire playboy. In fact, he isn't rich at all, holding down a low-wage job as a reporter for a second rate newspaper. But that doesn't stop him from wearing a domino mask and busting up gangs of criminals and uncovering murderers! In fact, I kind of liked the guy.

Pulpster Norman Daniels, while knocking out the Black Bat also kicked off the Crimson Mask, The Eagle and the Masked Detective—along with some other new characters along the way. Daniels had already been churning out Phantom Detective yarns, and probably some of the Dan Fowler tales that we're not aware of. He had started out slow in the mid 1930s, but by the 1940s was very prolific. Mr. Daniels was ideal as the scribe for the Mask, unfortunately he was busy with the Black Bat and other chores, so only turned out a hand full of the first novels, then the series was handed off to other authors, among them Sam Merwin, Jr., G.T. Fleming-Roberts, W.T. Ballard, and Laurence Donovan. Four stories remain unidentified.

Of the late entries, only the Black Bat was long lasting, continuing until 1952 and 61 issues. The Ghost (later changed to the Green Ghost) only lasted 14 stories. The Purple Scar had a worse record with only four stories and The Eagle followed with five stories. The Crimson Mask made it for 16 stories. Sadly, The Masked Detective could only survive for 12 issues in his own magazine, then he was relegated to the pages of *Thrilling Mystery* for a thirteenth entry, and then vanished.

Rex Parker has a lazy appearance, but that is deceiving. He is actually an expert at la savate, the French fighting technique of boxing with the feet, making him one of the first martial artist long before Bruce Lee's Kato. Although, the World's Greatest Detective, the Phantom often used this technique in his own battles with crimedom. However, after Daniels leaves the series, the Mask also eventually drops the use of la savate in the stories, making him just another masked vigilante. In fact, Donovan's later entry, "Candles of Murder" (Spring 1943) is merely a reworking of one of his Phantom Detective yarns, and barely resembles Rex Parker. Finally, in the *Thrilling Mystery* story, "Monarchs of Murder" (Fall 1944), he doesn't even wear a mask, and at one point uses jiu jitsu instead of la savate, and we're told that he was taught judo by Winnie Bligh, the love interest in the series. "Monarchs of Murder" may have started out as a novel-length entry, but ended up in a drawer when the decision was made to cancel the magazine title. An editor probably cut the wordage to novelette length to fit in *Thrilling Mystery*. A shame.

The characters involved in the stories are, of course, the formula for all such series: Rex Parker, the title's hero, Winnie Bligh, the love interest, and the ever-present bumbling police officer, Det.-Sgt. Dan Gleason of Homicide. The plots were regular run-of-the-mill murder mysteries for the most part, with the occasional Fifth Column Nazi stuff. All of it very typical fair for the 1940s pulp detective/super hero stories appearing in all of the titles.

Unfortunately, with the war starting in Europe and the paper shortage, it was a bad time for the pulp magazines, especially the new, untried single character titles that had recently hit the stands. Plus, it's likely that many of the writers were joining the war effort in some capacity. All of this resulted in fewer and thinner magazines. Perhaps, if Norman Daniels could have remained with the series, the Masked Detective could have survived as a companion title to Standard's other popular heroes.

Alas, it wasn't to be.

The Masked Woman

Madame Madcap was originally published as a serial in *The Washington Post* in 1921, this is another of Johnston McCulley's early costumed characters, appearing nearly two decades before The Domino Lady and The Black Cat. Like her future protégés, she brought beauty, brains, and sex appeal to the female vigilante long before they were popular.

Calling herself Madame Madcap, she wears a sexy evening gown, long black cloak with hood, and a black mask to cover her features. Appearing mysteriously, she recruits a gang of hoodlums to do her bidding, demanding complete loyalty. Then she sets them up for a fall, handing them over to the police with enough evidence to convict.

She was of medium height, dressed in an evening gown, jewels glittering on her fingers. Around her shoulders was a long black cloak with a hood, and a black mask concealed her face.

Bronze Shadows #11.

Twin sisters, Doris and Dorcas Darcan: twenty-four years old, with regular features, and charming. An adorable dimple where a dimple should nestle against the chin, and blue eyes with golden hair. They were the daughters of a notorious gentleman crook known as William Duncan. Seeking adventure, he had sent his daughter to be schooled in Europe, while he turned to crime. His men had betrayed him, and now Doris and Dorcas were turning the tables on his old gang. Although Doris originally dons the mask, her sister might work the trick to fool the police.

Professor James Xenophon Salwick: A professor of anthropology, he only stands 5 foot six inches tall, but besides brains, he is strong and an excellent boxer.

Sambo: A huge black man, he has wide shoulders and bulging muscles. He is also Madame Madcap's bodyguard and chauffeur.

The girls live in a mansion with servants, and are rich. Money left to them by their father's honest achievements. They also own a building in the underworld, where saloons and gangsters gather. With an entrance from the alley, there is a large room, well furnished, on the lower floor. On the floors above are rooms for guests, and a special room where two large cages are kept for prisoners. This is Madame Madcap's headquarters in the badlands.

"Red" Riley is a small time hoodlum, and safecracker. He is small, wiry, and tough, and is recruited to work with her.

This was an interesting story from the very first. As with most of McCulley's stories, his characters are heroes who act outside the law, but for the good of society—or for a purpose, like Zorro. Though there are no gun battles or sword fights, we see plenty of fisticuffs. Madame Madcap's chauffeur and bodyguard is a huge, muscular black man, and her right hand man is a professor of anthropology, who is studying the criminal element of society.

The Moon Man & Bronze Shadows

One of the first fanzines I ever read was Fred Cook's *Bronze Shadows* (Bronze for Doc Savage and Shadows for our hero, The Shadow), which ran for 15 issues, beginning with an undated Issue #1. Issue #2 was dated December 1965. Issue #15 was dated November 1968. Except for Issue #1, which was only a couple of pages of introduction, most of the succeeding issues were around 20 pages each. Printed for the most part on a mimeograph machine and pages stapled together, then folded and mailed without an envelope, it cost something like 35¢ an issue, and worth ten times that price!

Except for Doc Savage and The Shadow, there wasn't much known about the other pulp heroes at the time. *Bronze Shadows* set out to correct that lack of knowledge, even though the fanzine was a Doc Savage and Shadow hobby magazine. Nick Carr quickly started writing about G-8 and Operator #5, Bud Overn started writing about Bill Barnes, and soon there were other articles on some of the other great pulp heroes. Herman S. McGregor began his "A Critical Analysis of *The Doc Savage Magazine*," which, to my knowledge, was never completed. Robert "Bob" Kenneth Jones started his research into *Adventure*. He completed it later in *Echoes*, and then it was published in book form. Nick Carr's own research went on to be published in several books: *America's Secret Service Ace* (a study of Operator #5), *The Flying Spy* (G-8), *The Other Detective Pulp Heroes*, as well as *The Pulp Hero*, and others.

However, about this time, one of the first questions that intrigued all of us was in issue #8, dated January 1967. A letter from Robert Joseph asks: "Did you ever hear of a pulp series character by the name of Moon Man? I know it sounds unsophisticated even by the standards of the '30s and '40s. From what I can remember, he appeared in one of the detective pulps. He was supposed to wear a special helmet that made his head invisible. Any information that you can dig up would be appreciated."

Fred Cook answers him: "Good Gravy! A man with no head? Sorry, Bob, I can't place him, but I'm sure Gerry de la Rae, Dick Myers, Bernie Wermers, Lynn Hickman or some of the other collectors can pin him down for you. How about it—you pulp detectives?"

In Issue #10, dated June 1967, Jack Irwin responded with: "In response to Robert Joseph's query about the Moon Man: The Moon Man stories appeared in *Ten Detective Aces* and were written by Frederick C. Davis. I don't know the extent of the life of the series, but I have several issues between January 1935 and September 1936 that contain Moon Man stories. *Ten Detective Aces* was published monthly at this time but the Moon Man did not appear on a regular monthly basis. For instance, he didn't make an appearance in the February 1936 or October 1936 issues. Incidentally, the Moon Man's special glass helmet did not make his head invisible in the sense that it became transparent. Instead the helmet was one-way, in that the Moon Man could see out of the helmet, but none could see into it. So then, this was the reason that his head was not visible when he wore the helmet. The shape of the helmet together with its color gave rise to the name "Moon Man," since his helmet resembled a full moon. The rest of the Moon Man's costume consisted of a long black robe.

"The Moon Man, like many of the costumed characters of the pulps, worked outside the law and therefore was considered a criminal and hunted by the police. In reality, he was Detective Sergeant Stephen Thatcher, and was the son of the Chief of Police. In addition his fiancée was the daughter of a Detective Lieutenant. How's that for connections for a criminal?"

Fred Cook answers with: "Thank you for passing this information on to Bob in particular and the rest of us in general. It certainly is fascinating to trace down some of the answers to the questions that pop up. Let's keep it up and get all the answers that we can."

Well, by the time *Bronze Shadows* folded, all of the questions may not have been answered, but a good many of them had been. We eventually learned that Frederick C. Davis not only wrote the Moon Man short stories in *Ten Detective Aces*, he also wrote the Mark Hazzard and Ravenwood short stories over at *Secret Agent "X."* The Hazzard series lasted for six issues, from 1935 to 1936, and Ravenwood for five issues in 1936. Plus, he wrote the first 20 novels in the *Operator #5* series as Curtis Steele. Frederick C. Davis was a professional writer, even though most of his stories were shorts. It was rumored that he dictated his stories to a secretary, some times more than one story at a time. His Operator #5 novels were undoubtedly top-notch, and the best in the series. He shared the byline with Emile C. Tepperman and Wayne Rogers. But it's probably his short story series of the Moon Man that fans remember today, thanks in large part to *Bronze Shadows* and the question written in by Robert Joseph back in 1967.

Ten Detective Aces: When Ace bought out *Detective Dragnet* around 1932-33, they changed the title to *Ten Detective Aces*, and the new title ran for 161 issues, ending in October 1949. The title boasted ten stories per issue, or a cent a story, and most of the stories were series, or continuing characters by the same authors month after month. A typical early issue might consist of authors like Paul Chadwick, Emile C. Tepperman, Lester Dent, Norvell Page, and Frederick C. Davis. Many of these same authors went on to write the full-length hero novels in other series. Paul Chadwick went on to write *Secret Agent "X"* and *Captain Hazzard*, Emile C. Tepperman went on to write *The Spider, Operator #5*, and *Secret Agent "X."* Norvell Page went on to write *The Spider*. Lester Dent went on to write *Doc Savage*.

There were 38 Moon Man stories, from May-June 1933 ("The Sinister Sphere") to January 1937 ("Blackjack Jury"). All of these stories have been collected into two hardbacks: *The Night Nemesis: The Complete Adventures of The Moon Man—Volume One,* edited by Garyn G. Roberts and Gary Hoppenstand was published by The Purple Prose Press, Bowling Green, Ohio (no date of publication listed in my copy), and *The Silver Spectre: The Complete Adventures of The Moon Man—Volume Two,* compiled and edited by Robert Weinberg, The Battered Silicon Dispatch Box, 2004. Also with commentary by Garyn G. Roberts and Gary Hoppenstand, and an introduction by Will Murray. The character basically robbed from the bad guys and gave to the poor, like Robin Hood of legend. Later, Captain Satan would carry the plot to a series of five novels, although his band of men often kept a percentage of the take. Not so the Moon Man. Through his aide, Ned "Angel" Dargan, the money would be distributed to those who were in most need. The act of charity gave the character of the Moon Man his reason to exist. The reading public had just gone through a long Depression. Not only were they looking for a hero, they were looking for their very own Robin Hood of Sherwood Forest, and Frederick C. Davis's Moon Man character filled this bill perfectly.

As it was, it had been the Great Depression that brought on the pulp hero. For over ten years the pulps were dominated by gangster stories. Mobs, gun molls, and the Machine-gun Kelly's were the reader's fare. And readers were tired of the gangsters, real or imagined, and wanted to read about good winning out over evil. In 1931, *The Shadow* began over at Street & Smith, written by Walter B. Gibson under the Maxwell Grant house name. Shortly after that, *The Phantom Detective* appeared over at Standard. Soon, we had pulp heroes popping up at all of the pulp houses: *Doc Savage* in 1933 at Street & Smith. *The Spider* and *G-8* at Popular, etcetera. So it wasn't surprising to see pulp heroes over at Ace in 1933, even if they were short story series. In 1934, Ace would have *Secret Agent "X,"* and by 1935 The Moon Man

Mike Shayne Mystery Magazine, June 1968.

and a dozen other short story characters were going strong at *Ten Detective Aces.*

Mr. Jones

Pulp historians conclude that Captain Zero was the last pulp hero to be created during the pulp era, and perhaps basically this is true. However, Leo Margulies never lost interest in the pulp hero, or creating house names. For twenty years Leo was ramrod of Ned Pines' Standard pulp house, and he oversaw the hero line of character pulps for their magazines. He probably created most of them—though possibly through editorial committee. The pulp line included The Phantom Detective, Dan Fowler *(G-Men Detective),* Black Bat *(Black Book Detective),* The Masked Detective, Purple Scar, The Eagle, and probably a few I'm forgetting.

SOME ORIGINAL PULP HEROES 79

When Leo was let go from Standard as Head Editor, he quickly started his own publishing house, Renown Publishing, bringing out a slew of digest magazines. His mainstay was the *Mike Shayne Mystery Magazine*, but there were several companion titles: *Satellite Science Fiction, Zane Grey Western Magazine, Shell Scott Mystery Magazine, Charlie Chan Mystery Magazine*, and his highly successful *Man From UNCLE* and *Girl From UNCLE* titles; these latter were under the byline of one of his final house names, Robert Hart Davis, named in honor of an editor at *Argosy* who gave Leo his first job. Cylvia Kleinman Margulies, Leo's wife, told me the "Hart" came about because of Robert Davis' kind heart.

With the ending of the popular *UNCLE* series in January 1968, Leo was looking for a replacement title to fill the void. Keeping the Robert Hart Davis house name, he created his final pulp hero, Mr. Jones, The Man of a Million Faces. Mr. Jones was another wink at the old days, when one of Standard's widely used house names was G. Wayman Jones. A byline used on the Black Bat, among others.

Although Mr. Jones appeared to be a mixture of both The Phantom Detective and Purple Scar, he did not wear a costume. The days of costumed pulp heroes were gone. However, he is a master of disguise, bringing to mind Secret Agent "X," the Man of a Thousand Faces.

To test the water for a new magazine, Leo decided to publish the first story in *Mike Shayne Mystery Magazine*, and see how it went over with the readers. Preparing some notes on the character he wanted, he asked one of his prolific writers, Dennis Lynds, to come up with a good yarn.

Bon vivant and famed medic by day, scourge of the underworld by night, Mr. Jones is the man of a million faces! This is the story of Dr. Samuel Sears, brilliant society favorite, and successful plastic surgeon. Mr. Jones knows how to kill just as easily as Dr. Sears, his real self, knows how to live! As Mr. Jones, he can penetrate the inner circles of organized crime and bring his man to justice, dead or alive!

A Lt. Col. in the Army medical field, Sears had been transferred to OSS while in Korea. He has light brown hair and cool blue eyes, hard as sapphires. At 190 pounds, he is a shade under six feet tall. He was a deceptively slender man, with shoulders broader than they seemed. Mr. Jones could appear taller or shorter at will, and could control his facial muscles.

When his friend, the police commissioner, had bitterly raged against a high-and-mighty criminal the police could not touch, Sears had instantly realized something he had wanted to do for many years—catch and punish the hidden criminals who walked free and above the law.

He had caught that particular high-and-mighty culprit, and another, and Mr. Jones was born. Sears had never regretted his second life: the disguises pleased him, the acting challenged his mind, and the pursuit excited him. He was forced to admit that he had always wanted to be a detective, even in secret. Sounds a little like The Phantom Detective, doesn't it?

Kim Ree is Sears' Korean chef, valet, and general major domo. He was a sergeant in the R.O.K. Army when he met Sears.

Commissioner Angelo Pinto is a small, peppery man. He speaks as much with his hands as with his voluble old-country-style voice. He knows the identity of Mr. Jones.

Miss Agatha Bridge is his medical assistant at the hospital. She's a tough fifty-year old R.N. that runs the office like a chief petty officer.

Detective Captain Murry Brian is a short, stocky man. He wears an old gray suit, and battered felt hat over gray hair.

Sears lives in a plush apartment in The Carleton Towers on Park Avenue. The suite directly below his is rented year-round by Reginald Trott, a wealthy gentleman from Trinidad, but in reality belongs to Mr. Jones. Inside a locked closet in his apartment is a spiral staircase leading down to a secret room in the suite below. His offices are located at the Hippocratic House, a private hospital.

Leo's intentions were good, but Dennis wasn't comfortable with the pulp concept, even though he had written the Belmont *Shadow* novels ten years earlier. He told Leo the story didn't work, and he hated it. But Leo Margulies was determined to try for a new series. He ran the story in the June 1968 issue of *Mike Shayne Mystery Magazine,* and it met with poor response. The new magazine never got off the ground, and Mr. Jones died a silent death. A shame, I really think the time was ripe for a new character. Readers were still screaming for more *Man From UNCLE* stories. I'm afraid Dennis went into the story feeling the pulp style was wrong, and this hurt the story. Perhaps, if another writer had been given the task of writing the story, they might have put it over. Michael Avallone would submit a number of articles on the old pulp heroes for the *MSMM* a few years later, and the readers loved them. Five years later, Renown did launch a new magazine, the *Charlie Chan Mystery Magazine,* in November 1973. Although the title only lasted a few issues, it proved a new title might have worked in 1968.

But for pulp historians, Dennis Lynds goes down in the history books as not only bringing The Shadow into the 1960s, he was also tagged to write the final pulp hero novel, under the last pulp house name. Leo Margulies—the Little Giant of the pulps—saw to that!

The Purple Scar

The Purple Scar was one of the second-run series created in 1941 for Ned Pines' Thrilling magazines. Like most of the later series, The Purple Scar didn't fare too well, ending after only four stories in *Exciting Detective:* "Medals of Murder" (Fall 1941), "The Night of Murder" (Winter 1942), "Murder in Gold" (March 1942), and "The Chain of Murder" (Winter 1943), all bylined John S. Endicott.

The Purple Scar mystery still nags at me; it just doesn't fit that perfectly into the mold of Leo Margilies' costumed crime fighters at Standard. Oh, the character had all the traits that make a good pulp hero. But if we look at Standard's line-up: Dan Fowler, Phantom Detective, Masked Detective, Crimson Mask, The Ghost/Green Ghost, and the Black Bat, the main characters were all interchangeable. The Purple Scar is really Doc Murdock, a famous plastic surgeon, and his only assistant was his nurse, Dale Jordan; yes, he did use a number of slum dwellers once in a while, but they weren't really permanent characters. He is patterned closely after pharmacist, Robert Clarke, the Crimson Mask. Both had clinics/pharmacies in the slum districts. But something just isn't right.

I recently read "The Night of Murder" and "The

Exciting Detective, Fall 1941.

SOME ORIGINAL PULP HEROES 81

Chain of Murder," stories 2 & 4 in the Purple Scar series, and easily confirmed these were by the same author. Well written, and followed an outline very closely. In fact, after reading story 2, I knew when something was going to happen in story 4, because the author used the same outline in both. I also confirmed that this was the author of the Phantom Detective novel, "The Radio Murders" (April 1939). Too many clues connected the Purple Scar with that Phantom Detective novel. And there were clues to The Spider in "The Radio Murders" and the Purple Scar stories, so the author had to be connected to this series also. For one good scene, I'll refer the reader to Chapter 3 ("The Riot") of "The Chain of Murder." This scene was played out in just about every Spider story, where either Richard Wentworth or The Spider ("the master of men") stands before a mob to stop their advance, alone. After studying the writing styles of the authors involved in The Spider, I eliminated all but Emile Tepperman and Norvell Page. I had assigned "The Radio Murders" to Emile Tepperman, by the way, but it could have been by Page. But I felt that Emile Tepperman's stories seldom read like they were following an outline! And the Purple Scar stories were lacking the frantic emotional drain associated with Page's writing. I started looking at other authors associated with Popular and Standard at the time, and found a possible suspect in Robert Sidney Bowen.

Now Bowen never wrote a Spider, but was friends of Harry Steeger and the authors at Popular Publications, and probably read the Spider in case he decided to write one. It sounded good. But I still can't help feeling there is a skunk in the woodpile. I decided to approach the investigation from a different angle. If the Purple Scar doesn't fit the Standard line-up, what series does he most resemble? Again, Doc Clarke, the Crimson Mask is close, with several similarities. But to my surprise, I did find one that is almost a dead ringer for Miles Murdock and his nurse, Dale Jordan, and that is Jeffrey Fairchild and his nurse, Carol Endicott; curiously, the Purple Scar stories were written by John S. Endicott, a house name, and that's worth 99 points in my investigation. Now, let's read this from the first novel:

The pages of man's history are crowded with strange and awesome legends—weird, unauthenticated tales of monstrous beings and eerie happenings. Of them all, perhaps the most fascinatingly gruesome (author spells it grewsome) is the little known legend of the "Purple Eye!"

Of course, I'm talking about The Skull Killer, a Spider-like character that opposed both *The Octopus* and *The Scorpion* in 1939. The characters, hospital background, everything matches both series. There is a mystery surrounding the first story, "The City Condemned to Hell" *(The Octopus),* by Randolph Craig. A payment check was signed by Norvell Page and Edith & Ejir Jacobsson; the suggestion is that the Jacobssons wrote the story, but Popular Publications had Norvell Page rewrite it. The second story, "Satan's Incubator" by Randolph Craig was totally written by Norvell Page, but using the same characters, except for replacing The Octopus with The Scorpion, something that has long been a curiosity among the pulp crowd.

Okay, I'm going to stop short of claiming that the Purple Scar was either unpublished stories of The Skull Killer, or a continuation of that series, but I am curious as to why there are so many clues pointing to The Spider and similarities with the Skull Killer. So what happened? If there weren't so many clues to The Spider in the Purple Scar, I would suggest that someone at Standard simply borrowed some ideas from The Skull Killer to create the Purple Scar. I don't have any information on Edith and Ejir Jacobsson. As far as I know, they were not involved with any of the pulp heroes other than this one story, as their signatures on the check suggests. The pulp houses were notorious about borrowing ideas from other pulp houses, and authors often picked up plots from other writers. So anything is possible. But wouldn't it be fun to imagine that the Jacobssons brought the idea to Standard, and Leo accepted it, but without The Skull Killer, and had them introduce a milder Miles Murdock. Or perhaps that Norvell Page brought the character over to Standard, and toned down the action for Leo, thus we don't get that frantic emotional drain. Unfortunately, we will never know what really happened, but in the pulps anything was possible!

At this point, I still don't know who wrote the Purple Scar, but I have some pretty good ideas. After writing this, I glanced through the first Purple Scar story, "Medals of Murder," and without reading it, here are some things that jumped at me: The Web Hotel and Spider Kelly. That was just at a glance! I wonder if the author was trying to tell us something? If I were to go out on a limb, I think I would go with Norvell Page as the author. Oh, the Endicott house name? Remember the name of Dr. Fairchild's nurse? Carol Endicott! Leo Margulies had his own house names to use, why would he use John S. Endicott?

Red Finger

One of the most interesting pulp spy series appeared in the back pages of the *Operator #5* magazine. Written by prolific wordsmith, Arthur Leo Zagat, the Red Finger sagas ran in twelve exciting short stories, from October 1934 to March 1938. Several things made the character unique. First, spy series may have featured masters of disguise, like Secret Agent "X," Operator #5, and The Eagle, but Red Finger actually wore a costume similar to the detective heroes like The Spider, Phantom Detective, The Shadow, etc. The other thing that made him unique, he wasn't a rich young playboy from Park Avenue. Ford Duane operated an old bookstore dealing in rare volumes, and lived in a tiny back room of the dusty establishment.

Appearing in a magazine that already had a popular lead character, Red Finger was never featured on the cover, and the interior black and white images left a lot to be desired, so we never see a good representation of his costume. However, it is described thusly: a gray felt hat was pulled low over his forehead. A gray mask hid his nose and mouth. Only his narrow eyes were revealed. Skin-tight gloves covered his hands. The gloves were black, except for the finger curled around a gun trigger. This was a glaring scarlet "as if it had been dipped in blood." The gun is also somewhat special: "No report shattered the river quiet, but two jets of fine spray spurted from the muzzle, to become a vaporous cloud." If he was captured by the police, certain muttered words, and the furtive display of a secret sign, would set him free quickly. We are not told what the secret sign or words are.

Except for Ford Duane/Red Finger, there are few continuing characters mentioned. There is a girl, however. She is Patricia Ann Towndell, better known as Flower, another secret operative: Dark-suited and dark-hated though her slender figure was, she glowed somehow in the dusty twilight of the grimy shop. When she spoke there was a strange sweet huskiness in her voice. Ford was in love with her, for she was constantly in his thoughts: A face hovered there. A sweet mouth, formed for kissing. Gray, brooding eyes. Tawny hair in which the light glistened duskily. Red Finger once told her: "Flower, get out before it's too late. A girl has no business in The Force. Get out before a bullet finds its billet in your soft, sweet body. Or worse happens to it."

Arthur Leo Zagat wrote in a simple formula. His stories had a clear beginning, middle, and end, and he made writing look easy. When I started churning out short stories, I tried to copy his style, keeping my stories simple, with a beginning, middle, and end. I'm not sure how well I succeeded, but he was my influence, and I think it was while reading the Red Finger stories that I decided to also write short story fiction. There was just something about the character that I liked.

I hope the reader will discover that same magic I found in these little adventures.

Red Mask

Albing Publications sneaked into the pulp hero field in March 1941 with their first issue of *Red Mask Detective Stories*. There were four stories in the series, but by the third entry the magazine became *Red Hood Detective Stories*. Perhaps Ned Pines told them they

Red Mask Detective Stories, March 1941.

already had a character that wore a red mask (the Crimson Mask) so Albing changed the title for obvious reasons. But then the fourth story was published in *Movie Detective*. The editor was listed as Jerry Albert. I'll come back to him in a minute.

The reader was told right off that our hero, Perry Morgan, was an average "Joe," like you and me, but then we learn that he is a multi-millionaire, with enough money to last twenty lifetimes. Some ordinary Joe! The text claims that he wears a red mask, but the illustrations show him with a pull over hood. The covers also sport a red domino mask along with the title! Plus, he is affectionately called, "The Paladin of Law and Order." Perry Morgan is aided by the regular group of formula characters, naturally. Gloria Chalmers is the love interest; her father is Burton Chalmers, head of Chalmers Aeroplanes. Sound familiar? Try

84   ECHOES 30: THREE DECADES OF PULP FANDOM'S GREATEST MAGAZINE

Frank Havens and daughter, Muriel. The Police Commissioner is General Hugh Walters, retired military. There was also a Police Inspector named Sampson. Some other regulars pop up, but this is your typical pulp ensemble.

I'm not familiar with Albing Publications, but the "Alb" in "Albing" smacks of Jerry Albert, the editor, so I wouldn't be surprised if the Alberts are part owners of Albing Publications. I use "Alberts" in the plural because it's obvious Jerry isn't the only one involved. The author of the Red Mask/Red Hood stories is listed as Stanley Richards, an obvious pseudonym. If we had any doubts, a few years later (1944-45), a digest mystery series, *A Vulcan Mystery*, popped up and reprinted a slew of pulp stories. Two of the stories in the digest series are our Red Mask/Red Hood entries. However, the mask and hood are dropped, and so is the name of the hero, Perry Morgan. These two reprints are called, "A Paul Decker Mystery," and the author is listed as Andrew I. Albert. Who would have guessed?

There is considerable humor in the stories, which is an added treat. The author even makes fun of some of our better known pulp heroes of the period, as in these passages:

From "Tiger Claws," *Red Hood Detective Stories*, July 1941 (Perry Morgan is speaking): "A crook in a red mask! It sounds like a dime thriller!" Or this, "Well, he was no 'phantom' from out of a book," Voorhis assured him. Sounds to me like the author is having some fun with Ned Pines' Thrilling Group!

The stories were fairly short at novelette length, and might have fared better if they had been full novels, but as they were, the paladin of law and order was still an interesting addition to pulp hero line up. Unfortunately, like so many series that began during this late period, it was destined for a short life, and would not recover. By the time the war in Europe and the Pacific ended, the pulps were on a down hill plunge. In just a few short years, they would all be gone.

Secret Agent "X"

Secret Agent "X" was the ultimate spy! No one knew his name or face, and he only had one contact in government, a mysterious individual known as K-9. Only one woman was ever really close to him. Betty Dale, and she saw his face just once. But she loved him, and often assisted him in dangerous investigations. "X" was the unknown factor, and criminals beware!

I first found Secret Agent "X" when my father was in the Dallas V.A. Hospital waiting for his death. I was stationed in California in 1972, and drove into Dallas to visit my father for the last time. I had been collecting *Doc Savage* and *The Shadow* for several years, and even picked up a number of pulps out in Los Angeles earlier. Leaving the hospital for a while, I visited an older used bookstore in downtown Dallas, and was surprised to see thousands of science fiction pulps stacked on the floor throughout the building. I mentioned to the owner that I was really looking for the hero stuff, like Doc and The Shadow. He said, "Oh, those are upstairs, but nothing under two dollars. And first issues are four bucks! But I don't have any *Shadows* or *Doc Savages*."

He took me upstairs, and left me alone in a single room the size of the whole downstairs, filled with pulps and comic books from the 1930s and '40s. I swear, I thought I had died and gone to pulp heaven! Being in the military at the time, I didn't have a lot of money, so had to be careful how much I spent that day. The owner was wrong, though: I did find one *Shadow*. If I had had more time, I might have found more, maybe even a *Doc* or two. But time and money were both short.

I want you to use your imagination for a minute. Just think about going through stack after stack of pulp magazines, and finding so many beautiful gems that your heart skips a beat every few seconds. You find *Operator #5*, *The Black Hood*, *G-8*, *Masked Detective*, *Black Book Detective* (with the Black Bat), *Captain Future*, *G-Men Detective* (with Dan Fowler), *Public*

SOME ORIGINAL PULP HEROES   85

Enemy and *The Lone Eagle.* And comic books that I hadn't seen since the 1940s! Glorious covers, exciting titles, and I had to leave them all there!

I selected about fifty *Phantom Detective* issues, all from the 1930s, many issues of *The Ghost/Green Ghost* (including a first issue), that one *Shadow* issue ("Isle of Gold," August 1, 1939), and a dozen *Secret Agent "X"* issues! This was my first real pulp collection. And it took me some time to read all those wonderful old stories, but I finally got through them. And I was fascinated with the character of Secret Agent "X"!

I had to return to California before my father died, but I returned to Dallas later and went back to that old store with money in my pocket. Unfortunately, this time the upstairs had been pretty well picked over. The comics and most of the pulps were gone. I picked up a few issues of *G-Men Detective* and some other stuff, but was disappointed that I had missed the opportunity to go through those pulps one more time. The store later closed. I suspect the old gentleman had passed on. I can imagine some descendant tossing the books in a dumpster in the alley.

I began reading the Secret Agent "X" series and taking notes. Back then, there was very little known about any of the pulp heroes, except for Doc Savage and The Shadow. I also started looking through ads in magazines for missing issues for my collection. I paid four dollars for the second issue, coverless, from a book dealer somewhere. I was closing in on my set by the mid-'70s PulpCon, and I had asked Jack Irwin (I believe) to bring any "X" issues he had for sale, and let me look at them. He did, and I completed my set at that convention. However, those last few issues cost me something like $60.00 each! The prices had risen since interest for the lesser-known pulps were becoming greater.

It was prior to the convention that Will Murray contacted me. He had heard that I was researching the Secret Agent "X" series, and wanted to share data. I began sending him synopsis of the stories, and my notes, and thoughts, and Will started adding two and two together, coming up with little known facts and data from his sources. After the convention, we put the history of the series together and sent it to Robert Weinberg for his Pulp Classic books. It remained in Bob's hands until 1980, when it was finally published—missing a number of pages. An updated version was finally published by Altus Press in 2007, *The Secret Agent "X" Companion*, complete with missing pages, and more professional layout.

Today, everyone is familiar with the character, and there's not much that isn't known about the series. But everything being said seems to stem from the research that Will and I did in the book so many years ago. And because of that early research, new writers are churning out new stories about the character who may not have ever read one of the original novels. Will originally identified the rewritten Captain Hazzard novel as one of the Secret Agent "X" stories as far back as the early 1970s, but lately I've seen mention of someone else identifying the novel. Sorry folks, credit belongs to Will Murray.

Secret Agent "X," an enigma to the underworld, his face a mystery, ready to lay his life down for his country. This was the character I first encountered back in 1972. I have heard that this was one of the early influences of Ian Fleming when he created James Bond! Notorious gangster, Al Capone loved the pulp crime fighters of *Secret Agent "X"* and *G-Men Detective.*

Although the authors will change from time to time, the editorial control will keep the stories on a fairly even path, just alternating the theme from time to time. There is a possibility that Paul Chadwick, the originator of the series may have brought in a few ghosts in the early stages, but if so, he certainly went over their work and gave the final stories his own touch. It is only later that the publisher begins to bring in their writers to supplement Chadwick's stories, eventually replacing him completely. I think you will find the series as fascinating as I did back in 1972. ♦

Secret Service Aurelius Smith

By Tom Johnson

There's a lot of dime novel Nick Carter in Aurelius Smith, but there's also a lot more to the man dubbed Secret Service Smith than is apparent on the surface. In "The Black Magician," from *Complete Detective Novel Magazine* #13, July 1929, the reader finds many signs of coming trends.

The novel was written R.T.M. Scott, who, in a few years would create the character of The Spider in the first two novels of that exciting series. Although there has been some debate on whether The Spider was written by Scott Senior or Scott Junior, I don't think there is any doubt that the R.T.M. Scott that wrote the Aurelius Smith novels, also wrote the two Spider novels. The writing certainly appears the same, but the old saying, "Like father, like son…" could hold true in this case.

Smith was something of an ex-espionage agent with the CID, working for a man, Sir Oliver Haultain in London, but now only helped private citizens who truly needed his aid. Years before The Shadow and the pulp heroes graced the stands, Aurelius used his analytical mind to trap super villains bent on world domination. He even had his helpers who eagerly joined him in his fight against crime and evil.

Bernice Asterley was a young American girl from French parents who had studied acting, but was hired by Smith as a stenographer when she was down on her luck, and moved her into a room in his apartment. Bernice was the counterpart of all the females to stand beside the super heroes later.

Jimmie was a youth that Smith had rescued from the streets of Chicago and brought to live with him in New York. The boy was street-wise, and invaluable to the investigator.

Langa Doonh was his Indian manservant and old partner in many battles.

When Scott created The Spider, it was easy enough to transform Aurelius Smith into Richard Wentworth, Bernice into Nita Van Sloan, and Langa Doonh into Ram Singh. There was even a dog, Lemon, which would become a Great Dane in the later Spider stories. The only one not brought over was the boy, Jimmie. But I'll speak more about him in a minute.

The Aurelius Smith stories began several years prior to the hero pulps, but all of the elements are present, except for the masks and quick disguises. I think I read somewhere that Walter Gibson had read the R.T.M. Scott series, but I couldn't find my notes, so please don't quote me. But The Shadow would also have that analytical mind, and would face many similar super villains. However, so did all of the other characters, like the Phantom Detective, The Spider, et al. This current story under my microscope, "The Black Magician," involves an occultist named Jerome

The Black Magician, 1938 Triangle Books edition.

Cardan (often referred to as a devil) who, during the war had infected rats with a deadly virus to kill thousands of people in Asia. Smith had been there and discovered the plot, but they never arrested the devil. Now, he's in New York, and plans to blackmail a rich industrialist for enough money to return to Russia and set up his own government, and eventually rule the world. The plot, though not the story, is very similar to a later *Secret Agent "X"* entry, "City of Madness" (in which "X" battles a super villain called Shaitan—Satan) by G.T. Fleming-Roberts (this plot was originally tried in an earlier "X" story, "City of the Living Dead"). And "Plague of the Golden Death" had a strange connection to the story, as well. Oddly enough, Fleming-Roberts had a Green Ghost story titled, "The Case of the Black Magician." If I were a gambler, I would bet that Fleming-Roberts had read the earlier Scott story by the same title!

Jerome Cardan uses hypnotism to control the minds of his victims, pretends to bring people back from the dead, and supposedly controls supernatural forces (even voodoo). He also dabbles in poisons and deadly viruses, and uses five-pointed stars dipped in chemicals that either kill or knock out his victims. Early in the story both protagonists meet face to face over tea in friendly conversation, but when they depart it will be a "no holds barred" battle to the finish. Oh, in this early story, they discuss the splitting of the atom, and the theory of universes within the atom.

Not only did Secret Agent "X" and The Spider have similarities to the Secret Service Aurelius Smith series, so did Secret Service Operator #5. Z-7 was Sir Oliver Haultain, Jimmy Christopher (Operator #5) was Aurelius Smith, and Tim Donovan was the boy, Jimmy! Of course, Bernice Asterley became Nita Van Sloan, Betty Dale, and Diane Elliot. In fact, the Phantom Detective had Chip Dorlan, a young boy very similar to Jimmie. Truth is, the lad was supposed to be a draw for younger boys to read the stories. Tim Donovan was so important to the Operator #5 series that authors were not allowed to leave him out of a story.

I don't find it at all strange that R.T.M. Scott was asked to create The Spider. I'm just surprised that he didn't write more of the character pulps. After all, his Secret Service Aurelius Smith was a blueprint for them!

Surprisingly, *The Equalizer,* the 1980s TV series, had a very similar plot. Ex-CIA agent, McCall leaves the service to help private citizens. His old agency chief, Control continues to appear, just like Sir Oliver Haultine of the CID.

Aurelius Smith stories:

- *Murder Stalks the Mayor*
- *Aurelius Smith—Detective*
- *Secret Service Smith*

- *The Black Magician*
- *Ann's Crime*
- *Return of Secret Service Smith*
- *Smith Gets an Assistant*
- *The Case of Bernice Asterley*

There may be others.

Here are some titles I'm not sure of, but some could be Aurelius Smith tales. All are listed as by R.T.M. Scott.

- "A Tabloid Mystery"
- "Dr. Quintail's Case"
- "I Gamble With Lives"
- "In the Dark"
- "Magic"
- "Return of Sinbad Constantine"
- "Settled at Sea"
- "Solved at Midnight"
- "The Bird-Cage Mystery"
- "The Crushed Pearl"
- "The Egyptian Necklace"
- "The Missing Finger"
- "The Star of Death"
- "The Stubborn Heiress"
- "Tower of Doom"
- "Women Loathed Her"
- "The Spider Strikes" *(The Spider)*
- "The Wheel of Death" *(The Spider)*

Under Reginald Scott:
- "Eases Pip Seven"
- "The Trap"

Under Maitland Scott:
- "Death's Watchdog"
- "Doom Mountain"
- "Double-Exposure"
- "Eyes That Think"
- "Five Cents a Life"
- "Flowers of Vengeance"
- "Golden Suicide"
- "House-Guest From Hell"
- "Last Chance Ace"
- "Last-Mile Bargain"
- "Massacre Curse"
- "Priestess of Pain"
- "Satan's Armchair"
- "Satan's Bargain"
- "Shadows of Desire"
- "Something on the Side"
- "The God's Vision"
- "The Last Clue"
- "The Skeleton's Paymaster"
- "Time for Death"
- "Tunnel for Death"

The Maitland Scott titles are probably R.T.M. Scott, Junior, but I don't know that for a fact. There may have been other pen names by both father and son. And it's possible that one of the Scott's wrote some Phantom Detective stories. In fact, I believe a character named "Maitland" appeared in a late Forties novel, and Scott Junior was one of my suspects for the story. ♦

The Shadow's Ladies

By Tom Johnson

Many pulp historians are constantly putting together lists of the best novels in certain series. But, by putting as few as two different 'experts' together and asking their opinions as to the best story of any pulp character, you will probably get two different opinions. There is a reason for this. Personal likes, or particular favorites, will very often over-shadow a well written story, so the 'expert' is merely stating his opinion as to his likes when he prepares a list of any "Ten Best" of any series. True, many fans will very often have the same favorites as others, so there will be a duplication of certain novels being the best, but this fact doesn't necessarily make that particular novel "the best."

Believing that I was an "expert" in the field of pulp magazines, I recently asked a fellow collector… who was preparing such a list… why I had not been consulted for a contribution of my own opinions. I was somewhat shocked when he replied: "I didn't know you were an expert." After thinking about it for a while I started studying the question of experts and came to the conclusion that all of us relied on one particular ground rule—our personal favorites.

So, in preparing this article you are now reading, I decided to list a few of my favorites. Not because they were the "best," but merely because they stuck in my memory—and became a few of my favorites. Actually I must thank my good friend (a true expert) Nick Carr, for being my mentor. After all, he was the first to write about his favorites in *Bronze Shadows*, and influenced me to do the same.

Pulps were mostly dated stories, involving action around a theme popular at that time. Today, such series as *The Shadow* and *Doc Savage* can be read with equal fun as they were back in the 1930s. Such series as *Operator #5, Secret Agent "X,"* and *The Spider* were filled with such dedication as patriotism, love of country, protection of the weak—a theme sadly lacking in most character series today.

Many friends, and fellow collectors, have questioned my expertise on the main pulp heroes, as most of my articles deal with the lesser known character pulps, and short story-pulp characters. So there may be some surprise if they knew that I had read the complete sets of The Shadow, Doc Savage, The Spider and G-8. As I have only touched on a few of these characters in previous articles, I felt that this review for should deal with one of the main characters of the pulp magazines. And what better subject than The Shadow?

To set the record straight, let me say that The Shadow is my favorite pulp character, with Doc Savage a close second. My two favorite authors are Walter Gibson and Lester Dent. For years now, I have secretly been in love with Pat Savage and Ming Dwan (my wife doesn't know this, of course).

The Shadow was a fighter, a master manipulator of men and a human calculator, but he seldom had a romantic interest in the stories. He did have a girlfriend (supposedly) at the beginning of the series,

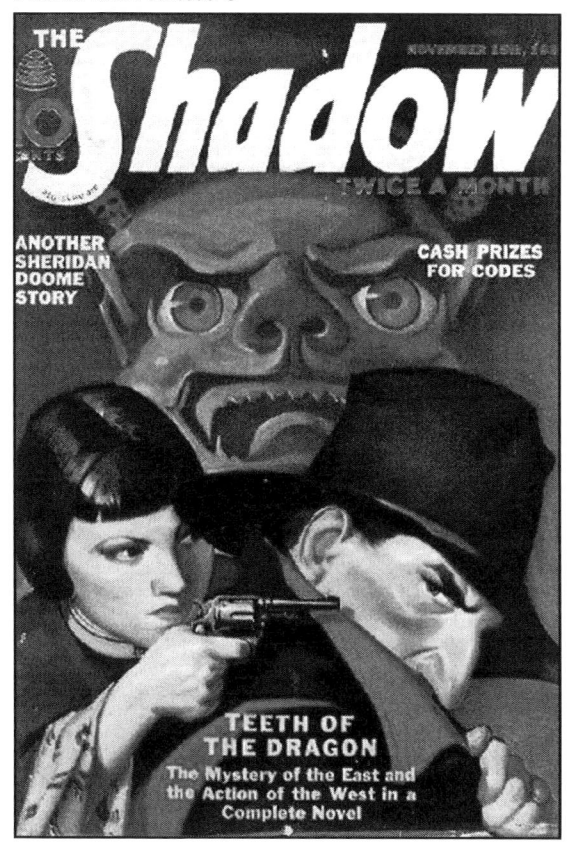

The Shadow Magazine, November 15, 1937.

but she was only using him. Then there was Margo Lane much later, but she was merely an aid. It was always my hope that The Shadow would marry Myra Reldon (Ming Dwan)... and The Shadow did, once, take Myra out on a dinner date. Though Myra captured the hearts of many fans, she failed to conquer the master of darkness.

Many a lady crossed the path of The Shadow. Most were young and beautiful; some were in love with a leading character in the story, while others were innocent victims of some criminal mastermind. Walter Gibson weaved fascinating mystery plots around these young ladies, and they were constantly being rescued by this extraordinary crime-fighter. However, The Shadow was a lone fighter. His life was dedicated to fighting evil... master plots and master criminals. Love just wasn't to be. Not for The Shadow.

But this doesn't mean that there were no suitable young women to capture his heart... or his many fans.

Many of our pulp heroes had their sweethearts from the very beginning, or met them during their first adventure; Operator #5 had his Diane Elliot, The Spider his Nita Van Sloan, Secret Agent "X" had Betty Dale, and the Phantom Detective had his Murial Havens.

The Shadow fought crime for ten years before he was given Margo Lane, his constant companion. But Margo wasn't his love. She would merely be an aid to The Shadow, and society date for Lamont Cranston. Introduced in "The Thunder King" (June 15, 1941), she still didn't become an agent until the novel "The Murdering Ghost" (November 15, 1942). Actually it was the radio series that gave Margo her role in the adventures of The Shadow, as she was created in that media, only later being added to his adventures in the pulp magazines.

Still, ladies were around before Margo Lane, women who would have made fitting mates to the Dark Avenger. It is concerning two of these ladies that this article is about. As mentioned previously, Myra Reldon remains at the top of the list as a suitable mate for our Dark Eagle. So she must be the first to take her bow.

Myra Reldon

Perhaps the most memorable lady to fight at the side of The Shadow was as much a mystery as The Shadow. And, unlike the rest of the young ladies, she was to be included in many of his adventures. Her name was Myra Reldon, and like The Shadow, Myra was a master with disguise. Introduced in the novel "Teeth of the Dragon" (November 15, 1937), she captured the hearts of many fans... and may have even touched the heart of The Shadow.

Myra was actually an undercover agent for the FBI. She had lived in China for a long time, and spoke the language fluently. Trying to break a Chinese smuggling ring in San Francisco's Chinatown, Myra, as Ming Dwan, has infiltrated the Jeho Fan (the teeth of the dragon), a powerful tong, in hopes of learning where the information leaks are coming from, which enables the tong to carry out their smuggling activities.

Meanwhile, unknown to the feds, The Shadow is also on hand. An important Chinese General (Cho Tsing) had recently been kidnapped and brought to America, to be held for ransom of ten million dollars by the Jeho Fan tong. The Shadow, as Lamont Cranston, meets Myra Reldon during a business meeting: She is posing as a secretary:

> A girl was seated in the reception room; her desk bore the nameplate: "Miss Reldon."
>
> She was Vayne's secretary; and she acted as receptionist. It would have been difficult to picture any young woman better suited to the double job.
>
> Miss Reldon had a distinct charm of feature and expression; her smile was the sort that would place any visitor at ease. With that graciousness, she also possessed a brisk business manner that contrasted with her social air.
>
> That marked her as unusual. Her appearance, too, provided contrast. The girl had the light complexion of a blonde; but her large, clear eyes were definitely brown. Her thin eyebrows were light in color; the fluff of her hair made it seem light brown against the sunlight. The Shadow noted, though, that it was darker when viewed from another angle.

After meeting with Vayne, Myra invites Cranston to dine with her at a Chinese restaurant, Cranston arrives at the restaurant as The Shadow, but he is captured by the tong… and a Chinese girl named Ming Dwan, who is a member of the Jeho Fan. The Shadow is taken before the Tao Fan (tong leader), but escapes through one of the tong's own death traps.

Who was this young Chinese girl that appeared to capture The Shadow?

> The mirror showed her light-hued face; her shapely shoulders and slender arms, smooth and white like ivory. That reflection told that Myra would have been extraordinarily attractive in an evening gown, thanks to the beauty of her skin.
>
> Yet the girl's first move was to obliterate that whiteness.
>
> From the make-up kit, Myra took a sponge and a bottle of yellowish fluid. Unsparingly, she daubed the thick liquid on her hands and wrists; swept the sponge up to her shoulders. Her face and throat were next; using a hand mirror, the girl dyed the back of her neck.
>
> She tapered the color downward from her neck and shoulders, until the yellow lessoned and blended with the whiteness. Above the bathrobe, Myra's face, neck and arms all possessed an even yellow tone.
>
> Still she would have looked well in an evening gown, but her complexion belonged to a Chinese beauty.
>
> Next came the facial make-up.
>
> Myra removed fluffs of false hair. Her real hair was darker brown. It seemed almost black when Myra combed it straight and pressed it thickly. From above her forehead, she combed short locks downward. Ordinarily hidden, they became short-clipped bang, dyed jet-black.
>
> The face that appeared from the mirror bore no resemblance to Myra Reldon's. It was the visage of a Chinese beauty—exotic, alluring, but with an expression that bore cruel malice.

At the turn of every event we are led to believe that Myra is an enemy, until the last when Ming Dwan saves The Shadow's life. Later Vic Marquette, the ace of the FBI discloses her real identity and purpose. But for awhile we were not sure:

> The Shadow's prowess was melting beneath the guile of Ming Dwan.

However, The Shadow knew from the beginning that Myra was on the side of law and order, The Shadow always knew! But Myra was not so sure that The Shadow understood her motives, and even told Vic of her fears, but Vic told her not to worry… she would never see The

Shadow again.

Myra returns to her apartment, where she shortly received a phone call:

"I am late?" she asked. "Late? For dinner…? Why, come to think of it, I haven't had dinner to-night, at all! I'm hours late… What's that? You say I am days late…?"

Myra's perplexity faded suddenly. She recognized the voice; something else, that the speaker mentioned.

"At the Yangtse Restaurant… Yes, I can make it in half an hour, Mr. Cranston. This time you can depend upon me…."

Myra's hand was motionless, still holding the receiver. That was why she heard the whispered sound that came from it—an audible, fading tone of mirth, an echo that seemed to nullify all menace of the past.

Myra would eventually become an agent of The Shadow's, but she, too, was not destined to become The Shadow's mate. The romantic interest only lasted for the one story. But she was not the only girl to cross the path of The Shadow, and leave her mark as a possible love for our hero, Nor would there be many more to come as close. However, in one story I detected a higher than usual interest in one of the ladies, on The Shadow's part, and this story has remained in my memory for years, and also becomes one of my favorites. She will now take her bow.

Geraldine Murton

Geraldine was tall, slim, with blonde hair, and very beautiful. She was an airline stewardess, and chance circumstances brought her into the presence of The Shadow, in the novel titled "Silver Skull" (January 1, 1939).

The Shadow, as Lamont Cranston, had been investigating several mysterious airplane crashes in which important men of money had supposedly been killed. Lamont Cranston has been captured, drugged, and put aboard a plane scheduled for destruction. When Cranston awakes he finds the pilots dead. The lone stewardess is alive, and with the aid of Cranston the two survive the plane crash in the Rocky Mountains.

At first Geraldine believes Cranston to be a criminal, but as they trek across the mountains she learns to trust him, and he reveals the criminal plot to her. They become close during their journey across the mountains, and when they locate a railroad track it isn't long before they are safe inside an empty boxcar, and on their way to Denver, where The Shadow plans to further his campaign against the plot… with the aid of Geraldine:

> … the girl was asleep, her blond head resting comfortably on Cranston's shoulder, while his arms, encircling her snuggled body, protected her from the lurch and swing of the jolting car.

The Shadow Magazine, January 1, 1939.

THE SHADOW'S LADIES 93

The Shadow Magazine, January 1, 1939.

When they reach Denver, Cranston leaves Geraldine, but informs her that she is to work with Kent Allard, and search for a hidden air base in the vicinity where their plane was shot down.

Geraldine compares the two men, Cranston and Allard, but can't decide which one she likes better.

> … of the two, Geraldine could not decide which she liked the better. She wished that she could see them together, and thereby make her choice.

At the end of the novel she has seen both men in action, and during a gun battle between The Shadow and a gang of crooks, she aids the man in black by giving him another gun as his thundering automatics fire their last bullet. The Shadow rescues Geraldine, and they escape in his autogyro before the local authorities arrive to pick up the wounded crooks. Within the autogyro The Shadow removes his black cape and hat, and reveals the Cranston identity to Geraldine. He explains the final points to the end of the case, answering Geraldine's questions:

> Geraldine had shifted to another question—one that she regarded as more important than any that she had put before,
>
> "Will you tell me, Mr. Cranston," she asked, "just where this present flight of ours is going to end?"
>
> "Somewhere near the Rockies," replied The Shadow, "where we can take another freight train."
>
> "Back to where we were?"
>
> "Or near there. So we can stumble, weary and ragged, into some mountain cabin, to tell how we survived the crash."
>
> Geraldine smiled. She'd forgotten that she and Cranston would have to explain their return to life. But she hadn't forgotten that day when they had trekked across the mountain slopes; a day that to her present recollection had been much too short.
>
> She didn't have to tell The Shadow that she was glad they were returning to the Rockies.
>
> The Shadow knew.

Ah! Was there a romantic interest there? I thought so. There was that certain hint that The Shadow, too, might enjoy that continued trek across the mountains with Geraldine. But the story ended there, and Geraldine never returned to the pages of The Shadow stories. Back in 1977, at PulpCon 6, I talked with Walter Gibson, and asked if there had been a romantic interest intended. I was informed that there hadn't been. So it looks like a beautiful stewardess, Geraldine had merely been one of many lovely ladies to cross the path of The Shadow… never to return. But to me these lovely ladies added a touch of romance to the adventures of the mighty avenger, and Myra Reldon and Geraldine Murton will always make those two novels a few of my favorites. ♦

An Essay on New Pulp Heroes

By Tom Johnson

I think the awakening of Pulp Renaissance began about 1965, less than fifteen years after the so-called death of the character pulps, with the fanzine, *Bronze Shadows*, by Fred Cook. The appearance of Doc Savage and The Shadow in paperback certainly helped in the awakening. This brought awareness to new fans, as well as reconnecting many old readers of the pulp magazine heroes. Many fanzines followed in the wake of *Bronze Shadows*, plus researchers began digging deeper into the history, including speaking with publishers, editors, authors and artists from the period, and the pulps were laid bare for the following generations. Numerous research books were published, making the data available not only to fans, but the general public as well. The Renaissance reached its peak around 1994 with Will Murray's new Doc Savage novels, and James Van Hise's short stories of Operator #5 and The Spider. Where the current Renaissance will take us, there's no telling, but right now it appears to still be strong and growing, not only with research books (mostly reprints of older books) coming out in newer and better editions, but there are more writers churning out new adventures featuring the old heroes, as well as many new characters in the pulp tradition. For the pulp fan, this is a great time to be alive, and I think the new generation of readers will carry the tradition into this new century with enthusiasm. In only twenty years The Shadow will be 100 years old. Did someone say the pulp heroes died in 1953? I think not. Many of the current generation will be around to see the anniversary of The Shadow in 2031. I hope there will be a big party! Following are essays on some of the new characters that have been created since the pulp heroes ceased in 1953.

The Black Cat

The Black Cat is a lone wolf, specializing in raiding dens of evil and removing their ill-gotten gains: She presented a startling figure of a woman. She was young, tall, and dressed all in black. On her head rested a black Robin Hood hat topped off with a feather. A silky mask like a Muslim yashmak covered the lower part of her face, but revealed long brilliant eyes that darted in quick alarm. She held a gun in each hand, and she knew how to use them! The dress and hat are reversible, red on one side, black on the other, making for an easy and quick change. The small guns are worn in holsters around her slim waist, and a scabbard rest behind her neck, holding a long, sharp throwing knife.

Nina Hastings is the daughter of Ronald K. Hastings, Railroad & Utilities magnate. She has dark raven-black hair. Her smile was open and frank, with dark eyes that seemed to laugh. Light as a feather, her movements were feline grace. A heady fragrance clung to her smooth throat, which was white and rippling. Nina had taken to sports early, becoming expert with knives, bow and arrows, and even guns, excelling in tournaments. She enjoyed the excitement

The Black Cat

of competition—and danger.

Ronald K. Hastings is a widower who raised his daughter alone after his wife died. Instead of remarrying, he devoted his time to business, becoming wealthy at a young age. Now balding, with gray tuffs at his temples, and a rounded stomach, he merely indulged in his daughters many whims.

Lieutenant Eric Lamont is the police official in the series. The lieutenant is tall and lean, with smooth slabs of gray hair and a fine, aristocratic face. His voice is soft and suave, while his eyes are a hard steel gray.

Rocky McFayne is the publisher of the Express, and the occasional romantic interest of Nina Hastings. He is compactly built with a square face, curly red hair, and light green eyes. His porkpie hat was tipped back from his face and his hands were thrust deep into his topcoat pockets. Rocky is a nickname he picked up while fighting professionally in the boxing ring. He inherited the newspaper after his father died, and is dedicated to cleaning up his town of crime and corruption. Though in love with Nina, he would turn her over to the law if he had proof she was the notorious Black Cat.

Marilyn is Rocky's aunt and his receptionist at the newspaper. She is elderly, gray haired, and very attractive. Ronald Hastings has been smitten by her charms.

Joe Roper is the Ace Crime Reporter for the Express. Joe is a wiry young man with his thin frame too small for the baggy clothes hanging loosely from his body. The fedora perched on his sandy head was tilted back at an angle, and a Press card was stuck in the band. His parents died from influenza while he was in Europe in WWI. Tough in a fist fight, and a good shot with a .45 automatic. He knew the badlands well. It's where he grew up. The Black Cat brings Joe into her confidence, and calls him Slim. When the police are closing in on Nina as the suspected Black Cat, Joe dons the guise of the notorious vigilante and draws suspicion away from her. By the second story, Joe is a partner and wears a black domino mask as Slim.

Nina lives in a comfortable apartment at the Empire Park Hotel. The apartment is equipped with a bar, lounge, and wall safe. Rich carpets covered the floors, and famous paintings adorn the walls. A large window overlooks Park Avenue below.

The Black Cat was a secondary character in the 1941 story, "The Totem Pole Murders," featuring The Angel Detective. The main character wasn't popular enough to carry the magazine, and the series only lasted the one issue. Tom Johnson took The Black Cat and added new characters, and gave Nina Hastings the lead role, and she seems to work much better than The Angel Detective. There have only been two new stories so far: "A Cat Among Dogs" and "Partners in Crime."

The Black Ghost

In 1994, Officer Malone is killed by a drug gang known as the Black Widows while on patrol, leaving a wife, Ruth, and 14 year-old son, Jimmy. Obtaining a minimum-wage job at a grocery story, they are forced to move into a Housing Projects beset with crime.

Jimmy Malone dons a black hood and, calling himself Compere, sets out to find his father's killers, at the same time protecting the area around their new home. Thus began the story. Although he had chosen one name, the gangs quickly adopted another to describe this nemesis of the night—The Black Ghost!

During the first story, "The Black Widows," The Black Ghost is rescued by an elderly couple who were once employed by the government as espionage agents. They take Jimmy under their wing to train him in the deadly fight ahead of him. In the second story, "Hunter's Moon," Jimmy is now about 24 and he meets Peggy Sue Simpson, a girl pursued by the mob. They would shortly be married. By thirty, gangsters have come to fear the name of The Black Ghost.

Jimmy Malone is tall, muscular, with blonde hair and blue eyes; he is trained in weapons and martial arts. Now independently wealthy from an inheritance left to him by the elderly couple that once trained him, his stepfather considers Jimmy a pain in the neck for his constant bother at his office.

Peggy Sue Malone is beautiful, blonde and blue-eyed, though she insists on wearing a red wig, which irritates her mother-in-law. But she laughingly explains that the red wig is Jimmy's idea. Peggy knows that her husband is The Black Ghost, and has often

The Black Ghost

donned the regalia to assist him in his fight against the underworld.

Ruth Malone Wheeler is Jimmy's mother. She is now married to the Chief of Detectives, Captain Wheeler.

Captain Wheeler is Chief of Detectives. He met Jimmy and his mother when Officer Malone was killed in "The Black Widows." A patrolman at the time, he has risen in rank to captain, and now runs the detective department. Usually grumpy, drinks two-day-old cold coffee, and his favorite expletive is, "Fiddlesticks!" Has suspicion that Jimmy is either The Black Ghost or has contact with him.

The Black Ghost is dressed all in black. He wears a black cape around his shoulders and a black hood pulled over his head. The hood has tiny lights within the fabric, which can be operated by a small battery. Once they are turned on, a ghostly face appears on the hood. He carries a brace of .45 automatics, either in shoulder holsters or on a belt around his waist, and is ambidextrous. He has several magic tricks literally up his sleeves. A compressed gas container will fill balloons in each sleeve at the press of a button, sending them screaming like Banshees to distract gunmen when necessary. He talks in an eerie whisper, and challenges gangdom with a weird laugh.

George Freeman is tall and broad shouldered. He wears his hair in a crew cut, and has a black widow spider tattoo on one arm. About 38, recently retired from the Army Rangers, skilled in weapons and martial arts, but prefers boxing. Served in Iraq and other hot spots. After retirement, he obtained a job as reporter for the local newspaper and was recruited by The Black Ghost in "Death and The Black Ghost." Freeman is married to Nancy, who doesn't know her husband is an agent of The Black Ghost until the story, "Carnival of Death." She works in a small boutique, owned by Paula Marsh.

Paula Marsh has dark hair, cut in a short bob, with dark, laughing eyes, but they were not always like that. Her husband, a helicopter pilot in Iraq had been killed soon after their marriage. Contemplating suicide one night, Paula attempted to a leap off the roof of a tall building when hoodlums attacked her. The Black Ghost happened along just in time to stop the hoodlums and prevent her from jumping to her death. While being treated in the hospital, George Freeman stops by the room, and she suspects he might be her rescuer the night before. Paula tells him she

The Black Ghost

has a proposition for the man in black. When The Black Ghost does visit her, she offers her services in his fight against crime. Paula was introduced in "Highways In Hiding."

Professor Josh Crandall is an elderly science teacher at the university, he had assisted the government agents who trained The Black Ghost, now he tells Compere he is training another young man to take his place when he is gone. He was only in "Highways In Hiding."

Professor Lamont Rogers is a young science teacher at the university, Professor Crandall had prepared to take over as a behind the scenes operative of The Black Ghost. He is introduced in "The Spider's Web," and becomes attached to Paula. He is tall and slender, narrow shoulders, not athletic, and is not an active agent.

Hui Yo Chae is a thirty-year-old electronic whiz trying to complete college when her money runs out. Yo is Korean, and she is recruited in "The Spider's Web" to run Control Central, the new contact and surveillance arm of The Black Ghost. She is a karate expert, but merely operates the monitoring systems, and answer calls coming in from agents and The Black Ghost. She is small and dark haired, with dark, almond-shaped eyes.

Tom Johnson created the series, and there have been about twelve novelettes or short novels in the series to-date.

The Devil B'Tonga

A monster of the woods meandered through the dense jungle of tall trees and thick vines, but this one had little shape to prove it was animal. It was not a man. Though at times it may have resembled a man in form, the creature took on the semblance of the forest itself. Depending on the shadows, it could have been green or gray, or even a dark brown. Its body was more like that of a tree trunk, its arms thick as limbs. Perhaps the feet and hands ended in claws, but who could tell with this shaggy brute?

The monster had been a man in the distant past, but its memory of that time was dim. He had been a fierce warrior of the Masai until a poisoned arrow from a M'Buto pygmy pierced his heart, cutting him down in the prime of life. There had been a small village, a wife and daughter, but memory slowly fades over time. His body had lain in the jungle marshes, merging with the vines, roots, and grasses that grew so abundantly in the rich soil, until he became a part of the very earth that had received him that fateful day. He may not have remembered that day, over twenty years in the past, when his hunting party had been ambushed by the pygmy headhunters, for his memory was only partly human now. Somehow the pygmies had overlooked his body, leaving it to rot in the jungle vegetation. But something had been different about this land, something that was magic. For the living plants covered him, becoming a part of him, and wouldn't let his body return to mud and clay, from whence it had come. Sometime, during the twenty years his body had lain there, the memory of the man guided the things merging with him, attempting to again form the body of a man. The ugly monster did have something of a human shape: two thick legs and arms, and something that resembled a head of sorts. There the resemblance ended. This thing was no man.

Though the natives thought of him as a monster, even monsters can prove to be a hero!

The Devil B'Tonga has appeared in two short stories so far, created by Tom Johnson.

Captain Steve Danger

Most of Captain Danger's universe is filled with the race of man, but they have encountered numerous alien races, many of which now belong to the Allied Command; the best of the fighter pilots recruited into the Space Rangers.

The rank structure within the Space Rangers: Pilots hold the rank of Captain. Copilots hold the rank of Lieutenant—though sometimes they might be Captains. Enlisted ranks are Privates for workers, and Sergeants for non-commissioned officers and the head of departments. There may occasionally be a Corporal bucking for promotion to Sergeant. Only commissioned officers are given ships. The Silver Raptors are powered by Null Drive engines, which propels through space at faster than light (FTL) speed.

Headquarters of Space Rangers is on The Crescent Moon, hidden somewhere within an asteroid belt. Their ships are Silver Raptors, each with its own designation.

Commander: Scott Perry's ship designation is unknown. The gutsy old pilot can usually be seen in his dress uniform of black boots, blue pants, light blue tunics, and a waist-cut blue jacket zipped to the stiff collars. A black leather belt stretched around his thick waist, with a large silver belt buckle carrying the fixed images of twin blaster pistols. On his waist hang a pair of deadly blasters. On his broad shoulders are the military braids of his rank, and on his left breast pocket was the insignia of the Space Patrol, which he commanded. Over his shoulders was wrapped a short, white cape, trimmed in black and gold, and his many military medals covered his chest.

Captain Steve Danger's ship designation is SR#1. He is tall and extremely handsome, and ruggedly built with soft blonde hair and flake gold eyes. Having visited the worlds of too many suns bronzed his skin. His Ranger uniform is similar to the Commander's, except he has gray pants and jacket, and light blue tunics On his right shoulder was a patch with his ship number, "1."

Professor Kela Kleeli is a Taegu-ma insect woman. She is also the adoptive mother of Captain Danger. She resembled a deadly preying mantis.

Lieutenant Cathy Rogers is a fantastic, statuesque, beautiful woman, with long jet-black hair, and bright blue eyes. However, she can change her appearance at a moment's notice with wigs and different color eye lenses. Cathy looks and functions like a human female, but stronger, faster, and nearly invulnerable. She is a robot, cool and emotionless, except when it comes to Steve Danger. She has a huge crush on her superior officer, and very jealous of him, though will quickly deny it.

Alien Races

- Jaspas—a race that evolved from cats, from the Jaspel star system.
- Taegu-ma—a race that evolved from insects, and have the appearance of a preying mantis.
- Zimco Robots—an android race, but their world was destroyed and few still exist.
- Trangonadans—a race of humanoids, not quite human, but can almost pass for them.
- Jareems—This is another humanoid race, also not quite human.
- Giacodon—a race evolved from lizards, with long tails and three eyes.
- Torabon—a race of three-foot tall creatures with blue fur from Torabonaborgugi star system. They usually work at manual labor.
- Pridonians—five-foot tall, purple-skinned humanoids, most work as space sailors because they are at home in zero gravity.
- Fadashka—an asexual race, neither male nor female, with pale yellow skin containing a metallic sheen.
- Deben-4 Robots—a renegade race of robots, once built by man, now built by robots, not yet in the Empire, but wish to join.

There are many races yet discovered. Most of the space pirates that prey upon the weak are humans, though sometimes a rogue alien will appear. As with the different races, there are still many unexplored worlds and galaxies in the far reaches of the universe. Some with binary star systems, some with giant stars, dwarf stars, red suns, orange suns, and even some ice planets without a sun.

The series is a creation of Tom Johnson, and there have been three stories so far.

Chu-Jung

From out of the mist of time to the fog of San Francisco streets, a visage appears to strike fear into evil hearts….

His face was utterly blank, with empty eyes. A long black cloak, lined with silver silk, and with many cleverly hidden pockets. Between the cover and silk were scales of armor. Scales and links of bronze and steel hung together in a complex net, as flexible as heavy leather, as intricate as clockworks. Catches disguised as decorations on the paldrons and gorget held the garment together. The collar concealed a hood that almost completely covered his head. The yoke hid armored shoulders. He slipped into the cloak, and tied a bronzed-bound wooden sword under his left arm. The mask was of red and black lacquer. He had smashed up crime syndicates at Oxford and in Chicago's Chinatown. Now he was in San Francisco's Chinatown to do the same thing.

Raymond Siu is American-Chinese. He is tall for his race. Worked as a stage magician while attending the university at Oxford. Trained in the ancient fighting technique of Chu-Jung, named after the Chinese Lord of Fire—the god who kept order on Earth. He is employed in San Francisco's Cultural Museum.

He lives in a small apartment in a Chinese flat. The courtyard consist of a maze of alleyways, the majority of which were not accessible from any of the main streets. He could hear the cluck and scratch of penned chickens around the corner.

Lily Wing is a famous archeologist and cartographer. She has traveled to Egypt, Greece, and other parts of the world in her studies. Her hair is elaborately piled atop her head and fastened with a gold butterfly pin, her smooth shoulders revealed by a low-cut evening gown. She is employed in the Asian exhibition at the museum.

Harry Marsden is the Chief of Police, the police official in the series.

Professor Black is Head of the San Francisco Cultural Museum.

Chu-Jung

Matt Bingham is the assistant director of the Northern European Exhibition Department, and is a racist.

Character created by Eric Turowski.

Colonel Jeremiah Custer

Colonel Jeremiah Custer is tall, thin, with a brushy mustache and long yellow hair, and stands with a military bearing. His flashing blue eyes denote a quick mind. Educated in the best schools, he claims to be a distant relative of General Armstrong Custer. Of mature age, he fought in France during WWI, receiving many decorations for bravery in the Intelligence Department.

After the Armistice, he worked for a secret government agency for a while, then tired of mundane assignment he set out on his own. A sharpshooter of great skill, he toured the southwest with a traveling troupe of acrobats and showmen, displaying his skills with guns of every sort. His act required that he wear western attire, including boots and ten-gallon hat. Around his waist was strapped a pair of Colt revolvers, and he enjoyed thrilling the audience with his quick draw act, shooting a cigarette out of the mouth of someone staunch enough to stand twenty paces in front of him.

When the traveling tent show disbanded, Colonel Jeremiah Custer found that he wasn't ready to give up his act. That's when he conceived of the Jeremiah Custer Wild West Show And Other Delights!

Chief Thunder Cloud calls himself a warrior of a lost tribe. The colonel wasn't sure if he was Indian or bear, but Chief Thunder Cloud was the largest man he had ever encountered. Dark skinned, he was a former wrestler Jeremiah had found in Saint Louis and recruited for his show. Long on muscle, he had very little education. The wrestling bouts had left him with a cauliflower ear and flattened nose. Small gray eyes were set in his round jovial face. His shoulders were as wide as a boxcar, and muscles rippled with his slightest movement. Calloused hands resembled large rocks, and were just as hard.

When not performing stunts for Colonel Custer's act, he delighted in showing off his great strength to an audience. His act consisted of bending horseshoes, and tying steel pipes into pretzels.

Mai Ling is a beautiful Oriental girl from China. She is a tiny piece of dynamite. Full of energy, she had come with Colonel Custer from the traveling tent show when it disbanded. Thrilling the audiences with her flying gymnastics, and death-defying stunts, she was only happy when performing. An exotic dancer, at times, she also performed the dance of the 7 Veils on the detachable platform, which brought in much of their coins. Her third persona was that of an Eastern princess, in which she wore a dark gown and veil that only covered her lower face, revealing almond-shaped eyes of black pearls.

Tom Johnson's relatives came out of the southern tent shows, and he always wanted to create a series in the mold of Doctor Thaddeus C. Harker. Colonel Custer is his answer. There has only been one story so far in the planned series.

The Dark Avenger

His calling card is a black bullet. Dressed all in black, he stood over six feet tall, and has a broad build. He had on a black trench coat, worn open, black shirt and pants, and a black fedora shadowed a full face-mask, also black. In his fists were two Walther P-38s. A low, menacing laugh, then "The price of crime is death!"

Robert Steele is the top investigator for the District Attorney's office. Gangsters had murdered his relatives in the '70s. His father and grandfather had been The Dark Avenger in their generation. Now it was his turn. Standing 6 feet four inches, and 210 pounds, he has the build of a wrestler. He has jet-black hair and his eyes are a cold, piercing gray.

Linda Aldridge is the District Attorney for Philadelphia. She had grown up with Robert Steele, and knew he was The Dark Avenger. Carries a Berretta .25 in her purse.

Lt. Richard Bruce is the police official, a Homicide Detective of the 115th Division. A large man at 43, he had been a cop for twenty years. Standing 6 foot three inches, he weighed 300 pounds, most of it muscle. He was very agile.

Elwood Jasper is Mayor of Philadelphia.

Henry J. Atkinson works for the Philadelphia City News. He's five foot six, with rumpled brown-black hair, under a battered brown fedora worn cocked back on his head. His wide black tie was twenty years out of date, and worn loose around his neck. His white shirt is stained and his pants were hopelessly scuffed at the ankles. His face was weathered, and his teeth stained by too much coffee and too many cigarettes. He has a raspy and annoying voice.

The series is written in Saturday Matinee serial style, with a cliffhanger at end of each segment. Created by T.J. Moore.

Deadline

The character was created from the pieces of the fictional characters that I enjoy from different mediums. Deadline is a masked vigilante in the tradition of the Spider and the Whisperer, with a dash of Mack Bolan, the Executioner thrown in.

Deadline's secret identity is newspaper reporter John "Ace" Brontes for the Guardian, in a later story. He received some combat experience as a reporter covering the Spanish Civil War in 1936. This was patterned by a newspaper ad from *The Equalizer* TV show from the 1980s and Matt Wagner used it in a *Sandman Mystery Theatre* story line that featured Hourman so it seemed to fit with the name and the reporter angle.

Deadline is of average height with a noticeable wiry build,. dressed in a black suit, black leather gloves, and a black fedora that concealed his features in shadows. A black domino mask covered his face to distort his features. The only color in this ensemble was a blood red rose in his lapel.

If he thought he would be getting into a fight he would change out of usual attire of his black suit and tie, and dress in a black turtle neck shirt, black pants, and black leather gloves. He carries two Colt .45s, a tool belt with a knife. He also carries a haversack containing various grenades and a gasmask. A grappling hook gun is strapped across his back. His face is painted black under his domino mask. Even with his face blackened, Deadline still felt the need to wear the mask. Other influences were by Marvel Comics' British pulp hero Night-Raven, who wore a black turtleneck with his equipment, and the Executioner's battle suit.

Lonny "the Gargoyle" Thomas is Deadline's mentor figure, and loosely based on Richard "Quick Trigger" Traeger from the *Whisperer* series. Since Deadline was not a criminal he needed someone to teach him his tradecraft. He also needed a confidant to explain his motives and actions in the series. He also designed and built some of Deadline's equipment.

Thomas had started out as a second story man and was acknowledged to be one of the best cat burglars in the business until an accident. One night, climbing toward the penthouse of the Shuster Building, he had miscalculated a leap and missed the balcony. He fell three stories and landed on a gargoyle waterspout, breaking both legs and his right arm. He lay there for two days contemplating his life before someone noticed him. He recovered from the fall, but it ended his career as a cat burglar. His still has a noticeable limp, and the denizens of the underworld started calling him the Gargoyle.

The Gargoyle had an apartment above a warehouse down on the docks where Deadline and he lived. It had tunnels and passages that ran underneath it and eventually connected with the sewer system that was created years earlier by rumrunners.

Morton Turner is a large man with an even greater appetite. He knew it was his destiny to be the crime boss of the country. Turner was in the process of consolidating the rackets of the city under his control. The private dining room in the back of the café was reserved for Turner and it was here that he conducted most of his business for his private fiefdom. If Turner could not be found at the café, then he could be found at his mansion in the suburbs. His description was influenced by Marvel Comics' the Kingpin because most of the gangland bosses at the time were small nondescript men. He was not going to have great strength just size and cunning. Big men are usually overlooked as non-dangerous type of people by society at large.

Larry "the Grinder" Thules is Turner's second in command. He is one of the most feared men in the city. Thules received his nickname, the Grinder, because he liked to place people's hands into a meat grinder to make them talk. The Grinder oversaw the day-to-day operations of Turner's expanding empire. He also handled the sensitive operations like extortion or removal of witnesses. He was never far from Turner's side during business hours.

Thules was created in the pulp tradition of a sadistic villain that everyone was afraid of. He was going to be like Turner, a self made man that had a veneer of culture that covered his sadistic side. He was going to be the main villain for the series but I did not decide if he was ever going to take over Turner's empire.

Toby Aikens is a small rodent of a man, who was one of the best pickpockets ever to grace the city. A nondescript man, who could blend in with any crowd. Any interesting tidbit that he found in a wallet he would sell to the right person. He had a photographic memory that retained all that he saw or heard and he would also sell for the right price. If you wanted information on anyone, you started with Toby Aikens.

Aikens was going to be my go to character if I ever had a plot hole or needed a jumping off point to move the story along. He was an amoral man that his decisions were based on any money that he might be able to make.

Dan "the Weasel" Jackson is a fumbling criminal in the Turner mob who was going to be an unwilling informant in Deadline's war on crime. Jackson accidently shoots the Grinder in the back and Deadline uses this to blackmail him for information.

Detective Clifford is on the police force. He is a large haggard looking man, and principled, he was willing to bend the rules in his pursuit of justice. He became an unwilling ally of Deadline's. He was the most decorated police officer in the city's history.

Phil's Bar is located in one of the worst slums in the city and owned by Phil Duncan, hence the name. It was a basement bar that was reached by a short flight of stairs. Phil's had the reputation that anything that anyone could ever want could be purchased within its four walls; the reality of the selection of merchandise was not that far off. Most of the villains that frequented Phil's would kill their own mothers for a sawbuck. Most of the patrolmen in the city would not have visited Phil's without a squad of heavily armed policemen.

The Carriage House is Deadline's base of operations in his war on crime. It was located in an upper income area that is now considered lower income, in which he owned property under a fictitious name. It is a modified apartment set above a garage that once was an outer building of an apartment that used to be a grand mansion. A secret basement workshop that housed his car and equipment completed the ensemble. The man in black would enter a walk-in closet in the master bedroom. He lifted a coat hook and the back of the closet slid open to reveal a narrow staircase spiraling into darkness. The stairwell ended in a subterranean library. The library contained reference books, criminal files, nautical charts, blueprints to public buildings, and various maps. There was also a cot in the library in case he needed a place to hideout. A small kitchenette with a hot plate and refrigerator was off of the library. A small bathroom was next to the kitchenette. The armory was where Deadline kept his weapons and equipment. The garage was barely wide enough to fit the dark coupe inside. At the other end of the garage was a ramp that opened from the floor of the carriage house's garage, leaving his coupe hidden from view in the basement.

Deadline's equipment was varied. His most important piece of equipment was the grappling hook gun, which resembled a large flare pistol with a lanyard. It contained a collapsible grappling hook that erupts from the gun barrel. The flanges of the grappling hook then expand umbrella-like into its normal shape as it unreels a silken cord. The point in the center of the hook embeds itself into whatever it is aimed at. When the trigger is pulled a second time, it activates an electric motor that rewinds the silken cord and lifts the shooter off of the ground.

The dark coupe had been donated to his cause from Crash McGhee, one of the best wheelmen in the business, before he died of tuberculosis. Deadline had saved his daughter's life in an earlier adventure. It was bullet proof with a large V-8 engine to pull its weight. Under the dashboard was a hidden toggle switch that disengaged the car's security system. The two-door coupe had been designed so that it could be started without a key for a quick getaway by a concealed button on the dash. In the trunk of the car there is a secret compartment for his equipment. The haversack contained extra magazines for his guns, a few grenades and other deadly instruments that he might need. A Thompson submachine gun rested in a customized gun rack in the secret compartment.

There have been two stories in the series so far, created by Jeffrey T. Zverloff.

Don "Daredevil" Donovan

Don Donovan had grown up in Dundee. His parents owned the Double D spread north of town, one of the largest ranches in the area. Don's father was a hard man and worked from sun-up to sundown to see that his family had everything they needed in life, and he pushed his son to excel in school, and college tuition had already been saved up by the time Don had entered high school. But Don had not chosen the easy way. He learned to ride and rope, and did all aspects of ranch work, as well as farming. He grew up straight, tall, bronzed of skin, and muscles that rippled beneath his metallic, leathery skin. Sports had come natural to him, and he displayed the strength of two men. He was a natural to win State.

Don had picked up the nickname of "Daredevil" because he was always trying to do something no one else would do—and succeeding! This might have had something to do with the stuff he read. For Don Daredevil Donovan read the Doc Savage adventures in the pulp magazines, and he had patterned his own life after the magazine hero. Don had read his exploits since the 1930s, and was well versed in all of the adventures. But the town folks just laughed at his reading habits. "Heck," they all said, "that magazine character is only fiction. Don Donovan can do anything he can, and Don is real!" Nevertheless, Don never missed an exploit of his favorite hero. After medical school, he became a world adventurer.

Tommy Tompkins is a big, two hundred and twenty pound linebacker. He eventually became a chemist, and joined Don in his many adventures.

Jerry Odom is a gangly individual who stands six feet tall and weighs in at 160 pounds—if he was soaking wet. Jerry was the team's running back. He would eventually become a lawyer and be part of Don's team of adventurers.

Created by Tom Johnson, there has only been one story so far, but his ranch plays a part in a second story.

The Forever Man

In the far distant future, when Earthmen have moved outward in the universe, a mysterious Galactic master thief has appeared to confound the world governments and police agencies. He has no name, but whispers circulate on the planets and moons where man and alien species have settled, of a man who appears suddenly, then disappears just as quickly—taking with him some great object of value. Their hushed voices mumble an odd name, The Forever Man! But who he is, and what he looks like, no one knows.

The Forever Man has dark hair and blue eyes and is part of a huge clearance house for returned valuables stolen from rich worlds and their leaders. He doesn't steal from them. He steals from those who have stolen their treasures. Then he acts as the ambassador, returning the valuable property—for a fee! No man—or world—can hold him, for he was born a mutant on a world that experienced a terrible catastrophe, giving him two brains. And the mysterious ability to teleport near and far distances. The one drawback is planet hopping. He is able to teleport short distances with no problem, but when jumping from planet to planet, he often arrives naked, and suffering from temporary amnesia.

The Consolidated Guard is a universal police force, with offices on every allied world, they have full authority among all the species. Within their organization are special espionage agents, known as Ghosts, who move about the worlds among their people, watching for unrest and criminal activity. They are well trained and highly efficient. They are also looking for leads to The Forever Man, but have no knowledge of the organization he works for. In "Planets In Peril," The Forever Man recruits a member of Ghosts to join the organization, named Paula Sinclair.

Paula Sinclair is a tall, slender woman, with dark hair and brown eyes. She flashes creamy white thighs to distract men, but is a highly trained and skilled agent of Ghosts!

There have been two stories so far in this science fiction series created by Tom Johnson.

The Fox

Based in Orlando, Florida, the Fox made her debut in "Trouble Times Three," where she teamed up with Debra DeLorme's The Scarecrow in an operation to take down one of the Corona's hierarchy members known only as Emerald. Little is known of her origins, though she does make mention in her first story that she once worked for the villains she now fights, ending with "I didn't know there were children until it was too late. That's when I decided to stop their kind." Making that decision, she began training with Ichikuro Komoyuki in martial arts.

The Black Orchid is a prominent nightclub in Orlando that is both a local and tourist destination as it hearkens back to the clubs of the 1930s, from appearance to songs. Her home base is referred to as the Fox's Den and is equipped with state-of-the-art computers, lab and so on. Her organization is small,

The Fox

but loyal, and serves not only the Fox but her alter ego at the nightclub. She tends to run a for-hire business but has worked in conjunction with the FBI on cases.

Kit Volpe—The Fox has dark red hair with deep green eyes, and is petite. As Kit, she's a blues and torch singer. As the Fox, she dresses as a ninja. Her weapons are primarily those generally used in martial arts, such as sai, sword and throwing stars, but she's also a crack shot and will carry a gun if the mission calls for it.

Justin Hawthorne is an ex-Texas Ranger, now serving as the FBI director in the Orlando region and is the Fox's federal contact. Despite his origins, he doesn't have a Texas accent. He hangs around the Orchid during his off duty hours, and hires the Fox when the case calls for a touch that isn't in the FBI rulebooks.

Ichikuro Komoyuki is Kit's sensei and father figure.

He works as a bouncer at the Orchid. Bonsai master. He perished at the end of "Trouble Times Three."

Jack Blacker is a computer hacker, communications expert, and so on.

Pete works as the bartender at the Black Orchid. Primarily, he is the go-to guy when it comes to transportation and he's good at procuring things, such as telephone company uniforms.

Created by Marilyn Morey, there were only two stories in the series.

The Hooded Hunter

The Hooded Hunter is a tall, spare man in a gray double-breasted suit, and a fedora hat. A tight-fitting hood covered his entire head except for his mouth and chin. From the hood a pair of steely gray eyes glared. A revolver was grasped in his right hand.

Barton Roberts is a special investigator for an anti-fascist group based in Empire City. He has authority and jurisdiction throughout the United States. When on a case, he often works as The Hooded Hunter to battle Nazis in the US.

Martin Terry is similar in height and weight to Barton Terry, and he has an aggressive thrust to his jaw. He assists The Hooded Hunter when called upon.

Harold Louis Wassermann is Head of the Board of the anti-fascist group that Barton and Terry work for.

The Hooded Hunter was created by Steve Mitchell, and is thinly based on the Matinee serial, The Masked Marvel. Plus, it is written in serial style with cliffhangers and dialogue. Each chapter ends with a fist fight or gun battle. The character also has similarities to Dan Fowler of *G-Men Detective*. Barton Roberts is Dan Fowler, and Martin Terry is Larry Kendal. There is even a girl in the story that plays the part of Sally Vane. Wasserman is the FBI Director, of course. So the story works as either a serial or Dan Fowler novel.

There have been two stories in the series so far, created by Steve Mitchell.

The Masked Avenger

Benson Roberts has dark hair and steel-gray eyes; he is tall and bronzed from a life of safaris. He was a wealthy young man-about-town, with no goal in life but traveling the world in search of pleasures. Then Claude Burks suggested he do something adventurous with his life. After his parents were killed in a plane crash, his father's dear friend, Claude Burks had seen to young Benson's education, raising him as his own son. Danger and excitement, and the thrill of the hunt took over as he reached maturity. With crime running amok, at Claude Burks' suggestion, he decided to adopt the guise of a masked avenger to fight the evil festering in the streets.

The Masked Avenger wears a domino mask with a dark hat pulled low on his forehead. Fiery eyes flashed as he whispered an eerie challenge in the form of a mocking laugh. Over his shoulders was a black cape. Matching the black of the clothes he wore. The cape covered two .45 automatics in shoulder holsters.

The ring: Reaching into a pocket, he removed a shiny object from within. It was a small ring with an emerald setting of blue-green, and the letter "A" emblazoned within the gem. This he gave to the children he helped.

Police Commissioner Kirk Stanley is the police official. He is a large man with military bearing. He was a retired three-star general. With dark, flashing eyes, a handlebar mustache, and a pointed chin and wide jowls, his family ties reached back to the founding fathers of the great city. Although not particularly rich, he was an accepted member of the exclusive Explorer's Club.

Curtis Van Leif is tall, lean, and powerfully built. Plus, he is the splitting image of Benson Roberts. He drives a Daimler.

Richards is Van Leif's elderly butler.

Wilson is Van Leif's chauffeur.

Jackson is Van Leif's personal doctor.

Explorer's Club: A private club for the rich, and named for their world-trotting safaris and explorations.

Character created by Tom Johnson.

Mr. Minus

He had been treated with radiation and various kinds of ray machines. He never did find out exactly what all they shot him with, or fed him, or put into his system. Nor what the experiments were supposed to prevent or cure. The doctor in charge, Dr. Bob Roberts, had been killed before completion of the research, and had not lived long enough to find out what caused this strange malady.

The first time it happened was fourteen years ago: Allan tried to calm himself, but that turned out to be impossible as long as he sat in front of the mirror! But he just couldn't move away! He had to watch! He had to know exactly what was happening to him. He had been sitting at the dresser writing a letter to a friend, when he had looked up and noticed that his reflection was looking a bit paler than before. He thought it was the lighting in the room. But no… he could still see the pen and paper and all other objects in the room. He looked down to his hands, and was shocked further! He could see his bones showing through his transparent skin!' He then looked up at his head and was amazed even more! He could actually see his brain! His skin was disappearing!

"Oh God! Even my bones are looking translucent! What is happening? I can't believe what I am seeing! I must be having a nightmare! But, when will I wake up? I'm turning invisible! This has to be a nightmare! Sure hope that this isn't true!"

Allan moaned and closed his eyes tightly, then opened them again only to see—or not see—the same thing! "There has to be an answer! I know. I'll go to bed and dream that I'm sleeping, and when I wake up, I'll know that this was a dream. I hope to God it's a dream!" he said to himself, as he got up out of the chair and moved over to his bed. He could still see his pajamas moving across the room in the mirror, and he could look down at his legs (or where his legs would be) and could see the legs of the pajamas move as he walked. But, he could not see his bare feet sticking out of the bottom. He checked out his hands again, and could not see them either. Not even the bones! He could feel them, but the actual 'seeing' didn't apply.

He panicked!! He tore off his pajama bottoms, and he could not see his shorts, which were all natural material! He then tore off his shorts! All he could see was his pajama top floating above the floor! He removed that and he could see nothing but his glasses floating about in the mirror!

He could still feel things. He could feel his feet with his hands, but could 'see' neither. He could still feel his feet on the floor! He went to touch things to prove to that he was actually still in the room! He touched the sofa, the chair, the bed, and finally the phone. He decided that he would call Dr. Roberts to see if he could still be heard! He could hear himself as he moved, and he had heard his voice as he talked to himself, but he had to be sure that others could hear him! He was so upset that he didn't even think of the time! He rose and went to his closet to dress. Even if no one could see him, at least he would know that he had clothes on his body! He picked out a pair of wool slacks and a synthetic shirt. He put his arm in the shirtsleeve and pulled it across his shoulders and buttoned it. Then pulled his slacks up his legs. He didn't tuck in the shirt, though. As he watched himself in the mirror, he snapped the waist. Then he did a double take! His pants disappeared! The shirt was still visible, but the pants weren't! He felt the pants with his fingers, but could no longer see them! He removed the pants, went to the closet and chose a pair of synthetic pants and put them on. They stayed visible! He looked at the pair of wool slacks that hung on a hanger and saw that they were again visible. There must be an explanation. He tried to remember what his underwear was made of. He knew that they had disappeared. He couldn't remember, but he checked out his other shorts. It turned out that he had several different styles in the drawer. He picked up a pair of woolen shorts and held them against his arm. They vanished where they touched his skin. He then got a synthetic blend and repeated the process. It stayed visible! He wondered what this meant. Maybe it had something to do with whatever the object was made of. He had the same reaction to all his clothing except woolen or natural products. And shoes. He found that none of his shoes would disappear! They were all made from synthetic materials. Or, at least, the additives made them synthetic. He really didn't know much about that sort of thing but he would check it out later. No leather shoes. All synthetic.

Thus, he became *Mr. Minus!*

Allan Lee answered an advertisement in the newspaper to participate in a research project in a small country in the southern hemisphere. He was supplied room and board and a wage, and told the research would be beneficial to mankind. He had taken the 'job' because his eyesight would not allow him to join the military. He was legally blind in both eyes.

Ed Cave was the red headed Chief of Police in the town of Pennton. He and Allan were friends and had no secrets from one other. At least none that counted. Now… they did have a secret between them, but neither one of them wanted this secret out. The fact that Allan was Mr. Minus was something they had both sworn to secrecy years ago. Even Kelli Door didn't know. And she was the romantic interest of both men. They often had friendly rivalry arguments over her.

Kelli Door was slender, but well built; tall at five feet, eight inches; shapely at 135 pounds, and was very athletic. She is an ace crime reporter for the Pennton World Daily Newspaper, where Allan also worked. She enjoyed the rivalry between Ed and Allan.

Ginger Johnson patterned Mr. Minus after Captain Zero. There have been numerous stories so far.

Nightwind

In 1967, Oregon City was just the name of a small community. Settlers had moved in after the War between the North and South, building small shacks near the Salt Fork of the Brazos River. Wagons had brought in lumber and furniture, and brave souls banded together to fight the Comanche and outlaws, and build homes while living in dugouts. The shacks finally got built, and soon other establishments started sprouting up. One of the first was a trading post that eventually became a general store, operated by an Easterner named Powell. Everything else sprung up around the general store.

Across from Powell's General Mercantile store was the Wild Skunk Saloon, set two feet off the ground on wooden porches, the swinging doors open for business. Down the wooden walkway was Scanlon's gun shop, and around the back was a set of stairs leading to an apartment on the second floor, with a sign reading, "Doc Benson." At the end of the street was an open barn, and a heavyset man was shoeing a horse. Evidently, the local blacksmith, though there was no name over the wide portal. A white sign hung from a two-story faded-brown building, calling attention to the Gibson Hotel.

Sheriff Steve Mason is tall and slender, with broadshoulders and dark hair. He is an hombre with smiling brown eyes and tough as they come. His pa was a white man, but his ma was a Cherokee squaw. Steve ran away from home after his ma died, learned to fight and shoot, cleaning up several border towns. When his pa died, he returned to the ranch to raise horses for the cavalry. He was lightning fast on the draw. After the war a lot of gunfighters showed up to draw on him! It became a regular thing, him being an Injun and all. And he was getting a reputation as a gunfighter. One day a gunman showed up itching for a gunfight and drew down on Steve in the middle of the street. Without hesitation, he drew and shot him smack between the eyes, then found out the kid was only fifteen years old, but big for his age and fast on the draw. But he was still just a kid. Steve took off his gun belt that day, and hung 'em up. He ain't worn his six-shooters since.

Deputy Johnny Southern was decked out with two guns, crossed on his waist, and tied down. His hair was greased and slicked back. A long rifle was in the saddle boot on the side. Johnny was only nineteen. His father had been killed in the war, and his mother died from a broken heart a year later. He didn't want to die for lack of shooting power.

Deputy Jerry Taylor was mature at twenty-four years of age. He had been a lieutenant in the Confederate Army. Shorter than the sheriff, he had sandy hair and blue eyes. His parents had sent him to the best schools before the war between the North and South, and he was well educated, though cocky. He only wore one gun in a holster on his right, though it was hung low on his side, and he was fast on the draw. In one boot was a small knife kept in a secret scabbard. He marries Karen G. Reynolds—Kagee—after the first story.

Kim: Sheriff Mason's cook at the ranch was a Priest in a Korean Temple before coming to America, and master of strange fighting techniques!

Bobby is the saloon bartender.

Nightwind: The giant black stallion called Thunder was standing in the moonlight with a rider dressed all in black, from wide brimmed hat, to black boots. A long black cape swirled outwards, blowing in the wind, and a 15-foot bullwhip curled in one hand. A black silk mask completely covered his face. Two pearl-handled Colt .45s were nestled in black holsters on his waist, the only thing besides the silver buckles on the belt that broke the scheme of black in his attire.

Imp is a small creature dressed all in black, a red sash wrapped around his waist. He rides with the mysterious masked rider of the plains.

A western series created by Tom Johnson.

Number Nine

Gray eyes behind a domino mask, Number Nine is a master of deception, and a man of countless faces whose own face was not known and never seen by friends, enemies, or the public at large for he was almost always in disguise. Long ago, after the Great War, he had established himself as a crime fighter. During the war he had been assigned to an elite group of airmen, ten men who were sent on a mission behind enemy lines to France. He was the ninth man, and

Number Nine

the only one to survive, but ten graves were left in France, leading the military to believe all ten had died. Only one man knew the secret, the officer who had sent them on the mission, Commander Paul Highland.

Vance is a sharp dressed man in fedora, pastel tie, pinstriped suit and leather gloves; the brim of his hat cast a shadow over his face. This was the only name revealed for the mysterious manhunter.

Paul Highland is now the assistant district attorney for the great city. He has a deep, commanding voice.

Danny is a police desk sergeant, and a spy for Number Nine.

Miss Reeves is Paul Highland's secretary.

The *New York Herald* is the city's newspaper.

Number Nine uses coded words to identify himself to Paul Highland with, "One from the grave." Highland responds with, "Who is lost to the living."

This interesting series was created by Sean Danowski.

Ravenshroud

Set in the 1880s, he had been a famous actor once. His stage name was King Raven, as he felt his true name, Ravenshroud was too morbid. His costar had loved him, but bargained her soul for eternal youth and life on the stage. He had saved her soul, but lost his in the process. He made another bargain of sorts, one for the return of his soul, but it too was a price.

Ravenshroud is a gentleman in flowing black mantle from beneath which peaked the last word in fashionable wear. He has jade eyes, an aristocratic face with an aquiline nose and thin lips. His lithe, long-legged frame unfolded, an opera hat set rakishly upon his slicked hair, and a golden serpent-head walking stick complimented the attire. A razor-sharp blade was concealed within that walking stick!

The Shroud's face was a stark chalk white, the lipless mouth a permanent grin exposing a skull's visage. The eyes were deep sockets from which peered white orbs that glared without blinking. Not quite human, his calling card is a miniature silver skull, tiny emeralds imbedded in its eye sockets.

The Carriage is fully a town coach of the most expensive model, with its midnight black exterior and its sable curtains, drawn by twin ebon stallions whose coats shown in the gaslight with a dull luster; only touches of gold trim broke the color scheme. Four oil lamps hung from the four corners of the carriage, their dullish orange glow flickering like funeral lights. The sumptuous but dim interior contained matching deep crimson leather seats and curtains. But perhaps most notable—and most amazing—was that the coach was driverless!

Foster is Ravenshroud's elderly servant.

Adele is a statuesque lady on the brink of middle age, her aristocratic features serene, her blazing red hair heightening her elegantly mature features. She believes Ravenshroud dead, sacrificed for the return of her soul.

Annie Julep is an elderly woman who runs a boarding house where Ravenshroud sends those he is helping to safety.

Created by Sean Danowski, there have been two stories in this exciting series: "The House of Somnus" (1996) and "The Headless Horrors" (1997).

The Scarecrow

Accepting the offer of rehabilitation for the crimes he had committed, an international jewel thief went from prisoner to law enforcer, serving his time in what his government refers to as the Shadowguard program. These carefully selected men and women undergo intensive psychological testing before training to become skilled combatants against the growing threat of the Corona, a multinational crime cartel. The Scarecrow has proven time and again to be the most successful of their prospects, focused on serving his time and bringing justice to those who would harm the innocent. He is also known as Karas Tengu—the Crow Demon—and "the Old Man'"as he's the oldest member of the Shadowguard. His first appearance was in the story, "Enter the Scarecrow."

The Scarecrow has operated in Charleston, SC and Charlotte, NC, presently calling the metropolis of Braxton, NC, his home, though he will travel to other locales, such as Orlando, FL in pursuit of the members of the Corona ("Trouble Times Three"). His base is in the sub-basement of a renovated 1901 textile mill presently used as apartments.

Forbidden to use guns, the Scarecrow is far from defenseless. His major weapon is his bo staff, or as he refers to it, a neurostaff. It's an unusual weapon as it responds to certain voice commands, can deliver a potent neurological shock capable of incapacitating whoever comes in contact with it, and will operate only for the person it's programmed for and no other. His other weapons include caltrops, throwing spikes, sai, nunchuks, blowgun, and other weapons, primarily those used by martial artists such as the ninja or samurai. He is a master in ninjutsu, bojitsu, karate, savate, and more.

Christopher Grant is tall, muscular and lean, with dark hair and dark blue eyes. He is one of the Scarecrow's many alter egos. Working part time as an instructor at the White Tiger Dojo.

Patches is another of the Scarecrow's disguises, Patches is a homeless derelict, well known in the streets of Braxton because of the distinctive malformation on his mouth and the worn, patch-riddled coat that he wears. This particular disguise is very useful as it allows him to walk in the seamy side of the city without being noticed.

The Scarecrow dresses in black garb like a ninja; his various weapons are hidden in the uniform. His eyes glow crimson thanks to the contacts that not only change eye color, but enhances his night vision. His voice is cold and gravelly with little emotion, and he uses a wild high-pitched laugh to catch his enemies off guard.

Deacon is actually John Munmulmara an aborigine from Queensland, Australia, the grandson of a shaman. Deacon isn't so much a nickname as it is a title—he's the Scarecrow's "warden," making certain his charge stays on the straight and narrow, as well as help him where necessary, whether as a driver, computer hacker or what not.

Though not part of the Shadowguard program, Michael Rourke, known as Torch, is also serving a sentence. The nickname fits him well as he's an arsonist and an expert with explosives. He works as a bouncer at an Irish pub in Braxton, and is doing "community service" as a volunteer fireman. His first appearance was in "Sidewinder."

Sarah Chapman is a reporter for the Braxton Bugle, and is trying to work her way up in the publishing industry. The Scarecrow has become her pet project, and she makes herself a nuisance by trying to dig up dirt on him to propel her career forward. Blond and rather pretty, she is quite capable of protecting herself, as well as being an excellent shot.

Created by Debra DeLorme.

Senora Scorpion

The Spanish possession of California, late 1700s. Riding a Pinto pony, Senora Scorpion was dressed as a caballero, wearing dark pants and jacket, with silver sequins running down the legs and arms. A wide, black sombrero, crested with silver buttons topped her head, and a black mask covered the bottom features of her face. In her left hand was a fifteen-foot bullwhip, and a deadly sword was grasped in her right hand. She feared no man, and willingly led her small outlaw band against Spain's soldiers.

Senora Alsiara Perez is the owner of a small café in San Francisco de Asis. She is a handsome young Mexican woman, wearing a large sombrero and brown riding suit. Her husband and family had been killed by the Spaniards, and her land stolen. Alsiara's father had taught her from childhood to ride and use both sword and bullwhip, and she was master of the blade and whip.

As the Scorpion, she was an outlaw, robbing from

the Spaniards, whom she wanted to drive into the sea and free Mexico from Spain's yoke.

The series was created by Tom Johnson.

The Scorpion

In this alternate universe, Germany won WWII. But after forty years of occupation they've finally been driven from America, leaving us to rebuild our cities. Five years later, we are now living in a world of Internet, email, fax machines and speakeasies, machine guns, and mob rule. While *The Lone Ranger* plays on the radio, MTV is on TV. Out of the chaos rises a paladin to battle the criminal element that the underworld knew only as The Scorpion. But the past has come back to challenge this defender of the city. This is Steeltown, PA!

The Scorpion is a tall, black-clad figure who resembles the Angel of Death. His features are hidden by a black veil that has been sewn to the brim of his fedora, falling to the level of his chin. His features are obscured and only his breath stirring the fabric. If anyone had possessed the power to look beyond such simple disguises, they would most certainly have looked away at the cold, blazing sight of the Scorpion's face and eyes. There was little of humanity there. And little of life. Beneath the heavy German coat cold blue metal flashed; black gloves are leather gauntlets, his black leather coat emblazoned with the images of the Deathstalker scorpions. His gun is a Luger, called the Sting.

Kurt Reinhardt is one of the richest men in Steeltown. He owns the largest newspaper, The Inquisitor. He has Nordic features, is six and a half foot tall, with long blonde hair, and drives a sleek black Mercedes roadster (black Silver Ghost). He carries a gentlemanly silver-headed cane. As a child he had been German born, and raised as a superman (#7101). He was one of the many clones of Dr. Reinhardt, who used the genes of his dead son to create monsters for the Fuhrer. And the evil that he must face is one of his own twins, a brother. Although a superman

Senora Scorpion

like himself, this one is pure evil. The genetic experiments had given the children many abilities. They healed quickly, and bullets were pushed from their bodies. Kurt's saliva contains the poison of a deadly scorpion. He had eventually escaped and worked his way across Europe into China, then to America where he was able to amass a fortune.

Suzaku is tiny, almost child-like in statue and delicate like a well-painted Dresden doll. She is gifted with a yard of blue-black hair that she wore down like that of a young unmarried woman. A mysterious Asian, she served Kurt Reinhardt and The Scorpion. They had met in a Chinese temple, The Golden Dog, where she became his sensei. She has high cheekbones and almond-shaped eyes. Suzaku appears to float in the air. She calls him, K-Chan, and he calls her, kami sama.

Captain Richard D. Barracks is Captain of the 27th Precinct, and is a head shorter than Kurt, but grew up a street fighter in Steeltown. He is lean and mean.

The Clock Tower is a graceful old building with a clock face built in the tower—the only one in the whole city!—with a wild, Bavarian design. The Inquisitor newspaper is located in the building. Kurt owns half of Clock Tower. Japanese investors own the other half.

Benny Herzog is chief editor of the Inquisitor, and does the lion share of the work for the boss. Has bulging muscles, drinks too much coffee, and there is always an overfilled ashtray on his desk, and cans of Red Bull crumpled in the wastepaper basket. Mobsters had broken his kneecaps, and Benny was begging on the streets when Kurt found him. Benny is totally dedicated to his boss.

Miz Emily is the Staff Advice Columnist for The Inquisitor. She is also totally dedicated to the boss.

Olga is Kurt's secretary. Like his other employees, she is totally dedicated to her boss.

Dr. Nobody was once Walter "Tex" Grayson. The Scorpion had stopped him from leaping off Jump Bridge to commit suicide, and then saw to it that he was eventually employed in the lab of the city morgue, where he is often of assistance to The Scorpion. Dedicated to The Scorpion, and knows his true identity.

Spike is the 12-year old leader of a street gang who often supplies information to The Scorpion. He has the habit of calling Scorpion, Spook.

Conceived as a possible new pulp magazine in 2006, titled *Scorpion*. This first story, *The Sting of the Scorpion*, was powerful, the concept fantastic, and the action moved at a furious pace. The writing was intelligent, but the syntax was awkward. It switched from 3rd person narrative to 1st person narrative constantly, sometimes even in the same paragraph. A second novel was advertised, *The City of the Living Dead*, and should appear soon. The author pays homage to the old pulps. There is an intersection named Robeson & Gibson Streets, another street is named Stockbridge. A Fortress of Solitude is mentioned, etc.

Created by Warren Stockholm.

Shadowhawke

Carlyle Alexander Tenebra is extremely rich. He had served as a pilot in the Great War, but in a crash had crushed both legs irreparably. While in the wilds of Australia Tenebra discovered "something." Whatever it was, it allowed him to overcome his weakness and use of his legs for brief periods of time. The power was given to him only for use in benefiting humankind, and he chose to dedicate his life to fighting evil. When he becomes Shadowhawke, his deep blue-green eyes turn a bright emerald green, and his legs straighten and grow strong. When not the nemesis of evildoers, he walks with the use of two steel canes to support his huge body on useless legs. Handsome, he is tall and distinguished.

Gilian Mars is an actress Tenebra had hired once, but found her courage to his liking. Now she acts as his secretary until time for Shadowhawke to go into action. She is a pert brunette, with dark eyes, and fresh pretty looks. A sharp mind, she is a quick thinker.

"Bruiser" Browser had once been a noted boxer, and a contender for the heavyweight title before joining the service to fight in the Great War, and ended up as a flight mechanic with the R.A.F. He had met Tenebra during this time, and became his bodyguard after the war. He has a good-natured face, not the slightest marred by a nose that changed direction three ways. He is tall, and heavy, with huge fists. He doesn't carry weapons, preferring to use his fists instead.

Wong Lei is a slender Chinaman who speaks in purest Oxford English, and has a dozen degrees in a dozen different subjects. He is also a master of jujitsu and hypnotism. He is employed as Tenebra's chauffeur and houseman. He and Browser enjoy a constant banter, but are the best of friends. Wong also collects an assortment of violent weapons as a hobby. When he goes into action, he prefers a pair of .45 automatics in shoulder holsters.

Wees Lea Changa Do (he who hides in plain sight), better known as Weslie. He is an Australian aborigine, small, dark, and a vicious fighter. Raised in the Australian Outback, he is at home in the darkness, and is a spotter for Shadowhawke. His weapons of choice are knife and spear, and he moves without sound.

The town house is a brownstone mansion that takes up a half block on 5th Avenue. It is a great size structure with an old ancestry. It contains his valuable art collection. There is a special room in the basement where only he goes, and it is here that he transforms into Shadowhawke.

Created by K.G. McAbee and Tom Johnson.

The Soul Stealer

Perhaps one of the oddest of all heroes, the Soul Stealer is a small person, sometimes a man, sometimes female. A sickly gray in appearance, they are very nondescript, gentle and soft-spoken. They appear to those who are about to die a violent death. Their mission is to help them cross over to the Afterlife.

The Soul Stealers feel a need to know their assignment before the appointed time, and the reader learns about the person along with the little gray being in gentle stories of passion before the violence that catches up with the victim. Perhaps a sudden car crash, or blazing weapons in the hands of killers, or the soldier on a battlefield. Wherever there is going to be a violent death, there you will find this strange little hero, the Soul Stealer.

There have been ten stories in this series created by Tom Johnson.

SSgt. Martin

SSgt. Martin leads a squad of well-trained soldiers through the Viet Cong infested jungles of Southeast Asia on reconnaissance for enemy activity. These men aren't suicidal heroes, they just want to survive the war and go home in one piece. It's Sergeant Martin's duty to see that they do! Here, death is their constant companion, and they learn about fear, and the dangers lurking in the night.

These are men who are faceless. Perhaps a son, a husband, or a father. Most are 19 years old, except for their leader, Staff-Sergeant Martin, a career soldier that began service to his country on the DMZ in Korea. Now he must fight a new war, and do his best to send his men back to wives and families.

There have been eight stories in this series created by Tom Johnson.

The Visage

Nicholas "Nick" Dane had gone off to war as a young boy, but returned a man—changed! Thirty, dark-featured with dark eyes. He brought forth black gloves that he slipped over his hands. From another pocket he produced a white cloth mask that he slipped over his face. Save for twin slits for the eyes, the mask covered his face totally. Then taking his gray fedora he donned that as well. Two automatics rested in shoulder holsters beneath his coat.

Blonde-headed Jerry Maxion was a former Federal agent turned detective, whom The Visage had saved from a frame up years before. The small agency Jerry ran in Lower Manhattan was merely a front, for he was an agent of The Visage.

Edward "Jazz" Bartler is all bulk, everything about him suggested squares, from his compact build to his chiseled jaw and wide shoulders. A former jazz cornetist in Kansas City speakeasy bands, ex Chicago gangster, one-time member of the Capone mob, and now an agent of The Visage.

Earl Wayford is a broker for the wealthy. His office is on the fourteenth floor of the Luthridge Building just off Wall Street in the financial district. He is the third agent of The Visage.

Dane lives in the penthouse apartment of the left tower of the Zaggurat Towers. Black and gold trim, the twin towers were almost invisible in the night sky.

Vladimir—Vlad, is Dane's faithful old Russian manservant. He had been with the Dane family for several generations.

Created by Sean Danowski.

Eddy Edwards–UFO Hunter

During his last hitch in the Air Force, Eddy Edwards was a supervisor in the North Dakota missile fields. One dark night strange lights had appeared in the sky above the silos, and the launch facilities lost all control of the missiles. There had been nothing his security could do about the UFOs, and the incident haunted him for the remainder of his career. Upon retirement, he went to work for AIM, a UFO investigative organization ran by a retired military officer. With his background in law enforcement, Eddy obtained a private investigator's license and became a field operative for the group.

Eddy is a retired Air Force Master Sergeant. He is about fifty, solidly built, graying hair, beard and mustache, dark eyes, with calloused knuckles from years of karate training. He drives a big Ford XL Van, equipped with desk and file cabinets in the rear, and all of the tools he needs in the investigation of UFO reports, including camera and other devices. The cab of the vehicle has a large cassette compartment holding his 1950s-era music collection of singers like Buddy Holly, Elvis, Fats Domino and Little Richard.

Brigadier Mitchell is a retired general who now heads AIM—Alien Intelligence Monitors, while experimenting on military equipment for the government. The government knows about his interest in UFOs, and keeps tab on the balding officer, but he has too much power to be shut down.

Stuanofu (not a true name) might be a young, foreigner hitchhiking across the states. Short, maybe five feet tall, and thin, people often feel like they are in a fog when around him. The truth is the creature calling himself Stuanofu looks nothing like that. He is projecting a mental image to those around him. He is s small gray being with large, almond shaped eyes, and the pilot of a flying saucer. He is strangely connected to Eddy Edwards without the investigator's knowledge, and appears in times of need to assist, then removes all memory of his involvement from Eddy's mind.

There have been three stories in this series created by Tom Johnson.

Martin Gort, Undertaker

Small towns can produce the mysterious corpse every now and then, and someone has to have a knack for investigating them, whether they turn out to be explainable or supernatural. In Oskaloosa, that's where Martin Gort, the local undertaker comes in. He has a penchant for solving hidden mysteries, whether it's a haunted chair or a corpse with the head crushed in—and the only suspect is a nearby statue.

Martin Gort is the Funeral Director for Oskaloosa, Kansas, located two miles off a major highway, with a population of one thousand souls. His description is left up to the reader, but hints at the old western frontier's black-clad, rather cadaverous characters of similar profession.

Wilkins is the train depot agent. He loves to play checkers, and always seems to beat the local undertaker.

Edward White is the local sheriff. He can never quite solve the strange mysteries that pop up every now and then. Emil Lotana is Gort's assistant at the funeral home.

Cytherea Lotana is a cosmetic professional who prepares the deceased for burial.

Oceans is the town coroner.

Several interesting stories in this series created by Nick Carr. ♦

The Coming of the Black Police
By Tom Johnson

Before we look at the trilogy with the Black Police, we need to start from the beginning with this whole "invasion of America" concept. At a luncheon with Popular Publication's president, Harry Steeger one day, Robert Sidney Bowen proposed a series in which Black Invaders invade America. Supposedly, it was agreed that the series would run for 12 issues. Bowen's *Dusty Ayres* began in July 1934 and ran for exactly twelve issues, ending in July 1935.

Over at *Operator #5*, Emile C. Tepperman had taken over that series from Frederick C. Davis with the December 1935 issue. Basically, Jimmy Christopher, Secret Service Ace, Operator #5 battled criminal elements, and evil masterminds bent on dominating the world. Or a little part of it in each issue. Tepperman continued the theme until the June 1936 issue, at which time the Armies of the Purple Empire invaded America. Almost immediately, not only New York, but the U.S. was under the booted heels of the Purple Empire. The invasion lasted for 13 issues, the 14th story, May 1938, begins the rebuilding of America after we were set back to horse and wagon technology. The following issue, Wayne Rogers then takes over the authorship of the Operator #5 series, and America goes through smaller invasions until the series ended.

Oddly, only a few months later, Richard Wentworth, The Spider, battles an invasion on a smaller scale when the Black Police capture New York. The similarities are many, though. With Tepperman, Operator #5 was the accepted leader of men. No matter where he went, complete strangers recognized him instantly. With America under invasion, Jimmy Christopher formed pockets of guerrilla fighters to set up resistance throughout the US. If he arrives in a location that already has a band of fighters, the leader immediately turns command over to him. If a battle takes place, Operator #5 must lead it, or it is destined to fail. Only Operator #5 can succeed. The same with secret missions. If someone is appointed to carry out an assignment, they are going to be captured, tortured, or killed. For the mission to succeed, Operator #5 must do it alone. But where Jimmy Christopher is a leader of men, The Spider is master of men, and Norvell Page takes the character a step farther. Richard Wentworth becomes a Messiah figure. And the Black Police trilogy becomes Armageddon!

> Isaiah 63: V 1 through 5
> Who is this that comes from Edon, with died garments from Bozrah? That is glorious in his apparel, traveling in the greatness of his strength? I that speak in righteousness, mighty to save. Wherefore art thou red in thine apparel, and thy garments like him that threadeth in the winevat?
> I have trodden the winepress alone; and of the people there was none with me: for I will tread them in my fury; and their blood shall be sprinkled upon my garments, and I will stain all my raiment.
> For the day of vengeance is in mine heart, and the

year of my redeemed is come.

And I looked, and there was none to help, and I wondered that there was none to uphold: therefore mine own arm brought salvation unto me; and my fury; it upheld me.

And He gathered them together into a place called in the Hebrew tongue Ar-ma-ged-don. Revelation 16: V 16

There were three very odd *Spider* novels that appeared in 1938, following Emile C. Tepperman's invasion of America over at *Operator #5*. The Black Police was not unlike the Purple Army from Tepperman's stories, but the Spider stories were written by Norvell Page: "The City That Paid to Die" (September 1938), "The Spider at Bay" (October 1938) and "Scourge of the Black Legions" (November 1938).

A recent election puts into offices of New York City and State, a group called the "Party of Justice." This will only be mentioned in the first novel, so evidently that was merely the slogan the group ran under. Richard Wentworth believes there are at least three men behind the political party; Angus Whitfield, head of utilities; Malcolm Nicol, leader of factories, and the holding companies of Martin Ducamps. These men, crooked or not, had backed the Party of Justice, putting their men in office. However, you can forget these names. Page forgot them, Wentworth forgot them, and the reader forgot them!

Now, after 30 days in office, the police department appears to be demoralized: criminal activity has increased, while policemen look the other way when a crime is in progress. And almost immediately, Martin Ducamps is murdered while in a conference meeting. Killed by a machine gun blast from behind a mirror, set by remote control to kill when activated by certain key words—"White face in the mirror."

In Albany, a law is about to be passed that will allow the poor to be taxed with a 90% of the tax burden, while the rich and powerful would be almost free of taxation. Not only that, but a rider to the bill would give the authority for property and possessions to be seized immediately upon demand.

The year is 1938, and the above scenario begins a three-part story in the Spider magazine featuring a take over of New York, that sounds like Hitler's Germany at this time. But like the Operator #5 stories during the Purple Invasion period, this was happening in America, and the people were Americans. Norvell Page, writing as Grant Stockbridge, was bringing the plight of the Europeans into American literature.

During special legislature at Albany, Governor Whiting request—and receives—authority to create a special police force (the NYBI), with special power to arrest and seize property by the special force. On paper, the special police sounded like the best solution to the states financial problems at the time. The police force was equal to their federal counterpart, the FBI Governor Whiting appoints Jervis Strong to head this organization, giving it power over local agencies. The head of the agency will only be mentioned in this one novel, and then only in passing, then quickly forgotten.

As the action begins, the owners of two stores were flogged into producing money, and their stores looted of all valuables. Richard Wentworth rigs up a truck with special communications equipment and takes to the road, where he comes across one of these acts in progress.

The special police force is given the name of the Black Police because of the black uniforms they wear (derived from the Gestapo uniforms). It is their duty to collect taxes; torture people; kill; and confiscate valuable goods from anywhere they wish.

The Spider appears on the scene and shoots it out with these crooks in black uniform, saving store owners from death or severe beatings at their hands; and that's exactly what these black policemen were, crooks: strong-arm men, gunmen, all type of underworld hoodlums. In fact, we are told that Jervis Strong was a big-time crime racketeer, though he had never been convicted of any crimes.

Wentworth enters the capital building in Albany and works his way into the assembly chamber, and uses his radio equipment to broadcast the governor's speech, detailing the criminal activities of his minions.

After a violent gun battle, Wentworth escapes the assembly chamber and hides in the governor's private offices, where he waits in darkness for the governor to return; he watches as the governor enters the office and speaks into a mirror. Presently a white face appears and a hidden voice gives instructions for the governor to follow. This mirror gives the reader an impression of early television, but really there is very little to the thing. It more resembles a movie projector and voice recorder. Later it will be revealed that the hidden mastermind has lights set up in the mirror, and a recorder with a pre-taped message on the machine. When the words, "White face in the mirror," are voiced, it activates the machinery, and the lights come on, displaying a face illuminated inside the mirror.

Wentworth and Commissioner Kirkpatrick are outlawed by the new regime, which means their property and money can be taken legally by the Black Police. Plus they are to be arrested, taken dead or alive, and a price of $10,000 is placed on each of them. They escape and rendezvous in Chinatown, where they are cared for by the Spider's old friend,

The Spider, September 1938.

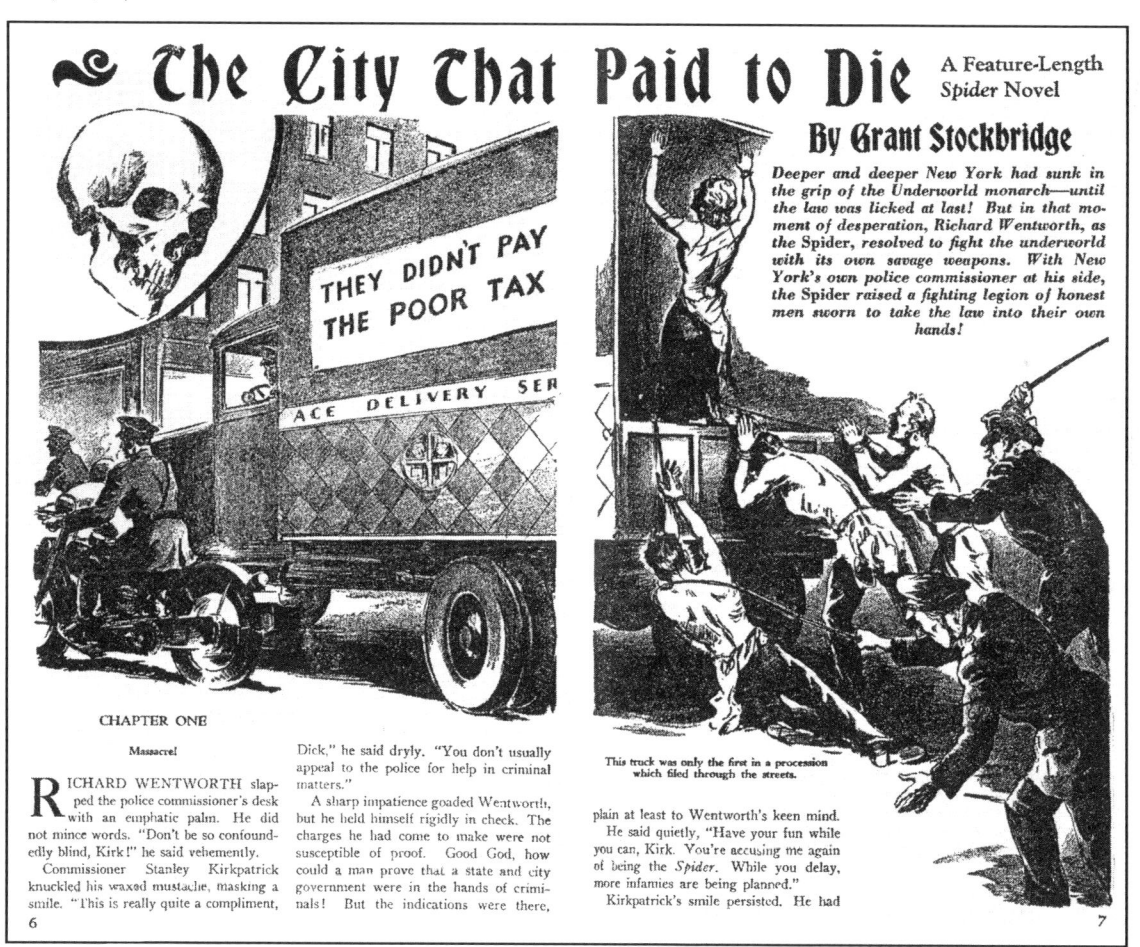

Hwang-yo, who, we are told, the Spider had helped previously.

Wentworth now makes appropriate plans. Tactics that will lead the honest men of New York against the criminal hordes of the Black Police!

After obtaining a few hours sleep at his hideout, the Spider is awakened by Chei Hwang-yo, who has learned of a public hanging that is to take place shortly. Those scheduled to die are Nita Van Sloan and Jackson, Wentworth's personal chauffeur.

Obtaining a Colonel's uniform in the Black Police, Wentworth rescues them and several others; they make their way to Chei Hwang-yo's Chinatown hide away, but don't stay there for long, as the Black Police have trailed them. Again they escape, this time heading for the mountain ranges between New York City and Albany, where they intend to operate as guerrillas in 'hit and run' tactics.

Wentworth performs several feats of 'daring-do,' for no other reason, apparently, than to impress upon everyone that he is the man to lead; this seemed more in keeping with Operator #5 than for the Spider, whom everyone already knew was a 'master of men,' and destined to lead!

His company of fighting men are forty strong. Many are former servants or helpers, others had been wounded or crippled. All of them are willing to do their share. Nine were Chei Hwang-yo's men, but they were quickly forgotten and the Chinese never mentioned again.

Meanwhile, back in New York, the hidden mastermind (remember white face in the mirror?) was cementing his power. People are being tortured and stripped of their wealth, while the Black Police hold authority over the city police; and the city police spend all of their time trying to Capture Wentworth and Kirkpatrick. Actually, out of the world's greatest police force, only one lowly policeman had cast his lot with the commissioner.

By the end of the first story, "The City That Paid to Die," Wentworth and his small band have succeeded in robbing the Black Police of millions of dollars, which had been collected from taxes and charities.

At the end of the story, the mastermind is identified as someone named Glass, a mere secretary to the governor. However, the identity itself appears to be a disguise. The man escapes, of course, so he can show up next month as someone else—to lead the Black Police through another episode.

This series of novels is very fascinating, though highly suggestive of the Operator #5 Purple Invasion series. The events could happen—and did in Europe—but for a hidden leader to take mere criminals and turn them into a "Gestapo" soldier overnight does not strike me as an easy task. After all, even Hitler's Nazi's were well-trained, and disciplined soldiers, not merely taken out of prisons and told to run wild.

But, given the possibility that this could happen, as recorded here, how a group of state government leaders, under control of criminals, could take over a complete state—to include state and local police departments—and pass a tax bill like this one, and seize personal property, and torture its citizens, could then be defeated by forty men, is beyond me. But to be honest, there was only man who defeated them. The Spider!

As the October 1938 story opens, the Black Police are now 100,000 men strong. Wentworth, fearing their mountain hide out is known to the enemy, initiates an immediate evacuation to another location; he has a mission elsewhere, and leaves the evacuation for Nita to handle.

Meanwhile, Titustown, a city nearby has been taken over by the Black storm troopers, and a terrible disease has struck the inhabitants—a disease that kills very quickly. Kirkpatrick and several followers have been stranded in Titustown. They had gone there to help its people, only to be captured and locked in cells. Now, only the Spider can save them. Even with the dread disease hovering always within their little group, ready to strike any of them, the

The Spider, September 1938.

Spider will not leave them. His men at the mountain hideout had cheered when Wentworth had declared he was going to Titustown to save his men. Has there ever been such a leader of men as was Richard Wentworth—besides Operator #5, that is?

Nor can the reader overlook the "Messiah" complex that ran throughout the Spider series; the Spider wounded for the sake of others. He only destroyed the evil within mankind; he alone was the way to safety; and on and on. Even when he reaches Titustown and destroys a squad of Black Police as they begin a mass execution in the town square, a shout rings out from the populace: "The Spider," voices cried. "The Spider has come." In reality they were saying, "The Messiah, The Messiah has come!"

Whatever beliefs Norvell Page had during his writing career, it is certain that he was given a Christian upbringing. The Spider was Norvell Page's "returning" Messiah to humanity. Even from the beginning, the Spider had been called the "Master of Men." Page just carried it a little farther; the Master of Men had became the Savior of Mankind.

And all of his stories take place, not really in New York City or America, but a mountain in the Middle East. A mountain called Armageddon. As Israel (mankind) is about to be destroyed by evil (the anti-Christ and his armies), the Messiah (Christ/Spider) comes in all His Glory to battle and save Israel (mankind/New York City).

The Spider leads the people out of Titustown on an Exodus through the wilderness, destroying all who come against them. Paragraph after paragraph, the narrative even takes on a Biblical story: (Page 19, Chapter 2):

> "... but these multitudes will be found as easily in the hills as in a city. And how in the name of God will they be fed?"

Why, the Spider would perform a miracle, wouldn't he? Just as Jesus had fed the multitudes, the Spider would see that they were fed, too.

The plague, called the "White Face" plague, hits some of his men. But the Spider knows it is merely a form of leprosy and, like Jesus, he remains with them. Soon he would have a cure for them, never fear.

Leading those he has rescued from Titustown to the caves in the mountains, he turned these tortured, plague infested men and women into a fighting machine that defeats everything in their path, including airplanes with bombs and machine guns.

Arriving at the caves where Nita was supposed to have evacuated from, the Spider finds a small group of people hanging from gallows (trees in this instance); they were all dead, except for one poor soul the Black Police had left alive to give Wentworth a message. The man's body had been crushed, but he managed to live long enough to deliver his message: Nita Van Sloan had been taken prisoner and was now being tortured in Albany by the Black Police.

Leaving Kirkpatrick with those he had rescued from Titustown, at the mountain hideout, which is no longer a secret from the Black Police, the Spider goes alone to Albany. There he learns that Colonel Rice, an old friend, is in charge of the national guard, keeping law and order in Albany at the orders of the governor. Wentworth confronts Rice, asking him why a dedicated, honest man like himself was working for the criminals. His answer, of course, was "Just following orders." The same answer the Nazi's later used at their trials. And, incidentally, the same thing Colonel North would say in the Senate Hearings.

Straight out of *Operator #5*, The Spider challenges Colonel Rice to a duel of sabers; the winner would have the allegiance of the other. And just like Operator #5, there was no better swordsman than The Spider! Naturally, Colonel Rice gives his command to The Spider, and follows him forever.

Wentworth dispatched one man secretly to Washington and the White House, but he was caught and hanged.

Another man is dispatched, and ends up dead also. Now the Spider will not sacrifice anyone else. He alone must carry the message to the President of the United States. Only with the help of the president can the Black Police be defeated. But in the end, only the Spider would be able to do it, for the president's help would never arrive. The trip to the White House was just to move the story along.

He steals an airplane and flies to the border, only to have his plane shot out of the sky. He survives, makes his way to Washington, secretly enters the office of the President, and gives him the details of what is happening in New York. The President listens to his story, promises help, and allows him to depart the White House. This time he charters a plane and heads back to New York and parachutes out over the state. He then makes his way to a secret spy headquarters in a magazine shop. Again, this sounds more like Operator #5 than The Spider!

The Spider, October 1938.

> When Wentworth enters the tiny magazine shop, the proprietor drops on his knees and tears trickle down his cheeks.
>
> "The commander!" the man stammered. "The commander! They told us you were dead. Oh, thank God!" (But he rose after the third day, don't you remember?)
>
> Even a priest has joined their ranks, and when he finds the Spider has returned: "We have done evil things since you have been gone," he said. "Evil things, though they were necessary."
>
> Yes, indeed, they had hanged fourteen men. Black Policemen. But The Spider will forgive them their sin and we knew he would, of course. Later, Wentworth is captured, tried for crimes against the state and sentenced

to die. In the meantime, his last stronghold is destroyed by the enemy. Only Nita and a few others escape, the rest are killed But as Wentworth is about to be executed, Nita and her small band arrive just in time to save him.

The Spider recruits hundreds of men dying from leprosy, and they march on New York City, calling themselves "the Army of Death!"

During a violent attack on the city, Wentworth splits his army into three divisions; Kirkpatrick was to take his men and capture the police department, Sailor Joe took another third and attacked the Black Police headquarters, and Wentworth took his men to the armory where the anti-toxin for the plague was being stored; the Black Police was not letting any of the diseased victims get the drug. Wentworth and his men succeed, and very quickly New York City is restored once more. It is a great victory, but the battle had been tremendous, with heavy losses.

As the Spider races across town to city hall, he comes upon a strange procession, we are told: Nita and the priest are leading the citizens of the city through the streets, and they are all singing:

"Mine eyes have seen the Glory of the coming of the Lord,

He is trampling out the vintage where the grapes of wrath are stored...."

How fitting, but I wonder if Norvell Page wasn't seriously thinking of the Spider when they were singing this Hymn? Maybe I shouldn't go too deep into the Messiah complex. After all, the Spider was mere fiction, and we must hope that Norvell Page realized this. But, just a few pages later we find this scene:

Wentworth mounted then to the window from which the body of the mayor dangled and managed at last to make his voice heard. A great waiting quiet fell upon the multitudes while their white faces turned upward to the man in the window, their savior from oppression.

With the city of New York once again in the hands of the good, the evil disappears; this time the Master is identified as a G-Man named Miller. But, again, this is merely a disguise: Page introduces several new people in each story, and at the end one of them will turn out to be the Master. It's one man disguising himself in each story, to become a different person from the last story. But the same man, never the less.

But, honestly, after this Armageddon, there is little wonder that there could have been a third story in this mini-series. But there is...

It is the November 1938 story, titled "Scourge of the Black Legions." The story no sooner opens than the Messiah image is once again provoked: thousands of plague victims are on the outskirts of New York City arriving from all over the state. However, they are being stopped at the city limits, to protect the folks in town that are not infected with the disease yet.

They begin crying out for Richard Wentworth. When he comes to them, we read this:

> White faces turned up to him incredulously. In the forefront of the crowd, a woman stared, and Wentworth saw her throat jerk convulsively. She dropped to her knees and her hands were lifted as if she prayed.
>
> "It's Richard Wentworth!" Her cry ran thinly through the chill air of early winter. "Richard Wentworth, our commander has come!"
>
> They had left the meager fires they had built for warmth and were huddled before him like sheep, like children frightened of the dark!
>
> The old woman saw the movement and, with an inarticulate cry, she flung her body in the path of a bullet meant for Wentworth!
>
> "My life," she whispered. "It means nothing. You... you are the commander!"

From page to page it continues. A woman looks up to heaven and proclaims: "Thank God. The Spider has come. Now we are saved."

And more and more, the role continues, as Wentworth/The Spider is proclaimed the savior of mankind. The long awaited Messiah, in who their only hope remained! Now that Armageddon was upon the world, they could only look to one source for their salvation!

Was Norvell Page really serious with all this silly stuff, or was he only laughing at his readers as he wrote these Armageddon plots, and messiah yearnings? Did he believe in the power of his own creation? I don't really think so. But who knows? Who cares, really? Page was having fun; the action is fast, the pace furious, incidents happen just to prove the power of the Spider. A lot of things really non-essential to the story line, but they pop up every few pages to keep the narrative plot moving, and again show the Messiah image of Richard Wentworth.

While Wentworth is with the multitude of lepers at the city limits of New York, having just recently left Kirkpatrick at police headquarters, a messenger arrives with the latest news from Washington DC. The White House has sent an ultimatum to the defenders of New York City; "Relinquish control, surrender or military troops will be sent in." Already military planes were in the air over New York City. So much for the Presidents promise to Wentworth in the last story. But that little scene was played out just to show off some more of the Spider's powers, and to extend the story by a few more pages. And they had only held the great City for forty-eight hours.

With no more than this, Wentworth gathers his men and tells them that they must retreat once more. Go back into hiding and turn the city over to the government troops (who will give it to the Black Police, of course). Remember Armageddon in the last issue? It meant nothing. What of all those valiant men and women who had died while worshiping Wentworth, I might add? Too bad. What about all those thousands of suffering Victims of the leprosy plague who were relying on the Spider to cure them? They would rely on him again. They would look up, white faced, and proclaim him their commander, their savior. Just wait and see. But for now Page wanted the Spider and his band to fight another guerrilla war, so off they go, into hiding once more. After all, this worked just fine in the last story, and kept the pace smooth, and the action jumping, so why not do it again?

Wentworth hears of another town in bad straights, like Titustown last issue. Here again, the Black Police have shut off the town from entrance and exit, and are torturing the people and robbing the banks, while the National troops are holding New York City for them! Oh well.

So what if the Spider and his band had secured New York City, and were protecting its citizens? The president would probably just say, "No comment."

The Spider mounts a motorcycle, wearing a green cape (never explained), and off he goes, to save this new town. Its name doesn't matter, because it's only another Titustown, or one like it. They are all the same. Alone again, but that's what we expected from the Spider. The Black Police had better look out. The green cape was flying behind him!

But we knew what was going to happen; the Spider was going to recruit another army, with a new town to join his ranks. Men and women to fight and be killed, to worship Richard Wentworth, and do his service, while he runs around saving everyone else.

Sure enough, he no sooner gets into town and he finds Black Police torturing five young girls at a roadblock. He shoots them dead and recruits the women, telling them to call every one in the telephone book and have them meet him in the town square.

Gathering the citizens in the town square, he comes across a woman holding a baby in her arms. She runs into the middle of the street and sobbed almost in his path.

As he rolled past, he heard the woman speak to her child: "Look, Junior. Look, and don't forget this ever! You have seen him! The Spider! The greatest man ever!"

The Spider, November 1938.

Another Biblical connection happens almost immediately. As the people gather in the square, he meets a woman the reader also recognizes. She plays the part of Mary of Magdalene, but her name is Maria Laplante in this story. She was in other stories, under different names. As Was Matthew, Mark, Luke and John. Not to mention the other image of Mary (the woman who took the bullet meant for Wentworth at the beginning of this third novel).

Nor does Kirkpatrick miss the savior syndrome in the Spider: "Sometimes, I think Dick must be the embodiment of all those ancient heroes. The Saviors of mankind. Only they died, and Dick lives on and on." And I'm only at the beginning of Chapter Three.

By the next action sequence, the Spider is seriously wounded, but secretly being cared for by Mary Magdalene. Er, excuse me, Maria Laplante, while he lies near death; the Black Police report his death. They even produce his green cape as proof. His men have been released from his command, and Nita believes he is dead also. But she goes on fighting. That's what he would want her to do!

Nita disguises herself and gets a job as secretary to the lieutenant governor, Marvin Rixson, the coordinator for the activities of the Black Police; she makes contact with Kirkpatrick, Jackson and Colonel Rice; Rixson had merely been baiting her; he and the Black Police raid their meeting. They are about to be tortured when the Spider arrives to kill Black Policemen, capture Rixson (who turns out to be Colonel Rice's twin brother: why sure, we knew that, didn't we?!) Rixson divulges that the Master (remember the guy in the mirror?) plans on destroying a dam in Pennsylvania to cause a diversion for the federal troops while the Black Police raid three cities in New York State.

The Spider, still weak from his wounds, not to mention Maria Laplante's care, as well as his inactivity, steals an airplane from the Black Police and off he flies to warn the people below the dam. There's no mention of problems with the telephones. He's running neck to neck with Black Police bombers. He destroys the bombers, but only after they have wrecked their damage on the dam. Stealing a car, he rushes ahead of a giant tidal wave, to warn the people in its path. Remember the Biblical story about the deluge? Well, the title of this chapter is "Deluge." Of course!

Fighting with the men, while saving women and children, he rescues an unknown number before his strength is entirely spent; fearing the local police are at his heels (that's what they are there for), he sees a plane landing. It is Nita, here to save him. But now there are the three towns in New York State that must be protected. Off they fly. How one man can protect three towns at once doesn't even enter his mind. He could do it, no matter what the odds were!

Later, the Spider attacks a concentration camp single-handedly, garrisoned by hundreds of Black

Policemen, destroys the camp and releases the prisoners: Kirkpatrick, Colonel Rice, Jackson, Ram Singh, and about a thousand others. With Colonel Rice, Wentworth heads for Albany and the headquarters of Rixson, the lieutenant governor, and twin brother of Rice. They capture Rixson, call in the governor and capture him. Rice takes over the identity of his brother and under the guidance of Wentworth, starts issuing orders that will disband the Black Police, and then brings in the national guard to restore law and order. A good plan, and it should have worked. However now enters the Master, that dastardly villain, disguised as the real Rixson (now we have three of them!), releases the original, captures the second (Colonel Rice); again has Nita, Ram Singh, and Jackson in his hands, and the Spider to top this off.

In a sudden change of character, Rixson (the real one, this time) attacks the Master (one of the Rixsons in the story), diverts his aim, so the Spider can get loose. It appears that Rixson has fallen in love with Maria Laplante. Are you following all this? The Spider starts shooting, gets shot, the Master (one of the Rixsons) escapes.

Delayed, The Spider starts laughing. Now he knows the identity of the Master (so do we, he's someone introduced in this story). Thank God! He grabs the green cape from somewhere, steals a motorcycle, and heads for the Master's home.

Entering a building, the Spider empties an automatic into the back of an easy chair. Seated in front is the mastermind of this whole mess. The Master dies. The series comes to an end as easily as that! Wentworth identifies him as someone named Francis Kepler, the inventor of the trick mirror. Of course! I should have known that! Just because he hadn't been mentioned in the first two novels, I should still have known who he was. Everybody else did! At least the Spider, and maybe Norvell Page.

All of this nonsense comes to an end. Kirkpatrick is put back in office. The Spider is again wanted for all those crimes. Marvin Rixson is re-instated as the governor. I though he was a criminal and had been instrumental in all of those deaths and crimes. He takes the beautiful, and faithful, Maria Laplante as his wife, and we are assured he will never again turn to crime. He had repented, and The Spider had forgiven him. The Spider can do that, you know.

The whole series was laughable, but it was good, nevertheless. It was typical Spider and Norvell Page. But sounded more like Operator #5 throughout. In the first story, crooked politicians are duly elected into office by the populace, and they quickly start killing, robbing, and torturing. The citizens are afraid to fight back until they are led by the Spider.

In the second novel, the best of the three stories, we have freedom fighters whipping the pants off the Black Police, and eventually capture New York City and, hold it for 48 hours.

In the third novel, the worse of the three, the Black Police take control back of New York City with the aid of the federal government. The Black Police then start looting all the banks in the State, and—well, I have already described the ending once. No need to do it again. Once was enough.

The whole trilogy reeked of Armageddon, but that was what every Spider novel was. Just read any story, and you're in the middle of Armageddon. It's the final battle. The Spider must save mankind. In each story we are told that this latest evil was worse than the one before,

And it really was, as hard as that is to be believed. If you were to start from the very beginning, when Norvell Page takes over the Spider series with the December 1933 issue, and read the stories in succession, or start with the December 1943 issue, and read the stories in order backwards, each new story is more terrible than the one before it. Page had a way of making each novel worse than the next one.

It was his Armageddon!

"And he saw that there was no man, and wondered that there was no intercessor: therefore his arm brought salvation unto him; and his righteousness, it sustained him.

> For he put on righteousness as a breastplate; and an helmet of salvation upon his head; and he put on the garments of vengeance for clothing, and was clad with zeal as a cloak. (Isaiah 59: V. 16 & 17)

A final question lingers in the back of my mind. One that won't easily be answered. There were incidents within these three stories that were almost identical to incidents in the Operator #5 stories by Tepperman, so I can't help wondering if the Black Police stories had not originally been outlines for the Purple Wars.

I am sure that Page read Tepperman's Operator #5 stories, as you can see the influence of that series. And the Black Police stories appear just as the Purple Invasion ends, and Tepperman leaves the series. This could be pure coincidence, but it is odd.

Perhaps Page merely styled the outlines after the Purple Invasion stories. That's certainly a possibility. But I have a strong feeling that Tepperman was tired of the Operator #5 series and wanted out. Harry Steeger may have been looking for a replacement writer, and Page read some of the Invasion for ideas. When Wayne Rogers took over the Operator #5 series, Page merely turned his outlines into Spider stories. An easy enough task. I would like to think the Black Police series from The Spider are three missing accounts of the Purple Invasion from Operator #5.

Regardless of how well they fit within the Spider's world, they were better suited for the invasion theme of Operator #5. ♦

Captain Satan

By Tom Johnson

In Michael Cook's *Mystery, Detective And Espionage Magazines* (Greenwood Press, 1983), Joe Lewandowski remarks in his profile of Captain Satan: "Imagine, if you will, a mixture of Doc Savage, The Saint, and The Spider. Throw in a touch of Raffles, season with a dash of Arsine Lupin and a pinch (a very tiny pinch) of Ellery Queen, and you have the essential ingredients for the pulp hero who bowed in as Captain Satan, King of Adventure, in the spring of 1938."

In truth, Captain Satan did resemble the characters mentioned above: the muscles of Doc Savage, the killing instincts of the Spider, and the adventuresome spirit of The Saint. Combined with these, you can also toss in Robin Hood and his merry men. For in truth, Captain Satan and his crew also resembled this bunch of rowdies from Sherwood Forest: taking a page from Johnston McCulley, they tracked down crime and robbed the gangsters of their ill-gotten gain!

Captain Satan was, in reality, a certain Cary Adair, who was described thusly: He had the look of a gentleman, a man-about town; a "clubman, a body without a soul, a sword without an edge." But this was merely the appearance he allowed others to see. He has gray eyes, set in a smoothly rugged face that was tanned by the winds of the seven seas. A strong chin and broad shoulders. He gave the appearance of a rich, lazy man-about-town. He spoke—and read at least seven languages, and could usually be found reading a classic (like *The Arabian Nights*) in its original language. It was said that he lolled around his many clubs, or attended first night movie shows, and haunted the antique shops, buying jade, rare coins, and other treasures from around the world.

Captain Satan is strong as an ox, cunning, daring, relentless. He wears a tight fitting black coat, buttoned over a black sweater, showing the perfect symmetry and powerful muscles. Black trousers and rubber-soled black shoes completed his attire, and it enabled him to blend into the darkness. He stood over six feet tall, in outstanding physical condition, and could ride, swim, fence and drive either car or speedboat as good as any professional.

His face was square, without being heavy, with a strong, well-rounded chin, slanting forehead, ears ample and flat against the head; a head that was cropped as close as a convict's. Stern gray eyes were framed in a face that was as brown as an Indian's. The nose was straight, over a slight, strong mouth. When he moved, his sloping shoulders and large biceps spoke of the tremendous power of the man. His age could have been thirty, thirty-five, even fifty or fifty-five. In a chronology worked out by Wooda N. Carr, in "The Devil You Say," *Nemesis, Inc.* #20 (August 1985), Nick places his birth in 1881. In These Ven's (Joe Lewandowski) article in *Echoes From the Pulps* #3 (Fall 1980), Joe lists his possible birth in 1895.

Here are a couple of scenes that I thought were interesting:

> Whistling softly to himself a popular air, he set his hat at a jaunty angle and whipped the door open.

Sounds a little like Richard Wentworth, alias The Spider, doesn't it?

> The banker's face was drawn, his eyes fearful. "Who—?" he quavered. "Who—?"
>
> "Are you imitating an owl, or are you trying to ask my name?" asked Satan.

I was slightly reminded of the *Secret Agent "X"* novel "Kingdom of the Blue Corpses," when this type humor was used.

Satan usually carried a brace of heavy .45 automatics, but would use whatever weapon was available to him, including machine-guns or knives. Once he allowed himself to be captured, the crooks shook him down-and found no weapons. Later, when Satan went into action, he shook his arms vigorously and two heavy automatics dropped into his hands. They had been hidden up his sleeves, attached to heavy rubber bands to hold them in place until he needed them! .

He smoked cigarettes, which he carried in an expensive case. He also used an enamel-and barrel-shaped automatic cigarette lighter. This lighter was also a flashlight in the bottom, which held his Satan seal that he would flash on a wall, announcing his entry to crooks. The seal was an image of Satan holding a three-pronged pitchfork. He used a large lantern, which served this same purpose and it was usually shined on the wall of the warehouse where his crew gathered. Or in the crooks' hideout! This trick worked very well, as it not only seemed to hold his crew in line, it also frightened crooks who saw it, as well.

Cary Adair lived in the penthouse apartment of a giant skyscraper. Below him also, but hidden from view by the wide terrace that circled the penthouse apartment, were the teeming streets of New York's financial district. It was a whim that led Adair to build his home atop one of New York's business skyscrapers… and the fact that he'd had to buy the building to do it hadn't deterred him; (Perhaps Cary was "The Shadow Over Wall Street"?)

In the living room were thick Turkish rugs covering the floor, Venetian blinds over the windows; Adair only had to touch a single button and the wide studio window folded back silently into a frame. Beyond, the terrace was colorfully tiled to its guard wall. The terrace itself held, among other objects, many rare and various plants. Black drapes covered the window frames also, usually kept open. Just beyond the living room was the foyer, with trophies from his hunting trips lining the walls. There was a dining room with inlay paneling, a guest room in addition to those occupied by Adair and his manservant, Jeremy. A doorway leading into what was probably the kitchen area was concealed by a rare Chinese screen. The living room also contained a fireplace, several chairs, and bookcases, all filled with rare and valuable tomes. There were two telephones, one being a private in-house line that connected him to the desk in the lobby. And a private elevator that led down to street level. The apartment did not have an alarm system, but the doors and walls were completely fireproof. This worked to Adair's advantage in the story entitled "A Ghost Rides the Dawn," in which a Chinese invader sets a fire in the hallway between the elevator and the apartment door.

However, the penthouse apartment was self-efficient, as we can see in this scene between Adair and Joe Desher of the FBI:

> "Once I thought you were crazy to buy a skyscraper," Desher remarked. "Just so you could take over the roof of it and live up here. Must set you back a pile of money to run it."
>
> "On the contrary," Adair replied, "the tenants pay me. I haven't a vacant space in the building."

Also, from the novel "A Ghost Rides the Dawn,"

we are given a description of the hallway: it contained two chairs, a table with a lamp, and a rug (these were all destroyed by the fire in the story). There is also a camera set up for recording any activity in hallway.

As Kokamori, a Japanese spy, remarked after the above incident, "Hard to understand," he said genially. "Building owner has spy traps, uses many guns when men come near."

Joe Desher of the FBI, who was also present (it was Joe who the Japanese spy was following, while the Chinese were following the Japanese spy), said derisively, "They came in sort of handy today, Kokamori." But his eyes were puzzled, agreeing, almost, with the spy's words.

There was also a warning system of sorts: when anyone entered the hallway, a lamp in Adair's living room changed from a pink color to a red! (This also taken from the novel A Ghost Rides the Dawn.)

Joe Desher was Chief Agent of the FBI in New York City, though he often followed cases across the United States. He was described thusly: he had a stubby, powerful frame, squat, powerful, dark, round of head and with a gleaming honest light in his brown eyes… and pudgy hands.

Satan had saved Joe's life twice in the past, once in Samoa when the FBI was running down a slave-trafficking gang (probably white slavery), and again when an international smuggling gang had got the drop on him.

Joe—the author used "Jo"—would always come to Cary's to discuss cases that had him stumped. It never failed that Joe would also bring up the subject of Captain Satan (Joe's mythical Captain Satan, as Cary would call him). After Joe left Cary's apartment, the "mythical" Captain Satan would shortly be on the case—sometimes Cary would even accompany Joe to some meeting or interview with people involved in the case.

On one occasion (the first novel), Joe does suspect Cary of being Satan; in the second novel we find this:

"The few times I've seen him at close range he's been masked," Desher remarked to Adair.

"Or at night, in a poor light. He was unrecognizable anyway." He stopped, his face breaking into a delighted smile. "You'd be surprised if I told you the man I suspected him to be on one occasion."

"Who?" Adair shook his head slowly. "One of your own men?"

Desher waved his hand, negligently, the smile still on his face. "Never mind that part of it, Cary. It was ridiculous."

But Desher felt that Cary was content to clip dividend coupons from various newspapers and magazines, as his only exercise. Though he also believed Cary to be a big-game hunter, as his many trophies would acclaim.

Joe also smoked cigars, referring to them as "wicked-looking and black." However, his voice was also full of vigor and energy.

When Satan completed a case he left Joe to take the credit. But Desher always swore he'd arrest Satan and throwaway the key. However, he often admitted that Satan was wiping out crooks, regardless of his methods. I was never comfortable with Joe's title; was he the head of the FBI, the head of the New York office of the FBI, or was he merely a special agent—or more likely, an Inspector, like Dan Fowler?

Cary Adair's manservant, valet, and butler, was Jeremy Watkins. He was described as "a tall, gangling man, whose severely black attire was as funereal as his long, sallow face. Sad, almost mournful eyes." And again, as "a square, somberly clad man whose serene face was contradicted by his wide humorous mouth. Aquiline nose, high, intelligent forehead, long jaw, unfathomable eyes; all these were in strange contrast to that wide, mobile mouth. But most remarkable of all was his long sensitive hands."

His eyes were also a steady brown, whatever that means.

He was an accomplished sleight-of-hand artist,

constantly picking the pockets of Joe Desher, removing important papers, or evidence, without his knowledge. He always removed Desher's cigars, putting them in his hat or on a table, giving Joe the impression that he himself placed the cigars there; however, in the last novel, The Ambassador From Hell, Desher seems to be wise to Jeremy:

> Joe Desher shook his head slowly. He patted his breast pockets, frowned. "Now, what the devil did I do with my cigars?" he muttered.
>
> Adair's manservant glided soundlessly onto the terrace, a Panama hat in his hand. He deftly produced half a dozen wickedly black cigars and proffered them to the FBI man. "In your hat, sir," he murmured.
>
> The FBI investigator riveted the gaunt man with a bleak stare. "I'm on to your sleight-of-hand tricks, Jeremy," he said severely. "But when you 'lift' my cigars, you might absently return me some of your boss' sixty-five cent wonders, instead of these ropes!"

Captain Satan, March 1938.

Adair grinned. "You cost me money that time, Jeremy. Give Mr. Desher a box of my specials."

Jeremy was often described as "moving with deceptive speed." In "A Ghost Rides the Dawn" we find this passage:

> …And Jeremy had materialized in the center of the room, his eyes riveted on those closed portieres, a hand at either side.
>
> "What of the comet?" Desher was talking to himself again. But his eyes bulged when he saw Adair slide an automatic from a shoulder holster… saw Jeremy tread back, catlike, and drop to a kneeling position on the floor in front of his master. Two heavy automatics had appeared as if by magic in the hands of Jeremy!

In *Echoes From the Pulps* #3, Joe Lewandowski conducts a fictitious interview with Jeremy, detailing the activities of himself and Cary Adair, along with a lot of factual history, as well as romantic fantasy, in the life and adventures of them both. Lewandowski also throws in lots of fictitious titles of stories that were supposedly chronicled prior to the five published Captain Satan stories, as well as some adventures afterwards. There were also some adventures of Captain Satan and Captain John Fury together in fictitious stories. John Fury, of course, was he Skipper. Cute, and very interesting. And it adds possible information on Jeremy Watkins, who was Adair's manservant, as well as Captain Satan's first lieutenant, the man designated as "Slim."

And what about Satan's crew? Those men who would assemble in a deserted warehouse on Pier Four of the East River? Each of them was a specialist in one field or another, and they craved adventure. Some would die, while others would turn traitor, but there were a few who were solely dedicated to Captain Satan, and would willingly die while in his service. Here was their code of honor:

"What is your purpose here, strangers?" he asked, intoning the ritual.

"To become blood brothers," they answered in unison, but with a tremble in their voices.

"Why?"

"To join with the others of Satan's Crew in fighting Satan's appointed enemies; to obey orders implicitly; to maintain the secrecy of our order and to refrain from attempting to discover the identities of other members; and to defend to the death ourselves, our brothers and our identities."

Only Captain Satan and Slim knew who their crew members were. But the crew members did not know each other in private life, nor in their professional capacities. When together they all wore domino masks, and were addressed under their code names, i.e., Jeremy Watkins was "Slim."

Slim called Satan "Captain" but the others had to call him "Cap'n." And when a roll call, or line up was called, each man would answer with yet another variance of this code; the use of their first and last letters from their code names, i.e., Slim was thus designated "S-M." The others had similar designations.

In the first novel, "The Mask of the Damned," two crewmen were mentioned as being "no longer with us," killed prior to this current case; they were Dutch and Paddy. Also, as the crew gathered, a character known as Sledge is found to be an impostor (and it's believed that he had probably killed the real Sledge and merely took his place). Satan shoots the impostor dead!

Below is a roll call of Satan's crew:

Happy (designated "H-Y") was short, stocky, with merry blue eyes that would have been darker in a less powerful light; a face that was round and dimpled in a smile as he stared steadily back into the beam. He was married and had children. He only appeared in the first novel, and nothing is said about him in future stories. The interior artist did not sketch him.

Mike (designated "M-E") was portly, with earnest eyes, red hair, and wispy mustache and a strong, wide mouth. He was Irish and spoke with a rich brogue. He was shot down in a hail of gunfire during the first novel, though a similar character would appear in the second story. The interior artist did not sketch him, either.

Frenchy (designated "F-Y") was very good looking, had a debonair mustache and glittering black eyes. Captain Satan discovers that Frenchy has turned traitor to him and his crew. As was the case with Sledge, Satan shoots him dead. There was no artist sketch of him.

Gentleman Dan (designated "G-N") was described as tall, blond and very graceful, with a waxed mustache, patent leather hair and a quiet smile. In The Ambassador From Hell, he admits to being a former member of the Secret Service, and a skilled pilot. He was also something of a ladies man, and ended up with the girl, Marianne Sarno, at the conclusion of "The Mask of the Damned." In the next novel, "Parole for the Dead," the crew members kidded him about how he got away from the 'Missus' for this latest assembly, so we can assume that he probably married Marianne, though this was never stated. He remained with the series throughout. There was an artist sketch of him.

Doc (designated "D-C") was a doctor of some kind in his private life. He was described as small, with keen gray eyes and capable hands. He was calm and dignified. It was up to him to obtain medical information during the cases, plus treat the crew for any wounds or injuries they may sustain during the adventures. He was featured throughout the series. There was an artist sketch of him, as well.

Kayo (designated "K-O") was a thickset individual with large shoulders and the form of a wrestler. His many abilities came in handy throughout the series. He was also a pilot, and flew planes in several novels. Among his other duties was being the chauffeur for the crew. Cary Adair is also mentioned as being a chauffeur, so Kayo may have done this work professionally. He is called "a regular Barney Oldfield," and had previously broken his nose. He remained with the series throughout. There was an artist sketch of him, also.

Pat (designated "P-T") was introduced in the second novel as "an old member returning from abroad." He was ruddy faced with a carroty mustache, and twinkling eyes. It might be suggested that the author, for some reason unknown to us, returned the character of Mike to the series- but under a new name. For Pat is an exact duplicate of the crewmember who was killed during the first novel. He also speaks with a touch of an Irish brogue. He appeared in the last four stories of the series. There was no artist sketch of him.

Big Bill (designated "B-L") was a seedy-looking, shuffling, oversized, bleary-eyed man with a toothless grin, and a soft, grave voice. He usually played the drunk, though he couldn't handle more than three drinks at any given time. Big Bill was killed in the second story, a knife stuck in his back. There was no artist sketch of him.

Soapy (designated "S-Y") was merely referred to as a rather nondescript individual, kind of short, and slinky. He might possibly have been a safe cracker as his code name might seem to indicate He was featured throughout the series, and there was an artist sketch of his character.

Solly (designated "S-L") was a small person, with a large nose, and stooped shoulders. He was also a former engineer, railroad worker, welder, machinist, lighting equipment troubleshooter, and radio worker. His hands were always moving. Because his name and that of Soapy both contained the same first and last letters, Solly was given the call letters of "S-L" for Sol. He was introduced in the second novel and remained throughout the series. He also spoke French, so he takes on something of the semblance of the past member, Frenchy. He was sketched with an artist profile.

The Dutchman (designated "T-D") was a thin, jolly-faced man. He had been a soldier, sailor brew master's assistant, insurance salesman, and dental laboratory worker. He had a college degree. He was introduced in the second novel, and remained throughout the remaining series. Again, we have something of a curiosity with The Dutchman: the original "Dutch" was never introduced, as he had died prior to the recorded series of five novels. But it is strange that the artist, in sketching The Dutchman, sketched "Dutch" instead. The author, William O'Sullivan, was just playing with his set of characters, killing them off, bringing them back (Pat not only replaced Mike, but Paddy, too), changing them every so often. And it is very likely The Dutchman had the same qualifications as those of his earlier character, Dutch. Anyway, onward.

Hank (designated "H-K"), sometimes called Big Hank (remember Big Bill?) was introduced in the third story, and only remained for the next story (the third and fourth issues), before being killed off in a volley of gunfire. He was described as big-handed, raw-boned, and a former railroad worker. He made his entry into the series about the time the crew needed a railroad man, for the current mystery surrounding railroads, so his character came in very handy for this one story. He was honored with a sketch by the interior artist.

Chink (designated "C-K") was the last crewmember to be introduced (in the last novel) at a time Captain Satan needed a man of his qualifications, and would have probably been killed off if series had lasted for another issue or so. He was described as small, an accomplished wrestler, a disguise artist without peer, a college graduate, and professor of electrical engineering at one university. Again, his only appearance was in the last novel. The interior artist did illustrate the character.

So, there you have a quick look at Satan's crew. The characters were not totally unlike other aides from the other hero magazines; you could probably argue, successfully, that they, in a way, resembled aides of Doc Savage—each being a specialist in one field or another. But the aides of Captain Satan were not averse to killing now and again—or turning traitor, something the Fabulous Five would not have done.

However, in only five novels it was very hard for author William O'Sullivan to build their characters to any degree, and even then he kept killing them off, adding new characters, and so on. In such a short series, they had little chance to make any kind of impression.

And how about the novels, themselves? For one thing, the crooks went for the big game, usually banks, gold supplies and counterfeit money. Any area where there would be big dividends from their robberies. So, too, this was one of Captain Satan's main interests: he went after these big-time crooks to relieve them of their ill-gotten gains! Already one of the richest men in the world, he operated in a big way. He would finance his men at the beginning of the case; they received two-thirds of the booty, after Satan took his one third of the loot, the expenses were taken care of by the good Captain, as well. He was no slouch when it came to taking care of his men, and the crooks.

Once a year, regardless of criminal activity, Satan and his crew would meet for the exercise and improvement of their skills. They always met at the warehouse, though this location was raided at least twice, once by the Feds, and again, by the Chinese who followed Satan and Slim there. The warehouse itself was described thusly: a room in the interior was fitted with a shower, a rubdown table and a desk. And on the wall, specific maps related to whatever was necessary to their current adventure. There was also a phone set up in a secret panel, that was connected to another building, so the line could not be traced; and even if it was, it would not lead the investigators to Captain Satan and his men. The ring itself was only a soft buzz, and the number was known only to Satan's men.

When the Federals raided the warehouse, we find

© Argosy Communications

Captain Satan, March 1938.

this scene: The crew moved to the room center. Slim, at the wall, pressed against a panel. A small wood square moved inward. Slim gripped a handle that had come into view, turning it to the right, then he snapped the panel shut, quickly joining the others. From the fissure at the base of the walls on all sides, jets of black smoke poured into the room. Simultaneously, there was a trembling of the floor. Slowly the flooring dropped away—down to the underground escape Satan had provided. Once the elevator had went below floor level, another square of wood, identical with the floor above, dovetailed perfectly and closed the opening above their heads. And it was fool proof as the elevator must be re-set before it could be used again. Next, Satan opened a floor trap. Another level. A section of the wall came open, revealing metal tracks. From there, the path led into the New York subway system, and escape.

The first novel must have given a lot of collectors a nightmare, as it began with volume one, number three, dated March 1938. And evidence within the first story left the impression that there had been previous stories. The demise of such characters as Dutch and Paddy were clues. The magazine publishers had merely re-titled an older magazine, *Strange Detective Mysteries*, which had contained the previous volume and numbers.

But, for now, let's examine the stories in order, from "The Mask of the Damned"; the first, to the last, "The Ambassador From Hell." And you consider whether Captain Satan and his crew deserve to be counted among our other greats.

> "He held in his hands the burning Brand of Hell and in his heart was locked the courage of the gods! Wise guys and tough mugs, crooks and their thieving mobs knew the Mark of Satan; and they knew the swift ghosts of Fear and Destruction that rode by his side; the many fierce hands of Justice that fought in Satan's crew!"

And thus we are introduced to Captain Satan. The title was "The Mask of the Damned" (March 1938). The author is listed as William O'Sullivan. The magazine is *Captain Satan*, subtitled King of Adventure. Although the contents said Volume One, Number Three, it was the first in a series of five stories.

The location takes place in New York City and Washington, DC.

The main characters were King Cal Merrill, US President Coyulter Kane, Secretary of Navy James Halding, Secretary of War David Garlock, Manse Mason, Louis Mesters, Hymie, Marianne Sarno, Professor Sarno, Dokey Martin, Mugsy the Fish, Lobo Louie, "Rowdy Bob" Cash, Joe Maganni, Secretary of the Treasury Harold Pettiman, Harman Jenkins, and Senator Day Marra.

Satan's Crew: Slim, Happy, Sledge, Doc, Frenchy, Gentleman Dan, Kayo, Big Bill, and Mike.

Police officials were Joe Desher (FBI), Inspector McCall (NYC), FBI agent Eastham, and "Tough Tom" Toomey.

Alter egos: Captain Satan used the following Willard Haskell and Jo Desher.

Synopsis: In high circles at the very top of American government, top officials are acting strangely. Joe Desher suspects something but can't put his finger on it. He takes his friend, Cary Adair, to a baseball game; Cary notices one of the players seems to be acting strange. There is an attempt made to kill the FBI Chief.

Satan enters the case, finds that just about everybody is being impersonated including the President himself. The real leaders are being kidnapped and impostors are taking their places.

And at the bottom of this mess is not world conquest, not even a touch of international intrigue. It all boils down to a notorious crook planning on hijacking a shipment of gold!

Interesting. In one scene, Satan is in a room with crooks when suddenly a door opens and in walks someone who appears to be the President of United States; he has a gun. Satan orders him to drop the weapon. He doesn't, and is quickly shot by Captain Satan!

Next up is "Parole for the Dead" (April 1938). Volume One, number Four. The author is William O'Sullivan. The magazine is *Captain Satan*, subtitled King of Detectives. It is the second story.

Crime walked the night, alone, unpunished when the dead were given their paroles! For prison bars and concrete walls can never hold a ghost! But Captain Satan talked with lead, a language that even a corpse can't ignore!

The grim rocks of prison walls had finally sprung a leak, but only the greatest of gangdom's chiefs could taste the fresh air outside. Crime!—with its many bloody fingers—Crime!—with a single master! Who was the man behind these prison breaks who fed the fat keepers of Hell and laughed at the Law? Satan

Captain Satan, April 1938.

came up with the answer—while hot guns spoke of Death and the Law held up its hands!

The locations of the adventure are New York City and San Francisco.

The main characters were Sam Klami, Joe Mikkle, Siggy Murrah, Denver Phil Gilkane, Burton Murnell, Dr. Anthony Leedrum, Dr. Harold Simmiss, Wanda Mellin, Dr. Costa, Davies Duggan, Benny the Fog, Micky Carfano, Pagan Lorando, Dr. Michael Giffontis, Nibs Mackley, and Jake the Dip.

Satan's crew: Kayo, Soapy, Pat, Doc, Gentleman Dan, Big Bill, The Dutchman, and Sully.

The police allies were Joe Desher and Carter Colley.

Synopsis: Cary Adair's old friend Joe Desher drops in to see him. It appears there are some strange goings-on at federal prisons: big-time crooks with plenty of dough appear to be murdered while secured in infallible prisons. But one of the mysteries is that the murdered men are burned beyond recognition, though their fingerprints match what is on their records, and dental plates identify them as well. What is going on?

Captain Satan wants to know, too. He starts investigating a dental office and immediately falls into criminal hands. He turns the tables, the crooks vacate the place, and Satan's crew takes over the dental offices; and once he figures out the set-up the big crooks are not really being murdered in prison; he appears to be taking over the operation; he agrees to infiltrate the prison system with an unknown corpse, burned beyond recognition, and to leave the body and take out the big-time crook leaving the impression that the crook has beer murdered. (False records are made up to make officials believe the real crook has been murdered.

All very simple. Satan upsets the apple cart, makes off with the big shot's dough, and leaves the bad guys in prison.

Our third novel in the series is "The Dead Man Express" (May 1938), Volume Two, Number One. The author is William O'Sullivan. The magazine is *Captain Satan*, subtitled King of Detectives.

Death, with its hungry hands, is the companion of Crime, and both are the enemies of the living! Now Satan returns with his steely fists and guns, climbing over the corpses of the damned. He's out to wreck the Dead Man Express and prove that not even the Hyena can laugh his way out of Hell! But who is the Hyena? And what means his bloody laughter?

There's a red light on the track for Captain Satan and his crew, and all Hell rides the rails with the dead Man Express! Here is a story you will not forget, when the gun smoke has faded and the hyena has laughed his last bloody laughter!

The locations of this story are New York City, San Francisco and Nevada.

Captain Satan, May 1938.

The main characters were Hassem, John Smith, Jake Largo, Larry the Dude, Doctor Vasili Vashte Sonya Kerstadt, Big Swen Kerstadt, Spike, and the Hyena (Doctor Vashte, of course).

Satan's crew: Gentleman Dan, Doc, Pat, Soapy, Kayo, Solly, the Dutchman, and Hank.

The police allies were Joe Desher and FBI agent Peyton.

Synopsis: Talk about a mystery. Freight trains leave California, disappear somewhere in Nevada then the same train is seen in three different places on the East Coast, thousands of miles apart! Joe Desher is going out of his head trying to figure it out. Can his friend Cary Adair help him get some answers?

Well, Captain Satan can. And he does. The trains are being high jacked after a gas puts everyone to

CAPTAIN SATAN   137

sleep and hidden in a cave in the desert. Satan and his crew fly out to San Francisco, meet a lovely airline stewardess, locates her father and half brother, shoots the half brother dead in front of her and her father, then hears from the father how he helped his son obtain the numbers on the railroad box cars.

They then head for Nevada where they locate a cave, find "living dead men," whose brains had been operated upon, making them the perfect workers, never tiring, never complaining, just work, work, work unloading box cars of their valuable cargo. In the meantime, the Hyena, the master criminal, is blackmailing everyone involved who want the cargo returned, making a big profit for himself.

Naturally, Captain Satan turns the tables, walks off with the swag, while the crooks and living dead men are blown to bits when the cave explodes from dynamite. Exciting!

By the way, Joe Desher had been on the last train. Satan puts him to sleep, sends the train on its way, and again Joe is given credit for solving the great mystery

Our fourth entry is "A Ghost Rides the Dawn" (June 1938), Volume Two, Number Two. The author is William O'Sullivan. The magazine is *Captain Satan*, subtitled King of Detectives.

Murder walks the bloody path and crime is a ripe and festering sore! Satan rides once more with his tight-lipped crew and the guns sing out in a leaden song.

A hot gun speaks above the streets of New York, and Satan returns to his kingdom of Hell! There can be no compromise with the men he fights, for the hot fires of hate are eating out lives; lives that mean much to Satan and his swashbuckling crew. There's gold at the end of this bloody trail and Satan intends to have it.

This adventure takes place in New York City and Colorado.

The main characters were Kikko, Ivan, Kanyo, Corsi, Datsu, Merku, Ishii Kokamori, Sanso, and Mr.

Captain Satan, June 1938.

Newton D. Phineas.

Satan's crew: Soapy, Doc, Gentleman Dan, Slim (Always present), Solly, The Dutchman, Pat and Hank.

The police allies: Joe Desher is the only police character mentioned by name. Satan uses the alias Emory at one point.

Synopsis: I thought this was probably the best story in the series. Joe Desher visits his old friend Cary Adair to discuss the murder of one of his own men, plus the strange activity of comets in the skies, and people burning to death—rich folks, that is. But tailing Joe is a Japanese Naval spy named Kokamori and following this gentleman is a man of possibly Chinese descent. They all meet in the lobby of Adair's penthouse and force the elevator operator to take them up. A warning system reveals them and a gun battle takes place. The Japanese spy is momentarily captured but the Chinese spy escapes. In his wake, he leaves a firebomb at Cary's door, but the penthouse is saved because of the construction of the apartment and hallway.

Captain Satan enters the case, but the Chinese spies follow him and Slim from Adair's apartment to the warehouse. Again, another firebomb. Again, Satan and his crew escape without damage, but the Chinese are killed.

What was it all about? Simple. An American crook, operating in Asia, gets on the wrong side of a bandit leader. The American loses both legs from the encounter. He obtains wooden legs, escapes from the warlord, and comes across a band of fire-walking cult men. He thrills them by walking on the fire. Being white and able to walk on fire was enough for the cult men, so they quickly make him one of their gods, which they believe him to be. He rules over them by "cleansing" them in the fire if they do not obey his orders.

He returns to America, where he begins to threaten rich Americans for their fortunes. If they don't come across, he sends a fiery comet to destroy them, and they die. Needless to say, after word of this gets around, the rich guys start coming across with the money! This crook now calls himself "The Emperor of the Dead." And if you don't want the dead part, you obey him.

Satan, while just coming out of one fight, accidentally runs across the home of our mastermind (out in the middle of nowhere). He and Slim are captured, but Satan speaks the cultists' language. He strips down to his shorts, flexing his Doc Savage muscles, shines his cigarette lighter turned flashlight (with the Satan emblem) on the wall of the underground cave where they are. And the cult men see—Satan! Their ultimate leader!

Guess what happens. Yep, old Emperor of the Dead gets dead, as in "cleansed." The cult men throw him into a hot furnace, and while he is burning for his sins, Satan walks off with all of his loot!

Our fifth, and last, entry in this series is "Ambassador From Hell" (July 1938), Volume Two, Number Three. The author is William O'Sullivan. The magazine is *Captain Satan*, subtitled King of Detectives.

Phony guys and phony money, protected by a squadron of killers with hot guns in their hands! These are the men that Satan must fight as he becomes the Ambassador From Hell! The rivers of blood flow swiftly through the Underworld where the law has lost its grip, and Satan alone has the guns and the fists, plus the courage and brains to defeat them!

Gun guys ride again and banks give up their gold while the police are helpless or dying of their wounds! This is a job for Captain Satan whose hard hands have broken the jaws of a hundred thieves!

This adventure takes place in New York: New York City, Braiton, Saugerville and Taylor City.

The main characters were Calvin Cossart, Gaynor Belman, Miss Pam Pollarde, Evans Arnleigh, Gink Lammartey, Ted Krantz, Raphael Gartano, Seth G. Saugers, Ezra Timkens, Tough Tommy Maddlin, Texas Twomey, Ollie Uppers, Tobias Ellert, Attorney-General Claxton, Dandy Joe Montori, and Skimp. Both Raffles and Jesse James are mentioned.

Satan's crew: The Chink, Slim, Solly, Gentleman Dan, The Dutchman, Pat, Kayo, Soapy and Doc.

The police allies were Joe Desher and an agent named Simmers.

Synopsis: Again, Joe Desher visits Cary Adair, where he tells his friend about some strange goings-on at some area banks in and around New York City. It seems that one banker has already been arrested for embezzlement; it appears that he has robbed his own bank to pay an extortion note.

Evidence is foolproof. But why would the banker make so many mistakes: leaving his finger prints all over the evidence, leaving the extortion note to be found, and then claiming his innocence to law enforcement officers? It did not make any sense.

Enter Captain Satan! He finds underworld kingpins involved, and funny money coming from the banks! The bankers commit suicide while in jail. More clues start turning up, and the trail leads Satan to the head of a banking institution that has control over the area banks.

It seems that the mastermind had hired crooked contractors to build several new banks. These banks, only a few years old, were equipped with fake walls, a faulty vault, and easy access. Becoming partners with a notorious counterfeiter, they were systematically taking real money out of the banks, putting phony money into the banks and framing the bankers of their particular bank. This is to throw the investigators off the real trail.

Satan rounds up all the crooks and gets away with the real money that had been honestly obtained by the crooks!

And another case came to a close.

Unfortunately, the series now ends. It had a short, but fun, life. Captain Satan and his crew were a fine bunch of adventurers, fighting crime, and being wonderful, while we, the readers, left the real world for a short while and joined them in their spoken code of honor, put on our black dominos, and checked our weapons for one more fight with the underworld; the same underworld where Richard Wentworth (The Spider), Lamont Cranston (The Shadow), and a dozen other pulp heroes fought to save humanity. Maybe Satan wasn't up to their greatness, but then, who is? He did flex his mighty muscles every now and then, so we got a glimpse of another Doc Savage imitator; one who had the killing ability of the Spider, though maybe not of the great quality of either. Still, the series was a lot of fun, and I think that's all that the publishers wanted from the series.

The publisher was Popular Publications, who gave us the greats, like The Spider, Operator #5, G-8, and so many others. The package was put together as only Popular could do it: bright colored covers, wild action on the inside, and a faithful following. And very few series starting so late ever made a long impression. For many of them it was nearing the end. The Spider

Captain Satan, July 1938.

was great in 1938, but his series would end in five more years. Operator #5 had just gone through the Purple Invasion, and it would end in 1939, the following year. G-8 would last until June, 1944, but G-8 was special.

The letter section never really got off the ground. In the first issue they printed a letter from a father who had watched his son put to death for crimes he had committed. Not a very good way to start off a new hero, I don't think, but maybe they were trying something different. In the last issue were several letters, but the only one to stand out was from someone who didn't think much of the new series:

> Listen! Please cut it out. I'm tired of these windy Sherlock Holmeses who go around showing their muscles to the public and doing things that are absolutely impos-

sible. What did I think of Parole For The Dead? It bored me to tears.

When I saw a new detective-adventure mag on the stands I said to myself, "Here's where I get lost for a few interesting hours in the armchair." I didn't feel like sleeping at the time. But believe me, sir, that after fifteen minutes with Parole For The Dead I was as sleepy as a chloroformed cat.

Why don't you people think up something new once in a while? Tell Satan to take off his mask; we know him! Tell Jeremy to stop stealing people's watches and cigars. He bothers me.

Yours truly, Edgar Hennessey, Kansas City.

The above makes me think that the next letter may have been written by the staff in the office:

Gentlemen: I have followed the adventures of Captain Satan from the beginning and find your magazine, by all odds, the best of its kind to be found on the newsstands. I do not make this statement carelessly, because I have, in my time, read practically every adventure magazine published in the English language.

I feel that Captain Satan has a new approach to thrills and adventures. His band of followers are like no others we meet in fiction. He does not talk like a stuffed encyclopedia, but like a human being, and the things he does, while spectacular and exciting to the last degree, always manage to keep within the bounds of possibility. My imagination is exercised but never outraged when reading Captain Satan. Let me offer my congratulations to William O'Sullivan who has, in my opinion, reached a new high in this type of writing.

Sincerely yours, John Quigley, Deerfield, MA.

Yeah. Well, maybe if we combined the two letters, we might come out with the true quality of the magazine and its new hero, Captain Satan.

The letters and news on upcoming stories appeared in a section entitled The Hot Seat. Some top authors were appearing in the back pages of the magazine: William R. Cox, Walter J. Higgins (?), Ralph Bennit (?), W.T. Ballard, Robert S. Bowen, Wyatt Blassingame, and Moran Tudury. The question marks mean that I don't know anything about those names; the other names should be well known to most pulp readers.

William O'Sullivan was a real person. He wrote at least one more full-length novel featuring another pulp hero. This was Dan Fowler in "Death on the Runways" in *G-Men Detective*, from November, 1947. I would think it very likely that Mr. O'Sullivan may have written other full-length novels, but maybe under house names or pen names. The Secret Agent "X" story mentioned could have been such a story, but there's no way of knowing. I have heard that he was still living; he supposedly quit writing to return to teaching. (I wonder how many Phantoms he may have written?)

A final note: Satan's car was armor-plated, and contained a compartment for hidden weapons. A lot like the car of Richard Wentworth. For more reading on Captain Satan, readers are urged to read "The Devil You Say," by Wooda N. Carr, *Nemesis, Inc.* #20 (August 1985). Nick added a lot that I have left out. His possible chronology on the good Captain is very interesting, and will undoubtedly be followed whenever mentioning Captain Satan in the future. ◆

The Belmont Shadows

By Tom Johnson

In 1963, Belmont Books brought back the greatest crime-fighter of the 1930s—The Shadow! Asking Walter B. Gibson to write a new story featuring the famous character of his creation over thirty years before, Walter Gibson responded with the novel, "The Return of The Shadow." This was to be the first story featuring the black-garbed avenger since 1949, and only the first in a new series of stories that Belmont Books had planned for the Shadow. Though Walter B. Gibson brought back the old character of the 1930's, the Master of Darkness was now caught up in the 1960's, a feat not impossible for either Walter Gibson or the Dark Avenger. The stories of the Shadow are as readable today as they were in 1931, and the character is as believable today as he was in 1931, and just as believable today as back then.

I think that the prologue of the first story, released in September 1963, must have caught the eye of both the old and new reader alike. This prologue was actually taken from the original novel, "The Living Shadow" (April 1931), in which The Shadow is recruiting Harry Vincent:

> "Your life," probed the hypnotic voice from the shadows, "is no longer your own. It belongs to me now. I shall improve it. I shall make it useful. But I shall risk it too. Perhaps I shall lose it, for I have lost lives, just as I have saved them.
>
> "This is my code: life, above all, with honor. And in return, I demand obedience. Absolute obedience."

"I promise," whispered The Shadow's new agent. "I swear absolute obedience...."

At the time of its release in 1963, I was a very impressionable young man of twenty-three years of age, a corporal in the United States Army with five years active service. I was stationed in Europe, France to be exact; but in 1964 I was sent to Turkey during the Cypress Crisis—the first crisis of President Johnson's administration. It was here that I found, and read, my first Shadow adventure, *The Return of the Shadow*. I would later be initiated into the Doc Savage adventures via Bantam Books when I returned to my Post in France.

I was a great fan of the James Bond movies, and belonged to the US Army judo and karate team; plus, had joined a French savate school where I participated in tournaments in France, and was registered in Paris. I was also teaching self-defense to the Army MP's. I was ready for my introduction to The Shadow and his agents. I have been a fan ever since.

My introduction was fairly simple; it was after an Army "free-for-all," in which I had ended up with a broken leg. With a cast on one leg, and walking around on crutches, I made my way to the Base Stars & Stripes bookstore where I found, "The Return of the Shadow." I had grown up with radio drama, and one of my favorite programs had been The Shadow. I quickly bought the last copy from the newsstand and hobbled back to my barracks where I commenced reading my first Shadow adventure. I must admit that I have read this series several times now, and each reading is as fun and fascinating as the first time. I find them enjoyable, exciting, entertaining, and hard to put down!

For those who may not know, The Shadow was created by Walter Gibson back in the early 1930s. The first story appeared in April 1931, under the Maxwell Grant house name, from the magazine published by Street & Smith. The series ran from 1931 to the Summer 1949 issue, a total of 325 stories, the majority of which were written by Walter B. Gibson. A few of the stories were written by Bruce Elliot, Theodore Tinsley, and one by Lester Dent. In 1979 and 1980, two short stories were published in small press books, both written by Walter Gibson.

The Belmont Books series began with the previously mentioned story, under Gibson's own name, but eight more stories soon followed, all with the Maxwell Grant house name. Will Murray was undoubtedly the first to identify these later stories as by wordsmith Dennis Lynds. And in these later stories, Dennis Lynds brings the Master of Darkness into the era of the super spy, with incredible abilities, becoming superhuman.

So return with me now, for a few minutes, to a small selection of Shadow stories, seldom talked about—to a series the collector usually turns his nose up at—to the Belmont Shadow!

Return of The Shadow

With a cover similar to that of the pulp image on "The Black Hush" (August 1, 1933), the Belmont Shadow series was underway. Written by Mr. Walter Brown Gibson, the story takes place on the Appalachian Trail, in New York State and along the Hudson River, with one brief, nostalgic return to the famous "Cobalt Club" in New York City.

Key men of international affairs, connected to the United Nations, have been acting oddly, which indicates to The Shadow that all is not as it should be.

Return of The Shadow, September 1963.

He believes that these men may be under duress, pressure, or else impostors have taken their places. His initial investigation reveals that these men had previously vacationed in the area of the Appalachian Trail prior to their odd behavior. Harry Vincent is sent to the area to investigate and an attempt is quickly made on his life. At the same time, a leading citizen is murdered. The victim may have held the key to the kidnapping plot.

The Shadow sent for several more of his agents: Clyde Burke, Cliff Marsland, Miles Crofton, Rutledge Mann, and Myra Reldon. Their job was to look for any spy activities that may have infiltrated the area.

In New York City, Moe Shrevnitz, Hawkeye and Burbank are assisting in the investigation, and Myra Reldon (as Ming Dwan) has infiltrated the organization of an individual whom The Shadow believes is next on the kidnappers list.

The chief suspects to the murder of Gregg Austin, the leading citizen who was murdered at the beginning of the story, are Irene Shallick, Gregg's niece, her husband Craig Shallick, Irene's boyfriend Rick Langdon, Peter Winstead the family attorney, and the owners of the Palomino Dude Ranch—Mark and Martha Wade.

Investigating the case is local county detective Fred Frisbee, who believes the murder was committed by a trail hiker named Donald Morland who has not been seen since the murder of Gregg Austin. Assisting in the investigation of the kidnapping is Commissioner Weston, Joe Cardona, and Eric Delka—Interpol Agent, and once a member of the CID Ghost Squad of Scotland Yard.

The climax of the story ends at Folly Castle, owned by Rufus Palford, where the key men are being held in cells. The Shadow enters Folly Castle disguised as Rufus Palford, releases the prisoners and unmasks Peter Winstead as the murderer of Gregg Austin, and the mastermind behind the kidnapping plot.

A battle begins between the prisoners, using ancient weapons, and Winstead's men using modern machine guns. The story was good, and typical of Walter Gibson's stories from the 1940s. But this was to be the only Belmont Shadow written by Mr. Gibson, as Belmont Books wanted to pay him reprint prices for new novels, which Mr. Gibson would not agree to. The next Shadow story would be released 13 months later, October 1964, and a new author would be at the helm.

As mentioned previously, the new author using the Maxwell Grant house name was identified by Will Murray as wordsmith Dennis Lynds, one of the many authors writing for Leo Margulies' *Mike Shayne* and *Man From UNCLE* magazines. The new Shadow novels read like the UNCLE stories in that The Shadow is now an international crime-fighter, fighting international spy organizations similar to those the Man From UNCLE fought. The Shadow now has more sophisticated weapons and equipment to combat these organizations. Although the old Shadow may not have needed the updated equipment to combat these organizations, at least it gave the new Shadow an advantage over the Shadow of the 1930s. The Shadow now becomes a superman of unequaled ability in crime fighting. Though the stories margined on the science fiction, and The Shadow's capabilities are a concept employed in many science fiction stories, the new exploits of the Dark Eagle are entertaining, with action, adventure, and pure reading enjoyment.

However, because of this new slant many of the Shadow fans of old refuse to accept the new series as being a part of The Shadow's history and adventures, preferring to remember him as he was in 1931—1949. But I disagree, and consider the Belmont books part of The Shadow's cannon; though the new series is by no means an improvement over Mr. Gibson's creation, they at least bring the mighty avenger up to his full capabilities. For The Shadow is now what was hinted at in the 1930s—a mysterious superman!

The Shadow Strikes

The Liberation Front, headed by Istvan Papescu, has been helping refugees from around the world to flee their countries and come to America. Some of the refugees are innocent, but others have a past to hide. Those hiding in fear are being blackmailed by Papescu. But he knows how far to push them, and how much they can afford to pay.

When three of the refugees commit suicide it throws light on the Liberation Front, and brings The Shadow into the investigation. It appears the refugees are being blackmailed by someone other than the Liberation Front. The Shadow has an agent trailing a suspect, Anton Pavlic, who is murdered in the town

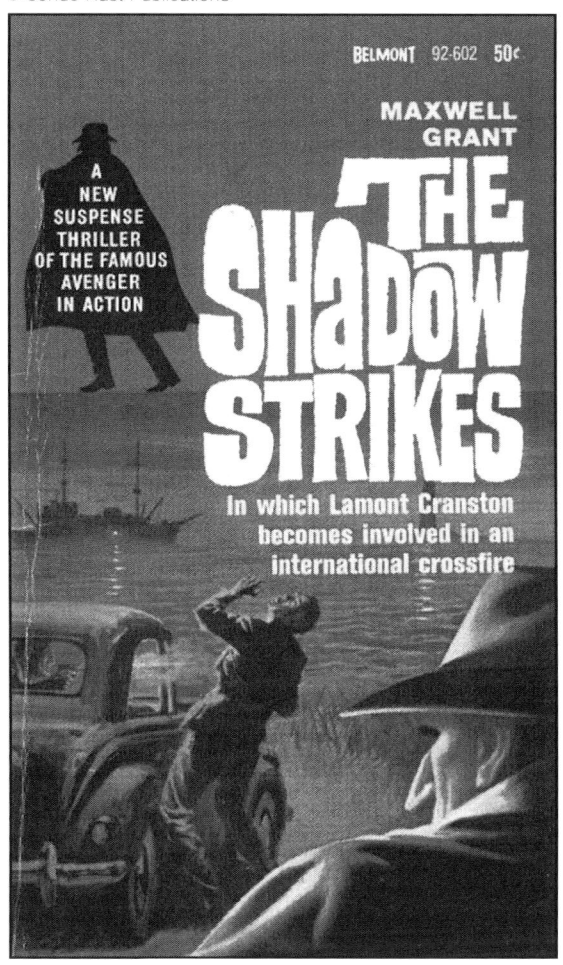

The Shadow Strikes, October 1964.

of Sea Gate.

The Shadow then moves his investigation to Sea Gate, where he finds a lot amiss, including Fred Morgan, a sergeant on the Sea Gate police force, who appears to be accepting payoffs to allow an illegal gambling syndicate to operate. Plus, the town appears to be populated by many of the refugees whom the Liberation Front has helped, and they are working in the gambling casino.

The Shadow learns that Pavlic had been the second blackmailer, and was killed by his partner/lover, Shirley Anders, the daughter of one of the refugees.

In the novel, The Shadow uses the alter egos of Lamont Cranston, Kent Allard and Phineas Twambley. His agents are Margo Lane, Burbank, Shrevvy, Clyde Burke and, now a full-fledged agent, Stanley (his one-time chauffeur).

Also investigating the case is Ralph Weston and Joe Cardona (both of whom seem to have jurisdiction outside of New York City). An FBI agent, Paul Altman, is also assigned to the case but is killed while in Sea Gate.

This novel was the first by Dennis Lynds, and was certainly an exciting story. And he becomes the fifth Maxwell Grant, as these novels bare the old house name.

Shadow Beware

In the next novel, Ralph Weston is called to London to identify a man identified as George Paulson, a Peace Corps supervisor who had been found dead under mysterious circumstances in a London alley, when he was supposed to be at his post in New Guinea. Paulson had formerly been with the New York City Police Force; and Weston was a member of the Peace Corps Board in New York City.

Weston brings his friend, Lamont Cranston with him to London, and there The Shadow takes over the investigation. The case leads The Shadow from London to Paris, Scotland and New Guinea, while using his major alter egos of Lamont Cranston, Kent Allard and Phineas Twambley.

The Shadow learns that Paulson was in reality an agent of the CIA, and was in New Guinea investigating the world-wide hijacking of medicine to underdeveloped countries, and the switching of plain aspirin in the place of more needed medicines. It was a multi-million dollar operation in which only the poor would suffer.

The Shadow trails Jasper Lorring, the head of the worldwide shipping organization, to Scotland where he uncovers the whole plot. He learns that Paulson had found a clue in New Guinea, leading to Jasper. He had left for London to contact his superior, Jeff Byrd, but learned too late that his contact and superior was in with the hijackers. Thus, he was killed when he met with Jeff Byrd in London.

Working closely on the case in London is Rufus Jones, a Scotland Yard CID agent, and Inspector Mong. An Interpol agent, Luigi Nenni, is also investigating for Interpol.

The Shadow's agents include Burbank in New York, with Margo Lane, Stanley, and Bombardier Bill Mace, agent-in-place, London. Plus, The Shadow, as Kent Allard, uses an old bush pilot, Max Halandann, to fly him into the jungles of New Guinea. Max is mentioned as being a friend of Kent Allard's.

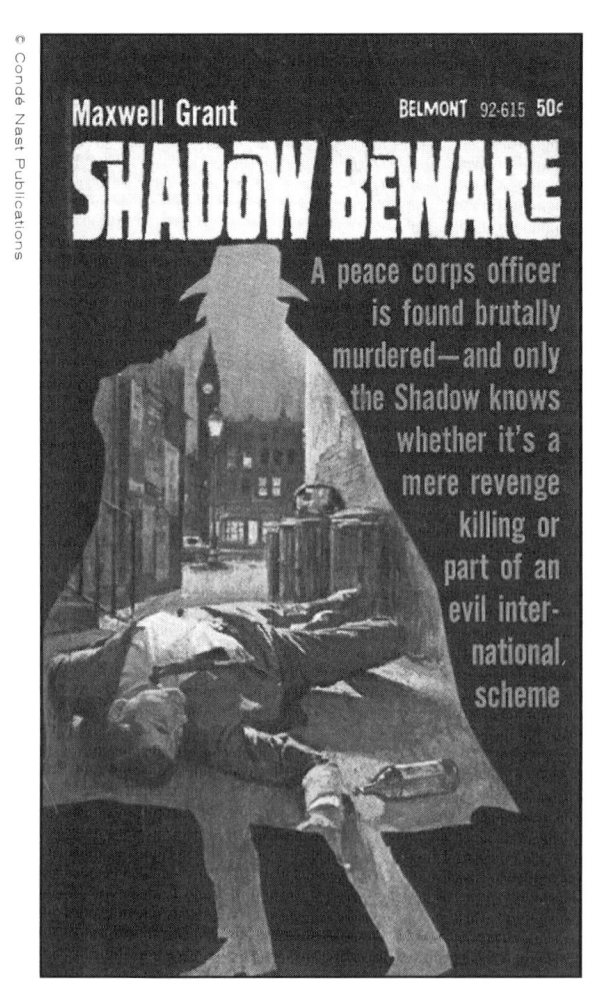

Shadow Beware, January 1965.

Cry Shadow!, April 1965.

Cry Shadow!

Strange art thefts leads The Shadow to investigate two minor crooks, Pedro Mingo and Morris Kitt. The Shadow spoils a robbery by the crooks, but Kitt is killed while being questioned by The Shadow. This leads The Shadow to believe that the plot is deeper than the mere thefts the valueless artwork would imply.

Hearing of a mysterious killer called Kolchov, The Shadow investigates deeper into the mystery and finds a worldwide ring of counterfeiters operating through an art gallery ran by Hubert and Avis Adrian.

The Shadow is captured, drugged, and his iden-

146   ECHOES 30: THREE DECADES OF PULP FANDOM'S GREATEST MAGAZINE

tity is disclosed to the gang as Lamont Cranston. He is sent to a watery death near Martha's Vineyard, in Edgartown, MA, but escapes after fighting to the death with a Tiger Shark, and is rescued by a salty old sea captain named Sulu Sea Calin.

The Shadow drops the Cranston identity for that of Henry Arnaud. With his private secretary Ellen Morgan (Margo Lane), he arrives in Edgartown to question old Gideon Coffin. Coffin owns an old castle where he maintains printing presses, and The Shadow soon learns that this is where the gang has been operating. But Coffin is merely a dupe, being used by his niece, Penelope Drake, who is actually the mysterious killer, Kolchov.

Ralph Weston and Joe Cardona are investigating the case, along with a T-Man named Ralston. The Shadow's agents are Burbank, Moe Shrevnitz and Margo Lane.

The Shadow's Revenge

Gerald Vickers, a missionary stationed in Africa, is killed under mysterious circumstances during what seemed to be a raid on the village where he was living. He was able to get a short-wave radio message through to the authorities. The short message was—"The Demon Flies…."

Lamont Cranston is contacted by his friend Ralph Weston, in New York, and requested to attend a meeting with Kurt Rhorback, an Interpol agent. At the meeting Lamont Cranston learns of the mysterious death of Vickers. The Interpol agent asks Cranston to go to Africa to learn more about the mysterious death, as well as the strange raid on the village.

The Shadow sends Bombardier Bill Mace to Africa as a soldier, to spy on the military authorities. With his chauffeur Stanley, and private secretary Margo Lane, Lamont Cranston travels to Africa to investigate personally. He learns of the government unrest in Africa, and of a mystery surrounding the forbidden area of the Kanda Tract, a region of jungle where a safari, years previously, had all died of jungle fever.

The Shadow's Revenge, October 1965.

And Vickers' village had been on the edge of the forbidden Kanda Tract.

In a village that acts as the area headquarters for the military, The Shadow meets Colonel Mnera, the regional government official; Doctor James Arthur who has been doing medical research for many years in Africa, and Angus McNair, the man who had led that ill-fated safari into the Kanda Tract years ago. During an evening discussion the men are attacked by an Israeli assassin squad, consisting of two men and three women. The raiders had wanted Angus McNair for questioning, but The Shadow foils their attack. Later the Israeli team does capture Kent

Allard, fingerprints him and then releases him after some questioning.

Later, The Shadow (as Lamont Cranston) joins Maria Berger, the leader of the Israeli commandos, and together they enter the Kanda Tract. Maria Berger explains that her team is searching for a Nazi war criminal that disappeared years ago.

Deep within the Kanda Tract they find a mysterious army training for world conquest under the leadership of ex-Nazi soldiers who plan to bring back the Third Reich.

The Shadow destroys the group and uncovers Doctor James Arthur as the German war criminal whom the Israeli war team had been searching for. He also learns that Vickers had escaped the night his village was raided, but was killed later when he contacted James Arthur and told him of the flying demon, which had turned out to be a one-man helicopter that was being used to scare the natives around the Kanda Tract. Also, the safari which was presumed to have died from jungle fever, were really Arthur's Nazi soldiers—or cadre—who were intended to disappear in order to begin training for world conquest once more.

Mark of The Shadow

A crime waves strikes Santa Carla, which brings a crime commission into being. The commission consists of Ralph Weston, his aid Lamont Cranston, Gerald Symes, Morgan Slater, Samuel Bauermann, with Walter Bedsole Bailey and his aid Allen Richards. All evidence leads the investigators to believe that the Mafia is behind the crime wave, but The Shadow is not satisfied. The Shadow believes that the Mafia of Santa Carla are merely dupes, being conveniently blamed for the crimes by another hidden organization—an organization as powerful as the Brotherhood of the Cosa Nostra, themselves.

The Shadow uncovers an organization called Cypher, and is captured by Allen Richards, whom he learns is actually a woman with extraordinary powers,

Mark of The Shadow, May 1965.

able to assume any identity at will—powers almost equal to that of The Shadow. Allen/Miriam Richards had studied under a student of the Master (Chen T'a Tze, who had taught The Shadow and trained him in his strange powers) and thought herself more powerful than even The Shadow.

The Shadow, as Lamont Cranston, and Margo lane while in the captivity of Cypher are taken to Mexico, a regional Cypher headquarters. Here, The Shadow destroys the headquarters, rescues Margo Lane, and steals a plane in which to return to Santa Carla.

Back in Santa Carla, The Shadow discovers that the mastermind is Walter Bailey, who had hopes of

Shadow—Go Mad, September 1966.

becoming governor after he had supposedly destroyed the Mafia with the help of Cypher. Cypher itself is just an organization, which hires itself out to anyone that can pay their price for services.

In a final confrontation between The Shadow and Miriam Richards, a battle of minds is fought high above the streets of Santa Carla, and the Richards woman discovers that she is no match for the powerful being facing her. For The Shadow has all of the powers of the Master, given to him by the Master himself. The Richards woman had only been instructed by a student of Chen T'a Tze, who did not have all the powers. The girl loses and falls to her death from the top of a high building.

Harry Vincent, Margo Lane, and Stanley assist The Shadow in this case. Burbank, as always, remains in New York, within the secret sanctum of The Shadow.

Shadow—Go Mad

Berlin, Paris, New York! Strange assassinations, robberies and incidents involving every country happen all over the world. In Vietnam a team of US Army Green Berets suddenly surrender to the Viet Cong, who they had already defeated. A man kills another in the streets. He is captured. He does not remember the killing, and did not know the man he had killed, and had no motive. A young man robs an old woman for a few dollars. He is captured—and remembers nothing! He is employed, with a savings account of several thousand dollars. He had never been in trouble before and did not need the few dollars he had taken from the old woman's purse.

What is the reasoning behind all of these senseless murders and robberies? The Shadow, too, wants this question answered. He begins his own investigation, bringing his crime fighting organization into the case. While in New York he, as Lamont Cranston, is assisting Ralph Weston, Joe Cardona, Erskine Parker of the FBI, and Mr. Hawkins of Interpol. At the same time Harry Vincent, Stanley, Moe Shrevnitz, and Burbank are carrying out their own investigation. Bombardier Bill Mace is on the job in Great Britain, and Marcel Guyot, a French taxi driver, and agent of The Shadow, is investigating in Paris.

A clue leads The Shadow, as Lamont Cranston, and Margo lane, as Ellen Morgan, to Paris where they capture Jary DuNeuf, an activist who had been spotted at several of the strange incidents. Jary DuNeuf is killed by agents of Cypher wearing flying belts before he discloses the reasons behind the strange events. But The Shadow learns of a secret meeting of Cypher leaders in Hong Kong, and is now aware of their involvement.

The Shadow attends the meeting and learns that this evil organization has developed X-2, a machine that acts as a movie camera-gun. The camera can project instructions into the mind of an innocent bystander to do whatever has been programmed into the gun. Cypher has this new weapon up for bids to any country that wants it—for the highest price, of course. The senseless murders and robberies are now explained—they had merely been simple field demonstrations. Men like Jary DuNeuf had been used to plant weapons near the scene of the demonstration, where the victim could obtain his instrument of death when needed. Anyone at the scene could then be picked.

Final bids for the weapon are to be taken in a mountainous region of California. The Shadow attends the meeting and turns this super weapon upon its own investors, and those that would bid for its ownership. Another of Cypher's campaigns and headquarters is destroyed.

The Night of The Shadow

Beginning like a Doc Savage novel from the 1930s, a dying man staggers into the corridor leading to the New York offices of Lamont Cranston's Park Avenue headquarters, closely trailed by three Malaysian killers. The Shadow intervenes, and captures the leader of the killers, but the dying man only speaks in gibberish and is unable to talk before he dies. The captured Malaysian can furnish no information for The Shadow, so he is released and trailed to his contacts by The Shadow.

The dead man's identity reveals his connection to a chemical corporation, and this clue takes The Shadow to Singapore, Rio de Janeiro and Brazil. Here The Shadow learns of operation "Windwar." A code name for a scheme to blackmail the whole world into slavery. Windwar is headed by an ex-Nazi German agricultural expert named Rudolf Mannheim. Doctor Mannheim has created a fungus that can be sent anywhere, riding the wind to lay waste to agricul-

The Night of The Shadow, November 1966.

tural lands everywhere.

The masterminds of Windwar plan to demonstrate its power by laying waste to the vast lands of the Jarro country of Brazil. Here, in a dramatic scene, The Shadow rises from the river as a water demon to fight the mighty "Red God" of the Jarro Indians. Doctor Mannheim wears the red robes of the natives' Red God, and uses magic to frighten their primitive minds. But the magic of the Red God cannot equal the power of The Shadow, and the savage natives turn on their Red God and his men.

Doctor Mannheim escapes from The Shadow, but while swimming to a waiting seaplane, bleeding from the wound of a Jarro spear, the water begins to boil. His bleeding wound has attracted the deadly little piranha fish, a cannibal fish that can devour a grown man within seconds.

Burbank, Stanley, Moe Shrevnitz, Harry Vincent, and Margo Lane assist The Shadow in this case, plus another agent is introduced to the series: He is Colonel Wilfred Price-Jones, working out of Singapore.

Destination: Moon

Project Full Moon, America's bid in the race for the moon, is being sabotaged. Ralph Weston is called to the NASA base in Utah to assist in the investigation. Lamont Cranston is also asked to assist, as his organization is a supplier of parts for the project at the NASA base.

The Shadow witnesses the latest rocket launch in which three American astronauts are killed when the rocket is aborted and explodes. He begins investigating another supplier, J. Wesley Bryan, and learns that Bryan is also being investigated by the Russians. The Shadow learns that the Russian project is also being sabotaged. A clue leads his investigating team to Bryan's laboratory in Idaho. There he finds Bryan's plant well guarded by civilian guards with military efficiency.

The Shadow, as Lamont Cranston, and his agents, Stanley, Harry Vincent, and Margo Lane are captured by—Cypher! This time The Shadow faces the head of the organization; a tall man wearing a golden mask. Lamont Cranston and his agents are court-martialed by Cypher, found guilty of spying and interfering with Cypher campaigns. They are sentenced to die by firing squad.

However, they escape with the aid of The Shadow's power, and learn of Cypher's own moon project. For here, in a hidden valley in Idaho, is another rocket ship, which has been built by J. Wesley Bryan. It is ready for launch, manned by Cypher's own astronauts. The Shadow learns that Bryan had hired Cypher to

Destination: Moon, March 1967.

aid him in his project. Cypher had agreed—for a price, plus they wanted their own men in charge of the moon. The Shadow destroys Bryan's rocket, and Bryan is killed. The leader if Cypher is unmasked by The Shadow and turns out to be General Calvin Rogers, personal aide of the President of the United States of America.

This third and final encounter with Cypher seems to have destroyed the evil organization. But, alas, it is also the final story in the Belmont Shadow series. Why the series was canceled is not known. Dennis Lynds had written an outline for another story, but it was not used—as a Shadow story. It appeared later in Award Books as a "Nick Carter—Killmaster" story in 1976, re-titled, *Triple Cross.*

During the time Dennis Lynds was writing the adventures of The Shadow for Belmont Books, he was also writing the *Man From UNCLE* magazine stories, and the *Mike Shayne* magazine stories for Leo Margulies' Renown publications, as well as his own paperback novels.

But, be that as it may, *Destination Moon* was a fantastic story, as was the Belmont Book series. That it ends here leaves the question, was this the end of Cypher? Evidently it was, at least in that incarnation. But I for one would love to see another story of The Shadow by Dennis Lynds, and the return of Cypher!

The Belmont Shadow

New background information is revealed on The Shadow within the pages of the Belmont series. True, it is information on a new Shadow, as created by Dennis Lynds, and not from Walter Gibson. At least Dennis Lynds was not afraid to add new information on an already long history of a character, which began in the Thirties. And we do find out a lot within a relatively few stories.

We learn that Dennis Lynds' Shadow had been a pupil many years ago of a man known as the Master, Chen T'a Tze. The Shadow was in Tibet when he studied under the Master, and it took many years to master the powers of this Oriental teacher.

Chen T'a Tze passed on all of his powers to The Shadow before his death, including the black cloak, black slouch hat, and the fire opal girasol ring. All of which were needed to enable The Shadow to cloud men's minds. This power was granted to only one man in each generation, and the Master had chosen The Shadow to carry on with this incredible responsibility.

The true identity of The Shadow is now said to be unknown. Only two men actually knew his real identity; one was the Master, now dead. The other was The Shadow himself. But now it did not matter who he had been, for The Shadow was now his true self, his past identity is dead, like the Master. However, The Shadow uses several alter egos. These are Lamont Cranston—his major alter ego, Kent Allard, Henry Arnaud, and Phineas Twambley. All of them have the super hearing and super eyesight, plus the muscular power and control of The Shadow. They have all of The Shadow's super powers, but one—that of clouding men's minds. The Shadow had to be The Shadow, with black cloak, black slouch hat, and fire opal girasol ring, in order to cloud the minds of men. About the only thing that wasn't taught to The Shadow by the Master was the art of safecracking; this was taught to him by Walter Pettibone *(Cry Shadow).*

The alter egos were built up and maintained by The Shadow at all times, as he never knew when he might be forced to drop one disguise and assume another. So he built up the reputation of each one, so that they would be known around the world: Lamont Cranston was a wealthy socialite and international businessman known the world over. He was also a close friend and aide of Police Commissioner Ralph Weston of New York City. Cranston had been a colonel with the OSS *(Cry Shadow)*, and had once been slipped into Japan, on a PT-boat, on a mission during World War II. This background is probably the reason that Weston enlists his aid so often. About his only distinctive features were the hawk nose, graying blond hair, and passive personality that he presented to the world. Plus, he had once been a boxer *(The Shadow Strikes).*

Kent Allard was the real identity of Walter Gibson's Shadow. In the original pulp stories, The Shadow often used the identity of a real Lamont Cranston, who was usually off globetrotting. But now, Kent Allard is just another alter ego, like that of Cranston. He is a famous explorer and adventurer (in the pulp stories he was a famous aviator). He limps from an old wound, which he received while exploring the High Himalayas and was attacked by a tiger. He has a broad nose, with dark hair combed straight back without a part, and has a mustache. The part of Kent Allard requires a disguise.

Phineas Twambley is an old man, and must use a walking cane. He is said to be worth 12 million dollars *(The Shadow Strikes)*. Curiously enough, Phineas resembles another character from the pulps, that of Elisha Pond, an alter ego of Secret Agent "X."

Henry Arnaud is taller than Cranston, with a broad and broken nose, the result of his early career in boxing. He also has a false, metal hand.

The power of The Shadow's mind can raise or lower his body temperature to offset the cold or heat *(Shadow Beware)*. He can open electrical circuits and locks merely by using his mind *(Shadow Beware)*. He can alter the lines and shape of his face by mere will power, or mind control *(Mark of The Shadow)*. The powerful resistance of his body can throw off the effects of drugs and poison, if he knows in time *(Shadow—Go Mad)*. The electrical engines of planes or helicopters can be stopped in the air by The Shadow's powerful mind *(Mark of The Shadow)*. The Shadow also mastered the art of shallow breathing from the Master. He can imitate death by slowing his heartbeat to almost nothing, and force his body to become rigid as in death.

Dennis Lynds kept the feel of The Shadow radio drama in his stories. He now uses parables when talking with the crooks: The Weed of Crime Bears Bitter Fruit. Evil Begets Evil and Dies of its Own Horror. Rot That Lives in the Shadows of Good, and Dies By the Same Shadows! He tells them that he is the Avenger of all evil, and he rights all wrongs. His life is dedicated to this end.

In Lamont Cranston's private offices, located on Park Avenue in the Fifties, behind a bookcase, is a hidden room not on any building charts. This is The Shadow's secret sanctum, the Blue Room. The room's location is only known to The Shadow's secret agents, and has never been entered forcibly by an enemy. This room is the headquarters of The Shadow and is manned By Burbank at all times. All of the agents' reports come into this sanctum in the form of tapes and are stored for future references. Within the room

Examples of Dennis Lynds' paperback output.

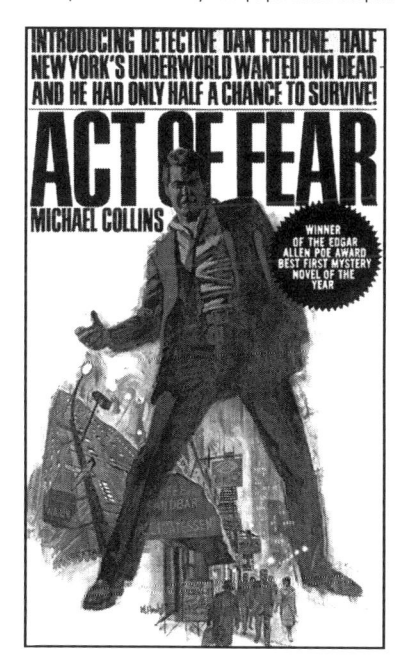

a deep bluish light glowed from an unknown source. Within the room was a long instrument half hidden in the bluish glow. The Shadow entered the hidden room and reached his long hand toward the silent instrument, and the fiery girasol glowed brightly on his finger. Without being touched, the machine began to hum and a face appeared on a screen in the center of the instrument, the face of an agent in another room, like this one, only thousands of miles away. In at least one major city of every country The Shadow maintained one of these hidden rooms with a similar communication system. He has instant contact with his far-flung crime fighting organization. All reports are made on micro-recorders, and then filed at the headquarters called Control Central.

All of The Shadow's agents wear a replica of the fire opal girasol ring. These rings can activate the organization's communication equipment. When The Shadow wants a secret contact with one of his agents, he merely rubs his own ring and the ring of his agent will glow as if it had a small light bulb inside.

With his powerful short wave radio set The Shadow can contact Burbank in New York from London. This radio is operated on a secret wavelength that is impossible to intercept.

Though Cranston's limousine is a long black Rolls Royce, when alone prefers to drive his small sports cars. He owns at least two—a small, black, custom-built Jaguar with a super-charged engine. A car telephone is installed for his many business ventures, plus for telephone contact with his agents. The car is also equipped with an electric eye system, which opens and shuts the garage door at his town house (this device seems out of place, as he should be able to work this electric door with the power of his mind alone). His second automobile is a small, powerful Austin-Healey, presumably with the same equipment as the Jaguar.

The Agents

Not only does The Shadow seem to have changed considerably from the 1930s, but so too have his agents to a certain degree.

Margo Lane is now Lamont Cranston's confidential secretary and helper. She is originally from Denver, Colorado. After leaving college and before meeting The Shadow, Margo had gone to the theater as an actress. This had brought her maturity and poise to go with her beauty, in addition to training her to assume the many disguises she uses to aid The Shadow *(The Shadow Strikes)*. When The Shadow must use the alter ego of Henry Arnaud, he takes his confidential secretary with him (another touch of reality for the character he portrays). In the guise of Ellen Morgan, Margo can fill the requirement as Henry Arnaud's private secretary and agent of The Shadow. She is The Shadow's number one agent, and carries a small, snub-nosed revolver under her skirt. Besides being an actress, make-up artist, and skilled intelligence agent, Margo can also read lips *(The Shadow: Destination Moon)*.

Stanley, who for so very long in the 1930s and 1940s was merely a chauffeur for the real Lamont Cranston, now becomes an actual agent of The Shadow. Though to all appearances he is still merely the private chauffeur/bodyguard of Lamont Cranston, he is really the number two agent in The Shadow's far-flung crime-fighting organization. Beneath his chauffeur regalia he carries an automatic, blackjack, and a complete set of picklocks. Besides his automatic, Stanley also keeps a .38 under the dashboard of the limousine, and another in the glove compartment. He is an ex-cop *(Shadow—Go Mad)* and a pilot *(The Shadow's Revenge)*. He is a Sixth Dan Black Belt expert of karate *(Shadow—Go Mad)*. Stanley was completely dedicated to his chief, as can be seen in *The Shadow: Destination Moon.*

> The Cypher Commandant's eyes turned to Stanley. "You, chauffeur! We can offer you far more than you appear to have. Who is the man in black?"
>
> "You can go to hell," Stanley said.

Harry Vincent changes very little, if any, with the switch of authors. In my personal opinion Mr. Lynds could have used Harry to better advantage, but he didn't. Now Harry acts more as an observer, and sees less action. He is even left out of a few stories. And, though Harry had been with The Shadow longer than any active agent, now he becomes merely the number three agent of The Shadow, being out-ranked by Margo Lane and Stanley, neither of which were actual agents in the original pulp stories.

With *Return of The Shadow,* many of the agents of the old made their last appearances; Rutledge Mann, Miles Crofton, Myra Reldon (my favorite of them all), Cliff Marsland and Clyde Burke (though Burke did make a small appearance in *The Shadow Strikes*.) However, Mr. Lynds did bring in a few new agents to add to the series:

Bombardier Bill Mace is a stocky man of average height with a broken nose that spread thick across his heavy-jawed face. His ears were thickened, and powerful muscles rippled beneath his clothing. He gave the appearance of a middleweight boxer grown inevitably too old for the ring. He had once held this title in England. The underworld and police knew him as a punch-drunk old battler, who stole, lied and cheated, and would gamble whenever there was a shilling in his pocket. He was a small-time hustler and vagabond like the other denizens of the London underworld. This was the reputation that he gave to the public—but he was not a punch-drunk, nor any of those things, for behind the battered face and shabby exterior was a keen mind, and the unimpaired skills of a professional boxer. In his army career he had reached the rank of Bombardier, and he was a man of purpose—he was an active agent of The Shadow! On the third finger of his right hand, a small fire opal ring seemed to glow when The Shadow was near. Bombardier Bill mace is officially agent number 109 of The Shadow's International crime-fighting organization.

Colonel Wilfred Price-Jones, VC, OBE, agent number 15 of The Shadow's organization. The Colonel was an ex-British Army, retired. He is a tall man, with a ramrod straight carriage, a thick mustache faded pale on his long upper lip. He has hard blue, piercing eyes, with a long scar on his left cheek. Price-Jones had not been an Army desk colonel in the service, but had seen action on many battlefields, and pinned to his lapel was the Victoria Cross. He was a decorated hero of his country.

Marcel Guyot was Moe Shrevnitz's counterpart in Paris. He was a French taxi driver, unequaled when it came to speeding through the back alleys of Paris. He was a trusted agent of The Shadow, but no official number was assigned to him (that is, recorded in those few issues from Belmont Books).

Besides the new agents of The Shadow, there were at least three other individuals introduced in the Belmont series that played minor roles. These were not agents, but more that of aides to either one, or all, of The Shadow's alter egos.

Madam DeLac was a hotel proprietor-concierge. She owned an apartment building on Rue St. Sulpice, Paris, where she maintained rooms for each of The Shadow's alter egos. These rooms were always available, at any time, should The Shadow come to France.

Joa da Cuhna is part-African, part-Portuguese, and over sixty years old, but he still stands as straight as a tree, and his muscled arms are as thick as branches. He is the caretaker of Kent Allard's base camp in Brazil.

Max Halandann is an old bush pilot whom Kent Allard has used many times to fly him into the jungles.

They are certainly an interesting crew to be added to the names of the many other agents, and associates of The Shadow. History is added to this great crime-fighter.

Cypher

Cypher—a secret organization. They work for a fee, and do not share in their client's profits or affairs. They do the work, fulfilling their contract and then leave. They do not blackmail or interfere with their clients after the service has been completed. They are hired for a service, and are contracted. They complete the account. Their services include murder, complete disposal of all evidence including the bodies. Kidnapping is another of their services. They will spy, assassinate or supply bodies to replace other bodies. They will supply any force a client needs, protect the client, eliminate his enemies, arrange any form of crime the client wants done without his participation or involvement. If required, Cypher can supply a squad or battle force. They have full facilities to offer all forms of violence in the service of a client.

Cypher will plan a complete campaign if the client

The Forgettable Shadow

After Belmont Books launched the new Shadow paperbacks in 1963, with "The Return of The Shadow" by Walter B. Gibson, Archie Comics (Belmont Books parent arm) began a series of 8 comic books featuring The Shadow as a super hero, running from August 1964 to September 1965. One look at the super hero costume turned me off, so I passed up the comic book series, and only learned of the 6000-word text story (not credited) that was included when I was contacted by Dennis Roy recently.

Dennis was kind enough to scan the text for me; it ran approximately one page per issue for the eight issues of the comic book, each segment ending in something like a cliffhanger. This meant that the beginning of each story recapped the ending of the last segment—in case the readers had forgotten what happened previously.

Basically, it's another origin story of The Shadow. Lamont Cranston's parents are killed in an accident, leaving him the Cranston business worth billions of dollars. Bored with life as a rich young man-about-town, playboy and business executive, Lamont leaves affairs of the business to his Financial Board, and heads for Egypt to find himself.

While in Egypt, Lamont discovers his power to control the minds of people and animals, and decides that this should be his true life's work. He departs for Greece, where he encounters an attack on a ship against a young man by ruffians; to protect his identity, he wraps a dark canvas tarp over his shoulders and intervenes, rescuing the young man. When asked his identity, he says, "I am The Shadow."

While in Greece, he again sees a man being assaulted by hoods, and steps in—as The Shadow. The man he saves is Weston; head of America's Secret Service. Weston is in Greece looking for a world menace. He is assisting an organization known as CHIEF (Command Headquarters, International Espionage Forces). Using mind control, The Shadow learns that the hoods are working for a man named Shiwan Khan. With this information, he prepares to depart, but Weston stops him.

"We need a man like you working with CHIEF," he tells The Shadow.

"I don't join others," The Shadow tells him. "But I have a friend, Lamont Cranston...."

Weston asks that Lamont Cranston come to his cabin the next day, but when he does the C.I.A. man is tied and gagged, and sitting calmly in the room is—Shiwan Khan.

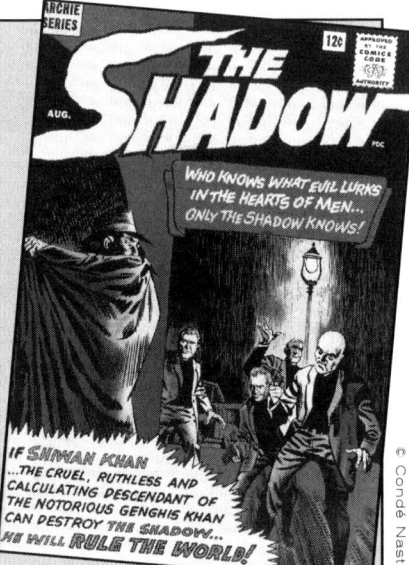

Unfortunately, this was the 8th chapter, and the story stops there. It wasn't a good story anyway, and quickly forgettable. Cranston was a champion boxer in college, a great athlete, and does laugh at least once. He never uses guns. He has 6 sets costumes made of silk by a Greek, who The Shadow hypnotizes into forgetting about making them. They are thin and compact, consisting of hood and cape, and can be folded small enough to fit in a pocket, like a handkerchief. He is still in Greece when the story stops suddenly.

supplies the ultimate result he desires. Efficiency is guaranteed, the fee is inclusive, no extras and no follow-up. Cypher!—Nothing! It is an organization of negation, an international violence for hire—an organization with no connection to either its clients or its victims, ruthless and efficient and completely organized. It is an agency of all violence—for a fee and no more.

Cypher is an efficient Army of well trained men: ex-Chinese Communist murder teams; American Special Forces misfits; ex-Smersh agents; Algerian terror team veterans; ex-Nazi soldiers; French officers disgusted with their weak leaders. The best—all trained, efficient! Soldiers that like their work. This is Cypher *(Mark of The Shadow)*.

Yes, Cypher was a military organization with many faces. Not belonging to any country, and responsible only to its leaders. Their uniforms are black coveralls with a round white circle, the badge of Cypher, on the chest of the uniforms. Each agent has a small destructive device implanted beneath the skin over their heart. This device will explode, killing the Cypher soldier if he is forced to reveal any information concerning Cypher or the client. Only the Cypher doctors can remove the device, as poison is released when it is removed, and Cypher alone has the antidote. The leaders of Cypher wear the same uniforms, except the tunics are grey, and the circle is gold instead of white.

The Shadow fought this evil organization in three adventures: *Mark of The Shadow*, *Shadow—Go Mad*, and *The Shadow: Destination Moon*. In each involvement it took the full, super powers of The Shadow to defeat this well-trained evil group. The most remarkable of the adventures was that which was recorded in *Mark of The Shadow*, in which The Shadow is opposed by the man/woman Allen/Miriam Richards. She is Group Leader 12, American Division of Cypher. She had studied under a student of the Master, Chen T'a Tze, and had powers similar (though not equal) to The Shadow. She had hypnotic ability, and was able to change her facial features at will, becoming a man or woman, whichever suited her present needs. She had once been a soldier of the Irgua Ha'n Avi, the feared Israeli killer-commando unit. In their final confrontation, the evil woman laughs evilly at The Shadow, thinking her powers are superior to his. But her will is not as strong as that of The Shadow, and her mere hypnotic powers are not equal to The Shadow's power to control the minds of men. She senses his power reaching into her mind and with a scream leaps backwards, to fall to her death many floors below in the streets of Santa Carla. The Shadow's laugh rings triumphantly out over the city of Santa Carla—a tribute to Walter Gibson's Shadow of the 1930s!

In The Shadow's final confrontation with Cypher, *Destination Moon*, he is challenged by the head of the organization, General Calvin Rogers, American aide and military advisor to the President of the United States. Rogers succeeded in capturing Lamont Cranston, Margo Lane, Harry Vincent, and Stanley. He wanted them to join his organization, but they had to tell him who The Shadow was. They refused, and in the end, knowing that he had lost his final battle with The Shadow, General Calvin Rogers took his own life. Thus ended the evil organization. Or did it? How nice it would be if Dennis Lynds would once again pick up pen and paper, and again pit The Shadow against this group for one more battle. I would read it with pleasure! (Unfortunately, Dennis Lynds passed away August 19th, 2005.)

When I first read the series, I did not know for sure that Dennis Lynds had written the Belmont Shadows after Walter Gibson had left the series, so made notes regarding the writing style in the stories hoping to identify the author later. After these many years, and with the knowledge that he had written the stories, it is fun looking back over the notes. Here are some of them:

A few final notes on the series: with the exception of *Return of The Shadow*, all of the remaining stories appear to have been written by the same author. The spelling of "gray" as "grey" appears in all of the stories; the spelling "yeh" is always the same except for one story, *Mark of The Shadow,* in which it appears as both "yeh" and "yeah"; similar to Ted Tinsley Shadow stories of the pulps, instead of a laugh, or a swift action at times, The Shadow merely commands the crooks to "stop!" In the early stories he is referred to as the "comic opera monster," and this is later replaced with "comic in black," or the "man in black"; with *Mark of The Shadow* and *Night of The Shadow,* sentences appear often in parenthesis, not common in the other stories; also, in the first two stories his fiery eyes are sometimes referred to as "the angry eyes of The Shadow." This was dropped in the later stories, but even with these few differences, I believe all of the stories were written by only one author; and my thanks to Will Murray for identifying that author as Dennis Lynds.

One last note on Cypher. As I have mentioned previously, Dennis Lynds was also writing the *Man From UNCLE* magazine stories at the time he was writing the Belmont novels, and the James Bond movies were a big rage, as well. It is no wonder then, that Mr. Lynds created an organization similar to Bond's SPECTRE, and *UNCLE's* THRUSH. And Cypher may have even been the most powerful of all the evil organizations that our heroes fought. An invisible Army, consisting of the best trained soldiers in the world, needing no authority from some local or national government, but responsible only to their own leaders. A super army.

Most of the Belmont series appear to have been based on the first story *Return of The Shadow,* or perhaps from notes that Walter Gibson may have given to Belmont or Dennis Lynds, when Gibson dropped out of the series. And Dennis did say that he was given some notes, though he did not really use them. And when references are made to a previous story, it is always to *The Shadow Strikes,* and the case of Anton Pavlic—the first story written by Dennis Lynds.

Some Final Thoughts

Perhaps the most that I miss from this Belmont Shadow series is The Shadow's swift entrance into an affray, his thundering automatics and, to a certain degree, his challenging laugh. No longer do we hear those thundering automatic coupled with his weird laughter as he challenges gangdom to do their best, as can be seen in this scene from Walter Gibson's "Death About Town" (July 15, 1942):

> That blackness gave an announcement of its approach in the form of a fierce, challenging laugh that impaled the men who heard it to swing in its direction. The sweeping mass materialized. It came like a living cloudburst, in the person of The Shadow! A cloudburst that delivered hail in the form of metal. Its lightning was the spurt of guns, its thunder their echoes. Sweeping in from the side passage, The Shadow was raking the lobby with bullets, and masked men were diving to escape his fury. Their own guns answering frantically, were too hurried even to annoy the intrepid fighter, whose attack had all the power and motion of a cyclone!

Such a play on words was a trademark for Walter B. Gibson. He was an expert when it came to creating scenes of action for The Shadow. But this is not to belittle the Shadow series by Dennis Lynds. He, too, was good with a fight scene, but his action consisted of more personal contact—that of hand to hand fighting, as can be seen with the September 1966 story, *Shadow—Go Mad!*

> Cranston moved. He was off the table in an instant. With each hand he chopped killing blows to the necks of the smaller Chinese and the Gestapo man. The smaller Chinese went down without a sound, his neck snapped instantly by the force of the Karate blow. The Gestapo man turned a hair as Cranston struck. The Gestapo man went down but he was not dead. The Negro Moroccan

half-turned to meet Cranston. The heel of Cranston's hand caught him beneath his chin. The Negro's neck snapped with a sickening sound and he dropped dead to the floor. The Chinese would have had a second to prepare, but when he turned and saw Cranston—alive and on his feet—the instant of shock paralyzed him. It cost him his life. Cranston struck the point of his hand into the solar plexus of the Chinese, and chopped his exposed neck as the Chinaman doubled over. Behind Cranston the Gestapo man moaned and half rose to his feet. Cranston broke his neck with a single blow.

What action! What fight scenes! It was enough to whet the appetite of any James Bond fan. Yes, The Shadow had come up from a crime-fighter of the 1930s to a superman of the 1960s. Thank you Walter Gibson, and thank you, too, Dennis Lynds. You are both a part of the history of the mighty avenger, The Shadow.

Code Name: Miriam

Whenever I research a series, or read them for fun, one thing I always look for—in any series—is a deadly female! Many of you who are familiar with my research into the Secret Agent "X" series, will remember the many vamps I uncovered from that series. Well, there happened to be such a woman in the Belmont Books Shadow series. We've already mentioned her, but I thought it would be appropriate to write a profile on her, too. This profile originally appeared in the legendary magazine, *Nemesis, Inc.* #18, back in September 1984. Here, then, is Miriam Richards:

She wore many faces—none of them her own. Trained by a student of a Tibetan Master who knew forgotten secrets of the mind, her powers were too great against normal men.

Her past was really no secret: She had once been a soldier—the secret mark of the Irgun Ha'n Zvi was on her left arm—the feared Israeli killer-commando unit. She had killed four Arabs after the war was over, which resulted in her discharge from the military. But she found another army to serve. One that was made up of soldiers from every country—soldiers that were killers, good at their work, and who were disgusted with their weak leaders.

She was… little more than a girl. Perhaps twenty, no more. Tall, slender, magnificently curved in the tight green dress. Long dark hair, a perfect nose, full lips and a face that would have done credit to any contest of female beauty. A face that could only be termed beautiful, and yet…the lips, at the corners, had a curve of cruelty. Her body was coiled and tense like some cunning and dangerous predator. Catlike, and with all the hidden muscles of the cat. And the eyes! Her eyes were cold, flat, hard and very quick—burning eyes! The power of the woman's mind was that of a very powerful hypnotist!

She was…Allen Richards, a well-known private detective; a small compact, slender man who had built his agency from a one-man operation into a powerful organization of trained investigators that operated nation-wide.

She was… both! The detective agency was a front. Her real organization was a group known as Cypher—a secret organization. She was Miriam Richards, Group Leader 12. Her uniform was black, slim and efficient coveralls with the round white circle that was the badge of Cypher on the chest of her tunic, and her rank was prominent on her shoulders.

In the story, "Mark of The Shadow," a crime wave had hit Santa Carla—without rhyme or reason people are murdered on the streets. The mafia is blamed. A crime commission is organized to end the battle. From New York City, Commissioner Ralph Weston is called in to head the crime commission. With him he brings Lamont Cranston as his aide to assist in the detective work.

The story was credited to Maxwell Grant (in this case, Dennis Lynds), published by Belmont Books in May 1966. Mr. Lynds weaves a tale of action and suspense as the plot unravels in this outstanding novel featuring The Shadow as a superman of right against this new evil of Cypher.

At the time Dennis Lynds wrote this novel, he was also involved with the *Mike Shayne* magazine novelettes, as well as the Man From UNCLE stories in the magazine of that title. The UNCLE organization was involved in fighting THRUSH, a worldwide organization of evil. Calling upon his familiarity with THRUSH, Mr. Lynds created Cypher to oppose The Shadow. *Mark of The Shadow* was the first story to feature this evil organization—and Miriam Richards would be his most dangerous foe.

Miriam Richards had studied under a student of the Master, Chen T'a Tze, and had abilities similar to those of The Shadow, himself. But The Shadow had been a pupil of the Master, and with the death of Chen T'a Tze, all knowledge and power was passed on to him. Miriam Richards had thought herself an equal, or superior to The Shadow. She was neither.

But her powers were magnificent:

> There was no time even for The Shadow to reach her. But in the flash of time in which he saw the object pointed up, he realized two things: the woman had heard him, and heard him an instant before he laughed, or she could not have acted so swiftly; and the woman could see him now, clearly, completely, despite the dimness of the office and the black garb that blended with the dark of the room. (Page 45)

And then on page 46:

> But he had been stopped for a matter of ten to fifteen seconds. It was enough for the woman. As The Shadow glided swiftly through the dissipating cloud of gas he saw that the woman was gone. The single window was open. There was no other way from the room except the door The Shadow had been standing in front of. The cloaked crime-fighter floated through the small office to the window. His burning eyes looked down into the alley clear as day in the dark night. The alley was two stories below. It was empty.

Cypher continues to operate in Santa Carla. The Mafia is still blamed. Still, The Shadow has not uncovered this hidden group. Though he has identified Allen Richards as being involved, he has not connected the girl with him. He allows Allen Richards to capture Lamont Cranston and Margo lane. In chapter 15, The Shadow learns of the dual identity, and watches as Allen, the man, turns into Miriam, the woman, before their eyes. Miriam was able to control her facial muscles and become a man, a woman, young or old, but her sex she could not change, except through clothes. She laughs, boasts of her power, and claims the ability to cloud the minds of men.

Then on page 131:

> The woman's eyes blazed, burned, and stared straight at Margo. For an instant Cranston felt suddenly as cold as ice. Was it possible? Had Chen T'a Tze given his ultimate power to some other person as well as The Shadow? Cranston looked at Margo. The dark-haired girl had gone rigid, her eyes blank. Then Margo seemed to relax, become limp, and stood there with her eyes staring at nothing.
>
> The woman's eyes blazed again and she stared straight into the eyes of Cranston. Cranston stood and his hooded eyes opened and burned in return. Within a moment he smiled deep inside, although his impassive face showed nothing. The power of the woman's mind was that of a remarkable hypnotist, but only that. She would be no match for the full power The Shadow!

Cranston pretends to be under her mind control, and allows the woman to take him and Margo to the hidden command base for the American sector. Here Cranston becomes The Shadow and penetrates to the chambers of the Area Leader of Cypher. There he takes control of the leader's mind and forces him to reveal information about Cypher. During the interrogation the Area Leader is killed by a bomb imbedded in the skin over his heart. An alarm is sounded and The Shadow races to rescue Margo Lane. They escape, and the Cypher headquarters is destroyed.

Upon returning to Santa Carla, The Shadow unveils the "client" and is forcing him to talk when Miriam Richards shoots the client in order to stop him from revealing their activities—she had returned to Santa Carla, not knowing of the destruction of her headquarters, and the escape of Lamont Cranston and Margo Lane.

Miriam Richards, alias Allen Richards, alias a thousand shapes and faces, alias Group Leader 12, Cypher Command, faced The Shadow in the deepening twilight:

> "So, we meet again," the woman said. The eyes of The Shadow blazed. "We do, Miriam Richards!"
>
> "Group Leader 12, Cypher Command!" the woman snapped. "And you?"
>
> "I am called The Shadow. I destroy all evil."
>
> The woman laughed. "No, I think not, Shadow. Perhaps you can frighten fools, but not me."
>
> The beautiful woman's eyes blazed out. The power of her eyes, and her skill and training, bored into the fiery eyes of The Shadow.
>
> The Shadow laughed his wild, eerie laugh.
>
> The woman seemed to shiver, to gather all her will, to concentrate on the great black figure before her on the silent roof. The Shadow laughed again, and his voice was mocking in the twilight above the city.
>
> "You know of the Master, Chen T'a Tze," The Shadow said softly as his eyes burned into the woman. "Then you know of his ultimate power!"
>
> For one instant the eyes of the woman flared in a final effort, but the shape of The Shadow mocked her, and then she seemed to stagger. She seemed to hear the words of The Shadow.
>
> "The ultimate… power!" she said, gasped. "Then you…"
>
> Fear appeared in the eyes of the beautiful woman. Perhaps the first fear she had ever felt. The power of The Shadow reached out now like long, soft fingers entering her mind. Thin soft fingers with the strength of steel that reached to grip and cloud her reeling mind.
>
> With a sudden, final effort, she hurled herself backward and over the edge.
>
> She fell to the street ten stories below without a scream or a sound.
>
> On the roof The Shadow glided to the edge and looked over. Below people were running toward her smashed form.

The Shadow's final laugh of revenge floated out over the darkening city.

The crime wave in Santa Carla was over. Cypher had been defeated in their first battle with The Shadow. But they would be back, again and again—always to meet defeat when they encountered the Dark Avenger. And that was to be expected, as there was no power they could muster that could stop the mighty avenger. But never again would they have an agent quite like Miriam Richards. She was unique, powerful, and a competent foe to match powers with The Shadow.

She will be remembered in the annals of crime as the woman who feared… shadows!

The Nick Carter Stories

Dennis mentioned that *Triple Cross*, a Nick Carter—Killmaster novel from Award Books was from an outline for the tenth Shadow planned for Belmont. But since I never cared for the Killmaster series, I put off reading the novel until 2008. Actually, I had tried reading some of the early Killmaster stories, but just couldn't get into them. They had tried to capture the James Bond mystique of the period, but filled the books with so much sex, they were little more than teenage erotica for young boys. The sex was something only a thirteen year-old boy, who had never experienced a sexual encounter, could imagine. It was completely unrealistic. The series touted, "20,000,000

Books in Print!" And all I could imagine were 20,000,000 thirteen year-old boys reading these things. Kind of like the kung fu craze with The Destroyer, where the hero could jump off a building's roof and land cat-like on the sidewalk thirty floors below—safely. I did read the Destroyer stories by Will Murray, but that was because he talked me into it. I passed up the other stories in the series. In both the Destroyer and Killmaster series, a warning should be put in the books—"Don't try this at home!" And I refer to the sex in Killmaster and the jumping off thirty floor roofs in the Destroyer!

Out of curiosity, I finally broke down and read the Killmaster stories by Dennis Lynds. I knew Dennis had intimated that *Triple Cross* was from a Shadow outline, but what about the other two: *The N3 Conspiracy,* and *The Green Wolf Connection?* I figured it was about time I checked all three stories for their plots.

We begin with *The N3 Conspiracy* from 1974. I was amazed to find that this story appeared to be something of a sequel to *The Shadow's Revenge.* Nick Carter is sent to Africa to kill the leader of a possible uprising, but no one knows whom this leader is. So Nick is told to kill everyone! Well, there are three suspects, and he goes after them with deadly intent. But before he can kill them, he has sex, is captured, escapes, has sex, captured, escapes, over and over again, until the mature reader gets tired of all the incredible sex, captures and escapes. But I digress. We meet one of Nick's fellow agents, an ex-female Israeli commando named Deirdre Cabot, who reminded me a lot of Maria Berger from *The Shadow's Revenge.* And then a group of mercenaries, consisting of soldiers from many countries (shades of Cypher!) show up. Cypher wasn't in *The Shadow's Revenge,* but I'm sure that's what this group was originally supposed to be in this story. Supposedly, Deirdre Cabot is murdered, but I'll leave it there in case you haven't read the story.

Cypher usually works for a person, being hired for an assignment, from a simple murder to a full-out war. That is, in most cases. However, in *The Shadow: Destination Moon,* although Cypher had a contract, they were essentially working for itself. In this current case, the mercenaries (Cypher?) are working for Russia (but remember, there was supposedly a "leader" behind the scenes somewhere), and they wanted to get control of Africa.

Whether or not Dennis intended this plot as a Shadow in the beginning, it certainly conforms to his Belmont Shadows in the 1960s. With the exception of all the incredible sex. With so many captures and escapes, I was left wondering if maybe there had originally been others in the case (like The Shadow's agents) who were being captured, and had to be rescued.

Overall, this story was confusing, as if hurriedly written, and possibly based on a loose outline. But I have to admit it's the first Killmaster story I've ever read completely through. Perhaps, that's the way they all read. But I would like to think that just maybe, Dennis had wanted to use this plot as a Belmont Shadow. There is something about a "Sleeping Lion," so could have been the original title.

Next up is *The Green Wolf Connection* from 1976. In a novel that reads, at times like *The Shadow's Revenge,* and other times like *The Shadow: Destination Moon,* a small American oil company in the Middle East plans on world dominance. With a disgraced Green Beret colonel from the Vietnam War as security chief, he is building a private army of ex American soldiers to rise up and control the Middle East and all of its vast oil supply. This novel wasn't hurried, or confused. It was much tighter than *The N3 Connection,* but again employs the plot elements of the Belmont Shadows. There is plenty of incredible sex, to give those 20,000,000 teenage boys a lot of dreams.

The final story is *Triple Cross* from 1976, supposedly the plot for the tenth Belmont Shadow. But, again, this novel is a throwback to a Belmont Shadow: *Shadow Beware,* in which a hidden power, the Blood

Eagle is operating under the auspices of a Peace Organization. In this case, it is a fanatical group wishing to assassinate world leaders and bring peace to the world. Strangely, they wear large rings similar to The Shadow and his agents, but these rings flip open, showing a signet with an eagle with a snake in its mouth beneath the stone.

This novel was also very good, tight, and moved smoothly. All three stories had throwbacks to the Belmont Shadows, at least in reused plots. But they left me with a couple of questions. First, Dennis told me that *Triple Cross,* the third story, which appeared ten years after the final Shadow, was from an outline for the tenth Belmont Shadow. I don't doubt it, just curious as to why he didn't use the outline for the first Killmaster story he wrote? Why did it appear last? Two of the stories had definite plot connections to the Belmont Shadows, *The Green Wolf Connection* and *Triple Cross.* The first Killmaster story, *The N3 Conspiracy,* was more of a sequel than a mere throwback. Could it have been the true outline for the tenth Belmont Shadow, instead of *Triple Cross?* It was published in 1974, before *The Green Wolf Connection* and *Triple Cross.* Odd. Unfortunately, I never got around to asking Dennis about this. In later years, he returned to writing Nick Carter—Killmaster novels, but I've never read any of his later stories. I wouldn't be a bit surprised to learn that some of the old Belmont Shadow plots resurface now and then. I thoroughly enjoyed his Shadow novels, and the Killmaster stories would have been great, if all those required sex scenes had been left out. They were merely there to entice young readers. Thirteen-year-old boys, to be specific. The stuff was laughable.

Dennis returned ten years later with four more Killmaster novels, *The Master Assassin, Mercenary Mountain,* and *The Samurai Kill* all in 1986, and *Blood of the Falcon* in 1987. And then in 1989, he collaborated with his wife, Gayle Lynds on two Mack Bolan (The Executioner) novels, *Blood Fever* and *Moving Target.* There could well be others that I don't know about. I have not read any of these. But I would be curious about the plots. I was told by a reliable source that Dennis was churning out the Nick Carter novels

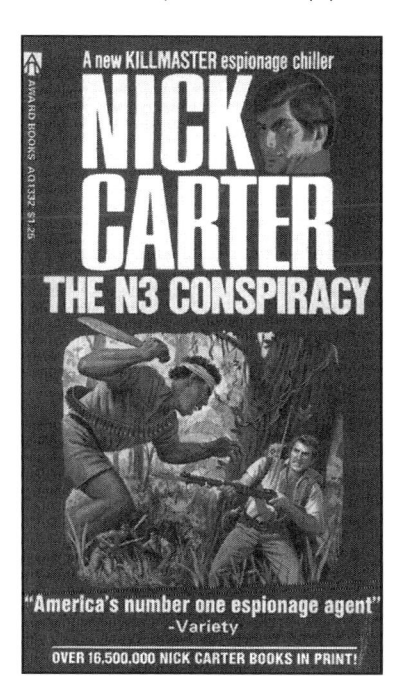

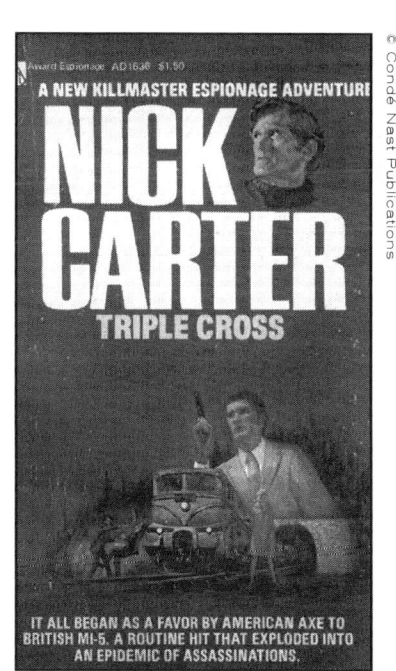

A trio of Dennis Lynds' Nick Carter paperbacks.

before they ceased. But I can't confirm this. I believe the series ended in 1990 or '91, with 260 or 261 novels published. I'm sure those thirteen-year-old boys have found something new to read by now.

The Story of Dennis Lynds

Dennis Lynds was born January 15, 1924 in St. Louis, Missouri, though he never really lived in that town. Upon his birth his parents moved to England for several years, then to New York, and finally to Hollywood, California in 1930. Later he moved to Denver for a while, then back to New York (Brooklyn) where he lived until he joined the US Army in 1943. Mr. Lynds served with the United States Army for three years, attached to the Infantry, the 12th Armored Division, in Europe. Dennis attended Brooklyn Technical High School, then the Cooper Union (night engineering), later Texas A&M, and finally Hofstra University for his B.A., and Syracuse University for his M.A.

After the war and his BA and MA, Mr. Lynds returned to New York (Manhattan) to live from 1951 to 1965. He had been writing fiction since his army days in World War II, and until 1962 wrote primarily short stories and poetry published in the literary quarterlies and the smaller literary magazines. (There were a few early "popular" stories in *Alfred Hitchcock Mystery Magazine* and *Amazing Stories*, but Mr. Lynds admits that he remembers neither the titles nor the name he wrote them under, except for one in *Amazing Stories* called "Test Rocket.") But he continued to write mostly literary short stories for such publications as *New World Writing, Hudson River, Epoch, Northwest Review, Minnesota Review*, etc., and in 1954 began to work on novels. To support himself during this period (1951—1960) he went to work as writer-editor for various trade magazines in the chemical field: *Chemical Week, Chemical Engineering Progress, Chemical Equipment*, etc.

In 1962 he published his first novel, *Combat Soldier*, based on his experiences and feelings in World War II, and in 1963 his second novel, *Uptown Downtown* appeared. This was a novel of the growing separation and conflict between the young and the establishment that was soon to burst over the country. At the end of 1960, on the strength of having sold his first two novels, he stopped full time jobs with the trade magazines and struck out on his own as a writer. He continued to write novels, do freelance writing for trade journals, and in 1962 began to write "popular" short stories for such magazines as *Mike Shayne Mystery Magazine, Alfred Hitchcock Mystery Magazine, Ellery Queen Mystery Magazine, Manhunt, Argosy*, and others. It was at this time, with his first popular story for *Mike Shayne Mystery Magazine*, that he created probably the cheapest, poorest, sleaziest private detective in literature: Slot-Machine Kelly! The adventures of the "one-armed bandit." Kelly lasted up to 12 stories before he was laid to rest and transformed into a more honorable and respectable alter ego, Dan Fortune, the hero of Mr. Lynds' novels under the pen name Michael Collins. Of the Kelly stories, Mr. Lynds says, "They were written with considerable tongue-in-cheek and intended to be half funny. Only half funny, because, in all truth, Kelly may be closer to the real private detective than anyone else!"

It was in 1962 also that he began his career of writing "for hire." That is, writing novels and stories that were his own creation, but were written under author's names, or so-called "house names." The first of these was "The Friendly Corpse" under the Brett Halliday name in the September 1962 issue of *Mike Shayne Mystery Magazine*. After that, Mr. Lynds wrote most of the Mike Shayne stories for *MSMM* through 1964, and from 1965 until February 1970 wrote all the Mike Shayne short novels for the magazine.

From 1962 through 1970, Mr. Lynds wrote the Mike Shayne stories in *MSMM*, one third of the Man From UNCLE adventures in the magazine of that title, his famous and controversial (to some fans) series about The Shadow for Belmont Books, and

Dennis Lynds

various other books and stories under different "house" names.

In 1967 he began still another career—his own suspense novels under his own pen names. The first of these was *Act of Fear* by Michael Collins, featuring the considerably more upright one-armed detective Dan Fortune, evolved from the earlier "Slot Machine" Kelly character, and that won the Mystery Writers of America's Edgar Award as the best first novel of 1967. (Mr. Lynds later won a second M.W.A. Award with a short story under his William Arden pen name.)

Since 1967, he has published nine novels by Michael Collins featuring Dan Fortune; six novels by John Crowe that take place in Buena Costa County, California; five novels by William Arden about the exploits of industrial spy Kane Jackson; four novels by Mark Sadler featuring Madison Avenue private detective Paul Shaw; and one novel by Carl Dekker. (Michael Collins has also written two science fiction novels.)

In 1965, after having lived somewhere in New York City most of his life (with time out for war and school), Mr. Lynds moved to Santa Barbara, California, where he now lives. He is married and has two children—both daughters—Kate and Diedre. In Santa Barbara he continues all of his various careers side by side.

His Michael Collins novels are all being brought out by paperback. His John Crowe novels about life and violence in Buena Costa County are still being published by Dodd Mead. His Mark Sadler novels may begin again soon. He still writes short stories for the literary quarterlies, with a collection of his stories scheduled to be published in September 1979 by December Press of Chicago (now in print).

In the period 1974 through 1976 he wrote three Nick Carter novels for Award Books (Nick Carter is probably the most famous "house" name in suspense fiction, having been written by dozens of writers.) In 1974 he wrote a Charlie Chan feature novel for Renown Publications for their then new magazine *Charlie Chan Mystery Magazine,* and did a Chan novel for a Bantam paperback series, the only Chan novel not written by his originator, Earle Derr Biggers. In 1975 he novelized a TV script for *S.W.A.T.* for Pocket Books.

Dennis Lynds still works part time as editor-in-chief of a trade magazine, *International Instrumentation.*

And at this writing, Mr. Lynds says he is about ready to finally write his third straight novel after more than sixteen years! This will be one to look forward to in the future! As for now, I would highly recommend Mr. Lynds' series of Dan Fortune, by Michael Collins. For the mystery genre, this series is one of the best!

Following is an in-depth bibliography of Mr. Lynds writing. There may be a few later novels not listed, but I believe it is fairly complete as of this writing.

Dennis Lynds Bibliography

Short Stories, Literary Magazines

"Trip West," *The Bridge,* August 1951

"Rites of Spring," *Prairie Schooner,* Spring 1954

"The Man With the Turned-Down Hat," *Embryo,* Vol. 1, #1, 1954

"The Island," *Interim,* 1954

"Just Once More," *New Voices* #2, Hendrick's House, 1955

"Monday Morning," *The Gent,* April 1957

"Yellow Gal," *New World Writing,* #11, 1957

"Victory," *The Gent,* 1958

"A Young Man Sat in Central Park," *Epoch,* Vol. X, #2, 1960

"Though Procurer and the Poet," *The Dude,* September 1962

"Freedom Fighter," *The Literary Review,* Vol. 6, #2, 1963, reprinted *The Best American Short Stories 1964,* HMCo 1964, reprinted Anthology *Crime Without Murder,* Scribners 1970

"American Landscape: The City," *Literary Review* Vol. 6, #4 1963, reprinted *The Best Short Stories 1964,* HMCo 1964

"A Blue Blonde in the Sky Over Pennsylvania," *The Hudson Review,* Vol. XVII, #2, reprinted *The Best Short Stories 1965,* reprinted *The Short Story, Fiction in Transition,* Scribners 1969

"The Glass Cage," *The Minnesota Review* Vol. 4, #3, 1964

"Why Girls Ride Sidesaddle," *The Minnesota Review* Vol. 5, #2 1965, reprinted anthology Short Stories From The Literary Magazine, Scott, Foresman 1970

"The Animal That Howls Unheard," *Northwest Review,* Vol. 7, #3 1966

"A Night in Syracuse," *Beyond The Angry Black,* Copper Sq., 1966

"Squares With Thin Red," *The Minnesota Review,* Vol. 7, #3 & 4, 1967

Short Stories, Science Fiction Magazines

Amazing Stories:
April 1959: "Test Rocket" (J.D.)
July 1959: "The Traitor" (J.D.)
May 1961: "Dead World" (J.D.)

Short Stories, Suspense Magazines

Manhunt:
Apr-May 1966 "Viking Blood" (D.L.)
The Man From UNCLE:
June 1966 "The Dirk" (D.L.)
Shell Scott Mystery Magazine:
July 1966 "Climate of Immorality" (D.L.)
Ellery Queen Mystery Magazine:
July 1969 "No One Likes to be Played for a Sucker" (M.C.)

June 1970 "The Bizarre Case Expert" (W.A.)
Argosy:
April 1968: "Success of a Mission" (W.A.)
Jan 1970: "The Savage" (W.A.)
March 1971: "Clay Pigeon" (W.A.)
Alfred Hitchcock's Mystery Magazine:
October 1963: "Nobody Frames Big Sam" (D.L.)
May 1964: "Silent Partner" (D.L.)
July 1964: "The Sinner" (D.L.)
October 1969: "Scream All The Way" (M.C.)
July 1972: "Long Shot" (M.C.)
August 1972: "Who?" (M.C.)
September 1972: "Occupational Hazard" (J.C.)
February 1973: "The Choice" (M.S.)
Mike Shayne Mystery Magazine:
August 1962: "It's Whiskey or Dames" (D.L.)
September 1962: "The Dreamers" (D.L.)
October 1962: "The Bodyguard" (D.L.)
November 1962: "Accidents Will Happen" (D.L.)
February 1963: "Death, My Love" (J.D.)
March 1963: "Man on the Run" (D.L.)
April 1963: "The Blue Hand" (D.L.)
June 1963: "The Price of a Dollar" (D.L.)
July 1963: "Harness Bull" (D.L.)
August 1963: "Even Bartenders Die" (D.L.)
October 1963: "Death For A Dinner" (D.L.)
November 1963: "The Heckler" (D.L.)
January 1964: "A Better Murder" (D.L.)
February 1964: "No Way Out" (D.L.)
March 1964: "Where The Lines Meet" (W.D.)
May 1964: "Winner Pay Off" (D.L.)
June 1964: "The Man Who Sold His Head" (W.D.)
July 1964: "Hard Cop" (D.L.)
September 1964: "Homecoming" (D.L.)
November 1964: "No Loose Ends" (D.L.)
January 1965: "Full Circle" (D.L.)
May 1965: "The Hero" (D.L.)
June 1965: "All Night Long" (W.D.)
December 1965: "A Well Planned Death" (D.L.)
March 1968: "A Murder From Inside" (M.C.)
June 1968: "The Man of a Million Faces" (RHD)
August 1968: "Hot Night Homicide" (M.C.)

Note: Regarding the novel, "The Man of a Million Faces," Mr. Lynds says: "It was something of a disaster. Leo Margulies dreamed it up, asked me to do it, and I broke my back, but as I told Leo at the time the concept just didn't work. It was old-fashioned and conceived backwards. That is, the wrong identity was the real one. It was pulpish, of course, because I made it that way. What was wrong with it was that the idea simply could not support a modern series—it was, as I said, backwards. The alter ego was less interesting than the cover personality. I couldn't get Mr. Jones to come alive. Leo was not happy with the piece, and the whole thing died—mercifully."

What with the new interest in series' heroes, like the Man From UNCLE, evidently Leo felt a return to those pulp days of old was right for the time. The character of Mr. Jones was a close similarity to those many masked heroes that Leo created for Standard Magazines in those bygone days, like The Phantom Detective, Masked Detective, Black Bat, and others: the house name of G. Wayman Jones was actually used on the first few Phantoms and the Black Bat novels. Perhaps it was Leo's last attempt to relive those glory days. Maybe the story did not come across, but I certainly enjoyed it, and (although it isn't likely) would like to see it reprinted some day.

Novels and Novelettes For "Hire"

NICE CARTER (Award Books):
The N3 Conspiracy
The Green Wolf Connection
Triple Cross

Note: Titles are by Award, not Mr. Lynds. Also, *Triple Cross* is from an outline for the tenth Belmont Shadow story.

CHARLIE CHAN (Renown Magazine)
May 1974: "The Temple of the Golden Horde"

Note: Title misprinted on contents page as "The Temple of The Golden Death." Robert Hart Davis house name used.

The Man From UNCLE (Renown Magazines); Robert Hart Davis house name.
February 1966: "The Howling Teenagers Affair"
April 1966: "The Unspeakable Affair"
June 1966: "The Vanishing Act Affair"
August 1966: "The Cat and Mouse Affair"
November 1966: "The THRUSH From THRUSH Affair"
August 1967: "The Genghis Khan Affair"
October 1967: "The Mind-Sweeper Affair"

Note: The first story, "The Howling Teenager Affair" was advertised in the February 1966 issue of *Sheel Scott Mystery Magazine*, by reprinting the first two chapters.

Neither Mr. Lynds nor Renown (Leo Margulies) had any connection with the television or paperback series, nor the comics, except that each manuscript had to be approved by MGM prior to publication. Mr. Lynds was paid $450.00 per story.

CHARLIE CHAN (Bantam #4) "Charlie Chan Returns" by Dennis Lynds
S.W.A.T. (Pocket Books #1) "Crossfire" by Dennis Lynds
THE SHADOW (Belmont Books) All under the Maxwell Grant house name.
October 1964: "The Shadow Strikes"
January 1965: "Shadow Beware"
April 1965: "Cry Shadow"
October 1965: "The Shadow's Revenge"
May 1966: "Mark of The Shadow"
September 1966: "Shadow—Go Mad"
November 1966: "The Night of The Shadow"
March 1967: "The Shadow: Destination Moon"

Note: Mr. Lynds was paid $1,500.00 per story. He was supplied a work sheet from Belmont to supply needed information about the character of The Shadow, and had a copy of Mr. Gibson's *Return of The Shadow* to go by. Dennis would submit an outline of each story to Belmont before writing the novel. Belmont would then either tell him to proceed, or wait on writing the novel, thus the long delay, at the time, for the stories to appear. About his Shadow stories, Mr. Lynds writes: "I had kind of a fact sheet to work from about The Shadow, and I did follow it closely as far as it went. (The Kent Allard change, for example, was given to me, obviously by someone who did not know the series too well which I had no way of knowing.) I had Walter Gibson's *Return* but I did not use it much—the style I found rather too old-fashioned. When you come to many of the differences I think you overlook a vital influence—the radio program. I had never read a Shadow, but I listened to it on the radio from the days of Welles—not religiously, but off and on—and the radio show became a part of our popular culture and so what I kept in mind as I wrote the books was the aura, the feel, the ambience of the radio show. I kept the voice, the sense of blue rooms, etc. If you will look at my scenes I think you will see the radio influence more than any other. In short, what goes deeply into my aura was always the sound of The Shadow. Obviously, never having read them, or very few of them, the automatics escaped my notice because I would guess they were not featured on a non-visual medium such as radio."

MIKE SHAYNE (Renown Magazine) Under the Brett Halliday name.
1962: September: "The Friendly Corpse"
October: "The Guilty Bystander"
December: "Miracle of Murder"
1963: February: "The Fourth Man"
April: Detour to Murder"
June: "Death of a Deadman"
September: "The Power of Death"

October: "The Dangerous Secret"
November: "Crooks Holiday"
1964: January: "Revenge for a Massacre"
February: "The Milk Run Murder"
March: "Drink Up—And Die"
April: "Killers Masquerade"
May: "Kill With Care"
June: "Scream in the Night"
August: "A Matter of Courage"
September: "Tragedy of Errors"
October: "Murder at Floodtide"
November: "Death in Cell Five"
December: "Murder On Berkeley Square"
1965: January: "Dead Man's Walk"
February: "Cruise for Murder"
March: "Requiem for a Killer"
April: "The Maghul Box"
May: "String of Pearls"
June: "Inside Job"
July: "A Salesman Dies"
August: "The Moving Target"
October: "Pressure Play"
November: "The Unnecessary"
December: "Accent On Murder"
1966: January: "The Spy Who Was Mike Shayne"
February: "In the Shadows"
March: "The Good Citizen"
April: "The Pattern Went Wrong"
May: "The Gothic Manuscript"
June: "The Big Frame"
July: "A Run of Luck"
August: "The Man Who Never Forgot"
September: "Kick of Death"
October: "The Innocent Victim"
November: "Voice of Blood"
December: "An End to Horror"
1967: January: "The Unseen Man"
February: "Thief in the Family"
March: "A Reason to Die"
April: "Hustle Death"
May: "Trail of a Phantom"

June: "The Wrong Room"
July: "Understudy for Murder"
August: "Dead Man's Message"
September: "Death is My Ransom"
October: "Murder of Fear"
November: "The Final Payoff"
December: "Die in Haste"
1968: January: "The Teddy Bear Murders"
February: "Death Times Three"
March: "Key to a Killer"
April: "Death Trap"
May: "The Baby Doll Murder"
June: "Detail of Death"
July: "The Lady Who Kissed and Killed"
August: "Affair of Death"
September: "Death is My Mistress"
October: "Spirit of Evil"
November: "Deadly Conscience"
December: "Deal Me Out of The Morgue"
1969: January: "Die Like a Dog"
February: "Rich Man's Blood"
March: "Kill in the Dark"
April: "Murder is My Accomplice"
May: "The Girl With the Tortured Eyes"
June: "The Night Was Made for Murder"
July "Cause for Murder"
August: "Youth is for Dying"
September: "Murder-Go-Round"
October: "Road to Nowhere"
November: "Killer of the Glades"
December: "Die in Silence"
1970: January: "A Wild Young Corpse"
February: "'Twas the Night Before Murder"

Note: Dave Dresser, the real name behind the Mike Shayne series, based a novel, "Too Friendly, Too Dead," from Mr. Lynds' story, "The Friendly Corpse."

Published Novels of His Own Series

Combat Soldier, New American Library, 1962 (D.L.)

Uptown, Downtown, New American Library, 1963 (D.L.)
Act of Fear, Dodd Mead, 1967 (M.C.)
A Dark Power, Dodd Mead, 1968 (W.A.)
The Brass Rainbow, Dodd Mead, 1969 (M.C.)
Lukan War, Belmont, 1969 (M.C.)
Night of the Toads, Dodd Mead, 1970 (M.C.)
The Planets of Death, Berkeley, 1970 (M.C.)
The Falling Man, Random House, 1970 (M.S.)
Hero to Die, Random House, 1971 (M.S.)
The Goliath Scheme, Dodd Mead, 1971 (W.A.)
Walk a Black Wind, Dodd Mead, 1971 (M.C.)
Shadow of a Tiger, Dodd Mead, 1972 (M.C.)
Another Way to Die, Random House, 1972 (J.C.)
Mirror Image, Random House, 1972 (M.S.)
Die to a Distant Drum, Dodd Mead, 1972 (W.A.)
The Silent Scream, Dodd Mead, 1973 (M.C.)
A Touch of Darkness, Random House, 1973 (J.C.)
Circle of Fire, Random House, 1973 (M.S.)
Deadly Legacy, Dodd Mead, 1973 (W.A.)
Woman in Marble, Bobbs Merrill, 1973 (C.D.)
Bloodwater, Dodd Mead, 1974 (J.C.)
Crooked Shadows, Dodd Mead, 1975 (J.C.)
Blue Death, Dodd Mead, 1975 (M.C.)
The Blood-Red Dream, Dodd Mead, 1976 (M.C.)
When They Kill Your Wife, Dodd Mead, 1977 (J.C.)
The Nightrunners, Dodd Mead, 1978 (M.C.)
Close to Death, Dodd Mead, 1979 (J.C.)
The Slasher, Dodd Mead, 1980 (M.C.)
Freak, Dodd Mead, 1983 (M.C.)

Pseudonyms:

(M.C.) Michael Collins
(W.A.) William Arden
(M.S.) Mark Sadler
(J.C.) John Crowe
(C.D.) Carl Dekker
(J.D.) John Douglas
(W.D.) Walter Dallas
(RHD) Robert Hart Davis

A wordsmith, a fantastic writer, a magician of the typewriter, Mr. Lynds has supplied his many fans with hours of reading pleasure. His novels of The Shadow, The Man From UNCLE, Nick Carter, "Slot Machine" Kelly, Charlie Chan, Mike Shayne, Dan Fortune, Paul Shaw, and Kane Jackson, will always remain a tribute to his writing talents. I for one will never forget his fantastic plots about a black-garbed avenger called "The Shadow." ♦

The Green Ghost

By Tom Johnson

Leo Margulies had a thing about masks. From as early a story as "Masked Men" he wrote for the May 5, 1928 issue of the *Argosy All-Story Weekly*, Leo was setting a pattern for his future work in Ned Pines' Thrilling Group in the 1930s and '40s. Leo was to become Mr. Pines' head editor who would be responsible for such pulp hero greats as The Phantom Detective, The Masked Detective, The Crimson Mask, The Black Bat, and The Green Ghost. All would wear some kind of mask, be it a domino, or complete face coverings and hoods.

Ned Pines' Standard Magazine Group or Better Publications, Inc., nicknamed the "Thrilling Group," was one of the big "4" in magazine publications: Street & Smith, who published *Doc Savage*, *The Shadow* and *The Avenger*; Popular Publications, who published *The Spider*, *G-8* and *Operator #5*; Ace Magazine Group, who published *Secret Agent "X,"* *Captain Hazzard* and *Ten Detective Aces*, were the other three giants.

In 1931, Street & Smith started a series of stories about The Shadow, a mysterious character who dressed all in black, wore a black cape and slouch hat, and fought crime with a weird laugh and a pair of heavy automatics. It was an instant success.

By 1933, Popular Publications had their Spider series, an almost identical character as The Shadow, and Standard had their version in a "masked" character called The Phantom Detective. In 1934, Ace came out with Secret Agent "X," who was a man of mystery and a thousand faces. They were all rivals of one another.

Walter Gibson, under the direction of Street & Smith, created The Shadow and authored most of the series, writing under the Maxwell Grant house name.

The Spider, over at Popular, was created by R.T.M. Scott, but the series was quickly turned over to Norvell Page, who would write most of the series under the Grant Stockbridge house name.

The Phantom Detective from Standard, was probably began under editorial committee—and authored (at first) by D.L. Champion, under the house name of G. Wayman Jones, then turned over to a multitude of authors—chief among them was Norman A. Daniels—under the new house name of Robert Wallace.

Over at Ace, again under editorial committee, the Secret Agent "X" series I was created by Paul Chadwick, writing under the Brant House "house" name. Other authors contributed stories until the series was finally given to G.T. Fleming-Roberts, who would write the stories until its end in 1939.

By 1939 & 1940, most magazine chains were set in their ways, not wanting to experiment with new characters. This was not the case at Standard. Leo Margulies, the "little giant of the pulps," was constantly looking for new characters—usually masked or caped crime-fighters. Norman A. Daniels had only recently created The Black Bat for Leo in July 1939, to appear in Black Book Detective.

After the demise of his Secret Agent "X" series, over at Ace, George Thomas Fleming-Roberts moved over to Standard, where he created for Leo, the magician-turned-detective, George Chance, alias The Ghost—Super Detective. This title would later be changed to The Green Ghost.

G.T. Fleming-Roberts was born April 17th, 1910, in Lafayette, Indiana, where he grew up in that town, attending his primary grade schools. Later, he would attend Perdue University. One of his first published short stories, "The Day It Rained Bodies," was bought and published in the pulps during 1932, shortly after his graduation from Perdue. The setting of this story was the locale of that campus.

Throughout his writing career, G.T. Fleming-Roberts tried to keep the setting of his stories in areas with which he was familiar. This was fine with his short stories, but where the character pulps were involved—usually the setting was New York City—Mr. Roberts had to write stories around locales in which he wasn't all that familiar. But his stories never suffered from his not being familiar with these locales, only that there was a vagueness as to where the story was taking place. His strong point was working on the characters and the plots, building them up, and the results were very realistic characters involved in… sometimes… highly unrealistic plots. But this was excusable as we, the readers, expected the unrealistic—the more far-fetched, the better.

In 1934, G.T. Fleming-Roberts moved to Indianapolis, Indiana, and his stories reflect this move. But through his agent, August Lenniger, he was selling short stories to the Ace Magazine Group, and by mid 1935 he had his first character series, Secret Agent "X."

The year of 1939 proved to be the end for Secret Agent "X," but not so for Fleming-Roberts. This was the year that he was to marry the lovely Miss Agatha Halcyon Amell, whom he had met in Marshall, Michigan. (Fleming-Roberts often explained his meeting with Agatha in a lengthily semi-fiction tale

© G.T. Fleming-Roberts

G.T. Fleming-Roberts

that involved William Wallace Cook's Chinese houseboy finding a mysterious letter in the wastebasket.)

While still at Ace, Fleming-Roberts had begun another series, Diamondstone, for *Popular Detective*, contributing stories as early as 1937. But in January 1940, he had his second pulp hero series, The Green Ghost. As a lead character, The Ghost ended with the Summer 1941 issue. At which time he started his third hero pulp series, The Black Hood, which only lasted for three issues. In the meantime, he continued writing The Green Ghost for *Thrilling Mystery,* another product of Standard.

For a short period, during World War II, G.T. Fleming-Roberts was called to active duty. He was assigned to the Army Air Corps, and stationed at Sheppard Field in Wichita Falls, Texas.

In 1947, with his wife, Agatha, and son James T. Roberts (born September 16th, 1941), they moved to the "Witch House" located near Nashville, Indiana. Here, one of his stories, "The Deaths of Laurie Ford" was written with a Nashville, Indiana rural background.

Until 1949, G.T. Fleming-Roberts contributed many short stories to various pulp magazines. Then, in November 1949, he created the last of the pulp heroes, Captain Zero, which only lasted for three issues, until March 1950. After this, Fleming-Roberts wrote for five more years, ending his writing career in 1955.

After he stopped writing, he became active in local politics and was Republican County Chairman for Brown County, Indiana for two terms. He also worked as Bailiff of the United States District Court until his death in 1968.

When the pulp market started to dry up in the mid-1950s, Fleming-Roberts went on lecture tours on how to write. His son, James, still has his father's notes that were used on the tours. James, now a lawyer in the Nashville, Indiana area, said it best when he replied to my question about the personal life of an author during the pulp era: "I must say that my strongest impression of my father was that he was writing all of the time, and he must have been to be able to support his family at pulp magazine rates." And, indeed, how true this must have been! G.T. Fleming-Roberts was an exceptional writer of the pulp magazines, and he supplied many hours of reading pleasure to the young readers of the Pulp Era. Whether he wrote of a secret agent with no identity, a ghost detective, a hooded detective, or a reporter who turned invisible at the stroke of midnight, we thrilled to the many exploits of his many characters. Below is a partial listing of G.T. Fleming-Roberts contributions to the hero pulp magazines. This listing is not complete, as there are many stories yet to be found.

- "The Corpse Cavalcade" (June 1935, Secret Agent "X")
- "The Golden Ghoul" (July 1935, Secret Agent "X")
- "Legion of the Living Dead" (September 1935, Secret Agent "X")
- "Ringmaster of Doom" (November 1935, Secret Agent "X")
- "Brand of the Metal Maiden" (January 1936, Secret Agent "X")
- "Dividends of Doom" (February 1936, Secret Agent "X")
- "Faceless Fury" (April 1936, Secret Agent "X")
- "Subterranean Scourge" (June 1936, Secret Agent "X")
- "The Doom Director" (August 1936, Secret Agent "X")
- "Horror's Handclasp" (October 1936, Secret Agent "X")
- "City of Madness" (December 1936, Secret Agent "X")
- "Death's Frozen Formula" (February 1937, Secret Agent "X")
- "The Crime Conductor" (March 1937, Diamondstone)
- "The Murder Brain" (April 1937, Secret Agent "X")
- "The Brothers of Doom" (May 1937, Diamondstone)
- "Slaves of the Scorpion" (June 1937, Secret Agent "X")
- "Satan's Syndicate" (August 1937, Secret Agent "X")
- "The Buddha Whispers" (September 1937, Diamondstone)
- "The Assassins' League" (October 1937, Secret Agent "X")
- "Curse of the Mandarin's Fan (February 1938, Secret Agent "X")
- "The Left-Handed Legacy" (March 1938, Diamondstone)
- "Claws of the Corpse Cult" (April 1938, Secret Agent "X")
- "The Corpse That Murdered" (June 1938, Secret Agent "X")
- "The Murder of the Marionette" (August 1938, Diamondstone)
- "Corpse Contraband" (December 1938, Secret

Agent "X")
- "Yoke of the Crimson Coterie" (March 1939, Secret Agent "X")
- "Three Wise Apes" (June 1939, Diamondstone)
- "Calling The Ghost" (January 1940, The Ghost)
- "The Ghost Strikes Back" (Spring 1940, The Ghost)
- "Murder Makes a Ghost" (Summer 1940, The Ghost)
- "The Case of the Laughing Corpse" (Fall 1940, The Ghost)
- "The Case of the Flaming Fist" (Winter 1941, The Green Ghost)
- "The Case of the Walking Skeleton" (Spring 1941, The Green Ghost)
- "The Case of the Black Magician" (Summer 1941, The Green Ghost)
- "Death's Five Faces" (September 1941, The Black Hood)
- "The Corpse Came C.O.D." (November 1941, The Black Hood)
- "The Whispering Eye" (January 1942, The Black Hood)
- "The Case of the Murderous Mermaid" (September 1942, The Green Ghost)
- "The Poison Puzzle" (Fall 1942, The Masked Detective)
- "The Case of the Astral Assassin" (November 1942, The Green Ghost)
- "Lilies for the Crooked Cross" (January 1943, Dan Fowler)
- "The Case of the Clumsy Cat" (March 1943, The Green Ghost)
- "The Case of the Bachelor's Bones" (June 1943, The Green Ghost)
- "The Case of the Broken Broom" (Fall 1943, The Green Ghost)
- "The Case of the Evil Eye" (Winter 1944, The Green Ghost)
- "The Plague of the Yellow Snakes" (Spring 1944, Dan Fowler)
- "The Case of the Phantom Bridegroom" (October 1944, The Green Ghost)
- "The Floating Coffins" (Fall 1944, Dan Fowler)
- "Death Takes Vanilla" (May 1945, Hillary House)
- "Remains—To Be Seen" (July 1945, Hillary House)
- "Death Walks This Beat" (March 1946, Hillary House)
- "City of Deadly Sleep" (November 1949, Captain Zero)
- "The Mark of Zero" (January 1950, Captain Zero)
- "The Golden Murder Syndicate" (March 1950, Captain Zero)

There are several time lapses between some novels, leaving the possibility of unknown stories. For instance, between the June 1939, Diamondstone story, and the Ghost story for January 1940, we have no listing for six months. There could have been some unknown novels between these dates, or merely a number of short novelettes. There are a few interesting Dan Fowler and Phantom Detective stories in this period, so who knows?

Due to lack of records, and the incompleteness of Mr. Roberts' own file copies, there could be many novels not listed that he wrote. To date, we've not attempted to compile a record of all of his short stories, and these were many!

George Thomas Fleming-Roberts was a very prolific writer of the pulp magazines, and is just now starting to receive his due. And it is with great pleasure that we now present his popular series about a magician-turned-detective, George Chance, alias The Ghost—Super Detective!

The Main Characters

Meet George Chance! Meet—the Ghost!

They're one and the same—and take their bow in this, America's newest and finest detective magazine—*The Ghost*.

> Mystery and magic—thrills and excitement—legerdemain and suspense—you'll find them all in the Ghost's repertoire.
>
> Follow the mystifying exploits of the most extraordinary manhunter the world has ever known! Roar through the pages of this super-detective's startling memoirs—appearing exclusively in *The Ghost!*
>
> Meet the Ghost's aid de-camp in his war on crime—Glenn Saunders, the double; Tiny Tim Terry, the Midget; Joe Harper, the Man About Town; Merry White, the glamour girl who has brains and courage, too; Ned Standish, the Commissioner of Police; Robert Demarest, the sharp-tongued Medical Examiner.
>
> Seldom has such a galaxy of characters been gathered within the covers of one magazine. Step up and meet then all—and above all, get to know the Ghost himself.
>
> You may not have believed in "ghosts" up to now, but you will have faith in this one.

And so, we were introduced to the new character in the January 1940 issue of *The Ghost—Super Detective*. One of the late arrivals of super hero pulp characters that were attempted. Published by Better Publications, a pulp magazine line from Ned Pines' Thrilling Group, thus nicknamed because of the many titles under that heading.

The editorial chief was Leo Margulies, who handled most, if not all, of the magazines under Ned Pines. Leo was probably instrumental in the guidelines for not only The Ghost series, but several others. There would be a number of similarities between the hero pulp characters created by the Thrilling Group. Just prior to the appearance of the Ghost in January 1940 was The Black Bat (written by Norman Daniels), which would influence a number of similar item's that would later appear in The Ghost. The Black Bat appeared in July 1939, six months before The Ghost, and suggests that both were created from a blackboard of suggestions.

But regardless, for a short tine, these new characters came to life and gave us many hours of reading pleasure while the series of The Ghost lasted. And on this note, we should take a look at the people who played their parts so well.

Robert Demarest was the chief medical examiner of New York City. He was described "as gloomy and saturnine an individual as ever came out of a morgue alive." He had sleepy, heavy-lidded eyes, and appears amused that someone with a good life (like magician George Chance) would want to put his life in danger by investigating crime and murders. He felt that someday he would have to perform an autopsy on George Chance if he kept meddling in the affairs of the underworld.

At first, he is called "Bob," but later on everybody would call him by a more personal nickname—"Demmy."

He actually had very little involvement in the stories, and always complained that he never slept "because people were always dying in New York City." He would be completely left out of several stories, and in one of them he was only mentioned. When he did appear he would merely speak one-liners, like "How's ghosting, George?"

Of all the main characters, he was least used—and least needed. If anything, he only added a few paragraphs to the story, and was not missed when he was not used.

However, his character was fairly unique in the pulp fiction annuls, at least within the pulp hero magazines. A medical examiner? I can think of no others, anyway. Stewart Sterling had a recurring ME character in the pulps later on, but not a pulp hero.

Commissioner Edward Standish, "Ned," as he was called by his friends, was the typical "father figure" in the pulps. Being the Commissioner of Police of New York City, he was to The Ghost, what Ralph Weston was to The Shadow. Or Stanley Kirkpatrick was to The Spider. But in this case, Commissioner Standish knew that George Chance was The Ghost.

He can also be compared—and probably more

closely—to millionaire-publisher, Frank Haven, of the Phantom Detective (another of Leo's responsible pulp hero characters) as the authority figure, as well as father figure. And like Frank Havens, Edward Standish had been instrumental in starting George Chance along the road as a crime-fighter; knowing Chance's interest in crime detection, Standish suggested that he try his hand at solving a seemingly baffling murder case that was annoying the police department at the time.

Chance quickly solved the case and brought the murderer to justice merely by employing a little magic. Thus the Ghost was born.

From then on, Commissioner Standish would call on the Ghost whenever he had a baffling case on his hands. For instance, in "Calling The Ghost," January 1940, a man leaps to his death from a tall building. When his body is examined, it is discovered that he had jumped to his death without his teeth! Standish feels that this is enough of a mystery for him to call in the Ghost.

Strange, indeed.

He had close-set, gray eyes, and was of medium height; with a taste for subdued clothes, heavy from the belt upwards. His was a typical cop's figure—hard, muscular, but spindle-shanked. He has pronounced chops, a black square of mustache. And though still only in his early forties, he has nevertheless grown gray in the service of the police department. But his legs were still thick, and his body stalwart.

He was loved and respected by every man in the department—probably because he had never forgot that he, too, had once pounded a beat.

Early in the series Standish would be involved in the stories, even active in the cases. But this was during the novel period (1940 & 1941). By the time the stories were moved to Thrilling Mystery, and the length of the story had shrunk, his role became less. Often in the later novels, his office would receive a message or phone call from some citizen, who reported a mysterious crime—or requesting, the New York City Police department to send a detective to investigate some crime. If Standish thought it could really be something, he would pass the information/request on to George Chance, alias The Ghost.

In the shorter, but tighter stories, Standish also become extra baggage and thus could be dropped from the action. The stories did not suffer.

Besides Commissioner Standish, one of the minor characters that were part of the police department was Inspector John Magnus. He made recurring appearances in the early novels. He led the crack homicide team of New York's finest, and could be found at all murder scenes.

Magnus could have been used to a better degree than he actually was. He thought very little of The Ghost, neither sanctioning him, nor condemning him. He would have arrested him if he thought The Ghost was the criminal.

Unlike McGrath, from the Black Bat series, Magnus could have cared less about who the Ghost really was. There was no inter-action between him and the others in the stories. There could have been something of a rivalry between The Ghost and Magnus, or at least a desire to unmask the mysterious crime fighter, but there was nothing.

He was left out of most of the *Thrilling Mystery* stories, and he wasn't missed.

He received little description, and even less characterization. He was little more than a name of a character who contributed to the action. Such a shame, as his character did have better possibilities than that!

Another of those non-entities, Hadley was mentioned as being the Commissioner's secretary, a man that set outside the office of the Commissioner, and announced visitors. No description was given to him. Nor would he always be named in the stories—just mentioned as "the Commissioner's secretary."

However, it is possible that Hadley was scheduled to be replaced in the series, as in the last published story, "The Phantom Bridegroom," there is a girl at the desk, and she even has a small part in the story. Her name is Janet Trees.

This story was originally written as a Green Ghost entry, then with the demise of that series, Fleming-Roberts deleted the names of the original characters, i.e., George Chance becomes George Hazard, etc. However, the part of Janet Trees called for a female role, so it is still possible that the girl appeared in the original manuscript.

Tiny Tim Terry is George Chance's oldest friend—and certainly the smallest. Nearing middle age, he still isn't tall enough to see over the average table. The midget, for such he is, had been a friend of George Chance since the old circus days, and now that he had retired—Tim had inherited a nice fortune that enabled him to retire from the circus—they kept in constant touch with one another. And Tiny Tim is one of the cleverest of the Ghost's agents.

He was usually immaculately clad in one of his tiny double-breasted suits, the largest of cigars grotesquely clenched in his babyish mouth.

Though he always complained against it, usually his part was to play a child to Merry, as they shadowed someone involved in the case. "Well," his child's voice piped, "whatever the answer is, I know my jab. I'm to have another kiddy role. I get pushed around in a baby carriage in Central Park. Merry pretends to be my nurse. Cops chuck me under the chin—and the next one who does that, damn it, will get his finger bit off, so help me."

Merry dimpled at the midget, "Tim, if you knew how adorable you are in a little lacy bonnet."

THE GREEN GHOST 177

"Quiet, frail!" Tim shilled.

His was a baby's face, somewhat spoiled by a wise-eyed expression of gravity. His was a man's sized brain in a child-sized body. As an agent of the Ghost, he was extremely valuable.

Actually, Tim's part wasn't all that strange. Again, I am sure that his part corresponded to the suggestions laid down by Leo Margulies. In fact, Tim can easily be compared to big Butch O'Leary from the Black Bat. Butch was a giant of a man, but sometimes he was identified with a child-like mind. Fleming-Roberts just chose a midget for the part, and it worked just fine.

Tim usually made one mistake in the stories; while on a stakeout, he was usually caught once he decided to light up one of his cigars. He was usually captured in every story. But he was also of great help because of his size. Being as tiny as he was, he could usually get into places inaccessible to the Ghost; thus he could enter a guarded house unobserved, and unlock a door that would give entry to the Ghost.

Joe Harper is also in keeping with other series' characters. In most past articles on Joe, myself included, we always made the point of saying how odd his character was. It wasn't, not really. Far instance, in referring back to the Black Bat series, we have Joe's counterpart; he was Silk Kirby, an ex- confidence man turned honest. He had entered the home of Tony Quinn, the fighting D.A., with the intent of robbery. While in the house he discovered another man, a killer bent on the murder of the master of the house. Silk awakens Quinn and tells him about the killer, which enables the master of the house to set a trap far his would be murderer. Tony Quinn then talks Silk into becoming his personal valet and aide-de-camp, in general.

Joe's entrance to the Ghost series was similar; we are told that he had appropriated George Chance's guest roan one night, years ago, to recover from a hangover—he had remained ever since.

Joe retained his life-style, and could always be found on Broadway—wearing a checkered suit, piped vest, snap-brim hat that was always offensively green regardless of what fashion prescribed. He was lean and wolfish, with black-beetle eyes connected with an agile brain, thin lips and thin nose, and the sort of chin that would break a fist.

He didn't believe in working for a living, when it was much easier to con some hick out of their money. He lived by the doctrine that everyone's money was his money if he could get his hands on it.

If you were a hick on Broadway, maybe the pitchman who tried to sell you a lifetime fountain pen for two bits was Joe Harper. Or if you liked the ponies, maybe Joe was the bookmaker you wanted to shoot after the race. Or if you were a glamour girl trying to crash Broadway, you might have met Joe sitting behind the desk in a booking agency. Anyway, it's certain that Joe knew you before you knew Joe. He'd make your business his, and he'd have done pretty well for himself at the same time.

His lean legs bridged the gap between a leather lounge chair and the top of a desk. His green hat rested on a plane determined by the tips of his close-set ears and the bridge of his nose. Except for the hat, he might have been asleep—he almost never went to bed with his hat on. His voice was crisp and a little nasal, not an unpleasant sound against the mushy stirrings of cars and pedestrians in the damp street outside.

Joe was also good with a gun or his fists, whichever was needed, and though he sponged off George Chance, magician, he was always ready to give his assistance to The Ghost during his investigations.

Lean and wolfish, coldly calculating, in some ways altogether unscrupulous, Joe Harper was nevertheless absolutely loyal to both George Chance and his alter ego, the Ghost.

Years ago, George Chance had discovered Glenn Sanders sitting on a bench in Central Park and had been struck by the similarity in their appearance.

He had approached Glenn Sanders with the idea of becoming his double and since Sanders was down and out on his luck he had promptly agreed.

By a curious quirk of nature, helped a little by plastic surgery, Glenn became the identical double of George Chance. Their height is the same at six feet—one inch; the sane broad shoulders and lean waist. Blue eyes, ruddy gold hair waving back from a fairly broad forehead, thin nose and mouth, prominent cheekbones.

Glenn gladly acted as George's double in exchange for all that George Chance could teach him about magic as an art and a business. Glenn gave up his own identity to become George Chance, when George himself was out ghosting.

In another passage, we read that he "was a fraction of an inch shorter than The Ghost's six feet. The same straight nose and high cheekbones, determined chin and twinkling blue eyes. A pair of lips that appeared always on the point of breaking into a whimsical smile. And lean, graceful hands."

When you looked at Glenn Sanders, you were looking at George Chance. A time or two Glenn also had an active part in the stories; he was even put in prison during "The Ghost Fights Back," in place of the real George Chance, and it was up to the Ghost to prove George Chance was innocent of murder, thus getting Glenn off death-row—which the Ghost did just as the hour approached for Glenn's execution!

Glenn was also invaluable when it came to magic illusions that required one George Chance to disappear at one point—and re-appear in another.

As with the case of Robert Demarest, I doubt that Glenn had his counterpart within any of the other hero pulp magazines. His character was unique to The Ghost series.

As the reader will quickly understand, with the Ghost using magic in his investigations, the underworld could easily guess that the Ghost and George Chance was one and the same. However, with Glenn to fill in for George, the illusion of the Ghost appearing at the same time that George Chance was around, criminals never caught the connection.

However, when the stories became shorter, there were a few cases in which Glenn was not used.

Unlike Robert Demarest, Glenn was missed in these stories.

Merry White was something of an enigma. Actually, she was a mixture of all those beautiful green-eyed vamps created by G.T. Fleming-Roberts in the popular Secret Agent "X" series over at Ace, when he was writing that exciting series. For one thing, Fleming-Roberts had a thing about green-eyed vamps. They were always present in the Secret Agent "X" series—at least when Roberts was writing the stories. Secret Agent "X" did have a girlfriend, Betty Dale, who didn't have green eyes. But Fleming-Roberts did not create the series characters. The series was actually created by Paul Chadwick. Fleming-Roberts merely took over the series after the characters had been worked out by Paul Chadwick. If Roberts had created the series, Betty Dale might have been given green eyes! With Roberts now at the helm of the series, the women that the Agent would meet most of the time would have green eyes. They were all green-eyed wonders, but one in particular will be quickly remembered by most readers. She was Felice Vincart, the Leopard Lady, and was described thusly:

Felice Vincart's face was small, nearly round, and dark complexioned (making her hair also dark, I would imagine). Her lips slightly voluptuous, were rouged a striking shade of red that was almost Chinese lacquer. Her nose was slightly tip-tilted, and her eyes were actually arresting; true emerald green they were beneath long, penciled brows that curved upwards at the outer extremities. Her every movement was feline grace.

After the demise of *Secret Agent "X"* in March, 1939, G.T. Fleming-Roberts moved over to Ned Pines' Thrilling Group, where he created The Ghost—Super Detective. This was shortly after Leo had asked Norman Daniels to create The Black Bat—the two series would be very similar in both format and, to a small degree, characterization of the main characters. The first story, "Calling The Ghost," appeared in January 1940, introducing the characters that would play their parts in this new series; the romantic interest for George Chance, alias The Ghost, was beautiful, green-eyed, Merry White. She is described thusly:

Tiny, black-haired, green-eyed, with a roguish smile that could make any man's heart flutter. She had a ten-thousand watt personality plus the sweetest face and the most graceful figure. Having little conception of the meaning of fear, she's a dark-haired angel stepping in where a fool would fear to tread; her abrupt, impulsive actions utterly unpredictable.

Or this:

She was a pretty little thing with clear green eyes and hair that was nearly black. Her figure would have met Rockette specifications, and theatrical-booking agents had always measured her personality in kilowatts.

A few times her name was misprinted as Mary, but the biggest mistake appeared in "The Case of the Black Magician," where she is described as having "blue" eyes. Why Fleming-Roberts made this obvious mistake is beyond me. But he may not have been keeping file cards on his many characters, and he was writing many short stories as well as long novels during this period, and merely forgot the green eyes. Or an editor made the mistake during edits.

Merry had performed on the stage with George Chance, magician, as his feminine assistant. But she had quickly became his love interest, and when George Chance, magician, retired from the stage, to become The Ghost, super detective, Merry became one of his most valued aides in his battle against crime. When The Ghost was on a case, Merry and his other aides: Tiny Tim Terry and Joe Harper would meet at the old rectory—an old church building considered to be haunted by the neighborhood kids—which The Ghost had turned into his home away from home when the case was active. Following are a couple of examples:

She came in wearing a sheer black dress and a wide-brimmed red hat that went well with her dark complexion. She flashed that million-dollar smile of hers, pulled off her hat, sailed it across the room. She skipped to the couch, stooped over, kissed The Ghost long and tenderly. Then she danced back, brushed upward with her narrow hand across her Madonna-like forehead and the backward roll of her dark hair. Her green eyes laughed at him.

Merry White curled up like a kitten beside The Ghost on the couch. She was the same charming girl who had provided the feminine attraction in the George Chance Magic Revue that had toured the world—a very lovely lady who someday was to become Mrs. George Chance.

And this:

Merry White ran across the room and threw her arm around my neck. Then she backed a bit, examining my ghostly get-up with her laughing green eyes.

"Old darlin' Ghost!" she said. "If you'll just take those nasty looking skull teeth out of your mouth, I'll kiss you!"

"I allowed myself to be led to the couch at one side of the basement room. There Merry contentedly curled into the crook of my arm."

It might be suggested here that Merry also takes on the similar identity with that of Carol Baldwin (from the Black Bat series). This was the same routine with Carol and Tony Quinn, alias the Black Bat, whenever the Black Bat was on a case, Carol and the other aides would meet in the secret room (not unlike The Ghost's rectory); there Carol would kiss the Black Bat and then she would curl up next to him on the couch. Both the Black Bat and the Ghost were created by Leo's editorial outline; there were many similarities between all of Leo's responsible series. The Ghost would have all of the suspects rounded up at the end of the story, where the Ghost then proceeded to identify the killer. This was the same with the Phantom Detective. And the Ghost's rectory was in keeping with the Black Bat's hidden room, which the aides entered by way of a storage shed in back of Quinn's estate, through an underground tunnel, which came up into the secret room. The rectory was reached by passing through a narrow walkway to the rear of the building, then a back door, and down stairs to a basement that was equipped like a modern apartment. When Leo had asked Norman Daniels to create the Black Bat, I am sure he gave Mr. Daniels certain specifics. It was the same instructions that Leo must have given to Fleming-Roberts. In any case, Merry White and Carol Baldwin were sisters in action, though not in looks.

A less likely answer to these similarities is that Fleming-Roberts read the Black Bat stories before creating his own characters. The Black Bat appeared in July 1939, and the Ghost came out in January 1940, six months later. A curious note to this is that one of the characters in the first Ghost story is named Theo Quinn, not a far off difference from the Black Bat's Tony Quinn. Perhaps Fleming-Roberts was trying to tell us something? Could be.

And like Carol Baldwin, Merry would be given her assignment while they are at the rectory. From there she usually ended up captured at least once during an adventure. But her captivity never lasted long. If she didn't escape on her own, then The Ghost was sure to rescue her. Yet she often came close to death. Once, in "'The Case of the Clumsy Cat," she is captured and placed in a building, the criminal then lights a fuse to set off a bomb to blow the place sky high. Fortunately, The Ghost arrives in the nick of time to rescue her. There were other situations. In one case she is imprisoned for several days before she was "allowed to escape" by her captors; she was being held for later use as a witness "for the criminals." However, The Ghost turned the trick on them. In another case, she was captured by one crook, who then lost her to another crook who had thought he was "capturing" her himself, instead of rescuing her. Anyway, she easily escapes from the second crook. But there was never any doubt that she would be rescued, and there was never any real danger of torture or other degradations.

Like all of the pulp feminine beauties, Merry was completely dedicated to George Chance and The Ghost. However, in one story, "The Ghost Fights Back," the crooks try to frame George Chance, making it look like he killed a man over her affections. There was nothing to it, of course.

However, Merry did have a little competition in one novel, and that was "The Case of the Clumsy Cat," in the form of the cat mentioned in the title; a Persian cat, to be exact, named Bangkok. I think this cat had to capture the hearts of the readers as well as George Chance. The case takes place in a rooming house, where everyone is a suspect—except the cat, of course. One resident suspects murder in the case of a dead tenant. He swipes some pills the man had been taking, gives one to the cat, which in turn makes the cat become a very clumsy cat, leading the tenant to send a message to Commissioner Ned Standish of New York City, who in turn sends down The Ghost to investigate the "case of the clumsy cat." A nice touch. The cat survived, by the way! Lots of fun, and Merry does take George Chance back to New York with her, and Bangkok remained at the rooming house. Oh well….

One scene does remain in my memory when thinking about our beautiful pulp lady, and that was from the novel, "The Case of the Laughing Corpse," when Merry is assigned the job of spying on a nightclub. She obtains the job of cigarette girl:

> Merry White didn't know when she had ever enjoyed one of the Ghost's assignments as much as this one. The Sixth Avenue club that was designated simply as Lafevre's, written in neon above the doorway, was one of the newest and swankiest places of its sort in town.
>
> Merry liked the band. In fact, she had a great deal of trouble to keep from dancing with her cigarette tray as a partner. She liked the brief and flaring skirt of her black satin costume, too. And being exquisitely feminine, she liked the admiring glances of the men patrons of the place.
>
> Neil Lafevre thought she had a find in Merry White. When Merry was refilling her tray with cigarettes at the back of the room, Neil came up to her and told her she was doing swell and to keep it up.

In this scene when a newcomer entered the club:

> Merry carried her cigarette tray over to his table. "Cigars? Cigarettes?" she suggested, waiting until the drunk looked up before she handed out her smile.
>
> The drunk looked her up and down appreciatively. In fact, she thought his cruel black eyes were a bit too attentive. She was somewhat relieved when the drunk shook his head. Merry started for the next table, but the drunk caught her by the hem of her skirt. She looked tack at him over her shoulder, one eyebrow raised, her green eyes as chill as a pair of arctic circles.
>
> "Don't," said the drunk, waving his right hand negatively, "don't get mad nor take any of thish pershonal. But d'you know what's matter with you, babe?"
>
> "I think I'm about okay," Merry said. "I was getting along peachy up to now."
>
> "Trouble with you ish," the drunk continued, "you got black hair. Go take a peroxide dip, honey, and you will be okay with Oscar."

Well, at least he didn't say anything about her changing her beautiful green eyes. And besides, there were enough blondes around—for instance Carol Baldwin. So I am very satisfied with Merry's black or "near black" hair. And it's for sure I like this green-eyed vamp just fine the way she was!

See Glenn Sanders for a description for George Chance: Born in show business, his father was an animal trainer and his mother a trapeze performer in a circus. When his parents died, leaving him a young orphan, he relied on his own ability in order to eat. Because of his early circus training, he was a fair tumbler and contortionist. He learned much of the secrets of makeup from a clown named Ricki (Ricki would later make an appearance in the story, "The Case of the Murderous Mermaid" (*Thrilling Mystery*, September, 1942).

To the grave-eyed man with the long black sideburns who traveled with the show under the name of Don Avigne, he is indebted for knowledge that has made the knife one of the deadliest of weapons in his hands. (He had never mastered the use of a gun.)

There was Professor Gabby, who taught him the principles of ventriloquism, which are today responsible for the hundreds of voices of The Ghost.

But most important of all, while he was hanging around the circus, he won the confidence of Marko the Magician. His sideshow sorcery caught and held George's fascination. Marko was German, and later died in a German concentration camp.

Magic was the ladder that helped George climb from the circus to vaudeville and from there to his own reviews. Magic had made him a fortune and he eventually retired from the stage to establish the New York School of Magic, where amateurs, bitten by the unending craze to create illusions, are taught.

While performing magic at a policeman's benefit party, George had met Commissioner Edward Standish, a man who he greatly admired, and had followed his career with interest. He had told Standish of his own interest in criminology—and how magic was similar to the other in that both depended on keen judgment of human nature and more than rudimentary knowledge of psychology.

They became fast friends, and George Chance was invited to take a hand in a current murder investigation that was giving the police department problems at the time. After solving the case, the two men decided that George was needed in police work. Thus was born the Ghost!

The Ghost: To create the character of the Ghost, he took small wire ovals and put them into his nose, tilting the tip and elongating the nostrils. For the somewhat ghostly effect proper to a ghost-character, he darkens the inside of each nostril.

Brown eye shadow goes on to darken the eye pits. Pallor comes out of a powder box. He highlights his naturally prominent cheekbones, then over his teeth he places shells the color of old ivory.

All that is left is for him to affect a fixed vacuity of expression and his face becomes something very much like a skull.

But, in roving about the city without attracting undue attention, he only needs to allow his eyes their usual animation and keep his lips closed over the yellow teeth, the Ghost is serviceably hidden beneath the exterior of an ordinary man who is merely a little less attractive than the average man on the street.

His clothes consisted of a black suit—black because the color apparently reduces the width of his shoulders and decreases his height. And, of course, renders him almost invisible in the darkness. The suit has other virtues in the way of secret pockets and clever holders of magical gimmicks he might find useful—even more useful than the small flat automatic he carries, as well as the nasty little throwing knife.

> "Before I went out, I put on a black felt crusher hat and took a look at myself in the mirror. The possibility of recognition as George Chance no longer existed. I looked like the ghost I had chosen to be—a rather husky, happy ghost, however—for the time being."

And then we have the following:

> The balloon he had inflated had a ghastly skull face printed on it with luminous print. The prowler saw the glowing skull face, utters a gasp....
>
> He gave the balloon a flick that carried it through the air toward the prowler. At the same time he called upon his powers of ventriloquism and gave the prowler the benefit of a derisive laugh.
>
> His reaction was the expected—he fired.

It was a good shot. The balloon burst, the sound of its bursting lost in the roar of gunfire so that the glowing head must have seamed to have vanished in mid-air.

Also included in the wardrobe is a flat pack of black silk. Folding the silk is no easy job, but unfolding it can be done with a flourish. Unfolded, it becomes a black domino suit with a mask hood, which will cover the Ghost from head to ankle. In the darkness the black domino is as good as the legendary Invisible Cloak. This suit also comes with black rubber gloves—all easily hidden and compact enough not to be found on his person.

As for the laugh:

Then came that gruesome chuckle that identified the Ghost. It was like no other sound in the world—a product of ventriloquism and masterful control of the vocal cords. It was a chill sound, a fearsome sound.

His fighting ability:

He saw a black gargantuan shape—a simian shape, hulking and menacing. Chance swung around. His left fist shot out like a piston, sank deep into yielding flesh and coarse, wiry hair. A grunt, and foul, hot breath exploded in Chance's face. Two thick hairy arms wrapped about the magician's body, lifting him to his toes in a mighty embrace that might have crushed the ribs of a man of flimsier makeup.

But the magician's arms were up so that they had escaped that powerful embrace. Fingers of his right hand clawed at hair on the back of the monstrous creature, while his left fist beat down like a hammer into the unseen face.

And those hammer blows hurt! The monster released his hold, plastered a huge, sweating palm over the magician's face and shoved Chance backwards to crash into the mirror.

And this scene:

The artist was in the act of searching out a pair of artificial eyelashes to glue onto the closed eyelids of one of the masks, when a chill, derisive laugh sounded within the room. Wilder turned, saw no one. He decided that his ears had tricked him—it had not been a very loud sound.

The laughter came again. Wilder turned, both hands resting on the edge of the table behind him. Were his eyes playing him tricks? Was there a black, shadow falling across the brown background of the canvas that stood against the easel?

A faint green glow appeared within a foot of the top of the long canvas. It had not been painted there. Armand Wilder knew that. It was a spot of green light about the size of a man's head, and the intensity of the illumination increased until actual features were becoming visible!

Alter Egos:

Dr. Stacey: In this role, he pretended to be an advisor to the police department, and was a familiar personage in the presence of Commissioner Standish. Following are a couple descriptions of Dr. Stacey:

He borrowed a look of wisdom by adding a pair of impressive Oxford glasses to his disguise, plus a sober dignity by virtue of a mustache. His hair was lightly powdered a dignified gray around the temples.

And this:

The man addressed as Dr. Stacey adjusted a pair of Oxford glasses to the thin bridge of his nose. He had rather a plump face for his lean body. He wore a severe black business suit. Lean, graceful fingers toyed with the black ribbon that was attached to his glasses.

Detective-sergeant Hammell (sometimes spelled Hammill): He wore a herringbone tweed suit, gray-green in color, which effectively widened and shortened the otherwise tall and lean George Chance.

He added a red toupee that bristled like a brush. Flesh-colored putty made a wide, flat nose, and a plastic plumper attached to his jaw teeth filled out the hollows of his cheeks and gave him a much wider mouth. He exaggerated this effect by touches of rouge at the end of his lips.

A badge on his vest, a black soft hat on his head, and he had become that chesty, swaggering police detective known as Sergeant Hammell.

Though he really had no authority on the police force, he seemed to be quickly recognized by other officers. In fact, Commissioner Standish actually assigned Hammell to the case in "The Case of the Walking Skeleton."

George Hazard: This character was George Chance, only in the last published story. The character of the Ghost was eliminated, and his last name changed to Hazard, a character who was an actor—and amateur criminologist who often aided the police department in their investigations.

Though all of the characters were given new names in this story, the commissioner is accidentally identified in chapter six as Standish. So, perhaps George Hazard was his greatest alter ego.

The House

Located on Fifty-fourth Street, there was actually very little action situated around this residence. However, there was some information given to it. We are told that one room has a stage in order for George Chance to perform magic for his friends at special parties.

It is a brownstone house. One room is where George and Glenn perfect their new magic inventions. One upstairs room has a closet with a trapdoor that leads to a lower floor.

He also had a series of mirrors set up which lets him see visitors to his house:

> The glass insert on top of the desk glowed, and he knew he was about to have a visitor.

> Through the medium of mirrors arranged in a periscope effect, he was able to see from his desk on the second floor, whoever approached the front door.

Again, as with the Black Bat series, it was not the main house that was important in the Ghost stories, but a "hidden" location, where he and his aides could meet to plot their course against the latest crime; here assignments were given out, and we see all of the aides together at one time. Once the assignments were given out, each agent went about their business, and then returned (or phoned) when there was something to report to the Ghost.

Very similar to the Black Bat's hidden room was the "rectory," and old church building located on East Fifty-fifth Street (about a block from his home). The old church has two lean spires that sway when a high wind sweeps across the city. In its shadow is a square brick house formerly used as a rectory. The gray brick house is always vacant, always displays a "for rent" sign on the front door. The rental is kept prohibitively too high for anyone to rent—and the owner of the rectory is George Chance.

The place has a bad reputation with small boys in the neighborhood. Its windows are always shuttered and it is somehow squat and evil looking in the shadows of the steeples that might be the home of Poe's ghouls. The place is said to be haunted—it is—by The Ghost! It is the headquarters of the Ghost:

"I turned into the narrow way between the walls of the church and the walls of the rectory. The walk led to a small court at the rear of my hideout. I mounted three steps to the back door, unlocked it, stepped into darkness and closed the door behind me. I went down basement steps unlocked another door and closed it before turning on a light.

"The basement is no spider's lair. No bones are lying in the corners and there are no chains for ghostly clanking. The basement of the house contains several livable rooms and it is home to the Ghost when he is working at his unique job of haunting criminals into the electric chair."

We are also told that tragic death had come to two successive ministers who had lived there and the place had been abandoned, its windows boarded.

It is not only furnished with couch and chairs, but contains a bar with the mixings for drinks. All appear to partake of these beverages!

The telephone number of the rectory is only known to the Ghost's agents, Commissioner Standish and Medical Examiner, Robert Demarest.

The Novels

The 1940 & 1941 period has a very interesting story. For one thing, the series changed title twice after the original one of *The Ghost—Super Detective*. It maintained the original title for only three issues, January, Spring, and Summer of 1940. With the Fall 1940 issue it becomes *The Ghost Detective*. Then the Winter 1941 issue becomes *The Green Ghost Detective*. A total of three titles, for a total of seven issues. Not bad, but possibly a little confusing.

The volume data ran three numbers per volume. The first issue, January, 1940, was Vol. 1, No. 1. The last issue was dated Summer, 1941, Vol. 3, No. 1.

The first four stories were written in the first person narrative, unique in the hero magazines, and the author was listed as George Chance, who "narrated" the exploits. This was a problem for the stories, as the Ghost had to be at the center of all action in order for him to narrate the movement of the action. There could be no breakaway to another scene where one of the agents is in danger. Instead, The Ghost had to be somewhere, like the rectory, where an agent could call on the phone, and tell The Ghost that they needed help. Fortunately, with the third issue, this began to change. The first person narrative began to slip to the third person every so often. And again, the same is true with the fourth story. By the fifth story, the more familiar third person narrative is complete—and the stories are much better; the scene can easily break away from the Ghost to another of his agents as they investigate the case on their own.

With these longer novels, the stories are very loose, too much narration, and a lot of useless dialogue. But the length of the story had probably been suggested to Fleming-Roberts by Leo Margulies, and being a writer, Roberts was happy to oblige. The shorter stories that would later appear in Thrilling Mystery and Thrilling Detective would be much tighter, better action, and less useless dialogue.

However, an eighth novel was advertised for Fall 1941, as "The Case of the Blind Soldier," but did not appear. Immediately after the publication of the seventh novel, Fleming-Roberts' Black Hood stories began. What ever became of this promised novel is anybody's guess.

The switch from "The Ghost" to "The Green Ghost" was sudden. From the first Green Ghost story, the crooks are already referring to him as The "Green" Ghost. What brings about this change is the adding (to his wardrobe) a black silk scarf with a tiny pen; this pen contains a small battery and a pail green light bulb. When turned on it gives his face a greenish tint. Also, in the heels of his shoes contain hidden cavities that, when pressed a certain way, releases a gas or mist, and used when the green light is on, causes the face to appear to wave or be non-solid to the viewer. This would carry over to the shorter stories later.

"Calling The Ghost"

By G.T. Fleming-Roberts, *The Ghost Super Detective* (January 1940, Vol. 1, No. 1)

Location: New York City

Cover: A young man, large on the cover, with New York City as the background, holds little people in his hands. One of my favorite covers among the pulps, this one was done by Rafael De Soto.

Principal Characters: Leonard Van Sickle, Theo Quinn, Hugo Wayne, Lulu Kurtzner, Fabian Deeming, Elmer Tanko, Gus Henning, Max Gerrich, Ken Vickers, Jonathan Marvin, Miss Rice, Arnold Smock,

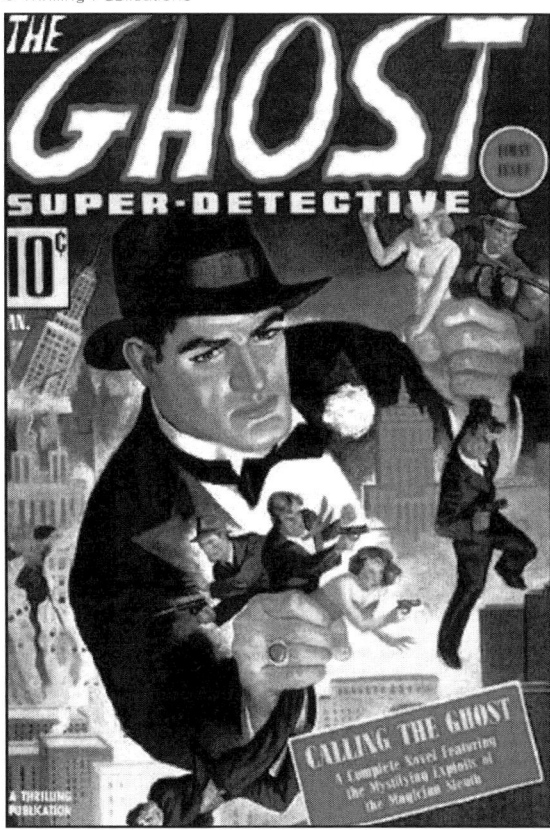

The Ghost Super Detective, January 1940.

Mrs. E.L. Long/Patsy Moore, Thomas Ivor, David John Hurst, Stephen Perkins, Dr. MacKay (dentist), Taylor Owens (Owens was the mastermind in an insurance scam).

Police/Allies: Detective Hullick, police secretary Hadley, Robert Demarest, Edward Standish, Joe Harper, Tiny Tim Terry, Merry White, Glenn Sanders.

Alter Egos: Dr. Stacey, Detective-sergeant Hammell.

The basic story plot involves the swindle of insurance companies—and innocent victims. A criminal mastermind tells unsuspecting victims that he will insure them for a lot of money, then a person who is already dying will commit suicide in their place. They can then collect the insurance money and split it. However, the victim actually becomes the victim and the criminal collects all of the insurance.

Notes: We are told that George Chance has baffled the best psychologists, and entertained the crowned heads of Europe.

The newspaper is named the *Herald*—the same newspaper where Betty Dale of Secret Agent "X" worked.

There are three clues; a person's teeth; bonds in a fictitious name; and a wire spiral.

Tiny Tim is captured.

A rope trick is used; in most stories the Ghost will use a rope trick at some point.

The next story is advertised as "The Ghost Strikes Again." It will be "The Ghost Strikes Back."

"The Ghost Strikes Back"

By G.T. Fleming-Roberts, *The Ghost Super Detective* (Spring 1940, Vol. 1, No. 2)

Location: New York City

Cover: Two men and a woman on a railroad track, one man and the woman hold guns in their hands, while the second man appears to be derailing the track. Another cover by Rafael De Soto.

Principal Characters: Dr. Seer, David Palmer, Irene Kalaban, Robert Martin, Margaret Palmer, Jimmie Calswell, Michael Holland, Harold Hackness, Augie McTeeg, Eric Emboyd, Dr. Mathew, Salvo Livingston, Randolph Curtis, Oscar, Artie Meyer, Carl Van Borg (Van Borg was the mastermind in this story. He wanted the deeds to some property in Mexico that was believed to contain large deposits of helium.

Police/Allies: Inspector John Magnus, Detective-sergeant Hullick, Hadley, Merry White, Joe Harper, Glenn Sanders, Tiny Tim Terry, Robert Demarest, Edward Standish.

Alter Egos: Dr. Stacey, Detective-sergeant Hammill (sometimes his name listed as Hamnill, and other times as Hammell).

The basic plot is the deeds, or stocks, controlling interest to a helium deposit in Mexico. George

The Ghost Super Detective, Spring 1940.

The Ghost Super Detective, Summer 1940.

Chance is framed for murder, but it's Glenn Sanders who sits in prison waiting for the death sentence to be carried out. In the mean time, The Ghost is looking for a leper. Great action!

Notes: Tim is captured again, and again uses phone in time to get the Ghost on his trail. He is saved from a burning car headed for the river.

The clues, appearing throughout the story were; a leper coin, a Mexican map with cryptic pencil notes, a light globe from the murder scene, and a typed note taken from a seer's crystal ball.

Again the rope trick—this time to carry a light bulb through a room.

"Murder Makes a Ghost"

By G.T. Fleming-Roberts, *The Ghost Super Detective* (Summer 1940, Vol. 1, No. 3).

Location: New York City

Cover: A dead man is slumped in his chair, with his desk drawer half opened. Another man looks on while holding a gun. A girl is rolling up a map of the city. Cover artist is unknown.

Principal Characters: Peter Kendle, Samson Andros, George Paton, Calvin Pieper, Dr. Stockbridge, Ronald Wicle, Stephan Orestes, Gimp Taylor, Hank Roscoe, Lefty McKay, Jules Kalkis, Jack Galema, Carol Bricker, Owen Marsh (Owen Marsh is after stocks that will net him a fortune).

Police/Allies: Inspector John Magnus, Tiny Tim Terry, Merry White, Glenn Sanders, Edward Standish, Robert Demarest, Joe Harper.

Alter Egos: Dr. Stacey, Detective-sergeant Hammell, Dillon.

Basic plot involves four Greek brothers who were

© Thrilling Publications

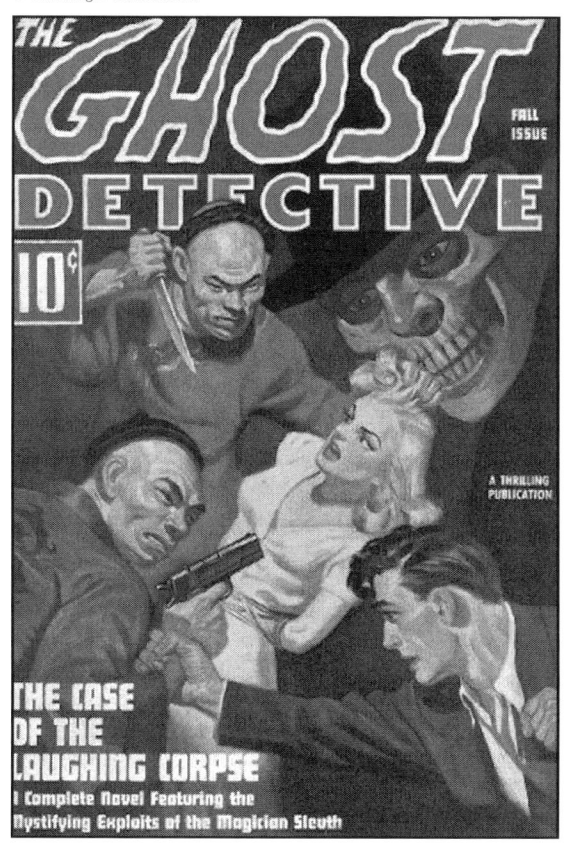

The Ghost Detective, Fall 1940.

trying to hide from a man who had sworn vengeance on them years ago. However, this man no longer wished to cause them harm. Instead, another man is after their stocks—and he is doing away with them one at a time—putting a metal hat on them and then turning on the juice—electrocution!

Notes: Merry & Tim are captured this time.

Again, the rope tricks.

Merry is held captive by one crook, when another man shows up to also take her captive. She eventually escapes from the second man.

"The Case of the Laughing Corpse"

By G.T. Fleming-Roberts, *The Ghost Detective* (Fall 1940, Vol. 2, No. 1)

Location: New York City

Cover: Two Chinese gentlemen threaten a young man and woman; one Chinaman holds the girl by her hair, while he threatens her with a knife. The young man holds the other Chinaman's arm that has a gun. Nice cover, and the artist is again Rafael De Soto.

Principal Characters: Frank Dyer, Emery Faust, Barton Clay, Julian Hornaday, Henry Fu Chang, Carter Nash, Nell Lafevre, Stanley Wilkins, Mike Pennard, Dorothy Handel, Oscar Gruder, Laura Nash, Claude Alfred, Dr. William Mallais (Dr. Mallais was the mastermind, and he was trying to steal millions in drugs).

Police/Allies: Edward Standish, Robert Demarest, Inspector John Magnus, Tiny Tim Terry, Glenn Sanders, Joe Harper, Merry White.

Alter Egos: Dr. Stacey, Detective-sergeant Hammill

The basic story plot involves the death of a man everybody hated. This man, the laughing corpse from the title, fakes his own death at first, then somebody really does kill him—a knife cut to the throat. In his will, he had left certain people (all people who hated him) brass keys. The killer wants these keys because they open a secret door that holds millions of dollars worth of narcotics.

Note: In this one, The Ghost and Joe Harper are imprisoned at the end in a room full of dynamite—and a wire recording telling them what it is all about before they are to die. Fortunately, the mastermind shows up before the bombs go off, and our heroes are able to escape; they in turn capture the mastermind.

"The Case of the Flaming Fist"

By G.T. Fleming-Roberts, *The Green Ghost Detective* (Winter 1941, Vol. 2, No. 2)

Location: New York City

Cover: A nice cover, with another man slumped in his chair dead. While a young man and woman look on: the man holds a gun in his left hand and

The Green Ghost Detective, Winter 1941.

the girl in his right. The cover artist is unknown.

Principal Characters: Samuel Thompson, Lanny Farmer, Ivan Gregory, Frank Luther, Eddie Thompson, Betty Thompson, Chester Oslow, Mel Slocum, Arthur Frame, John McNeile, Tony Luther, Gort Max Varna, Simon, Terry McNeile (McNiele was the Big Guy" who always threatened that his invisible bodyguard, Simon, would kill those who did not obey him).

Police/Allies: Edward Standish, Inspector John Magnus, Standish's secretary is mentioned, someone named Apperson is mentioned in connection with the police department, Tiny Tim Terry, Joe Harper, Glenn Sanders, Merry White, Robert Demarest.

Alter Egos: Dr. Stacey, Count Leopold del Sartos

Basic story plot is that the Big Guy is after stocks again. His bodyguard, Simon, is a magic trick, which The Ghost discloses. He is also blackmailing families for their insurance money—using a crooked gambling house to set up his suckers.

Notes: Merry White is said to use the alias of Bessy Miestnest.

Tiny Tim uses the alias of Harold Luscomb.

The string (rope) trick this time is used to return his thrown away gun; used many tines in these stories.

Merry is captured and spends four days in a basement cell of an abandoned building. She was allowed to escape, as the criminals had planted evidence against someone else, and she was supposed to release this information.

George Chance now rents the city's Drama Club Theater to bring the case to a close; in the past he had used his own home, or the home of someone else involved in the story.

The mastermind uses atropine to enable his eyes to see in the darkness—the Black Bat should have looked into this possibility, although he could already see in the darkness without atropine.

The third-person narrative is totally in effect now, and the stories move along much better.

"The Case of the Walking Skeleton"

By G.T. Fleming-Roberts, *The Green Ghost Detective* (Spring 1941, Vol. 2, No. 3)

Location: New York City

Cover: A girl is tied to a chair, while one man faces her with a gun, and another man appears to be trying to untie her from the back of the chair. The cover artist is unknown.

Principal Characters: John Turrin, Martin Drawes, Rurik Jones, Frederick Werges, Gabe Burton, Hubert Casselman, Patricia Wilder, Russell Gilbertson, Marvin Noble, Langa Doonh, Dr. Boonstray, Armand Wilder, Ian McClosky, Kenneth Leander (Leander was our mastermind behind murder and blackmail).

Police/Allies: Edward Standish, Robert Demarest, Joe Harper, Glenn Sanders, Tiny Tim Terry, Merry White.

Alter Egos: Dr. Stacey, Detective-sergeant Hanmill

The basic plot involves a comic strip in a famous studio, in which the characters in the strip are based on real-life people, who are being blackmailed. Suddenly, the artist of the comic strip turns up as a skeleton, and then others also end up the same way. While at the home of one of the original real-life adventurers there is a swimming pool set in a tropical surrounding, and within the pool is a family of man-eating fish from the jungle of Guiana.

Notes: This is one of the best of the Ghost stories in this series, and reads like a Secret Agent "X" novel from his earlier days!

Standish assigns Detective-sergeant Hammill to the case.

The case involves a comic strip version of four real-life adventurers: John Turrin, Martin Drawes, Fredrick Werges and Ian McClosky, who had once traveled to French Guiana on an expedition; because of an accident, Ian McClosky had been killed by the others. Someone was blackmailing the remaining three men.

"The Case of the Black Magician"

By G.T. Fleming-Roberts, *The Green Ghost Detective* (Summer 1941, Vol. 3, No. 1)

Location: New York City

Principal Characters: Soul Brokhage, Wayne Parks, Jerome Weeden, Ralph Sands, Donald McKay, Miss Sarah Light, Dr. Maxim Conder, Robert Nineva, Jimny Kent, Eva Johnston, Mrs. Van Bergen, Mal Foss, Ahern, Mr. Swain, Wilson, Harry Hasket, 'Winy' Jeff Wienhardt, Ben Orpington, Anson Torey (Anson Torey was the mastermind behind the plot; a member of the anti-crime commission, he really wants to control the underworld as its boss).

The Green Ghost Detective, Spring 1941.

Police/Allies: Detective Wendt, Standish' secretary, Ned Standish, Robert Demarest, Marcus, Glenn Sanders, Joe Harper, Tiny Tim, Merry White.

Alter Egos: Detective-sergeant Hammil, Dr. Stacey, and Mr. Campbell

The basic plot involves the group of an anti-crime commission that are supposed to be fighting crime; however, one of them loses evidence that is uncovered that can put one gangster out of business. Meanwhile, this particular crook is being blackmailed by someone hidden behind a mask, and made to follow orders.

All evidence points to a magician who had been brought to trial by this same commission years before, and now is back in society and appears to be after the members of the crime commission, killing them one by one.

The Green Ghost Detective, Summer 1941.

But actually the killer is one of the members of the crime commission; he plans on leading the organized crime of the city.

Notes: The interior illustrations are signed C. A. Murphy, a regular at Thrilling.

The Ghost has blue-gray eyes; normally they were just blue.

Merry White has blue eyes! What happened to her green eyes?

The Ghost is captured, his feet weighted, hands tied, and thrown into a watery grave.

Clues consist of a green soapstone figurine and false artificial eyelashes.

Joe Harper now calls The Green Ghost "Gee Gee." Says things like, "Haunt your way over here and boo him into talking."

This story has a similar plot to Norman Daniels' September 1940 Black Bat story, "The Black Bat's Triumph," in which 7 men of wealth are sent valueless trinkets (clay figurines) with hidden jewels inside that are worth millions. Our mastermind is also after these clay figurines.

The next novel is advertised as "The Case of the Blind Soldier," but it does not appear. In fact, the character now loses his own magazine and will be assigned to the long-running *Thrilling Mystery*, and the stories will now be shorter.

Thrilling Mystery began in October 1935 as a similar publication to Popular Publications' *Dime Mystery*, *Horror Stories* and *Terror Tales*. In the beginning, this magazine published the same type stories. But by 1942, it became the outlet for some of Standard's off-the-wall titles, even continuing such series as The Masked Detective and The Green Ghost stories.

The publication ended with the Fall 1944 (Vol. 22, No. 2) issue, finally printing the last Masked Detective story.

The last novel had advertised the next story as "The Case of the Blind Soldier," but almost immediately G.T. Fleming-Roberts started his Black Hood series, so it is doubtful that "The Case of The Blind Soldier" got any further than the planning stages. Or perhaps it ended up rewritten into something else.

But The Green Ghost was not dead. Beginning in September 1942, and appearing in six issues, the last appearing in Winter 1944. G.T. Fleming-Roberts wrote some of his best Ghost stories in short form.

"The Case of the Murderous Mermaid"

By G.T. Fleming-Roberts, *Thrilling Mystery* (September 1942, Vol. 19, No. 2)

Cover: The cover features a man holding a woman in his left hand while his right hand is firing a pistol. The girl is tied and gagged. A movie camera is in the background.

Location: Fulton Heights, N.Y.C.

Thrilling Mystery, September 1942.

Thrilling Mystery, November 1942.

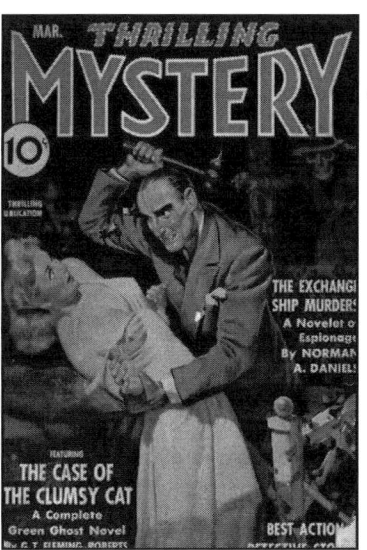

Thrilling Mystery, March 1943.

Principal Characters: Martin Hess, Ricki, Harry Marquand, Jerry Haines, Fay McKay, Tanko, Margaret Hess, Gregor Latour/Max Conrad (Conrad, in the disguise of Latour was the mastermind).

Alter Egos: Detective-sergeant Hammel

Police/Allies: Ned Standish, Robert Demarest mentioned, Merry White, Joe Harper, Tiny Tim Terry, Captain Bushman.

The basic plot takes place around a circus, where a criminal named Max Conrad is hiding under the alias of Gregor Latour. The case involves counterfeit money and murder.

Notes: Glenn Sanders is captured, thought to be The Green Ghost.

Ricki, the clown that was mentioned from the beginning, who had taught George Chance the art of makeup, makes an appearance in this story. This was nothing new for G.T. Fleming-Roberts. When he wrote the Secret Agent "X" stories over at Ace, he brought into the series the Agent's boss, a man who had always been called K-9. Roberts used him twice. Also, we were told that ten wealthy men were financing the Agent in his battle against the New York criminals; in one novel, Roberts brought in two of these men—they were Rex Dumont and Maurice Biers. They appeared in the last story. Also, Roberts was the author who disclosed the Agent's true face in "City of Madness." And the doctor who had treated a young officer for shrapnel wounds on the battlefield in France, was given a part in Roberts' "Brand of the Metal Maiden," and could identify the Agent we were told. (More about this doctor later.)

"The Case of the Astral Assassin"

By G.T. Fleming-Roberts, *Thrilling Mystery* (November 1942, Vol. 19, No. 3)

Location: New York City

Principal Characters: Monty Folkstone, Peter Creighton, David Hurley, Steve Parkinson, Charles Polk, Herman Blackfore, Dr. Leonard, "Legs" Maloney, Madame La Strange, Kenneth Deene (Deene is "the Invisible Man. ")

Alter Egos: Sgt Hammill

Police/Allies: Ned Standish, his secretary not named, John Magnus, Merry White, Glenn Sanders, Tiny Tim.

The basic plot is borrowed from the Black Bat

Thrilling Mystery, June 1943.

again, this time from "The Black Bat's Invisible Enemy," from September 1941. In this case an invisible man appears to be killing people. But the Green Ghost figures it out easily enough, and does some invisible tricks of his own.

Notes: Robert Demarest does not appear in these shorter stories, though he is sometimes mentioned.

"The Case of the Clumsy Cat"

By G.T. Fleming-Roberts, *Thrilling Mystery* (March 1943, Vol. 20, No. 2)

Cover: The cover featured a man holding a young girl with his left arm while he swings a hammer with a nail on the end towards her head. The Green Ghost looks on in background.

Location: Edgarton, N.Y.C.

Principal Characters: Edna Gravens, Dorothy Gravens, William Philmore, Doc Roy Lex, Frank Lannagen, Arthur Stuart, Jasper Maynard, Tom Huston, Mother Beel, "Little Jeff" Jeff Humber, Peter T. Smith/ Humphrey Rennard, Rosa Hillhouse/Helen House, Q. T. Annaman/Harry Coe (Harry Coe was the mastermind, blackmailing the tenants of the boarding house).

Alter Egos: Dr. Stacey

Police/Allies: Ned Standish, Robert Demarest mentioned, Merry White, Joe Harper, Tiny Tim, Glenn Sanders.

The basic plot in this fine little story involves blackmail. The mastermind forces his victims to live in a boarding house, and then charges them blackmail through the rent they are forced to pay.

Notes: This later out-of-town adventures may have been suggested by Leo Margulies, as they can also be found in the Black Bat series as well as others.

The cat, Bangkok is part of the story.

The Green Ghost is buried alive in a half-filled grave.

Most of the story takes place at Harmony House—probably a fictional house that is patterned after Roberts' own "Witch House" where he once lived. It should also be noted that he had another series that takes place exclusively in Hillery House.

Glenn & Merry are captured and imprisoned in a warehouse set to explode.

Glenn had taken George Chance's place as a guard at the warehouse.

"The Case of the Bachelor's Bones"

By G.T. Fleming-Roberts, *Thrilling Mystery* (June 1943, Vol. 20, No. 3)

Location: Amboyd (probably New York State)

Principal Characters: Roy Bartlet, William Simmons, Hugh Burkey, Edith Muns, Shag Hemphil, Dr. Hereford, Gabby Burns, Lanky Leyton, Raymond, Dr. Jefferson Hall (Hall was the mastermind behind this gambling house murder.)

Alter Egos: None

Police/Allies: Sheriff Clasner, Merry White, Joe Harper, Glenn Sanders

The basic plot involves the hunt for illegal gambling houses that are taking advantage of our young soldiers. During the investigation in Amboyd, the Green Ghost comes upon a fire that has killed several people, including a crook in hiding. The clue of the "bachelor's bones" were a pair of crooked dice.

Notes: George, Joe and Merry are already in Amboyd. Merry is sent back to New York City where she is to stay, and Glenn Sanders is sent by Merry to the town to assist George in the investigation.

Tiny Tim does not make an appearance; nor does Standish, nor is Demarest mentioned.

This could be the missing story, "The Case of the Blind Soldier."

"The Case of the Broken Broom"

By G.T. Fleming-Roberts, *Thrilling Mystery* (Fall 1943, Vol. 21, No. 1)

Location: N.Y.C., Wescott

Principal Characters: Wendal Bishop, Reed Kelmar, Doc Stuart Halsey, Rice, Whitman, Miss Billings, Fred Rodehaas, Edwin Q. Markham, Mort Bishop, Milly, Tom Seeley, Matthew, Mrs. Thomas, Joe Thomas, Henry Shallot (Shallot is our mastermind who was being blackmailed by Wendal Bishop before he killed him).

Alter Egos: None

Police/Allies: Ned Standish, Robert Demarest mentioned, Joe Harper, Merry White, Tiny Tim, Glenn Sanders.

The basic plot involves a man being blackmailed, who decides to kill his tormentor. The secret of the broken broom leads the Green Ghost to a graveyard.

Notes: In this story, George Chance stays at a hotel, the Shallot House, which is a lot like the Harmony House from "The Case of the Clumsy Cat."

Thrilling Mystery, Fall 1943.

"The Case of the Evil Eye"

By G.T. Fleming-Roberts, *Thrilling Mystery* (Winter 1944, Vol. 21. No. 2)

Location: N.Y.C.

Principal Characters: Tony Rex, Benny Akers, Ralph "Tinhorn" Gabriel, Iggy Miggs, 'Tiger" Mullin, Dorothy Bishop, "Sailor" Mack Hollis (Hollis is our murderer).

Alter Egos: None

Police/Allies: Merry White, Joe Harper, Ned Standish mentioned, Glenn Sanders mentioned.

Boxing is the basic plot line for this story; while a match is going on, a man in the front rows stands up and gives one of the boxers the "evil eye," at which time the boxer falls over dead.

Merry and George are at the boxing match and witness the strange event. George sends Merry home,

Thrilling Mystery, Winter 1944.

calls in Joe—who is already at the match watching one of the suspects. Within a few hours time, they have unraveled the mystery, and find that poison, not the evil eye, had caused the death.

Of the complete series, this one story I rated the least enjoyable, but it did have its moments.

Notes: In these later stories from *Thrilling Mystery,* about the only involvement that Ned Standish has is that he receives strange messages from concerned citizens that a crime—or mystery—is going on, or about to happen; Standish then contacts George Chance, who investigates if he deems it necessary.

Thrilling Mystery had advertised the next story as "The Case of the Phantom Bridegroom." However, it did not appear. In all appearance the series had finally came to an end. Fortunately, the story had been written, and G.T. Fleming-Roberts sold the story to Leo Margulies. Like the last Masked Detective story, "Monarchs of Murder," it too would appear.

However, it was given to the pages of *Thrilling Detective,* a magazine that Ned Pines had brought out in November 1931 as a companion to his *Thrilling Love Stories.* It was one of his longest running publications and was also published under the Better Publications. From Vol. 1, No. 1 to its demise in Summer 1953, the publication lasted at least 213 issues.

The one main difference between this publication and that of Leo's other magazines, *Thrilling Detective* did not run the more visible "masked" type of detective. Instead, the main line of story was that of the hardboiled, hard-nose detectives. The Green Ghost would have actually been out of place here.

However, it is within the pages of this magazine that our last Green Ghost story did appear! The title was "The Phantom Bridegroom," and George Chance magician-detective, becomes George Hazard, actor-detective. The Green Ghost was dropped.

"The Phantom Bridegroom"

By G.T. Fleming-Roberts, *Thrilling Mystery* (October 1944, Vol. 11, No. 1)

Location: New York City

Cover: Girl laying on a couch, tied, while a man kneels at her side, gun in right hand, knife in left hand. Artist is Rudolph Belarski.

Principal Characters: Grace Hathorn, Harry Evans, Mike Claney, Jack Gullan, Ronald Innes, Catherine Innes, Eddie "Duke" DeLisso, Abu'l Faraj, Simon Fennwick, Giles Fennwick, Rahman, Basil Randino (Randino is our master criminal this time. He killed for vengeance).

Alter Egos: Mr. Nero

Police/Allies: Police Commissioner Lawrence Cornish, Sunny Rogers, Goliath Sanders, Will Hobart, Inspector Murphy.

The basic plot lies in an age-old con game of dashing, handsome men who prey on wealthy widows.

Sunny, an actress who has taken a job at a sanitarium believes one of the patients, a woman who claims that she had been married, but her husband had disappeared on their wedding night.

Sunny brings in her actor-boyfriend, George Hazard, who starts his own investigation into the affair.

Notes: George Hazard is George Chance!

"Lawrence Cornish is Ned Standish! In chapter 6, page 26, column one, the editors forgot to change the name, and he is named "Standish."

Standish' secretary is now a girl named Janet Trees. She has a small active part.

Hazard lives in a modern apartment on East 55th Street; the "rectory," of course.

Goliath, called "Goly" for short, was a pint-sized former jockey who frequently played kid parts on the stage (!), smokes big cigars, and calls Will Hobart "a chiseler." Tiny Tim Terry & Glenn Sanders inhabit his body.

Will Hobart is a "muscle" man, a powerful dark skinned gent, with a prodigious appetite, who had once been a professional boxer and showed the signs of it around his ears. Hobart was "a chiseler," as he was really Joe Harper.

Sunny Rogers was, of course, green-eyed vamp, Merry White!

Inspector Murphy was Inspector Magnus.

This final entry was a far superior story to the previous one.

Hazard wore a black suit, black hat and scarf. Yeah!

"The Phantom Bridegroom" would have been a nice Green Ghost entry. It is a shame that the Green Ghost was dropped. However, with very little imagination, one can easily see our hero in this new disguise of George Hazard.

Some Final Thoughts

When the series first started, the narrative was in the first person, and the story signed George Chance (as the author), but all were written by G.T. Fleming-

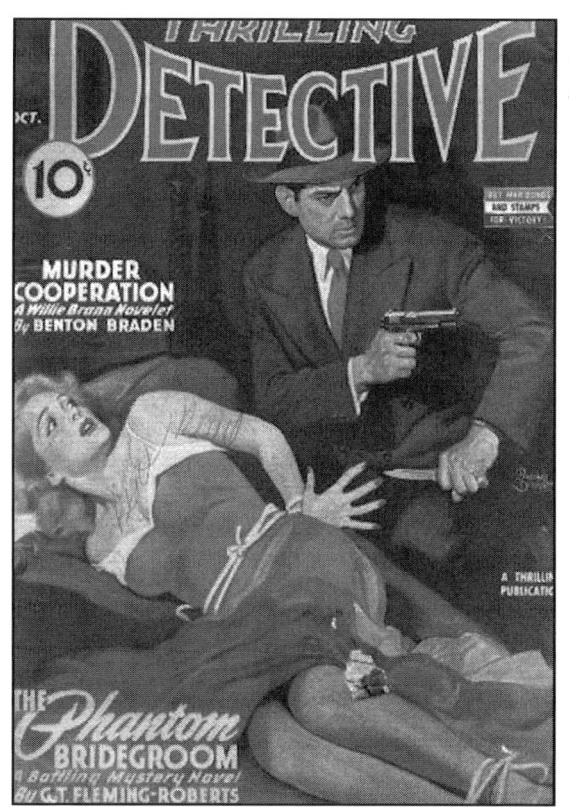

Thrilling Mystery, October 1944.

Roberts. The first person narrative did not work well, making it necessary for George Chance to have center stage at all times, so the story could not break away to another scene involving his other aides. The camera was always on George Chance.

The third and fourth novels did start switching from the first person to the third person narrative, but the main text was still first person.

All of this changed with the fifth story; the magazine became The Green Ghost Detective, the authorship was now listed as G.T. Fleming-Roberts, and the third person narrative was in effect—and would stay.

My favorite novel was "The Case of the Walking Skeleton." My favorite shorter pieces were from Thrilling Mystery, "The Case of the Clumsy Cat," and "The Case of the Broken Broom." The Thrilling Detective story, "The Phantom Bridegroom," was an equally nice entry, but the character of the Ghost had been dropped for the publication of the story.

G.T. Fleming-Roberts, as an author, was very imaginative, and his quality as a writer cannot be questioned. Two of my all-time favorite stories, "City of Madness," and "Claws of the Corpse Cult," one of which was the most exciting story I have read in the pulps, and the other was one of the best written pulp stories. Both were Secret Agent "X" entries, and both were written by G.T. Fleming-Roberts.

Some of the clues that were listed in the stories were actually silly things; why there was such a mystery behind a person jumping from a tall building without his false teeth is beyond me. Not to mention why the Commissioner of Police thought this fact alone was enough to baffle his own police force, and brought in The Ghost, is another question for the reader to fathom.

Actually, the stories were just starting to improve when the character was delegated to the pages of another magazine.

The proof is within the quality of these Thrilling Mystery stories themselves. The letter section of the magazine was possible proof that the character was not working. There were a few letters, but there wasn't much to be said in them; a fellow magician had a few words to say about the disclosure of some tricks. Others wrote that they liked the characters. But the feeling just wasn't there. Not like it was with, say the Black Bat or Phantom Detective.

So I don't think the problem was with Robert's writing, but very probably in the character of the hero. The Green Ghost just did not come across.

Another factor in attributing quality to the stories is the number of appearances—or births—it had. From the very first, it started as *The Ghost—Super Detective*, changed to *The Ghost Detective*, then to *The Green Ghost Detective*, and finally to *Thrilling Mystery* and *Thrilling Detective*. Then in 1950 & 1951 it was back; this time in *5 Detective Novels*. The stories were Winter 1950 (Vol. 1, No. 2) "The Case of the Astral Assassin," the Summer 1950 (Vol. 2, No. 1) "The Case of the Murderous Mermaid," Winter 1951 (Vol. 2, No. 3) "The Case of The Clumsy Cat," and Spring 1951 (Vol. 3, No. 1) "The Case of the Broken Broom." Nice entries all.

Another strange crossover from the Secret Agent "X" series to the Green Ghost series, is the alter ego of Dr. Stacey from The Ghost. In the "X" series, Agent X had been wounded on the battlefields of France. Shrapnel was removed from his chest, but it left a large scar in the shape of a crude "X" thus giving him his identifying nark. The Agent was in the intelligence service, but the doctor that treated the wound felt that only a man of great evil could have suffered such a wound and still live.

The doctor who possibly saved the life of the future Secret Agent "X" was Doctor Malcolm Palmer. Nothing else is mentioned of his combat duties or rank, but he did make an appearance in "Brand of the Metal Maiden," and the doctor was afraid that "X" would kill him—because he could identify him, and he thought that "X" was some super criminal. Here is his description:

> Remarkably broad across the jowls, his head tapered to a narrow forehead. Oxford glasses, fitted with a broad black ribbon, pinched the bridge of his button nose."

The Oxford glasses gave him away. Dr. Stacey had a habit of fingering the black ribbon that was fitted to his "Oxford" glasses.

I am sure that there were many such crossovers between his many series. Including the last pulp hero, Captain Zero, who G.T. Fleming-Roberts created for Popular Publications in 1949, which included a green-eyed vamp named Doro Kelly as the love interest for our hero.

In fact, even the red hair of George Chance was nothing new. Diamondstone was not only a magician-detective, but sported red hair also. And if this wasn't enough, we can go back to the Secret Agent "X" series for "The Assassins' League" (October 1937), in which the Agent uses the following disguise:

> "Red" broke away from a window and came toward the dour-faced man. Red was all that the name implied. He was perhaps the youngest man in the group. He had a turned-up nose, a laughing mouth, countless freckles and a shock of unruly red hair. He had a lean waist and broad-shoulders. The pocket of his coat sagged by the weight of his flash lamp. He had a camera and a tripod over one shoulder. An otherwise sad hat was given an air of jauntiness by the way it was tilted on the back of his head.

Green-eyed vamps and red headed heroes were something of a trademark for G.T. Fleming-Roberts it would seem. I would be curious to know how many other such characters appeared in his many short stories. More than a few, I would imagine.

Fleming-Roberts' files listed three Secret Agent "X" stories that were never printed as such. Whatever became of them may never be known. The same can be said about a Green Ghost story; the Fall 1941 issue of *The Green Ghost Detective* was announced with a lead story titled "The Case of the Blind Soldier." The story did not appear—as a Green Ghost story. However, it is very possible that the story was re-titled when Roberts thought his series had been canceled, and changed the character into someone else. It's also a good possibility that "The Case of the Bachelor's Bones" is the missing title. In the March 1942 issue of *Exciting Detective*, a Fleming-Roberts story, "Dance With a Dead Man," appears. A blurb stating, "by the author of The Black Magician" and "Diamondstone Returns." We already know about "The Black Magician," but what about the story, "Diamondstone Returns?" This story was not on Roberts' records, nor do I know exactly when it appeared; however, it would have been after June 1939, and before March 1942. A good guess would be sometime around the disappearance of "The Case of the Blind Soldier." And since Diamondstone was a red headed magician-detective, it would have been very easy for Fleming-Roberts to make a few changes and presto! But this is mere speculation on my part.

If Roberts wrote three unpublished Secret Agent "X" stories, I would be surprised if they did not appear somewhere, albeit with some changes. And I believe the same true for the unpublished "Blind Soldier" story. If it were indeed written, it would have surely been printed somewhere—with some changes, of course. And until someone comes up with "Diamondstone Returns," my thoughts are merely speculation. But wouldn't it be nice to locate those three Secret Agent "X" stories—and wouldn't it be nice to locate that missing Green Ghost story—even under a different title, with another name for the hero?

Fleming-Roberts used a lot of rope tricks, not only in the Ghost stories but in numerous other series, one of the best scenes appearing in the Captain Zero series. It has also been suggested that Fleming-Roberts may have written the last Masked Detective story, "Monarchs of Murder" (*Thrilling Mystery*, Fall 1944). He had written a previous Masked Detective story, "The Poison Puzzle," so it's possible. However, it isn't listed on his partial records. ♦

The Black Hood

By Tom Johnson

The Black Hood had a short pulp life. Beginning with "Death's Five Faces," September 1941 in *Black Hood Detective* (Vol. 2, No. 6), and written by G.T. Fleming-Roberts. The publisher was Columbia Publications, Inc., 1 Appleton Street, Holyoke, MA, with the editorial offices located at 60 Hudson Street, New York City, N.Y. *Black Hood Detective* was probably a continuation of *Detective Yarns*, which had ended in April 1941 (Vol. 2, No. 5). This magazine had been published by Blue Ribbon Magazine Inc., same address as above. In April 1941, most of the Blue Ribbon—most likely all—were put under the Columbia Publications imprint. (1)

The character of the Black Hood first appeared in comic book form in *Top Notch* #9 (October 1940), which was also a Columbia Publications, Inc. line of comics. But by September 1941, they had hired G.T. Fleming-Roberts to write a series of novels (actually novellas, as they were approximately 35 pages each) for their pulp magazine line, beginning with Vol. 2, No. 6 of the *Black Hood Detective*. This magazine was re-titled later as *Hooded Detective* (Vol. 3, No. 1) in November 1941, with a second story, titled "The Corpse Came C.O.D." A third story, "The Whispering Eye," was published in January 1942 in the new magazine title, *Hooded Detective*. And though the character would have continued life (off and on) in the comics, the pulp series would end with the third story.

The Characters

Kip Burland: Topping six feet, lean, broad-shouldered, his smooth cheeks seemed to be molded in bronze. He was of slight build, rather tall. Beneath his more generously fitted clothes was a body stripped of beef, steel-sinews, with smooth muscles of latent power. He had a strongly formed chin, humorous lips that sometimes broke into a flashing, friendly smile. His cheeks were smooth and bronzed, his hair a deep brown. There was something compelling in the glance of his dark eyes, something intense and very earnest.

And this: It was a pleasant face, sun bronzed and well formed, with waving brown hair and eyes that could be gentle and compassionate.

The Black Hood: From a voluminous pocket on the inside of his dress coat, he removed a flat black packet of dull silk. Then he removed his coat, vest, shirt and trousers. His clean-limbed, well knit body was clothed in brilliant yellow silk tights such as an acrobat might wear. The wide black belt about his middle served a dual purpose. Not only did it lend him support but served as a secret container for numerous small articles which he had found useful in his many battles with criminals.

He removed his dress shoes, revealing an inner shoe that was ounces lighter, made of strong black linen and gum rubber-soled. He unfolded the packet of silk. The body of the package was composed of a black silk hood to which was attached a long black cape of the same material. Inside the folded cape and hood was a pair of black latex supporter shorts. He stepped into the shorts, drew them up to his waist. He put on the black hood. It combined head covering and also a mask that concealed his face to the tip of his nose. The long cape trailing from the back of the hood could be used to envelope him if he desired to conceal himself in the shadows. (Later, the cape would be attached to his shoulders, not the hood.) His final move was to take from the pocket of his discarded trousers, a pair of gauntlet gloves of strong black leather.

He was no longer Kip Burland. He was the Black Hood, the 'man of mystery,' enemy of crime. His spectacular figure was known the country over, but his was the face that no one knew.

The Black Hood wasn't like the cops at all. He didn't trail a man with screaming sirens and blasting whistles. He hunted like a panther in the night, alone and silently. And you never knew when the shadow of this master manhunter was to fall across your path:

> "Black Hood sprung out from the pole, swooped down upon the messenger like a huge black bat. The man turned to flee to late. Black Hood caught him by the coat tails, dragged him back. The messenger turned, grappled with Black Hood. Then followed one of those grim, silent struggles, too deadly serious for oaths and threats. Rat this pawn of the Eye may have been, but even a cornered rat will fight with the courage of a lion." ("The Whispering Eye."

Joe Strong: He was muscle-conscious. With all the money he could possibly use at his disposal, he nevertheless bought suits that were a size too small for him. The great Strong biceps, which had rowed his college team to victory bulged the sleeves of his dress suit coat. The powerful thighs that had driven him tirelessly across the goal for many a touchdown, strained the seams of his trousers. His red hair bristled in defiance to any comb. His nose looked as though it had been hit a few times in its owner's lifetime. He also had the misfortune of being about as graceful as a steam shovel. In the third story, Joe had been hired by *The Daily Opinion*, as a newspaper cameraman to assist Barbara Sutton, who was also a reporter for the newspaper.

Barbara "Babs" Sutton: There was plenty about Barbara to excite jealousy. She was a slim, graceful girl with honey-colored hair and violet eyes. There was a certain unspoiled sweetness about her mouth that had awakened the desires of many men. Also from a rich family, she traveled the society route, being invited to all of the big events in the city, and was accepted among the society crowd. She resided at the old Sutton mansion on West End Avenue. She had been hired by The Daily Opinion as a reporter (though she did not need any kind of job). However, this was in the last story, and as the mastermind of the story turned out to be the owner of the newspaper (he was going broke, thus he turned to crime), it is doubtful that Barbara or Joe would continue as reporter and cameraman after this one novel.

Barbara was the constant companion of Kip Burland and Joe Strong, and though it was never mentioned that Joe was in love with her, he was constantly trying to impress her with his deeds. On the other hand, Kip Burland was in love with her. However, Barbara loved another—a certain man of mystery, wearing a black hood. And the Black Hood had confessed his love to her many times, we are told.

Sergeant McGinty: Assigned to the homicide squad, he was the bumbling detective who was always after the hero. He was red-faced, potato-nosed Irishman of the homicide squad. He had a habit of jabbing people with a forefinger that resembled a sausage. He was short, beefy, and the most ardent enemy of the Black Hood on the police force. He was present in each of the novels, but saw very little action. In the second story, he only appeared towards the end, after the case had been wrapped up.

The Skull: He had once been a workman at the Barnsdal shops until an accident had thrown a retort of caustic chemicals into the workman's face. The chemicals had eaten away the flesh, destroying all that was human on the man's face. He had become so hideous that none could look upon him without shuddering.

When Kip Burland had been on the police force, he had come up against the Skull. The Skull had framed him and Kip was thrown off the force. While out on bond, Kip went after the Skull, only to be met by the Skull's men who sent bullets into his young body, leaving him for dead.

In the comic book stories, I understand that the Skull was a recurring villain, but in the first pulp story, "Death's Five Faces," Black Hood tangles with him only once, and this time he is stopped. The Skull made a good villain, and would have worked nicely as a recurring criminal in the pulp series, too.

The Hermit: Very little is mentioned about this character in the pulp series, but he had found Kip Burland after Kip had been shot and left for dead by the Skull's men. The Hermit had nursed Kip back to health, at the same time building a new body on his already powerfully built frame. He only appeared in the last novel, "The Whispering Eye," though he was mentioned from the very beginning of the series:

> At the fringe of dawn the next morning, Black Hood was high in the Catskills, in the mountain fastness of that whiskered old man who had been his teacher—the man known simply as the Hermit. There in the Hermit's laboratory, Black Hood and the old man made a careful analysis of that scanty sample of powder, which Black Hood had scrapped from the coat of the murdered man.
>
> Finally, the old man straightened from the microscope over which he had been bending.
>
> "My son," he asked of the Black Hood, "what are your findings?"
>
> "The stuff is face powder," Black Hood said. "But it's something else, too. Mixed in with the face powder is another substance,"
>
> "Naphthionate of sodium," the Hermit said.

And This: It was the Hermit's vast store of scientific knowledge that had brought the half-dead cop back to health. It was the Hermit who gave the ex-cop a body with the strength of steel and a mind that was a veritable encyclopedia of scientific knowledge. It was the Hermit who had sent the ex-cop back into the world to live a useful life, to strike back at the denizens of the underworld who had harmed him.

So the Black Hood was born to life in two identities. By day he was a pleasant, mild-mannered young man known as Kip Burland. But at night Kip Burland became the Black Hood, man of mystery, hunter of killers, and it had been the Hermit who had given him this second life.

The Vamps

One of the main things I like about G.T. Fleming-Roberts' stories are those beautiful vamps he liked to introduce into his novels. This was more evident in his stories about Secret Agent "X," but once in awhile these same mystery women were brought over to his other series. Two such vamps appeared in the Black Hood stories, namely the first and last story in the series. Though there were several women mentioned in the second story, none were mysterious vamps; they had nothing to do with the crime. But let's take a look at the two who were present that do fit into that category:

Countess Anna Odinstov: From "Death's Five Faces." (The first scene is a two-bit flophouse, probably around skid row.)

> One of these miserable beds held one who appeared to be little more than a youth. He was fully dressed in ill-fitting trousers and a turtleneck sweater. He wore a battered cap on his head. His soft, rounded cheek was pressed close to the filthy pillow, and his deep blue eyes were very wide.
>
> A man bunked on the mattress next to the one the youth had left, whispered to one of his companions.
>
> "The Skull gave the kid an order."

The other man moistened dry lips.

"Something funny about that kid, Jones. He's too dammed good-looking to be a man."

Later, at a birthday party that was being given for the son of a wealthy industrialist:

The woman was beautiful. She was tall, and wore her thick gold hair in heavy braids that were wound about her shapely head like a turban. She had unusually long, almond-shaped eyes, surmounted by slender brows that slanted upward at the outer extremities, giving her face an element of the exotic. She was dressed in black satin that fitted her perfect figure like a coat of paint. Slender shoulder straps of turquoise crossed her milk-white shoulders. She was Russian, probably some exile of Czarist days—and she was presently a spy of that country!

She was the youth from the flophouse, and was working with the Skull under orders from her foreign government.

Vida Garvais: From "The Whispering Eye." The woman was beautiful. She wore a white evening gown. Her beautifully molded face was nearly as white as her dress. Her hair was black as India ink, drawn back from her rounded forehead to knot softly at the back of her head. Her eyes were cool green with an exotic lift at the outer extremities of the lids. She smiled—a smile that did not quite reach her green eyes.

Two things were always popping up in a Fleming-Roberts story; one would be a man with red hair. In this case, Joe Strong had the red hair. The second case would be a woman with green eyes! Both appeared in the Secret Agent "X" stories, and both appeared in the (Green) Ghost stories. I would imagine the same two identifying descriptions occurred in his other series. Merry White from the Green Ghost had green eyes. Doro Kelly from Captain Zero had green eyes. The Leopard Lady from Secret Agent "X" had green eyes, as well as several others in that series.

George Chance, the Green Ghost had red hair, Diamondstone had red hair. The Secret Agent used an identity that had red hair! It was a certainty that when one of the women in his stories had green eyes, she would be unforgettable.

The Novels

Our first story is "Death's Five Faces," September 1941, from *Black Hood Detective*, Vol. 2 No. 6. The author is G.T. Fleming-Roberts.

A hundred thousand dollars in valuable cutting tools disappear; tools so essential to a nation engaged in a gigantic defense effort that factories will be forced to close without them… A millionaire's son is kidnapped… Murder follows upon murder… And one lone mysterious figure, The Black Hood, grim avenger of crime, sets out to solve this perplexing riddle of murder and kidnapping….

Location: New York City.

Main characters: Mr. Gautier, Phillip "Waxie" King, Harry Shane, Barbara Sutton, Joe Strong, Kip Burland, Alan Hadley, Countess Anna Odinstov, Hugo Barnsdal, Miss Pike, Billy Shane, Mary Logan, Sergeant McGinty, police officer Dunlavey, The Skull/Blinky/Gregory Leeds.

Notes: Kip Burland has a little flat in Greenwich Village. In his apartment he has a small printing press. In the living room is a closet containing a large cabinet that rolled on casters. Within the cabinet were numerous glass instruments, reagent bottles, finger print powder and a fine comparative microscope. In the kitchen was a small darkroom for developing photographs.

The Skull, whose face had been destroyed in a factory accident, uses several rubber masks to hide his own identity; one was that of a resemblance to "Napoleon," and another is that of Blinky, a half blind stool pigeon used by Sergeant McGinty. A third is that of Gregory Leeds. The other two masks (from that of the "Death's Five Faces") were probably no more than non-entities just to allow him to disappear

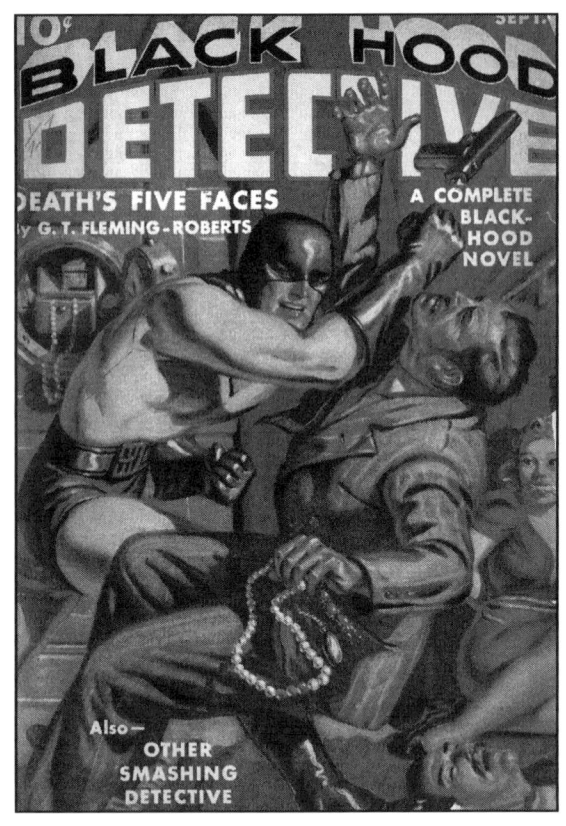

Black Hood Detective, September 1941.

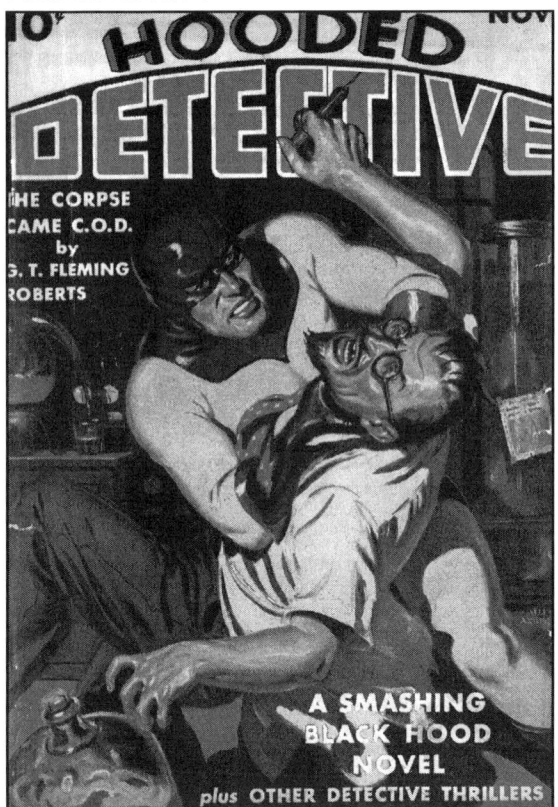

Hooded Detective, November 1941.

into crowds: In "The Corpse Cavalcade," a Secret Agent "X" story from June 1935, Fleming-Roberts wrote a story involving seven criminals—unfortunately, the "seven" were not all identified in the story.

Synopsis: The Skull, aided by Countess Anna Odinstov, kidnaps the son of a wealthy manufacturer of cutting tools, in order to force him to turn over these important tools that he had contracted to sell to Russia through the Countess. Kip, Barbara and Joe are among the guests at the birthday party for the boy when he is kidnapped. Kip changes to the Black Hood and almost stops the kidnapping, but the Skull shows up and pins the Black Hood to the wall of a garage with an automobile, leaving the engine running.

Barbara and Joe follow the Countess to her apartment, then to the flophouse where she was staying. They wait until she re-appears and follow her once more, at which time Barbara is captured while Joe bungles the simple task she had assigned him.

The story concludes on a boat where Barbara is being held captive by the Skull. In a shoot out, the Skull escapes, but the Black Hood has found a clue that leads him to the offices of Gregory Leeds, where he encounters both the Skull and the Countess, captures them both and rescues Billy, the kidnapped son of the industrialist.

Our next entry is "The Corpse Came C.O.D." November 1941, from *The Hooded Detective*, Vol. 3, No. 1. The author is G.T. Fleming-Roberts.

Arthur MaQuire wanted someone killed… killed so that he could collect a fortune and live in luxury for the rest of his natural life. Arthur needed a killer… so he hired Kazzar the mysterious, killer extraordinary.

Hooded Detective, January 1942.

Kazzar made killing easy, for a price, and he delivered C.O.D.… But the Black Hood, the merciless hunter of criminals, showed him that you pay the price for murder to the state and your receipt is the electric chair.

Location: New York City.

Main characters: Kip Burland, Barbara Sutton, Joe Strong, Sergeant McGinty, Deputy Wynn, Arthur MaQuire, Paul MaQuire, Ruth Himes, Rima Clark, Meeker, Max Goldrich, Dr. Colby, Manny Schulte, Arnold Best, Peter Raymond, Harry McQuade, Mr. Kamp, Gephart, Archie Ruddle, Larry Hastings/Kazzar.

Synopsis: Arthur MaQuire had visited Kazzar, a local fortune-teller and mentions that he wishes his stepfather were dead. The fortune-teller asks if he will pay for the deed, then names a price. The boy agrees. Two weeks later, Arthur is throwing a party and invites some friends, among them are Kip Burland, Barbara Sutton and Joe Strong. When they arrive at the party the old man appears to have been murdered.

The Black Hood follows Arthur to the fortune-teller's shop, where he is captured by Kazzar and his men, and taken for a boat ride—with a pair of cement boots—and tossed into the deep water. He escapes easily and again visits the scene of Kazzar's shop where he investigates and finds plenty of clues.

He also discovers that an aluminum manufacturing plant—that is going broke because the government has taken the aluminum for the war effort—is being threatened to turn over thirty thousand dollars from each stock holder, or be killed. None of the stockholders have that kind of money and are being killed off.

The Black Hood discovers that Kazzar (Larry Hastings) actually wants to kill them off so he can obtain the stock they control, as he is aware of an invention that will bring in millions for the company. By killing the elder MaQuire and then blackmailing the stepson, he can obtain the needed money to buy the stock.

Our last story is "The Whispering Eye, January 1942, from *The Hooded Detective*, Vol. 3, No. 2. The author is G.T. Fleming-Roberts.

Hunted by the police… framed for robbery and murder by the Eye, master fiend and vicious ruler of the underworld… Loathed by Barbara Sutton, the girl who loves him… The Black Hood had to face the blazing purgatory of the murder master's guns to win back Barbara's love and clear himself of the framed charges.

Location: New York City.

Main characters: Kip Burland, Barbara Sutton, Joe Strong, Sergeant McGinty, Officer Bricker, William "Old Bill" Weedham, Jeff Weedham, Ray Delancy, Shiv, Squid Murphy, A.J. Burkey, Jack Carlson, Major Paxton, Harold Adler, Vida Garvais,

Biggert, Ron "The Bug" Brayton.

Synopsis: The Eye, a mysterious king of the underworld is trying to combine the underworld under one rule—his. He plans the robberies, then provides a getaway system for the crooks. During one of the robberies and killing, the Black Hood comes across the killers and follows them to one of their hideouts. In the mean time, Joe Strong has taken a picture of the Black Hood standing over the murdered watchman. He is now working for a newspaper and they use his photo to splash across the newspapers with damning evidence that the Black Hood has indeed murdered an innocent man. The newspaper owner needed to improve the papers failing sales. Barbara believes that the Black Hood did kill the watchman and will have nothing to do with him.

In a complicated twist, the original Eye is murdered and another takes his place, causing our hero to believe he may have made a mistake in his original deductions as to who the murderer is—but not for long. He unravels the mystery, discovering that young Jeff Weedham has taken over the identity of the Eye with help from Vida Garvais, in order to make back his money already lost in the newspaper he had recently purchased—as well as making some more money while he was at it.

The Eye originally received ten percent of the take from all robberies, then with his help of transporting the criminals out of the immediate area, he would force them to pay another large sum—sometimes as high as fifty percent of the take. He was getting rich quick.

The Black Hood identifies him because young Jeff stutters, and the Eye stays away from using words that would make him stutter.

Thus ended the short-lived series about a fascinating character. The Black Hood began as a comic book hero, and switched over to the pulps for a few stories, then back to the comics. Though the stories were only about thirty-five pages each (a fairly normal length novel would be around seventy pages), they were still a lot of fun reading. That G.T. Fleming-Roberts wrote the series is credit to the editors of the magazine, as well, for he was one of the top pulp writers of the day, having written several series under his own name as well as a few under house names, most notably of these, the Secret Agent "X" series.

Some Final Notes:

The Black Hood told Barbara this: "We've got to forget love, you and I. We've got to forget that we've ever kissed."

The Black Hood did not want to die in bed, but rather he wanted to go out in a blaze of glory, fighting crime and injustice.

In the third novel, he did tell Barbara that he loved her.

The Black Hood never carried weapons, but usually took guns away from crooks to use against those he was fighting.

In the second novel, an intended victim lives on East 54th Street, the same location as the home of George Chance, alias the Green Ghost.

The covers are signed Allen Anderson. The only interior illustration I found that was signed seemed to be "Kinn." In Will Murray's article, he states that Allen Anderson also did a number of covers for *Private Detective Stories*. Will also states that the interior illustrator was Paul Reinman who did the comic book illustrations.

The Black Hood is one of the few pulp heroes to come over from the comic books, keeping his comic book image as well. ♦

The Missing Red Finger

By Tom Johnson

We are aware that many of the prolific pulp authors often had stories rejected. Even Lester Dent had stories, or parts of stories, rejected. We're only now finding rejected Dan Fowler and Phantom Detective stories. So it shouldn't come as any surprise that Arthur Leo Zagat faced the rejection slips as well. Matt Moring of Altus Press recently procured a list of Zagat's manuscripts donated to Temple University. Among the list were many stories with new titles; one of these was "Red Finger and the Murder Trio."

On reading this story, we found that some of the material had been used in other stories, but this particular story was never published. Obviously, an editor at Popular Publications had rejected it. There are numerous reasons. There were numerous stories with "murderous trios," usually involving Germans, Japanese, and even Mexicans. However, in this one we have an American Negro, Japanese, and German. Political correctness was often tossed out the window in pulp stories, but in this adventure the Japanese speaks in "ve'ly, ve'ly poor English:

> "But fi'st," the Oriental continued, smoothly. "I must ask who this woman is. I have not met he'befo'."

From the story, "Death Rides the Sound," we have:

> "But you must admit that it was the East that brought that gift to its perfection. Just so, when Asia conquers the world, we of the East will make it a far better place in which to live, even for you whites."

There is no pigeon English by the oriental, and readers have no trouble following the line of speech.

Now, let's look at the black man in "Red Finger and the Murder Trio":

> "Ah tailed heh to heh hotel, Misto' Krasnitch," the colored man, simian-armed, gorilla-faced, was saying. "But ah couldn't get in 'cause it wuz de Dolly Madison an' dey don't have nothin' except women he'p dere. Ah done spotted heh room, dough."

The black man is a killer:

> "De Moorish Ahms is nex' doah. One uv ouah comrades is a pohteh deh. An' deh wuz an empty flat right crost de couht f'om heh room. She wuz writin' a lettah an' we got a good shot at heh." He chuckled. "She neveh knew whut hit heh."

There were a lot of black readers of Popular Publications' *The Spider* and other titles, and I don't think the editors wanted to belittle them with this kind of dialogue. But we'll never know, as I've seen worse in the pulps. In the Red Finger series, blacks were usually portrayed as elevator operators, not crooks or killers.

But one thing we are sure of: "Red Finger and the Murder Trio" was rejected, and Zagat used bits and pieces of the story in other tales. This scene for instance in "Murder Trio":

> "Duane; gaunt and cadaverously lank, and stooped under the weight of a lassitude dreary as his stock-in-trade; appeared utterly oblivious of the pulse-stirring sound. But the pencil in his long, slim fingers halted, abruptly, in its idle tracing of a rose on the dust-filmed blotter covering the desk in whose chair the bibliophile slouched. Beneath their covert of drooped lids his eyes slid to an apparently accidental aperture in the window display, that gave them a clear view of the sidewalk. And of anyone who might seek entrance to the store."

Now let's look at from "Death's Toy Shop":

> "Ford Duane, alpaca-coated, lank, stooped under a lassitude too dreary for his apparent youth, sat at a shabby desk near the front of his second-hand bookstore. A pencil in his long, slim fingers idly traced a rose on the dust-filmed desk-blotter, and he seemed half-asleep."

It was always made clear to the readers that American spies died in their battle against foreign agents. He had warned Flower (the rose) that she should get out of this business before something happened to her:

> "Flower, get out before it's too late. A girl has no business in The Force. Get out before a bullet finds its billet in your soft, sweet body. Or worse happens to it."

She was constantly stepping into danger, and usually captured with the threat of death, only to be saved at the last minute by Red Finger. In this rejected Red Finger story, we read:

> "Krasnitch's hand on her mouth, stifled Lola's (Flower) cry of agony. The Negro ran a loving thumb along a razor edge.
>
> "Beneath the bleasts," Ho Chien lisped. "She will not bleed much, there, and we can lay he! in the bed, cove' he' up with the sheets. She will be thought to be sleeping."
>
> The glittering knife lifted. Its thin sting point pressed slit the tight-stretched silk of Lola's dress, pressed against white, quivering skin.
>
> The window sash thumped up in its frame! A black swirl bellied the shade inward. There was a fifth figure in the room, a startling, ominous figure, cloaked in swirling black draperies that made it incredibly tall, incredibly ominous.
>
> "Drop that knife," a sepulchral voice intoned. "Drop it!" The apparition was gray-masked, topped by a gray felt hat. It was a specter of sudden dread. A pistol with a curiously thick barrel jutted from a hand that was gloved in black, except for the one finger that curled about the strange weapon's trigger. That was scarlet, hideously scarlet as the finger of doom."

But women agents did die in this deadly game they played against foreign assassins. In this passage from "Red Finger and the Murder Trio," he's brought to a crime scene, thinking the corpse is that of Flower:

"The other men moved apart, making a path for Duane. There was something feline in the way they watched him. They seemed ready to pounce, to claw. But the book dealer was scarcely aware of them. He knew only that a corpse was hidden under that incongruously cerulean pall, and that in another second he would see its face. His throat was dry; a dull hammer thumped his skull. But his expression showed only bewildered curiosity, a timid wonder at the grotesque proceeding.

He stood above the shrouded body. "Who is this?" Collins barked, and jerked the blanket away.

She was slender, utterly feminine, in the big chair. One slim hand was clutched to a shirt-waisted breast, as though to repress a twinge of pain. The other lay in her lap, ink-splotched, its dead fingers tight on a pen. Duane forced his eyes upward—to a small, pallid chin, to a face gleaming with death's waxen pallor—To a face utterly unknown to him! Breath hissed sharply from between his teeth.

"No." His voice was tight, thin. A cloistered seller of old books would be expected to be appalled by the sudden sight of death. Of murder! A dribble of blood had dried on the woman's cheek, blood that had trickled from a tiny black hole beside her right eye. "No. I have never seen her before."

No, it wasn't Flower, but another female agent. One who knew Ford Duane was the deadly Red Finger, terror of foreign spies, and seeing that she was about to die had left a coded message to be found on her corpse bringing America's Ace spy after the foreign agents.

As for the story, the plot is about foreign and domestic agents preparing workers to strike and shut down America:

"Ve'ly well," The Mongol seemed satisfied. "Then we may plocede. As I unde'stand it, we are leady. You, Ivan Klasnitch, have reported that the Slavic wo'kers in the steel mills and mines ah plepa'ed."

"That's right. They'll quit work the minute they're told."

"And you, Mees Lola. You speak fo' the female opelatives in the facto'ies. They are leady fo' a gen'al strike?"

"They are ready." Her voice was throaty, deep chested. There was a drowsy voluptuousness about her that was as seductive as the stretch of a tigress, and as infinitely dangerous.

"And you, Washington Jones?"

"Mah folkses is allus ready to go on strike. Dey'll do Just whut ah tells them."

Ho Chien's fingernails rasped on wood, as though he clawed some helpless victim. "Good! Ame'lica is at our me'cy, com'ades, as Flance, was at Ge'many's mercy last June, when he' labole's folded thei' a'ms. Flance, despite her a'my, ent'enched in thei' implegnable fo'ts, capitulated to Ge'many then, and fo'ced England to remove the sanctions against Italy."

As a Red Finger story, it wasn't bad. Ford Duane even kisses Flower at the end:

"Flower!" the suddenly quivering counter-spy husked. "How did you…?"

"I didn't know anyone else was working on this case. You know how Headquarters is sometimes. Check—and double-check. But they didn't need to—with you."

"Headquarters doesn't know I'm on it.—" Red Finger was abruptly conscious of the soft, yieldingly warm body in his arms, of the heart thumping in his arms. He shoved up his mask. His lips slid across a satin cheek, found warm, sweet lips….

Such was the life of a spy, I guess. I can only hazard a guess as to why it was rejected. Surely it wasn't the story or plot. I can only assume that it had something to do with the black man in the story. As I mentioned earlier, the magazines were aimed at an Americans audience, and blacks were part of that reading target, along with whites. ♦

Pulp Ladies

By Tom Johnson

Now, let's face it, what do you men really like about those old pulp stories? Do you read and collect wonderful old magazines purely for the enjoyment of reading their fast action, adventure, and mystery, and thrills from a bygone era? Is it really the heroes you are interested in, or the locale of the adventure? Is it because The Shadow wore black and had a weird laugh? Is it because The Spider wore those terrible fangs and shot people dead? Or was it those bronze muscles of Doc Savage that drew you to the pulps? Well, I guess there was probably something that hooked you for life into reading those great adventures. As for me, I must confess, it was the fantastic ladies that could always be found within the adventure: remember all those lovely things that were featured in the Doc Savage adventures? I bet most of you can name a bunch of them, and tell me what adventure they appeared in, too! That's what I mean! Deep down you liked those ladies too. Now admit it.

Now there were a goodly number of beautiful young ladies in the Doc Savage adventures, as I mentioned above, and most of them were innocent victims of some terrible criminal mastermind, and Doc had to run around saving them from the insidious clutches of an evildoer—and he always did.

Or ask Nick Carr about the beauties that appeared in G-8 or Operator #5, or just about anywhere else in the pages of his favorite pulp magazines. They were there, and I know that Nick liked them. He's told me so. And he's always writing about them. Just check out his article, "The Silver Witch" in the *Doc Savage Club Reader* #11.

As for me, I liked them all, but in particular I liked those beauties found in the adventures of Secret Agent "X." Back in 1975, when I was researching this series for the book, *Secret Agent X—A History* (coauthored with Will Murray, for Robert Weinberg's Pulp Classic series), I fell in love with all of the ladies. So, if you don't mind, let me borrow from that book and take another look at these ladies for the benefit of those of you who did not read the book.

Secret Agent "X" was published by the Ace group owned by A.A. Wyn, publisher of such series as *Ten Detective Aces* and *Detective Dragnet.* His wife, Rose Wyn, was listed as editor of the *X* series. The reason that's important is the fact that women interest was very big with Rose Wyn, and the *Secret Agent "X"* series was no exception. Now these ladies were not always the pure and innocent type found in *Doc Savage* or *The Shadow*, but again, they were not always evil, either. They were "stock" Mata Haris, and they could always take care of themselves. They were not the type who were constantly getting into trouble, and had to be rescued by the hero. These women were usually international spies or adventuresses. They generally worked for themselves, but at tines were employed by foreign countries. In many cases they were after some secret invention or weapon: destructive rays, super weapons, a new gas, etc. Or else they would appear to be working for a master criminal here in America. However, most of them were controlling the American mastermind for their own purposes (or on orders from a foreign power). Many of these women were the actual cause of their mastermind-boyfriend's downfall. Many of these beautiful femme fatales met their death at the hands of the men they thought were under their control.

They were all gorgeously beautiful, wore exotic clothing and expensive perfume. They had flirty eyes and a voice that could melt the heart of any man. They were true "vamps," with low-cut dresses and shapely legs. They were the pulp's version of Marlene Dietrich, Greta Garbo and Mae West.

First we must take a look at the Agent's love interest in the series. Her name is Betty Dale. We will go into greater detail with this lovely because she was a leading character throughout most of the series. Her blonde hair, blue eyes and petite figure made Betty Dale a vision of loveliness; the daughter of a police captain who was killed in the line of duty, she was left alone in the world but for Secret Agent "X," who had been a friend of her father. The Agent aided Betty in completing her education, then saw that she was well placed as a reporter for a daily newspaper (the Herald). Many times the Agent has found occasion to enlist her services in his battle against crime.

Betty lives in a small apartment on 23rd Street (#63), on the 6th floor of the Belleville Apartments. He visited her many tines and donning many disguises while she lived there. She loved the Agent, and he certainly felt the same love for this courageous young girl. But like all of our pulp heroes, marriage and love were something that had to wait until the world was free from crime.

Betty was with the Agent from the very first, although a few novels featured her in no active part, she merely gave the Agent information over the phone. However, she was usually right in the middle of his cases, and getting captured, being drugged, put in dungeons and tortured. At least once in every novel, Agent X was forced to penetrate a criminal stronghold to rescue the young reporter. She saw the Agent's true face for the first tine in "City of Madness" (December 1936). She remained with the Agent for another year of the magazine, making her final appearance in the December 1937 issue, titled "Plague of the Golden Death." At that time she was dropped from the series (but the Agent still finds other fair damsels to rescue).

Betty had relatives in a town named Branford (no State given, but assumed to be New York), an aunt and cousin. The cousin, Paula Channing, is very wealthy in her own right, and popular in the community ("City of the Living Dead," June 1934).

Also important to the series was the love interest for the Agent's two aids, Jim Hobart and Harvey Bates, though the two ladies involved were only featured in one novel each, their parts were very important and deserve mention:

Leanne Manners ("The Murder Monster," December 1934): Leanne was a red-haired young girl from a mid-western town. The fiancée of Jim Hobart, she was refined and educated (and also a graceful dancer). Agent X got her a job at the Diamond Club, where she quickly became the star of the nightclub show. However, she actually had another job there, which consisted of keeping tabs on the mobsters that frequented the club.

Leanne and Hobart were soon to be married, but she only appeared in the one novel and was never mentioned again. However, as Jim Hobart only remained with the Agent for two more years it might be assumed that they did get married and, due to the dangerous work he was involved with, he was released from active service by the Agent.

Charlotta ("City of Madness"): Darkly beautiful, her narrow velvety-lidded eyes were almost black and extraordinarily shrewd. High cheekbones accentuated a small, pointed chin. Her rouged lips suggested determination without in any way detracting from her beauty. She wore a short, flared black skirt and the postage stamp apron of a housemaid.

Though American born, nature had endowed her with brains as well as beauty, and she had served Russia in the early days of the war. Her mastery of foreign languages and her love for adventure had enticed her to seek fortune in strange lands at an early age. She later left Russia and transferred her abilities to the French Intelligence Service. Wherever adventure and intrigue could be found, there too was Charlotta.

Harvey Bates fell in love with her (and so did I) in the novel and she returned his love. But after this novel Bates was only active in four more cases and seldom placed in a position of danger. Thus, it might be assumed that Charlotta added the name of Bates to her own—and Agent X once again lost another very capable operative.

Nina Rocazy ("The Spectral Stranglers," March 1934): She was blonde and dazzlingly beautiful, with a voice sinister as the purring of a sleepy tigress. She was a killer, a murderess at heart, a plotter of evil and an international spy.

Rosa Carpita ("The Death-Torch Terrors," April 1934): A strikingly pretty girl with hair as black as jet like agate and a smooth, olive complexion. She knew of the plot and wanted in on the money.

Lili Demora ("The Ambassador of Doom," May 1934): A stunning, lithe-bodied brunette with luscious, pouty lips and the languorous air of a society belle. Yet she, too, was an international spy, murderess and schemer.

Princess Ar-Lassi ("Hand of Horror," August 1934): A gorgeously beautiful woman; slender, sensuous, seemingly taller than she actually was, with jet black hair. She was a schemer—taking whichever side the money was on.

Tasha Merlo ("Octopus of Crime," September 1934): A redhead, beautifully molded in face and figure. With violet, heavy-lidded eyes. The lines of her face showed little outward character and were deceptively mild, almost babyish. Her laughter was a silvery tinkle. She was a jewel fence of international fame and had two fierce leopards Satan and Nero. She was the forerunner of another femme fatale, Felice Vincart, The Leopard Lady.

Greta St. Clair ("The Hooded Hordes," October 1934): Chestnut haired, slim of figure and delicately beautiful; her lips were touched with crimson and she possessed a stunning figure and soft features. She had been on the movie screen until she had become the paramour of a notorious gangster.

Mabel Boling ("The Murder Monster," December 1934): A beautiful, hard-faced, dark-haired woman; she was vivacious and had been a very good actress at one time. She was working with one gangster, trying to get in good with another mob and was killed for her scheming.

Paula Rockwell ("The Sinister Scourge," January 1935): A fluffy-haired, doll-faced debutante dressed in blue chiffon. She had beauty of a sort: red lips, dancing eyes, an exaggerated coyness about her. Her face mirrored a shallow, empty mind. She drove 12-cylinder cars and had a 1-cylinder brain. An innocent girl, though she had fallen in love with an international criminal and happened to be the ward of "The Big Boss," mastermind of gangland.

Goldie LaMar ("Curse of the Waiting Death," February 1935): Notorious nightclub hostess and underworld queen. A glamorous blonde… a handsome, alluring figure of a woman with the free swinging grace of a female panther. She was merely the "moll" of gangland gangsters.

Vivian De Graf ("Devils of Darkness," March 1935): Society beauty, arresting and exotic. Her tailored clothes subtly accentuated the perfection of her statuesque figure. She had a caressing smile on her crimson lips, coyly arched eyebrows, a silvery, rippling laugh, dark hair and long, slim legs. She was married to an inventor but played with men like a cat with a mouse. She was with the gang before her jealous husband killed her (and then did himself in).

Lola Lollagi ("Talons of Terror," April 1935): A gorgeously beautiful woman with the sharp, clearly cut profile of a dark, lovely face. With black, bobbed hair combed back behind her ears. The Agent had known her before, in Asuncion, South America. She had been a Paraguayan dancer. A mysterious woman, but her only desire was to free her brother, Laurento, from the clutches of Doctor Blood.

Alice Neves ("The Corpse Cavalcade," June 1935): A strikingly beautiful brunette, scarlet lips and warm, dark eyes. She was one of the "Seven Silent Men," and even killed for her leader. But in the end she helped Secret Agent "X" as she lay dying.

Drew Devon ("The Golden Ghoul," July 1935): A strikingly beautiful blonde, with wide, violet eyes. Once an actress, she was tall and statuesque—and played her part well. She worked for the "Ghoul" but loved another. Both were criminals and deserved their deserved fate.

Carlotta Rand ("The Monarch of Murder," August 1935): Dark and glamorous, with a touch of hauteur in her easy, graceful carriage. The graceful curves of her pliant body were revealed by her wind-blown dress. She had dark eyes, jet-black hair and ivory skin. Though an innocent tool, she was married to the fiend, Doctor Marko. He had made her his accomplice through fear. The Agent saved her at the end, when Marko would have killed her.

Felice Vancart ("Legion of the Living Dead," September 1935) and The Leopard Lady ("Dividends of Doom," February 1936): Her face was small, nearly round, with a dark complexion. Her lips were slightly voluptuous and were rouged a striking shade of red that was almost like Chinese lacquer. Her nose was slightly tip-tilted and her eyes actually arresting—true emerald green beneath long, penciled brows that curved upwards at the outer extremities. Snatched from the variety stage by an ardent young millionaire who had fallen in love with her, Felice Vincart had found herself a widow after a few months of marriage. She was called The Leopard Lady and had a grace and manner that was actually feline. The Leopard Lady graced the pages of Secret Agent "X" twice, making her character unique to the series. In these novels she had two pets—giant leopards. She was an adventuress, seeking excitement wherever she went. But she was evil, too, and trained her pets to kill. She confesses to the Agent that she could have loved him:

> "… I could have loved a man like you madly," she whispered. "But I am as easily turned to hate. Now you shall know the agonizing fear of the electric chair, even as I have known it because of you." Her voice seemed very far away now. "X" could no longer see those tantalizing red lips. "Goodbye, Agent X"… came the distant whisper. Then he knew no more.

Holly Babette ("Horde of the Damned," October 1935): A dazzling, willowy girl with gray-green eyes and pitch-black hair. She was a lovely woman and aided the criminals in gathering ransom money only because they had her brother held captive and forced her to comply to their will.

Donna Magyar ("Ringmaster of Doom," November 1935): She was considered the most dangerous woman spy in all of Europe. She wore a glove-fitting evening dress and the perfume from her hair was peculiar, seductive and intriguing. She had titian hair, the delicate, oval face and large hazel eyes that were somehow too worldly-wise for the eyes of youth. She was a lieutenant in the service of Thoth.

Electra Barker ("Kingdom of Blue Corpses," December 1935): Her voice was low, deep and liquid. She had dark fathomless eyes; was tall, lithe and moved with a supple grace. Her hair was the blackest "X" had ever seen, and her lips the reddest. She admitted to killing—however, her mind and will were not her own. The Blue Spark completely controlled her. The Agent sets her free so that she can marry Detective Sergeant Mallory and move to the west coast.

Countess Savinna ("Brand of the Metal Maiden," January 1936): She wore a creamy, clinging evening dress. Her beautifully arranged hair was the blue-black of a raven's wing. Her nose was delicate perfection, her lips petulant. Her dark eyes burned with a light that might have been kindled by an intense love—or an equally intense hate. She had been involved in several plots that had shaken the very foundations of certain countries of Continental Europe. She is a lieutenant in the service of Emperor Zero and is accidentally killed by him.

Sandra Phelps ("Dividends of Doom," February 1936): This auburn-haired beauty was actually the sister of the man who had married Felice Vincart. She believed that The Leopard Lady had killed her brother and was out to avenge his death.

Blossom O'Shean ("The Fear Merchants," March 1936): A Woman with a dazzling beauty and made-up face. Her features were a mask of synthetic beauty, giving no indications of her true age. Mascaraed eyes that held guile and ruthless cunning, she walked with swaggering hips. She was the ex-moll of a famous gangster. Now she worked for a new mastermind.

Mimi Clarice ("The Faceless Fury," April 1936): There was a worldliness about her undeniably beautiful face and mascaraed eyes. She had a hint of henna in her dark red hair. She had been a member of the notorious "Ghost' gang. She is killed (along with everyone else) by the Faceless Man.

Ann Dryden ("The Faceless Fury," April 1936): She was a fragile, lovely thing; boyishly slender, with blue-gray eyes and pale, wavy hair. She had tried to blackmail the Faceless Man and was killed for her efforts.

Vina Tremaine ("Horror's Handclasp," October 1936): She was dazzling, a beautiful woman whose poise was perfection itself. Slightly above average height, her black hair had the same silken sheen as the simple, black gown she wore. Her eyes of brilliant green held a ruthless glint. When the Agent's eyes met hers, it was like the crossing of swords. She was dangerously beautiful. Vina Tremaine was a widow recently over from Europe. An adventuress seeking excitement and danger. In meeting Agent "X," she had found the life she craved. Though at first appearing evil, she turned out to be an image of the Agent himself. This woman would have been a more fitting companion to "X" than Betty Dale. Their lives were the same; both seeking adventure, excitement and danger. She could have stood beside the Agent, as Nita Van Sloan had done beside The Spider, and Myra Reldon beside The Shadow. No Betty Dale was this woman. She was a woman of the world and could usually get out of any fix she got into. Where Betty Dale accidentally walked into a trap, Vina Tremaine went looking for them. She even assumes the identity of Secret Agent "X" in this novel:

> … standing in the door of the laboratory was a slim, boyish figure… a very' young man in evening clothes and a silk hat. His features were completely covered by a mask of black silk. "I am Secret Agent "X," " said the Man of the Silk Mask haughtily…

Zerna ("Death's Frozen Formula," February 1937): This woman was exotically beautiful. She possessed a dark, secret beauty that warmed to gay colors and daring costumes. Her dark, soft skin had a faint yellowish coat that suggested mixed bloods. Her lips were warm and scarlet; her eyes cold and sea green. She was as evil a woman that Agent X had ever faced. She dispensed drugs and death while never displaying any emotion. She was a cold and heartless woman.

Sally Vergane/Pamela Dean ("The Murder Brain," April 1937): Sally Vergane was a blonde, her hair clipped and combed like a man's. Her clothes were cheap, sleazy imitations of dresses worn by movie queens. She had been a queen in her own right—a gun-toting moll of an infamous gangster. Pamela Dean was breathtakingly beautiful. The blue material of which her gown was fashioned had been particularly created to match her eyes. Her skin had a dark, warm flush. Her hair was deep brown and wavy. She was the particular passion of enough wealthy businessmen to make the front-page news seven days out of the week. She supplied tips to the G-Men, which resulted in some very good raids. However, Pamela Dean and Sally Vergane was one and the same woman—and the tips that she gave to the law were for her own evil purpose.

Edna Cory ("Slaves of the Scorpion," June 1937): The lighting brought out the red-gold glint in her dark hair. Her dark eyes gleamed with excitement. She was bored with her riches and soft life and wanted excitement; even if it meant joining the criminal gang. She thought that she loved the mastermind, but it was only the love of excitement and danger that surrounded him. She even confuses Agent "X" with the master criminal, thinking they were the same:

> … the girl came toward him with lithe, swaying steps. Her eyes were shining, her wondrously soft lips smiling lazily. When she was so close that the bosom of her dress touched him with every breath she drew, she whispered: "This is the greatest moment of my life. I have hunted the world over for such a man as you, Mr. X. The Scorpion, feared by criminals and police alike; the most powerful figure in the world—yet a lonely figure. That should not be, Mr. X," She raised her head; her eyes warm pools of passion. She swayed slightly forward….

Perhaps hers was not the complete desire for danger and excitement, as was Vina Tremaine's, but rather the loneliness she felt and the need to be with a strong, exciting man.

Jane Lenox ("Satan's Syndicate," August 1937): A tall, slim girl with a pretty face and dark, wondrous eyes. Secret Agent "X" found this girl to his liking:

> "… Wait!" Jane Lenox put a detaining hand on "X"s arm. "You…you're going?"
>
> He nodded, "I must. There's more ahead—more adventures, more criminals."
>
> "Can't I… " She dropped her eyes and whispered… "Would you take me with you? I mean, perhaps I could help…."
>
> X took both her hands in his. "No." he said gently.

"You've done more than your share already. I have my duties—you have yours. Some day, perhaps, our paths nay cross again. Until that time…."

Sheila Landi ("The Assassins' League," October 1937): She was wearing a low-cut evening dress of flame-colored material that hugged her tall, svelte figure. Blonde, the waves of her straw-gold hair were unusual. Her eyes were so deep a blue that in the parchment-shaded lights of the lounge they appeared almost black. She was known as the "Moll" and was always involved in high crime, political intrigue and espionage. When the secret police of Europe smelled scandal in high places, or heard of smoldering revolt, they sought her out. This woman had the ability of penetrating any disguise the Agent wore, and she had been hired for this purpose alone. No matter what new disguise the Agent was wearing, she was to identity him for her boss, or to Sabin, the revolutionist. She was good at her work, and identified the Agent, but she didn't reveal his identity to the criminals. She turned out to be innocent and was permitted to go free. Secret Agent "X" was to miss her beauty and loyalty.

Janet Lane ("Claws of the Corpse Cult," April 1938): Janet had the freshness of youth. Her dark eyes reflected her innocence. Married but a few months to a G-Man, she was afraid that her husband was seeing another woman. He was on assignment, and was killed early in the story. Secret Agent "X" takes over his identity. Janet watches as Secret Agent "X" battles a gangster while in her husband's disguise. The two combatants drop from her sight, and the Agent kills the criminal, but before coming back into view he assumes the identity of the criminal. When the criminal appears to have been the victor, Janet believes that her husband was killed during the fight. Ronald Holme, K-9, is with her. He docs not explain the situation to her. Instead….

> . . . Something like a tear glittered in the hard eyes

of K-9 as he carried the unconscious Janet into the cabin of the cruiser. He placed her gently on one of the bunks and returned toward the hatchway. His footsteps less light....

Erlika ("Corpse Contraband," December 1938): Rapacious! Nearly black, narrow eyes with their obliquely slanting brows. There was cruelty in those eyes. Her costume was sheerest witchery, sleeveless and cut low. She was startlingly beautiful. Curls of blue-black hair were carefully coiffured. She had made love to a young boy who was a nobody. She had been raised as a goddess, so she wanted to elevate this young boy into the leadership of all criminals. Then he would be fit to sit beside her on her thrown while she ruled America.

Madam Death ("Yoke of the Crimson Coterie," March 1939): Only her first name is known. It is Naida. She had blue eyes, hair the sun had gilded piled high upon her lovely head. She had perfect features and slim, graceful hands. The white uniform she wore could not hide the perfect symmetry of the form beneath. She was a woman of exquisite proportions. An innocent girl, her mind and actions were completely controlled by another. He was the Doctor, a European scientist, who had found an unknown substance, which he had used to take over the girl's mind and body. She could kill with a mere touch of the hand. The Doctor forced her to kill those who were marked for death. At the end she kills the Doctor with her deadly touch, but he fires a bullet into her body before he dies. As she lies dying too, Secret Agent "X" approaches:

> "Naida, "X whispered. He knew that the girl was dying. He took a short step forward, repeated her name.
> She looked at him, a sweet, sad smile on her paling lips. "Someone else I do not remember calls me by name. Can you help me? There is something within me that burns like unholy fire. It has burned for so long. It began in the laboratory. Won't you do something for me to stop the pain?"
> The girl's head sagged. Her body wavered forward, flattened on the rocks. Her deadly hands pressed to the surface of the stone. She said: "Cool."
> X stepped nearer. "Naida," he whispered, "you are going away. It will be cool where you are going. Is there anything I can do? Have you a father or mother somewhere who would like to know where you are going?"
> "No," the girl whispered hoarsely. "A father—yes, once I had a father. In the laboratory, the Doctor showed me my father. He said I was to catch my father with my two hands. Like I caught a rat. Ugh!" A slight shudder convulsed her. "I hate rats."
> She jerked up her head, looked squarely at X. "Don't—don't touch me. Once I touched my father. He—he died. I am not like other girls. I am poison. My touch—- " she turned her head, seemed listening intently. "What is that rushing sound?"
> "Only the surf on the rocks below," X said kindly.
> "Water. Water down there? Cool water?" Breathing in shallow gasps, the girl dragged herself to the edge of the cliff. "Cool water," she repeated, "to quench the fire within me." And with her last ounce of strength, Madam Death rolled herself over the edge of the cliff. There was no scream, no sound below save the deep, eternal voice of the sea....

Okay, there you have it. Just a few of the reasons why I like pulp magazines! The girls! Some I expanded on, while others I did not. They were all magnificent. Each deserves her own story. Maybe another time. However. I have cheated a little with this article; several of these ladies have been profiled before in other publications. If the reader would like to learn more about of few of them, please refer to the following articles: "Erlika: Daughter of Satan" in *Doc Savage Club Reader* #11; "Lade X" in *The Age of The Unicorn* #6, and "Madam Death" in *Doc Savage Club Reader* #11. But since I wrote those articles, maybe I'm allowed to cheat a little bit. Hope you folks don't mind. ♦

The Lone Wolf Detective

By Tom Johnson

Will Murray recently suggested that a check of the above titled magazine might reveal the final resting place for three unpublished Secret Agent "X" stories that have eluded researches for a number of years. With this in mind I decided to look up an issue with a title that sounded strangely like a G.T. Fleming-Roberts entry. The following is my findings. I may not have located a lost Secret Agent "X" entry but I did enjoy my search.

In Michael L. Cook's *Mystery, Detective And Espionage Magazine* (Greenwood Press, 1983), we read, *"Lone Wolf Detective* was published by Ace Magazines, Inc. (A.A. Wyn) commencing in 1938, and running through at least April 1941 (Vol. 4 No. 1). The illustration on the front cover on this last issue noted was the same as used on the December 1935 issue of *Secret Agent "X,"* another Wyn publication. A typical issue of *Lone Wolf Detective,* containing five novels, was "Merchant of Menace" by Robert Turner, "One Escort, Missing or Dead" by Roger Torrey, "Homicide ledger by Clifton T. Holmes, "The Corpse Maker" by Eric Lennox, and "Bullet Banknight" by Paul Adams."

The issue I reviewed was October 1940 (Vol. 4, No. 1). The cover for this issue was by Norman Saunders. The stories were "Three wise Corpses" by Chester Brant, "Curse of The Cloven Hoof" by Paul Adams, "Suicide Close Up by John Gregory, "League of Doom" by Eric Lennox, and "Deep-Sea Sepulcher" by Arthur Flint. The first story was the one that caught my eye: Fleming-Roberts had a similar title in his Diamondstone series, in particular "The Three Wise Apes" from June 1939, only a year previously. The author for this story is listed as Chester Brant, which reads like Chester (Hawks) Brant (House), certainly a house name from Ace. The five novels were each between 20 and 25 pages long, falling quite short of novel-length, so I was quickly discouraged in my hope of finding an unpublished Secret Agent "X" story, as too much would have been deleted to give me any clues. But please read on.

The main character of this story was "lone wolf" Assistant D.A. Blaine. The other characters involved in the plot were Commissioner Leeds, Wilbur Hough, Carol Wilkes, Martin Wilkes, Miles Stuart, Gen (a Japanese butler), Frank Platt, Rourke, and Richard Grant.

When I first read that Frank Platt worked for a private detective agency called Habor Detective Agency, I quickly became excited. Those who followed the Secret Agent "X" series will quickly recall the "Hobart Detective Agency," not far removed from the present detective agency; just switch the letters around and you have Hobar(t) from Habor. Interesting to say the least.

But the story was slow, little action, and D.A. Blaine was no Secret Agent "X." I was disappointed. In fact, none of the stories were of top quality, giving me the impression that maybe the *Lone Wolf Detective* magazine published the stories that were rejects from the more popular magazines from Ace, Ten Detective

Aces, which did publish top-notch fiction. This notion would soon change, however.

The plot was interesting, however: Fifteen years previously four men: Frank Platt, J.S. Rourke, Richard Grant and Martin Wilkes (his name had originally teen Martin Wilson), had been bunk mates on a ship with the Merchant Marines. While in Korea, Frank Platt robbed a religious temple (Secret Agent "X" curiously enough trained with a Korean fighting sect after he had helped defend their temple) of a set of jade figures. Returning to the ship, he is seen by Martin while hiding the stolen jade. He is also heard by J.S. Rourke. Later, when the police investigate the theft, Richard Grant tells them that Frank Platt stole the jade. However, the three men Rourke, Grant and Wilson—recover the jade and hide it elsewhere. The police take Platt into custody where he is tortured, then jailed for fifteen years.

Upon release, Platt returns to America where he hires the Habor Detective Agency to locate his three cohorts. He also obtains employment with the agency, as they appear to be somewhat questionable themselves.

Finding the three men, at first he attempts to blackmail them, then kills them off. One of the pieces of jade was the famous figure of the three wise monkeys: "See No Evil, Hear No Evil, Speak No Evil." Platt kills Wilkes (Wilson). First, placing his hands over his eyes; Rourke is next, and he dies with his hands over his ears; and last comes Grant, with his hands over his mouth. In death they represented the three wise monkeys, see no evil, hear no evil, and speak no evil.

It is up to the "Lone Wolf" D.A., Blaine, to unravel the mystery of the three murders before an innocent man is sent to jail, which he easily does with very little suspense or action.

The plot does read like a Fleming-Roberts story, though the writing does not. In fact, it has some similarities to his Green Ghost story, "The Case of The Walking Skeleton," as well the Dan Fowler story,

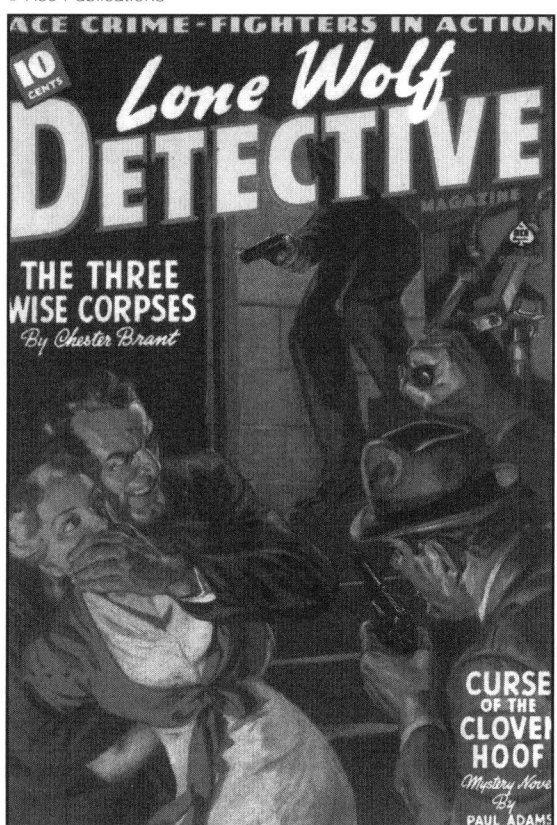

Lone Wolf Detective, October 1940.

"Crimson Crusade," and a number of Phantom Detective plots. As for this to have been an unpublished Secret Agent "X" story, I am highly doubtful. I think that we may be grasping at straws in trying to locate those missing "X" novels. Actually, I believe those three unpublished "X" stories may very well be hiding right under our nose. For instance, Fleming-Roberts was already writing other series, and could have simply made a few changes in character names. Not only did authors reuse their plots, they often borrowed plots from other writers. Oddly, immediately after the demise of Secret Agent "X," a story appeared in Diamondstone in June 1939, titled "Three Wise Apes." Notice the similarity in this title and "Three Wise Corpses"?

As already mentioned, in Spring 1941 was a far superior story titled "The Case of the Walking Skeleton," which did read like a Secret Agent "X" story. In fact, I was often reminded of Secret Agent "X" as I read this fascinating Green Ghost story. How's this for a plot?: Many years ago, four adventurers; John Turrin, Martin Drawes, Fredrick Werges, and Ian McCloski had been traveling through French Guiana on an expedition; because of an accident, Ian McCloski had been killed by the other three men. Now someone appears to be blackmailing them.

Sound familiar?

Evidently, as can be seen through the plots and titles, G.T. Fleming-Roberts recycled a lot of stuff. No disgrace in that. But if I were a betting man, I'd gamble that "The Case of the Walking Skeleton" was one of the three unpublished "X" stories, and that *Lone Wolf Detective* was merely a reprint magazine (more on this shortly).

What did I think of the *Lone Wolf Detective?* Not much. The dealer charged me thirty bucks for one issue. Given a second chance, I would have gladly bought a *Ten Detective Aces* issue. The only redeeming aspect of the issue is that beautiful Norman Saunders cover. By the way, the December 1935 *Secret Agent "X"* cover that appeared on the last issue of *Lone Wolf Detective* was by Rafael De Soto, another outstanding artist who contributed to the Ace Magazines, Inc. And if the publisher applied a previously used cover on one issue, it is possible that the Norman Saunders cover was also a recycled piece of art. Who knows?

Recently, John Dinan sent me an issue of the *Lone Wolf Detective* magazine for research purposes. This particular issue was the June 1940 (Vol. 3, No. 3) issue. The magazine is a product of Ace Magazines, Inc., published by-monthly, and subtitled "Crime Fighters in Action." This issue contained the following stories: "Laughter in the Morgue'" by Ronald Flagg, "Corpse's Understudy" by Harris Clivesey, "The Devil's Dormitory" by Chester Brant, "Crimson Cord of Doom" by L.B. Sharkey, "Big-House Phantom" by Frank T. Gilmore, and "The Death Curse" by George Ramey. The front cover is by Norman Saunders, featuring a room scene with a fat man apparently attacking a young girl who has one leg up to hold off her attacker. Appearing at the window is our "hero" who is about to come to the young girl's rescue. Another beautiful piece of art from Norman Saunders.

In the past, I have stated that I believed the *Lone Wolf Detective* was merely used as a place for Ace to print either rejects or reprints from their more popular *Ten Detective Aces*, but after further research into this rare magazine, I think that maybe I should redefine this belief. What I have found more recently is that this was very likely just a reprint magazine—but reprints without the readers' knowledge. That, or the stories were written by the main stable of writers from *TDA*, taking their series characters and turning them into new stories. I'll see if I can explain it in this review, because I am not all that familiar with many of the authors and characters that were running in the more important *Ten Detective Aces*.

First, let's look at the stories:

"Slaughter in the Morgue" by Ronald Flagg: When Clay Trant undertook the job of mouthpiece for the condemned, he did not know he was in for a morgue-watch assignment. But when the baffling corpse laughed a horrible requiem in the "Haven for Chair Cheaters," Trant had to turn super-sleuth to double-cross Death.

Situated in a lonely house away from civilization, on a dark stormy night, is a group of killers—all having cheated the electric chair when they had been found not guilty in their trials. The house is suddenly cut off even more from civilization when the electric lines and telephone lines are knocked out during the storm. And with the new darkness comes… murder. These self-admitted killers are now being killed themselves. Only Clay Trant can unravel the mystery before all are murdered.

Actually, I thought this was a very minor entry, even though it attempted to include a little mystery, something more than the "lone wolf" designation would imply. However, the story is a word-for-word re-write of Harry Widmer's "The Corpse Laughs," from the October 1933 issue of *Ten Detective Aces*. Only the name of the original hero, Jack McKee, was changed to that of Clay Trant.

"Corpse Understudy" by Harris Clivesey: Investigator Mark Hall, Who was a greater crime expert than drama critic had to don Doom's makeup to play… corpse's understudy.

"Mark Hall" is in reality, "Wade Hammond," and there is little doubt about who the series character or the actual author is. This is a Wade Hammond entry, and the actual story comes from Paul Chadwick's "The Face From the Grave," a Wade Hammond story in the January 1934 issue of *Ten Detective Aces*. Though I have only read a few of the Wade Hammond stories, I am at least familiar with the character, as well as the writing style of Paul Chadwick so this one was quickly identified.

A stage show in which our hero, Mark Hall, is attending on a night off, suddenly erupts in murder. A horrible monster in the show, played by one of the actors, is killed by a hard blow to back of his neck. Mark, who has special privileges with the police department, takes charge of the investigation. The clues lead to the morgue, and yet another murder, then back to the theater where Mark dons the guise of the monster in the play for the next scene.

Wade Hammond fans will like this little entry. I know I did!

"The Devil's Dormitory" by Chester Brant: Private Detective Don Taylor began his sleuth career in the G-Man's crime college. But when he took the case of the fatal feud, he discovered what it was like to live in the devil's dormitory.

Don Taylor appears to be something of a Hollywood detective. The narrative is first person, the story is hard boiled, and Don Taylor seems a little too much like Dan Turner. I wonder if this might not be Robert Leslie Bellem? There is no telling, but we do know that Chester Brant is a house name (Chester Hawks/Brant House), the one used on the *Captain Hazzard* novel, and the second on the *Secret Agent "X"* series. A check of *Ten Detective Aces* during this time period will probably quickly identify this author and story! I did check several issues of *Ten Detective Aces* during the 1941 period, and there is an author contributing during this period named Robert Turner; again, a Hollywood detective type, so I wouldn't be a bit surprised if this is not our man.

"Crimson Cord of Doom" by L.B. Sharkey: Captain Marvin Flagg was as tenacious as a wolf on a manhunt trail. And when Sir Cedric was brutally murdered, Flagg had to sharpen his homicide fangs to cut through the crimson cord of doom.

Again, fortunately, a slip of the editor's pen, and Captain Marvin Flagg's true identity is laid bare. Once in a while the editors use the character's original name of Captain John Murdock. A very popular series running in *Ten Detective Aces* was the Carl Mck. Saunders series about Captain John Murdock, so we know where this story originated. But I don't know if Carl Mck. Saunders was a real person or not. However, we do know that Captain Marvin Flagg should have been named Captain John Murdock, and though I do pot know what the original title was, nor when it appeared, it is not likely a new story, but chances are it is a re-write from *Ten Detective Aces*.

"Big House Phantom" by Frank T. Gilmore: Behind the grim prison walls, terror gripped the cell blocks. For one by one, wealthy convicts had their terms cut short by the Grim Reaper. And even Jim Hanlin, lone wolf investigator, had to get off the case—or meet the big-house phantom.

Hired by the girlfriend of a jailed crook to find out why her boyfriend had been killed—supposedly poisoned while in prison, Jim Hanlin had to go to prison himself to solve the mystery.

Not a very good story but it was interesting. Again, this is very likely a regular contributor to *Ten Detective Aces*, and I was reminded of Emile C. Tepperman's Marty Quade stories, but I can't be sure about this, so don't quote me as saying this belongs to him.

"The Death Curse" by George Ramey: A curse stalked the rubies of doom. And when private detective Ed Denison followed the treacherous trail of the stolen stones, death pointed a way out—by the bullet route!

A gang robs a rich man of famous jewels, kills the man, then everybody double-crosses each other. One, who now has the jewels, approaches the insurance investigator to offer the return of the famous jewels for a reward. But his partners want the jewels—and him dead!

In a fast-paced entry, and nice story, Ed Denison of the insurance agency goes after the jewels, and the crook. And again, there is no doubt as to who this author is. It is Emile C. Tepperman, and the story was originally printed in the April 1934 issue of *Secret Agent "X,"* and it was titled, "The Eyes of Durga." This is a nice little entry, and this proves that the editor was also taking stories originally printed in their other magazines, not exclusive to *Ten Detective Aces* alone.

Some Final Comments

After reading this issue of the *Lone Wolf Detective,* and the discoveries of some interesting information concerning the publication and the authors, I thought it would be appropriate to review some of the stories in the previous issue I reviewed in the first part of this article. A very interesting discover that I came up with on my second look at the October 1940 issue was "Curse of the Cloven Hoof" by Paul Adams; this is a word-for-word re-write/reprint of Norvell Page's "Satan's Hoof," featuring Ken Carter from the October 1933 issue of *Ten Detective Aces.* Did Norvell Page authorize this printing? Maybe sell it to Ace a second time, merely dropping Ken Carter for another character? Or did Ace reprint his story without payment or his knowledge?

"Suicide Close-Up" by John Gregory is another Hollywood detective-type story, and could be Robert Leslie Bellem (or Robert Turner) again. But I have no proof of this, so don't quote me.

"League of Doom" by Eric Lennox "might" have been another Captain Murdock story, but I don't know for sure.

"Deep-Sea Sepulcher" by Arthur Flint is a story with similarities to Emile C. Tepperman again. This could have been a rewritten Marty Quade story, but it also had a bit of the Ed Race character from the back pages of *The Spider*.

Finding a Wade Hammond story during this period is very exciting. To my knowledge, "Murder Bride," published in the August 1936 issue of *Ten Detective Aces* was the last Wade Hammond entry. Wouldn't it be nice to find some more stories, especially a new tale we don't know about, hidden in *Lone Wolf Detective?* Unfortunately, as nice as that sounds, I don't think we will be that lucky. These stories appear to be nothing more than reprints from Ace's other magazines. I just can't help wondering if the authors were paid for the second printing? Somehow, I doubt it.

Wade Hammond, like Secret Agent "X," was a master of disguise—at least in this incident. With no forewarning he becomes a character named Mark Hall, and who was the wiser? Look at it from A.A. Wyn's point of view. A new magazine with a new lineup of authors (old ones in disguise, of course), and new titles to old stories, and the unsuspecting readers had a new magazine on the stands. New? Heck, the covers were even re-used from other magazines. There appears to be nothing new about this publication except for the title!

Except for the possibility of finding a Lester Dent in this mess, albeit one that had previously been printed, suggestion to the collectors of today would be to save your money on this magazine. Put your money on *Ten Detective Aces*. At least here you get the original storics, not merely re-writes.

Special thanks to John Dinan for letting me look at this interesting issue! ♦

The Caretakers From Hell

By Tom Johnson

The pages of man's history are crowded with strange and awesome legends—weird, unauthenticated tales of monstrous beings and eerie happenings. Of them all, perhaps the most fascinatingly grewsome is the little-known legend of the "Purple Eye."

All the evils of mankind (so runs legend) can be blamed upon the men with purple eyes. During every great social catastrophe in history, purple eyes have made their appearance as harbingers, destruction. They have been either the cause or effect of terror among a people already ravaged by war or pestilence, inducing an unaccountable mass hysteria, often leading to wholesale atrocities.

Regardless of the truth or falsity of this ancient legend, it is distinctly interesting in a world that at present seems to be crumbling beneath the suddenly burgeoning hatreds of mankind. Randolph Craig—an author of national reputation has assumed this non de plume for purpose of this series—has, in the pages that follow, revived this figure out of ancient legend. He has made of him a modern super-criminal who, for protective purposes, has assumed the name of The Octopus. And he has given him all those truly weird and terrifying powers that modern scientist can bestow upon a great intellect.

Revelations: 7 thru 9: And there was war in heaven; Michael and his angels fought against the dragon; and the dragon fought and his angels (8) And prevailed not: neither was their place found any more in heaven. (9) And the great dragon was cast out, that old serpent, called the Devil, and Satan, which deceiveth the whole world; he was cast out into the earth, and his angels were cast out with him.

"*The Octopus* and *The Scorpion* are sequential issues of the same magazine. Both dated in 1939, they are linked by identical characters, similar backgrounds, similar themes, and closely related plots. They differ only in title and depiction of the villain." That was how Robert Sampson described them in Michael L. Cook's *Detective, Mystery And Espionage Magazines*.

Author Robert Sampson, writing in an issue of *Dime Novel Round-Up*, said: "It was inevitable that the pulps would experiment with single character villain magazines. They did: none lasted long. In 1939, another pair of costumed madmen appeared: The Octopus, a brilliant criminal Napoleon wearing an octopus suit and dominating the underworld. And The Scorpion, a brilliant criminal Napoleon in costume." Author Robert Kenneth Jones mentioned both novels in his book, *The Shudder Pulps*.

The first novel was "The City Condemned to Hell" (February/March 1939). Here The Octopus transforms men and women into deformed, purple-eyed monsters.

The second novel, "Satan's Incubator" (April/May 1939), carried forward the legend of the purple eyes.

Both novels were reprinted by Robert Weinberg in *Pulp Classics* #11 & 12. He wrote in his introduc-

© Argosy Communications

The Octopus, February/March 1939.

tion to The Octopus: "Here is escapist literature at its most unbelievable, The Octopus is pure pulp."

I agree.

The Octopus: He was a weird, sea-green creature with cupped, weaving tentacles, hideously malformed legs and a mask from which glowed those purple, luminous eyes.

We first encounter him in Chapter Four: one of the figures picked her up, held her at arm's length—and then hot air seared her lungs as she gasped it in and began to scream—but regularly, repeatedly, an evil staring mask wavered before her eyes, seemed to grow larger and more hideous just as the body beneath it seemed to swell. A million, tearing pains shot through her tortured flesh, seeming to rend it asunder, and she knew that not one but four arms encircled her, some that held her not by a grip, but by powerful suction. Then words floated into her consciousness: "The Skull's nurse. She'll be a good object lesson by the time he finds her."

The Octopus was... Satan!

The Scorpion: He wore a dark, swathing cloak. A black hood covered his hair, but not the face. Those were human features, however a birthmark extended from forehead to chin, a black, shadowy outline of a... scorpion!

Those who worked for him wore black robes and were branded with small scorpion emblems. Here is an example: He was of normal height, but his body was unnaturally lean. His dark face was vicious, a wrinkled, screwed-up area on an enormous head. The hands were covered by gloves of flexible brown metal; the fingers ended in claws. Under the gloves, the palms of the hands were branded with the mark of the scorpion.

The Scorpion was... Satan!

Jeffrey Fairchild: The man who fought both The Octopus and The Scorpion was a rather unique individual for one reason—because he resembled in many ways another pulp character—The Spider! Jeffrey Fairchild was about thirty years of age, son of the deceased Dr. Henry Fairchild who had achieved medical fame and fortune in the process before his demise. (His mother was mentioned, but no name given to her.)

He was described as lean-cheeked, black haired, with keen brown eyes. During his college days he had played football. A medical school graduate, at the head of his class incidentally: however, he never entered into active medical practice. Most thought of him as just another wealthy bachelor, residing in a Park Avenue apartment. But his were the athletes trained and rippling muscles.

Dr. Skull: Actually, Jeffrey Fairchild was just one of three personalities. The second was that of a rather kindly old physician, Dr. Skull, who lived and worked in the New York City slums as well as the area hospitals. He was white haired, with deep wrinkles embedded in his forehead, jaw and cheeks. (This was accomplished by two padded wires set in the lower jaw which served to alter the shape of his face. That, plus makeup and a gray wig, finished the disguise.)

In addition to being a qualified surgeon on the staff of Mid-City Hospital in New York City, his practice in the slums took most of his time. He had also written for the American Medical Journal a few articles. He was indeed no stranger to the practice of medicine. (He knew ju-jitsu, and did not hesitate to use it when necessary.)

"I am at home among the victims of poverty and ignorance where crime has its breeding place," he said, referring to his work on the East Side.

He was introduced almost immediately in Chapter One of the first novel, which had a most appropriate title of "When The Beast Hungers."

The Skull Killer: The last, and probably most important of the personalities, was The Skull Killer, who indeed killed without mercy, leaving his mark imprinted between the eyes—the outline of a human skull. This was accomplished by a steel stamp with a hollow handle containing an acid that moistened the dye. The results, when he pressed the stamp against flesh, was a red brand burned into the forehead with a skull outline. He carried this stamp in his suit pocket. (I guess it wasn't any more dangerous than the cigarette lighter that Richard Wentworth always carried around.)

For six years he had moved among the underworld. At the beginning of his career there had been three insurance policy racketeers who were found with raw outlines of the skull burned into their foreheads. Thus the legend began.

The police apparently regarded The Skull Killer a benevolent individual, but with each additional killing, the Commissioner of Police became more upset and vowed to bring him to justice.

Actually, nobody had ever seen him up close until a morgue attendant by the name of Angus

Burke was given that honor. He would later describe The Skull Killer as "a young man." Nobody suspected a connection between the old East Side doctor and The Skull Killer, regardless of the similarity of names. But from time to time a few criminals did apparently make the connection. But they now rested in a world from which none returned. (More about Angus Burke later.)

There are a couple of things that need to be mentioned. One is that he drove what was described as "an old tight-jointed jalopy" that resembled a high-bodied sedan. Under the hood was the chassis and motor of a racing car. We are also told that it was a 1922 make. This car was driven by Dr. Skull. Jeffrey Fairchild's private car was not described, except that it had a Diesel motor, which he had designed and installed himself, and there was nothing to mark his car as different from a thousand other sedans on the street. And also, like Dr. Skull's jalopy, its smooth painted sides were of heavy plated steel.

Jeffrey Fairchild also kept a trim little two-seater at the Newark airport; it had a lofty wing spread, which gave it some of the qualities of a glider, and a powerful little motor. At the airport he was known as a wealthy and idle young man, with a penchant for playing with air-currents and the scientific side of flying.

However, the media guessed The Skull Killer to be some lone fanatic crusading against crime. Or, as one newspaper guessed, he might be a higher up in the Police Department, for he knew so much about criminals and where to find them. He must be a gangster said another, for it's the gangsters who kill their own kind. A prominent psychologist, when interviewed, explained technically and at great length, that a killer who left his mark was an incurable exhibitionist. He had probably had a thwarted childhood, said the prominent psychologist, quoting effectively from Freud and Jung.

But, for Jeffrey Fairchild, there was an aura of health, strength and competence about him. And contrary to erudite psychological opinion, that "brand" was no mere braggart gesture. In Jeffrey's ceaseless war on evil, he had found that the brand gave him a definite authority over his enemy. Some times, indeed, it acted as a deterrent, for those marked corpses were proof to the living that The Skull Killer was alive and active.

But even with the close similarities between The Skull Killer and The Spider, in no way could the former compete with the latter; for one thing, The Skull Killer wore no black cloak, no slouch hat, no nothing in the way of a costume! The character killed while in the guise of Dr. Skull, or in his own identity as that of Jeffrey Fairchild. There was no horrible, hunchback, fanged terror to menace the criminals who he fought—only the brand on his victim's forehead.

As for the novels, there was a fierce intense heat about the scenes of horror and terror. But they did not contain the urgency that ran rampant in the Spider stories. Indeed, with these novels, the reader is kept at arms reach from the action, as if seen from afar; you are not drawn into the fierce action, as the narration seems to speak to everyone, not just you. With The Spider, you were pulled in. With The Skull Killer, you experience it happening to someone else, and you are not involved personally. But that was just as well, as you see the terror, but are not drained from the experience.

Nor is there any reality to time. Does the action take place within only a few hours, or does it drag on for days, or weeks. The reader cannot tell. The story opens, there appears to be a new horrible crime wave racking the city; did it just start, or has it been going on for months? The reader cannot tell. But suddenly Dr. Skull is involved and the reader sees the horror unfolding within the precious sanctum of the kindly old doctor. Before you take another breath, the action is hot, tense, and you forget about tine; and so does the author. You follow Dr. Skull as he races against time to stop this latest horror.

And not only does the doctor become involved, but so, too, does the people he loves. Now, let's take a look at the characters:

Robert Fairchild: He is the brother of Jeffrey Fairchild. A cripple, age eighteen, he idolized Dr. Skull, and in the first novel maintained residence at Mid City Hospital. At the moment he was there for a series of operations. He never really got along with his brother, Jeffrey. Some thought of him as "a spoiled, ungrateful brat." He was in a private suite on the eighth floor of the hospital. (Incidentally, the hospital is owned by Jeffrey Fairchild.)

Robert had been away from home, attending a college when he was approached by insurance racketeers who offered him easy money if he would fake an accident and sue the insurance company. He agreed, but before the trail, decided against the crooked racketeers. But before he can testify, the racketeers break his back, leaving him forever confined to a wheelchair.

After the Mid-City Hospital is destroyed by fire in the first novel, Robert is transferred to Jeffrey's own rooms. Where he would switch back and forth from his brother's residence to the rooms maintained by Dr. Skull.

Carol Endicott: The girl involved is a nurse hired by Jeffrey Fairchild to care for his invalid brother. However, she was usually to be found assisting Dr. Skull when not caring personally for Robert. She was a most capable person, raised in the New York City slums. She was young, lissome, with dark lustrous hair that held a reddish tint, an ivory-toned face, and pert little nose. She was a cigarette smoker. Naturally, she found herself in trouble from the beginning.

We also find this: Her white uniform had grease smudges on it, and a large smudge bridged her freckled, pert little nose, while there was a rather unprofessional competence about her movements. She was again the independent and rather harassed New York slum girl, whom Jeffrey Fairchild had persuaded to trust the old East Side doctor in order that she might have a home, decency and security.

Decency had always been one of Carol's attributes, though often, in the old days, she had had to fight for it. Young, tall, with a clear ivory skin and lustrous dark hair that carried in it a reddish glint, she had attracted considerable attention in the tenement district where she lived. The tough look that came over Carol's piquantly lovely features had nothing lady like about it. Rather, it reflected a portion of her life she had nearly forgotten—her upbringing in a rough-and ready slum neighborhood, and the battle she had waged continually not only for respectability among the worst elements of humanity, but for her very survival.

Wexler: Jeffrey maintained one servant whose name was Wexler. He was short and good-natured; had red hair, and he liked to cook. His attitude toward Jeffrey was benign and fatherly. He only appeared in the second novel. Other minor characters appeared, but had little substance. There was a Police Commissioner, named Tom Wiley, and a police captain in the first story named Manning. These characters were not explored, but they were friends of Jeffrey Fairchild.

Angus Burke: Although not really a principal character in this drama of life and death, Angus did strike a cord. As stated previously, he did see The Skull Killer, but under some odd circumstances. Angus was the morgue attendant at the Mid City Hospital, and had been handling "the stiffs" for a long time. He liked Dr. Skull because he treated a man fair and square and didn't mind because he kept dead stiffs instead of dying ones. One day two men came into the morgue asking for one particular corpse. Old Angus hobbled up to the latest stiff, and lifted the sheet from its face. And the corpse yelled at him to, "Duck, they'll kill you!" And a bullet sang above the old man's head. He hadn't really ducked; it had been more like his knees gave way. Angus tried to whine for help, but nothing audible was coming out of his windpipe. Like nothing dead, the stiff was letting the two others have it with a revolver. Old Angus shut his eyes, and his brain busied itself with a prayer.

When the shooting stopped, he peered about. The two visitors were dead, and the corpse was doing something to their faces. The corpse then glanced at him. Later he told newsmen about it and identified the individual as The Skull Killer.

The Novels

"The City Condemned to Hell": The story starts out in confusion; scenes are switching every few pages. The pace moves fast, no reality to time. Dr. Skull is caring for a patient at Mid-City Hospital when the patient turns into a monster; it tries to suck the lifeblood from the attending nurse—Dr. Skull arrives in time to save the nurse, but the patient escapes (just after an operation), then is re-captured. There is an attempt to murder Dr. Skull by the patient's purple-eyed husband.

Across town, while at Dr. Skull's office in a poor neighborhood, Carol Endicott receives a very strange message; shortly afterwards she is almost killed by more purple-eyed corpses, but is rescued by The Skull Killer. (Though she doesn't see him.)

She rushes to Mid-City Hospital to rescue Robert Fairchild and/or Jeffrey Fairchild from some pending doom. But the hospital is already burning; Jeffrey, unknown to her, has already rescued Robert and others from the burning building. But she rushes into the flames, only to be captured inside by purple-eyed men wearing gas masks… and The Octopus!

Jeffrey hears her scream, and rushes back into the burning building, finds Carol, defeats her abductors, takes her and Robert to his own apartment.

A new skyscraper has recently been built, and now a giant spotlight shines a purple bean into the heavens. Also from this new building—The Victory Building—a radio message goes out to the people—a portion of their weekly pay, or they would become monsters, too—and already there are thousands of these human monsters walking the streets: Dr. Skull is accused as the person responsible for their creation.

The triple identity of Dr. Skull/The Skull Killer/

Jeffrey Fairchild is discovered immediately.

In a final scene, the action terminates in a room of the new skyscraper—a room in Hell, with the Deathless One, Satan, Octopus, at the head of his demons—men and women he had turned into purple-eyed monsters. His own words send the monsters at… himself! For the monsters now know that he is their tormentor!

There is no criminal motif, no reason for the atrocities. The requested city ransom appears merely to be a homage to the Octopus. There is no profit to be gained for criminal cohorts. There is only evil to accomplish a "Hell" on Earth. Satan's own kingdom seems to be his goal! The novel felt out of place as either a hero or villain magazine. It read more like something the reader would find in *Horror Stories, Terror Tales,* or *Dime Mysteries*.

"Satan's Incubator": Mothers are killing their own children, husbands are killing their wives, men their girlfriends, wives their husbands, girls their boyfriends. The city is in riot, police are searching for killers; meanwhile, the workers of the sanitation department appear to be carrying off people… and evidence.

All is confusion again in this new novel of terror as Jeffrey Fairchild/Dr. Skull/The Skull Killer rushes from one scene to another—again, time is not real—it doesn't exist.

Again, an evil, unspeakable evil, is leading purple-eyed creatures in a mad play out of Hell itself! Torture, dismembering victims and forcing them to eat their own legs and arms in order to survive. Women chained in dehumanizing positions and offered as live art with large frames to promote the idea of portraits—portraits of shame, of horror.

Beneath the city dump, in caverns befitting Hell itself, resides The Scorpion (Satan) and his demons. Again, the scene of Hell, its master in the guise of The Scorpion, his demons, the purple eyed goons that torture, maim and kill—for the pleasure of it.

This time there is a semblance of possible profit to be gained—individuals connected with the Department of Health appear to be profiting from a "Blue Law." A law that forces people to eat and shop at establishments that display a blue/purple tag. But these crooks are destroyed by the Skull Killer, and The Scorpion/Satan is not pleased or angry—it is only a mere set back.

Again, the Evil is not identified. Could it have been Jan Devanter? Or was Devanter merely a stooge, as had been Dr. Borden from the previous novel? Very likely, as the real Evil cannot be killed by man!

In this final novel, we are told that Jeffrey Fairchild had bought the New Victory Building (from last novel) and turned it into a new hospital.

The Authors

The author for these two novels was listed as Randolph Craig, and for years everyone thought this name hid Norvell Page, so for years collectors wanted these two pulps for their Page collections. But as far back as 1976, Robert Weinberg knew that husband and wife writing team of Ejler and Edith Jacobson were connected somehow. In *Pulp Vault* #5, Robert Weinberg disclosed in his fine article, "The Problems With Pulp Research," that Norvell Page had not written the two novels, and that, indeed, Ejler & Edith Jacobson had written them. It appears that they had written numerous stories for Popular Publications, and their writing can be found in such titles as *Dime Mystery,* as well as others. There is still some question about how much Norvell Page did contribute to the stories. As I understand it, the check for the first story was signed by Page and the Jacobsons. Rumors consist that Page rewrote the second story almost verbatim from the first one, and that the second one is actually his alone. I don't know.

While making notes for this article, I looked for odd phrases that might come in handy later on as we continue research into such series as The Phantom Detective, where the full story of who wrote what is still not close to being solved. A slim possibility exists

The Scorpion, April/May 1939.

that these two authors may have written for other houses, and used other house names besides Randolph. Craig.

Here are a few examples of what I came up with:

> It was night, a cold starry November night, with Orion making a clear pale pattern above Manhattan, as it had done for the last five thousand Novembers.
>
> Dim but unmistakable in the darkness, the walls glowed like a new earthbound star.
>
> … there was something almost unearthly in the boy's sculptured profile.
>
> For a second her heart went acrobatic…
>
> Heat and gas rolled like ocean waves through her body…

The Mid-City Hospital was destroyed by fire in the first story, to be relocated in the Victory Building following its purchase by Jeffrey Fairchild. It was originally a fifty-story skyscraper on Columbus Circle in New York City.

There was a secret exit at the hospital basement. Jeffrey Fairchild went through a maze of abandoned gas and water mains under the New York City streets. Relics of the past, now forgotten, he had stumbled upon them as a boy. The terminals were in the basement of Dr. Skull's office. Inside the basement was a chamber containing a cot, a chair and bureau. A wall amplifier kept him fully aware of everything happening in his office. Here he exchanged the personalities of Jeffrey Fairchild and Dr. Skull. Once through a coal-bin door, up the cellar steps, he would emerge at the rear doorway of Dr. Skull's office proper.

Dr. Skull's office held a desk, bookshelf with a bust of Galen's. Once he employed a cleaning lady known as Mrs. Kitty Timiny. She and her son are both killed in the second novel.

Villains using the names of Octopus and Scorpion were not new to the pulps. Whenever any mastermind took over the head of the criminal underworld, he would most likely be called an "octopus of crime." Meaning, he had many arms to aid him. And for logical reasons, scorpions brought to mind a horrible image, so many "horrible" crime lords would be called The Scorpion. Most pulp series used them; from the Secret Agent "X" series alone, we have these two novels: "Octopus of Crime" (September 1934), and "Slaves of the Scorpion" (June 1937).

Nor is it difficult to find criminal Satans in just about any series. The pulps were full of such characters. It isn't any wonder. After all, purple prose and colorful characters was a trademark of the pulp action adventures from the Avenger to Captain Zero. And the two novels by Randolph Craig were merely following an old family tradition. If you haven't read these two novels, then give them a try. You will be in for a treat! ♦

Yesterday's Man of Tomorrow

By Will Murray

When Julie Schwartz and Paul Kupperberg paid tribute to the late, great science fiction writer Edmond Hamilton in *Superman* #378 ("The Man who Saved the Future"), they probably left a lot of comic readers wondering about the inspiration for their Ed Hamilton, a NASA scientist who became Colonel Future in emulation of the real Hamilton's pulp hero, Captain Future.

As nice as their tribute was, there was not enough room in the pages of Superman to fully explore the Edmond Hamilton/Captain Future legend and some of the more interesting ways it touched comics. It's a story worth telling in full.

Edmond Hamilton was possibly the most famous name in pulp science fiction during the Thirties. He was a pioneer, a master of a then-new form called "space opera." In an absolute sense, he was to pulp SF what George Lucas is to film SF today: A giant. As such, he was the logical choice to write Standard Publications' new SF hero, Captain Future, who was created by Editorial Director Leo Margulies and Editor Mort Weisinger in response to the First World Science Fiction Convention held in New York in the summer of 1939.

Margulies, the story goes, attended the convention out of curiosity, and was struck by this early manifestation of organized fandom. "I didn't think you fans could be so damn sincere," he blurted. Huddling with Weisinger, they created a character they called "Mr. Future, Wizard of Science" who would best be described as a futuristic version of Doc Savage.

Weisinger, still years away from editing Superman, wrote a long prospectus for the character, which he outlined as a genetic superman who battled evil in the 21st Century along with a trio of alien sidekicks. An extremely gimmick-minded editor, he must have thought Doc Savage the greatest series in history because, everywhere he went, he brought Doc Savage ideas with him. (He was a friend of Doc's main writer, Lester Dent.)

But Weisinger had ideas of his own, too. A couple of them appeared in the Mr. Future prospectus and were never used. They later showed up in Superman when Weisinger took over that comic. One was Mr. Future's device, which intercepted light rays that had traveled off into space, thus enabling him to see events in the past. Superman needed no such device to accomplish this handy feat, however. One of Future's sidekicks, as outlined by Weisinger, was a robot constructed in Future's likeness, designed to substitute for him in emergencies. This idea later was used with Superman's robots.

This unnamed robot, along with the other supporting characters, which included a tiny, rubylike alien named Otho, which Future wore set in a ring (!) and Simon Wright, a walking encyclopedia with a photographic memory, but no initiative of his own, were an unwieldy group. When Margulies and Weisinger hired Hamilton to take on the series, the latter objected loudly to this supporting cast and, over a

Captain Future, Spring 1943.   Captain Future, Winter 1941.   Captain Future, Summer 1943.

series of meetings, Hamilton and the others refined the entire concept. The robot became Grag, a hulking mechanical man who combined strength and good-natured loyalty; Otho was turned into a white-skinned, emerald-eyed android who possessed the wit and intelligence Grag did not; and Simon Wright was recast as an elderly scientist who, at death, had his brain encased in a transparent box fitted with artificial eyes and force beams for mobility. Hamilton dubbed the trio the Futuremen, and somewhere along the line, Mr. Future was rechristened Captain Future.

The end product of all this work was a novel, "Captain Future and the Space Emperor," which appeared in the Fall 1939 issue of Captain Future. The quarterly was subtitled "Wizard of Science," which became "Man of Tomorrow" not long after Superman acquired that particular nickname. Hamilton's first Captain Future novel attracted its share of attention.

Lester Dent read it, probably at Weisinger's urging, and decided Hamilton had done such a good job imitating the Doc Savage style that Dent asked Hamilton to ghost-write Doc Savage. Hamilton declined. He was too busy. Humorist S.J. Perelman also picked up that premiere issue and it inspired him to pen an article for the New Yorker titled "Captain Future, Block That Kick!" It consisted of a rather arch plot synopsis of the novel designed to make Hamilton and his hero look silly. Still, Perelman did admit that "Beside Captain Future, Wizard of Science, Flash Gordon and the Emperor Ming pale to a couple of nursery tots chewing on Holland rusk." But perhaps even that much was not meant to be complimentary.

"Captain Future and the Space Emperor" may not have been the greatest SF novel of all time, but it was good, escapist pulp, recounting Captain Future's battle with the evil Space Emperor, who is fomenting unrest on Jupiter where Earthmen coexist peacefully with the native Jovians. The Space Emperor is the first of the many super-criminals Captain Future chased around the solar system. Others included the Wecker, the Life-lord, Dr. Zarro (also known as Dr. Doom) and Future's eternal adversary, Ul Quern, the Magician of Mars. More on him later.

As explained in that first novel, Captain Future was really Curt Newton, the orphan son of scientist Roger Newton who fled to a secret laboratory on the moon in order to escape an enemy named Victor

Corvo and to conduct experiments in artificial life. These experiments led to the creation of Grag and Otho, and the technology which preserved Simon Wright as the Living Brain. But after Newton's son, Curtis, was born, Victor Corvo caught up with the Newtons and killed Roger and his wife. In revenge, Grag and Otho killed Corvo barehanded, and a dying Elaine Newton entrusted the upbringing of her infant son to the inhuman trio.

True to her wishes, Simon Wright, Grag, and Otho raised Curt Newton in the solitude of the moon, teaching him, acting as surrogate parents and ultimately transforming him into a physical and intellectual superman along a program obviously borrowed from Doc Savage—but which really goes back to the 1880s and Nick Carter. When he reached maturity, Curt Newton, scientist and adventurer, dedicated himself to preserving the future of the solar system against the forces of evil, and took the name of Captain Future.

He was not a Doc Savage clone, however. He was a bright, boyishly cocky redhead who may have owed much to C.L. Moore's grim space farer, Northwest Smith.

As Captain Future, Newton patrolled the solar system in his tear-shaped ship, the *Comet,* which could perfectly imitate the look of a comet in flight when necessary. He always wore a gray or green zipper suit (although the Earle Bergey covers invariably showed him attired in red or blue spacesuits) and carried a worn proton-pistol cowboy-style. The rest of the system, including the Planet Police, had to content themselves with crummy blasters known as atom-guns, while Future's unique sidearm had a discretionary stun capability, much like a phaser.

Eschewing a disguise, he was known by his special signet ring, whose jewels revolved in their setting to represent the nine worlds. A good friend of Earth's President, James Carthew, as well as various members of the Planet Police, including special agent Joan Randall, his main squeeze, Captain Future operated without official interference. His headquarters was a sort of Fortress of Solitude on the moon.

Initially, Captain Future concerned himself with just our solar system—an editorial requirement as iron-clad as those which demanded three big capture-and-escape scenes per novel and a futuristic sports game in every issue. With the ninth novel, "Quest Beyond the Stars" (Winter 1942) the Futuremen finally venture beyond Pluto to the Birthplace of Matter, which may contain the only method of regenerating Mercury's dying atmosphere. The Birthplace of Matter is somewhere beyond Sagittarius, they discover, and it contains an artificial world built eons ago by a strange race known as the Watchers, who have since vanished. Naturally, Captain Future's mission is a success.

As the series progressed, the scope of Newton's adventures broadened. He discovered a hidden world in a comet ("The Comet Kings," Summer 1942), and in "The Lost World of Time" (Fall 1941) traveled back in time to the lost world of Katain, where he discovered that all human life in the Universe originated with a race from the Deneb system. In "The Star of Dread" (Summer 1943) he finally went to Deneb. Author Hamilton, nicknamed "the World-Saver" because his heroes often rescued entire planets from awesome destructive agencies, created a consistent milieu for his characters to romp in. Often, old characters, places, and backgrounds were revisited. One of these characters was Ul Quorn, the renegade scientist whose red skin, ageless looks and black hair and eyes reflected his mixed Martian, Venusian, and Terran blood. He first appeared, along with his sultry Martian girlfriend, N'Rala, in "Captain Future and the Seven Space Stones" (Winter 1940), returned in "The Magician of Mars" (Summer 1941) and finally met his end in "The Solar Invasion" (*Startling Stories,* Fall 1946). The enmity between Captain Future and the Magician of Mars was not limited to good-vs.-evil. Ul Quorn was the son of Victor Corvo. Theirs was a blood feud.

Captain Future, Winter 1943.

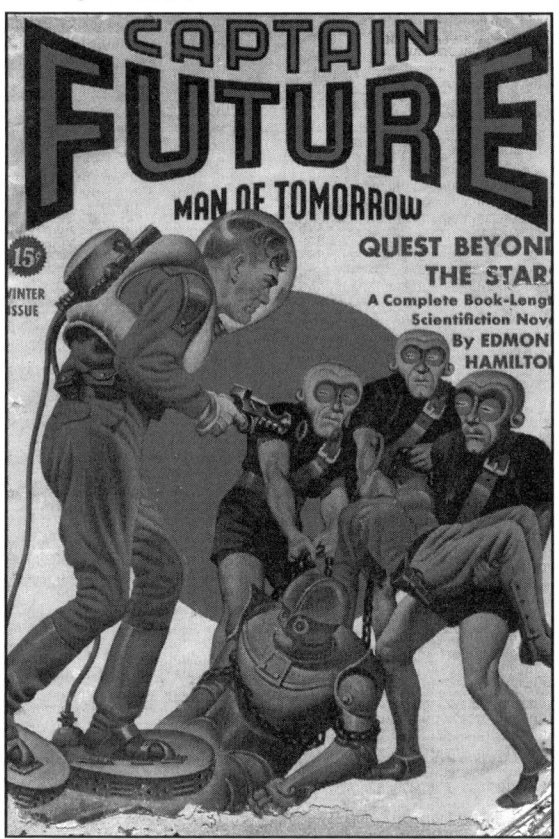

Captain Future, Winter 1942.

Captain Future was a wonderful magazine, but Hamilton's stories were considered too juvenile by many in the SF field, which was beginning to mature at that time. A number of story elements were pretty childish. For one, Grag and Otho were always bickering. This was another Doc Savage gimmick. Doc's aides, Monk and Ham, acted the same way. In that series, both characters acquired silly pets. So did Grag and Otho. In one story, Grag adopted a metal-eating moon-pup and dubbed him Eek. Not to be outdone, Otho later found himself a meteor-mimic, Oog. Oog is described as a white, doughy creature with four legs and two big eyes. It's called a meteor-mimic because it could change its shape and impersonate any creature or object near to its size. The idea for these pets may have been Weisinger's, but when Hamilton later went to work for Weisinger writing the Legion of Super-Heroes, he dug back into the pages of *Captain Future* and dusted off Oog, for that series, rechristening him Proty. Weisinger and Hamilton worked well together wherever they went. Even when Hamilton reworked the original Mr. Future idea, he kept as many of Weisinger's ideas as possible. The original Otho was obviously the inspiration for Captain Future's signet ring, and as for the robot which was to have been Curt Newton's double, that idea was carried over in Otho, who often made himself up as his "chief."

During World War II, *Captain Future* hit its stride, but ran into problems. Edmond Hamilton resigned from the series because he expected to be drafted. Leo Margulies hired two writers to replace him, Manly Wade Wellman, who sometimes wrote Captain America, and Joseph Samachson, who wrote under

232 ECHOES 30: THREE DECADES OF PULP FANDOM'S GREATEST MAGAZINE

the pen name of William Morrison. To cover this change, a house name was summarily attached to the series while Hamilton was still writing it, and the "new" author became Brett Sterling.

Then Hamilton discovered he wasn't going to be drafted after all. He continued the series as Brett Sterling, but that wasn't the end of his troubles. Once, customs agents seized the manuscript to his story, "The Magic Moon," because they were concerned over the maps and diagrams which were part of two background features he also wrote for the magazine, "The Worlds of Tomorrow" and "The Futuremen." They were seized as he crossed the Mexican border and relayed to Washington where Hamilton's map of the imaginary planet Vulcan was closely examined by war-wary censors. *Captain Future* had to skip an issue; later, he got his story back.

Another time, he was shocked when he read Joseph Samachson's *Captain Future* novel, "Days of Creation" (Spring 1944). It contained the same plot—Captain Future loses his memory—as a story he had just turned in, "Outlaw World." Not wanting to appear to be imitating "Brett Sterling," Hamilton hastily rewrote "Outlaw World." His editor, who approved all outlines in advance, must have been asleep. It wasn't Mort Weisinger; he joined National Comics (now DC) in 1941, from which he was drafted into the Army himself.

"Outlaw World" never appeared in the pages of *Captain Future*. The paper shortage killed the magazine. Leftover novels were dumped into a companion magazine, *Startling Stories*, then Captain Future was retired in 1946.

But not for long. Four years later, starting with "The Return of Captain Future" in the January 1950 *Startling Stories*, Curt Newton returned. This time it was in a series of sharp, poignant novelettes heavy on character and short on action. Hamilton's reputation in the SF field had taken a beating due to the space opera aspects of Captain Future. He had already redeemed himself by 1950 with many good, mature stories, and now he was out to clear the good Captain's name.

This he did with a vengeance. Through seven novelettes, each focusing on a different character, he explored the Captain Future cast. Simon Wright briefly regained human form in "The Harpers of Titan" (September 1950), Grag's loyalty was explored in "Pardon My Iron Nerves" (November 1950), and Curt Newton's character is tested in a beautiful final story, "Birthplace of Creation" (May 1951), when he returns to the Birthplace of Matter to stop a scientist from tampering with the power to create worlds and finds that even he is not immune from the corruption of power. Captain Future had grown up.

Having closed one phase of his SF career, Edmond Hamilton moved on, ultimately going into comics where he scripted Batman, Superman, and a series probably best suited to his skills, the Legion of Super-Heroes. He enjoyed working on the series, but claimed that Triplicate Girl drove him up the wall. All the while, he continued doing science fiction stories and novels, up until his death in 1977.

As for Captain Future, he did not die. Exactly. In the early Seventies, Popular Library reissued 13 of the novels with nice Jeff Jones and Frank Frazetta covers—although most of the covers were awful reprints from the German dime novel series, Perry Rhodan. Better packaged reprints appeared in Swedan and Japan, where the character remains popular.

The Japanese produced an animated TV series of Future's adventures. Someone should show it in America. Maybe it would lead to a resurgence in interest in one of our earliest—and best—space opera heroes. Captain Future deserves a comeback. Not long ago it was 1990, the year in which, according to Edmond Hamilton's origin story, Curtis Newton was (or will be) born. ♦

The House Name That Fell Off

By Will Murray

Sometimes you get lucky.

Sometimes you get real lucky.

I was visiting my friend Chuck Juzek in Florida when I made an arresting discovery. I make a lot of interesting discoveries prowling through Chuck's massive and well-organized pulp magazine and book collection. This one was a beaut.

Chuck had purchased a short stack of pulps at the previous PulpCon, and I was going through them when my eyes fell on a Canadian edition of *Exciting Detective*. I almost skipped past it. Chuck had other Canadian editions of *Exciting* and at first glance I thought this was an issue I'd seen in his collection before.

Indeed, the cover looked familiar. It was a crude line drawing, rendered in that weak two-color printing process Canadian pulps sometimes used during the war when they were obliged by their government to repackage US magazines instead of merely reprinting them. The line work was printed a strange chocolate black, while the rest was a sickly green. It was not the most appetizing pulp cover I had ever beheld.

The art depicted a scene similar to that of an early issue of *The Masked Detective*. Indeed, it was basically the same action, but posed differently. A hurtling car slams into a taxicab. A masked man, poking his head out of the taxi's roof hatch, appears about to retaliate with his Tommy gun. It was done better in the American original, which was the Fall 1941 issue of *The Masked Detective*.

My eye fell to the list of stories printed at the bottom of the cover, confirming my impression. It read:

The Threat of the Violent Men
A Complete Book-Length Novel Featuring the Daring Exploits of Rex Parker, Crime Avenger

This was a Masked Detective novel. No question about it.

When my gaze fell on the author credit, my brain almost short-circuited:

By SAM MERWIN, JR.

The byline in the Masked Detective series, as everyone knows, was C.K.M. Scanlon, a house name that had graced the Dan Fowler novels in *G-Men Detective* until 1940, when they decided to identify the authors by name. Whereupon, it resurfaced on the Masked Detective. What was this, I wondered? A typo? Hastily, I undid the mylar bag and pulled the issue free.

The contents pages showed this to be December, 1941 issue of *Exciting Detective*, Vol. 2, No. 3. The lead novel was trumpeted as:

A Complete Book-Length Novel Featuring A New Mysterious Crime Avenger in
THE THREAT OF THE VIOLENT MEN

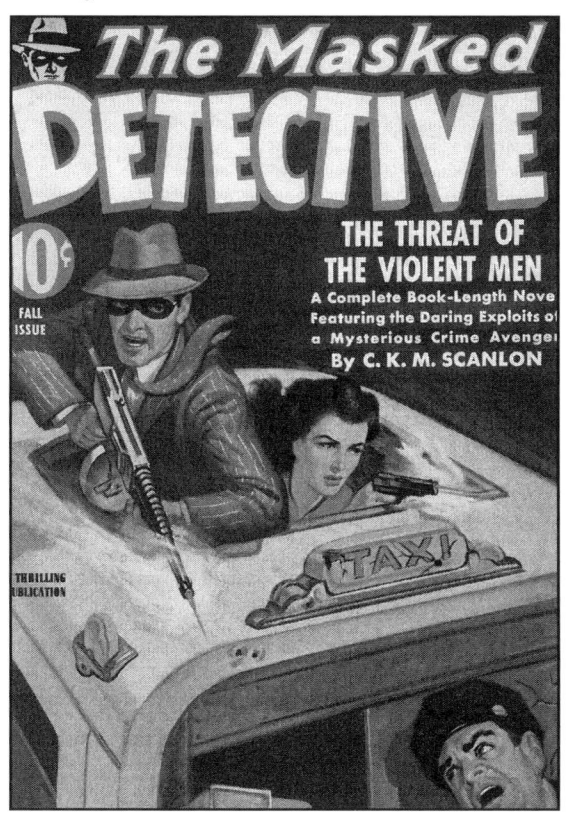

The Masked Detective, Fall 1941.

Exciting Detective, December 1941 (Canadian edition).

By SAM MERWIN, JR.

There was that name again. My excitement mounted.

The "new" suggested that this was the first Masked Detective tale to grace the pages of the Canadian edition of *Exciting Detective*. But I had no way of verifying this supposition.

Turning to the title pages, there was further confirmation. Sam Merwin, Jr. was listed as the author. C.K.M. Scanlon was nowhere to be seen.

More importantly, the author credits clearly listed two non-Masked Detective stories as among his prior work: "The Game of Death" and "Physician, Heal Thyself."

Pulling out Chuck's copy of Fred Cook and Steve Miller's *Mystery, Detective, and Espionage Fiction*, I looked up the titles. Both "Physician, Heal Thyself" and "The Game of Death" were listed under the byline of Sam Merwin, Jr. They appeared in *Thrilling Mystery* and *Thrilling Detective*, respectively, in 1940.

Chuck also had a reprint of "The Threat of the Violent Men," and I sought that out. On the title page, it duly listed C.K.M. Scanlon as the author, adding: by the author of "The League of the Iron Cross," "Alias The Masked Detective," etc.

Clearly, this was not a case of a house name falling off the page, or being confused with another byline by accident. This was deliberate. Intentional. Calculated to reveal the true culprit behind "The Threat of the Violent Men."

This was also an exciting discovery. Sam Merwin, I had been told by writer Sam Mines, ghosted *Phantom Detective* novels, but they had not been

THE HOUSE NAME THAT FELL OUT   235

identified, other than a suggestion by Tom Johnson that "Murder Set the Music" read like a Merwin tale. Merwin had written one Dan Fowler novel in 1941, "The Strange Shapes of Murder." And it was suspected he might have been involved with the short-lived *Masked Detective* series around this time. But here was proof positive of his involvement.

How did this happen? How could it have happened? I have a theory. First, we need to clarify something. There were two Sam Merwins. The elder, who signed his work Samuel Merwin, wrote a brief series about an obscure character named the Hornet in *The World Adventurer*, in 1934. That Merwin died in 1936.

The son, who wrote as Sam Merwin, Jr., joined the staff of Standard magazines 1941 as a sports and mystery editor. Later, he edited *Startling Stories* and *Thrilling Wonder Stories* successfully, as well as becoming a notable writer of pulp science fiction.

As one of his duties in 1941, I suspect Merwin had the task of preparing the contents of various Thrilling pulps for Canadian publication. Being the provider, he cleverly swapped the Scanlon byline for his true one, and thus it was innocently published by an unsuspecting publisher in the northern latitudes.

I looked through more of Chuck's collection. He had two other issues of the Canadian *Exciting Detective*. Later issues. There was no trace of the *Masked Detective*, but the April and July 1942 issues reprinted two Purple Scar tales from the American issues of *Exciting*—with the John S. Endicott house name intact, alas. Another Purple Scar story was promised in the issue to follow, July, 1942, indicating the Scar had established residency there.

This left only one issue between Merwin's novel and the Purple Scar's first appearance. The lead novel promised for February 1942, was blurbed as "We Sell Murder," by John K. Butler. The Mask—as he was alternately called—was not intended to be a regular feature, it seemed. If any more appeared, they have yet to be discovered. In any event, clearly the Masked Detective did not go over very well in Canada, for the Purple Scar soon supplanted him.

So by a fortuitous stroke of luck, we have the true identity of one of the Masked Detective C.K.M. Scanlons. I suspect Merwin did others as well. The story that immediately followed "Violent Men," "Death Island," reads a lot like Merwin's style. If Merwin did two, he may have done more. In fact, we know the true authors of most of the Masked Detective novels. After Norman A. Daniels did the first four, Merwin's tale came along. Other authors included W.T. Ballard, G.T. Fleming-Roberts, and Laurence Donovan. Few it seems cared to write more than one Masked Detective outing. Apparently rotating authors did the series no good, either. It died after less than three years of only quarterly publication.

Still unidentified are the author or authors of "The Crimes of Stilicho" and "Curse of the Living Corpse." One lone tale, "Monarchs of Murder," escaped the magazine's cancellation, only to appear in *Thrilling Mystery*, Fall 1944. It was severely trimmed, turned into a Rex Parker tale with all mention of his masked alter-ego blue penciled out.

I wonder: might Sam Merwin, Jr. have written that poor orphan, too?

Maybe the answers can be found in the pages of *Exciting Detective*, Canadian edition. If the house name fell off one novel, maybe another did, too! One can only hope. ♦

The Mysterious Dr. Zeng

by Will Murray

Dr. Fu Manchu made an indelible impression upon the popular writers of Sax Rohmer's day, who went on to produce a procession of faithful but spiritless imitations of the Yellow Doctor—so many, in fact, that listing them would be the work of a diligent bibliographer. The mystery-thriller field soon became so crowded with Fu Manchu *doppelgangers* that mere imitation no longer sufficed, and variations and inversions on the theme of the evil Chinese villain began to appear. Earl Derr Biggers' Charlie Chan was introduced in the 1920s, with E.A. Appel's Mr. Chang following a couple of years later and, in the 1930s, John P. Marquand's Mr. Moto. A more slavish imitation was Wo Fan, a stereotypical evil Chinese who appeared in a series of seven stories in *New Mystery Adventures* in 1935-36 under the obviously spurious byline "Bedford Rohmer." (Rumors that this pseudonym concealed the illustrious H. Bedford-Jones have so far been unconfirmed.) And of course, there was Donald E. Keyhoe's well-done Dr. Yen Sin and Robert J. Hogan's juvenile Mysterious Wu Fang—both short-lived.

But perhaps the most obscure pseudo-Fu Manchu was a character known as the Mysterious Dr. Zeng Tse-Lin. He was also one creation who stretched the Devil Doctor idea about as far in directions *different* from Sax Rohmer as could be imagined. For one thing, he was a good guy. For another, he was not even Asian.

Dr. Zeng was a pulp magazine character whose exploits took place during World War II, a time when the Chinese were our allies against the Japanese and pulp editors were encouraged to depict the Chinese people in a positive light by the Offie of War Informaion. Zeng first appeared in Standard Magazines' *Thrilling Mystery* in November 1941, in a story called "Fangs of Doom." The story was set in San Francisco's Chinatown and was the work of E. Hoffmann Price, the premier Orientalist of the pulp magazines. Price appears to have created the character of Dr. Zeng during an odd moment—a very odd moment.

Supposedly a merchant from Peiping who has taken up residence in San Francisco's Chinatown, Dr. Zeng Tse Lin, although young, is by all accounts a Chinese gentleman of the old school, who affects a pork-pie hat, quilted silk jacket, long tunic, and felt-soled shoes. While respected by the community, he is considered by the younger inhabitants of Chinatown to be hopelessly old-fashioned. Zeng is a scholar and also a detective, although of the amateur variety, and he limits his sleuthing to Chinatown and the Chinese community. He is on friendly terms with, and often works in association with, retired police captain Brian Carter and the tatter's daughter Anne.

Captain Carter knows Zeng's secret, although Anne, whom Zeng secretly loves, does not. Zeng's secret is a bizarre one. He is in reality Linwood Lawton, a white man who, through plastic surgery and other aids, disguised himself as a Chinese and became a scholar, apparently simply for the love of doing so. But when his parents, Dr. and Mrs. Hartford Lawton, were killed in the interior of China, he went to China to bring their murderers to justice. Afterwards he returned to Chinatown with his Mongol servant, Lai Hu Chow.

"Fangs of Doom" involves a bloody fight over a scroll which reveals the resting place of Genghis Khan. Despite the presence of many pulp-fiction cliches, Price depicts the Chinatown milieu and inhabitants with sensitivity, pointing out the many subtle ways in which Dr. Zeng is discriminated against because he is perceived as being Chinese. This is one of the reasons Zeng never declares his feelings for Anne Carter.

Price, widely traveled throughout Asia, made his protagonist as believable as the basic premise allowed. Even so, Dr. Zeng is an atypical pulp character.

Despite that fact. Dr. Zeng proved popular enough that he was transferred over to another Standard title, *Popular Detective*, where the real series got under way. Price, it seems, chose to allow his creation to pass into other hands: in *Popular Detective* the stories were bylined "Walt Bruce," a joint pseudonym for Robert Leslie Bellem and Willis Todhunter Ballard. At this time Bellem and Ballard were also writing the adventures of Jim Anthony, a Doc Savage imitation running in *Super-Detective*, and, not possessing Price's unique background (he was not only an Orientalist but a practicing Buddhist), they Doc Savageized Dr. Zeng to make him more heroic and presumably more acceptable to the pulp audience. Ballard recalled that "The stuff was pure formula and I did most of it on a dictaphone. I could dictate anywhere from thirty to forty pages a day."

The first of the Bellem-Ballard Dr. Zeng stories, "Blood Cargo" in the June 1942 *Popular Detective*, revamps the character's background. Dr. Zeng Tse-Lin (his name suddenly acquires a hyphen) runs the Mandarin Emporium in Chinatown. In addition to being an M.D. and Ph.D., Zeng has evolved into a scientist, as well as having studied in the lamaseries of Tibet. He is endowed with the strength of ten men and even though he still dresses the part of a Chinese scholar, the authors have decided that he is "a tall hawk of a man, with eyes like black coals glowing in the ascetic mask of his face." His secret headquarters above the Mandarin Emporium are tricked out with the latest in scientific equipment, including Zeng's own modification of television.

More significantly, Zeng has a new American name! He is, according to Bellem and Ballard, really Robert Charles Lang. Other background elements were changed also, as the following passage from "Blood Cargo" attests:

> Nobody suspected [Zeng's secret], not even the dwellers here in Chinatown, who considered him a sagacious member of their own race. They never knew that his parents had been affluent American missionaries, and that Zeng was born in China and had spent the first twenty years of his life there. But this was so; and it served Dr. Zeng in good stead now, in his assumption of the role of an Oriental.
>
> It was no idle whim that motivated his chosen way of life. Ten years before, while he was in the United States completing his education, bandits incited by Japanese had murdered his parents outside Shanghai, The grim tragedy had seared its mark on Zeng's soul. Since that

238   ECHOES 30: THREE DECADES OF PULP FANDOM'S GREATEST MAGAZINE

dark day, he had been a voluntary crusader against crime in all its aspects, masquerading as a Chinese merchant and physician, the better to give battle to the forces of evil.

Most of these changes were clearly designed to bring the character more in line with the pulp formulas of the day, and the Japanese wrinkle was no doubt fallout from Pearl Harbor, which took place shortly after E. Hoffmann Price introduced Dr. Zeng. In other respects, Dr. Zeng's adventures continued pretty much in the vein established by Price. Captain Carter somehow rejoined active police duty, and his daughter Anne became his niece Ann, but their relationship with Dr. Zeng was otherwise unchanged. (The magazine's editors must have initiated some of these changes in the belief that readers of *Popular Detective* had not read about Dr. Zeng in *Thrilling Mystery* and therefore would not notice any of the discrepancies—a supposition which makes one wonder why they chose to continue the character at all, unless they saw a commercial value in Dr. Zeng which was not fully realized by E. Hoffmann Price, prompting them to start the series afresh. Price himself might have wondered the same thing. I was in touch with him before his death in 1988, and he seemed unaware that the character had continued beyond his single opening story. "As my business was writing and selling fiction I wasted no time reading fiction, and have already given my skimpy knowledge of what others wrote—i.e., I was a professional, not a fan.")

A total of six Dr. Zeng stories appeared in *Popular Detective* over a period of slightly more than two years. *Writer's Digest* reported that this series was a regular one, even though they called him Dr. Zong by accident.) "Blood Cargo" (June 1942) is concerned with a theft of valuable blood plasma during which a Chinese-American ambulance driver is killed, thus bringing Dr. Zeng into the case. "Sinister House" (October 1942) deals with a supposed haunting on Nob Hill; there is no Chinatown connection. In this story a new character appears—Jimmy Calvin, a newspaper photographer who is one of the few who knows Dr. Zeng's secret. Just why he is in on the secret and poor Ann Carter is not is a mystery—but then they do call him the Mysterious Dr. Zeng Tse-Lin. Dr. Zeng continued to appear at roughly four-month intervals. Next came "Camelback Kill" (February 1943) and Lion's Loot" (June 1943). There was a slightly longer gap until the appearance of "Blackmail Clinic" (December 1943), and an even longer one before the final story, "Corpse Cargo" (August 1944), appeared. One of the stories, "Sinister House", was reprinted in *5 Detective Novels Magazine*, Summer 1950, this time under the ubiquitous house pseudonym, Robert Wallace. Ultimately, Dr. Zeng Tse-Lin is more a curiosity than a character of lasting importance. Certainly he had about as checkered a career as a fictional character could have. Probably the idea for Dr. Zeng grew out of E. Hoffmann Price's great love for things Oriental (I can easily see Dr. Zeng's transformation into an accepted and respected member of the Chinatown community as wish-fulfillment on Price's part. Price told me, "Classmate Wong Zen-Tze suggested Zeng Tse-Lin," adding, "I had not today's Chinese associations." This cryptic comment does not make clear whether Wong Zen-Tze personally suggested the character, or Price simply based Zeng on Wong.). By the time Bellem and Ballard started collaborating on the series, Dr. Zeng was simply another pulp hero, albeit a more improbable one than most, unless that honor belongs to the Green Lama, an American who became a Tibetan lama. By World War II, exotic Chinese characters of any type were pretty much passe in the pulp magazines, and Dr. Zeng Tse-Lin had to be close to the last of the long chain of imitations of, and reactions to, Sax Rohmer's original and still-memorable creation.

If Dr. Zeng is remembered at all, let it be in that light. ♦

Reprints

Tom Johnson

For this anniversary issue of Echoes, we thought it would be appropriate to include a couple of pulp fiction reprints. The first story up is one of Johnston McCulley's costumed characters from the mid 1930s. He had many such characters, though their costumes were usually simple hood affairs.

During the 1934 and '35 period, one such character appearing in *Thrilling Detective* was The Green Ghost. There were seven stories in the series. We are presenting the first story in the short series, "The Green Ghost." Like many of McCulley's other series, Officer Danny Blaney had been framed and kicked off the police force. Now he was after crooks. His simple disguise was a green hood pulled over his head, and a nom de guarre intended to frighten evil-doers.

Our second story is something of an oddity. "The Red Sword" was published in the February 1945 issue of *Popular Detective,* bylined John Drummond. Not to be confused with the Fiction House byline on the Ki-Gor stories, John Peter Drummond. In fact, when we reprinted this story in *Behind the Mask* #54, Fall 2000, I noted that the author of "The Red Sword" was C.S. Montayne. Now, a decade later, I have no idea where my information came from, nor if, in fact, Montayne is the author. I can tell you the writing sounds like his. Maybe so, maybe not.

If the author is a curiosity, so too is the story. The Red Sword is the British counterpart of *Popular Detective's* sister publication, *Thrilling Spy Stories,* featuring The Eagle. They could almost be the same character, except one sports a British personality. The Red Sword only appeared in one story, that I know of, and he only uses a sword cane as a weapon. It is encased in his walking stick. He also reminded me a bit of John Steed of *The Avengers.* His real identity is kept secret in the story until the very end.

Although the story was written after June 6th, 1944, the basic plot takes place prior to D-Day. A German spy has obtained information on Eisenhower's planned landing zones, and is taking that information back to Germany when The Red Sword intercepts him and takes over his identity. A secondary plot is the rescue of Count & Countess de Salle, a man and wife involved in the French Underground, held captive in Germany. Although the story never tells us who The Red Sword is working for, there is a strange correlation involving a real brother and sister who worked for the French Underground, Claude & Lisa de Baissac, and were members of the British SOE. So it's a good bet that The Red Sword is with the SOE. ♦

The Green Ghost

By Johnston McCulley

First in an exciting new series of stories of Danny Blaney, freelance avenger of crime.

Chapter One

Six feet from the mouth of the alley, it was pitch dark. At the edge of the darkness, Danny Blaney waited. He was keyed to a high nervous pitch. Crouching against the wall of the apartment house, he watched carefully. In his right hand, he held a blackjack.

"Snoopy" Carns was the first to appear. A distant tower clock had just struck two when Blaney saw Snoopy slip furtively to the mouth of the alley. He glanced in both directions, then darted into the darkness. Blaney gripped his blackjack and crouched closer to the wall.

Snoopy Carns had to pass within a few feet of him to get to the side door which opened into the basement of the apartment house. Danny Blaney knew the exact path he would have to take. He did not need a light to accomplish his purpose.

Shuffling steps, scarcely heard, came along the pavement of the alley.

"Carns!" Blaney spoke the name softly.

Snoopy Carns stopped abruptly. Blaney knew he was trying to peer into the darkness, and that he could see nothing.

"Who is it?" Carns' words were mere whispers.

"Here!"

Blaney crept forward cautiously, extending his left hand. It brushed against Snoopy's shoulder. And suddenly it thrust Snoopy back against the wall—and then Blaney struck with the blackjack.

The blow fell true. Snoopy Carns had started an ejaculation of surprise, but it ended in a gurgle. Blaney caught his sagging body and lowered it to the ground.

Now, Blaney worked swiftly. He searched the pockets of Snoopy's clothes, but did not find what he sought. He ripped open waistcoat and shirt, and an instant later had in his possession a money belt, its compartments filled with jewels.

Blaney stuffed the jewels into his own pockets, and tossed the money belt away. Then he bound Snoopy's wrists behind his back, and fastened his ankles together using cords that were as strong as wire. He gagged Snoopy with a gag previously prepared, and rolled him over against the wall.

Crouching against the wall again, Blaney waited. In less than ten minutes, Bill Sorsten appeared. He, too, stopped at the mouth of the alley to glance up and down the street, then slipped back into the darkness.

Bill Sorsten was not like Carns. Bill Sorsten was a thug, a master in the art of rough-and-tumble fighting. Rendering him helpless would be a more difficult job.

Blaney stepped out from the wall and waited. Bill Sorsten lurched toward him through the black night.

"Bill!" Blaney hissed the word.

Sorsten did not reply. He was too cautions, too suspicious for that. He stopped suddenly, was silent and motionless, waiting for the unknown in the darkness to speak again, so he could locate him exactly.

But Blaney did not speak. He scarcely breathed. He did not move enough to cause his clothing to rustle. There, within only a few feet of each other, the pair stood, each trying to locate the other.

Blaney sensed that Bill Sorsten stepped closer to the wall. In a lull in the wind that swept through the alley, he heard a man's deep breath. Then a sleeve brushed against his sleeve.

Blaney whirled and grappled with the man. Bill Sorsten grunted a curse. The blackjack fell, but glanced off a shoulder. Sorsten cursed again, aloud.

Once more Blaney struck, and the blow brought a cry of pain. Bill Sorsten was trying to put up a fight. Blaney evaded a bearlike hug that probably would have been his undoing. He struck again, and this time the blackjack cracked against the side of Bill Sorsten's head. Blaney lowered him to the ground and worked swiftly to get his wrists tied securely. He fastened the ankles, also, and then began going through Bill Sorsten's pockets. In a chamois bag fastened in Sorsten's left armpit, he found more jewels.

Blaney took them, returned a few to one of Sorsten's pockets, and retained the others. Then he crouched against the wall again and waited. Presently, Sorsten moaned. Snoopy Carns had been gurgling for some little time, showing that he had regained consciousness. Blaney heard both of them squirming and twisting. Both were conscious and aware of their bonds.

"Sorsten, can you hear?" Blaney asked.

"Who is it? What's happened?"

"It's the Green Ghost, Sorsten!"

Chapter Two

There was silence for a moment, save for the rustling of the wind as it swept through the alley. Then Sorsten spoke in a tense voice:

"The Green Ghost! Who are you? What's this mean, anyhow? You'll be put on the spot for this!"

"Yeah? How can you put on the spot a man you don't know?"

"Maybe I do know you."

"If I thought you did, Sorsten, I'd stick the muzzle of my automatic in your ear, and pull the trigger. But you don't know—you can't."

"What's your game?"

"I hate crooks, Sorsten. I know a lot about 'em. I'm out to wreck 'em, and their plans, and turn 'em in."

"Workin' for the cops, huh?"

"I hate the cops, too. That's enough—I'm not giving out a lot of information. I sent a note to Max Ganler, told him I'd be after him next."

"He thought it was somebody's joke."

"It's no joke, Sorsten. You pulled off a neat jewel job at the Carstairs house a short time ago, didn't you, Sorsten? I knew all about it in advance. I know who was on the job. It was big, and it'll be a sensation. Max Ganler's done it again. But the fool cops wouldn't be able to pin it on him."

"Whoever you are, you're crazy!" Bill Sorsten said. "I ain't seen Max Ganler for ages."

"You just said you knew about my note."

"I was told about that. I was just comin' to see Max

now."

"Why sneak in to the alley entrance?" Blaney asked.

"Max don't like to have some of us go through the lobby late at night."

"You're not fooling me a bit, Sorsten. Max was on that big job himself tonight. So was Snoopy Carns. I tapped Snoopy on his head, and he's over there against the wall. Gagged him so he couldn't yell and warn you when you came into the alley."

"I say you're crazy! I'll bet Max has been home all this evenin'. I know he was intendin' to have a little party. It's his girl's birthday—Lily Ratch's. That's why I waited so late to come and see him."

"If it's any of your business, I wanted to borrow a little jack off him."

"I just took a lot of jewels from you, Sorsten. You could have peddled them to a fence, if you needed jack. But you were bringing them to Max Ganler, so he can handle 'em. I got some off Snoopy, too. You were carrying home the swag. Max wouldn't run the risk of packing them himself."

"**Who** are you? How'd you know? What's the percentage in your racket?" Sorsten asked.

"I'm the Green Ghost, and that's enough to you. I know a lot of things. Knew you were going to pull off that Carstairs job. And I'm going to turn you in for it! About percentage—I keep some of the swag for expenses, and give the rest to charity."

"I'm tellin' you—" Sorsten began.

"Tell me nothing!"

"Untie me, and let me go. You've got the loot."

"Can't think of it, Sorsten. Howl for the cops, if you like. Somebody may hear you and call 'em, and then you'd have a lot of explaining to do."

"You goin' to leave Carns and me here, tied up?"

"You've guessed it, Sorsten. Somebody will happen along and pick you up, I imagine."

"But what's the idea? What've I ever done to you?"

"If I told you too much, you might guess my identity," Blaney said. "Good-by, Sorsten!"

Blaney backed away through the darkness. It swallowed him. Silently he crept along the wall of the apartment house toward the basement door.

He knew that Bill Sorsten would get loose soon, and free Snoopy Carns, and that they would hurry into the building and carry news of this double outrage to Max Ganler, the boss crook the cops were unable to catch.

But that was exactly as Danny Blaney wanted it.

Chapter Three

Blaney had taken a bunch of keys from Snoopy Carns' pocket. Now he hurried to the little basement door, tried the keys, and found that the third he tried did the work. He went through the door and locked it behind him.

An instant later, he was creeping quietly along a basement hall, alert, ready to dodge to cover if he heard anybody coming.

He got to a service stairs and up to the first floor, went unseen along a hall to a rear stairway, and began ascending. Max Ganler's apartment, his objective, was on the fourth floor.

Almost directly across the hall from the entrance door of Ganler's apartment was a supply closet. Blaney got in among the mops and brooms. He unbuttoned coat and vest, and from around his body took a garment made of thin green silk. Slipped over his head, it became a hood that came down to his shoulders, and had slits for eyes. He drew on a pair of thin green gloves. His suit was of inconspicuous black, not unlike thousands of other suits in the city. His shirt was dark, his tie black, his shoes black and of ordinary pattern.

With the hood enveloping his head and throat, the gloves shielding his hands, Danny Blaney had no fear of being identified. In size and general build he was not unlike thousands of other men.

Inside the closet, where it was hot and stifling, he waited. He had ceased being Danny Blaney for the time; he was the Green Ghost, the man who hated the crooks, who was out to run them down, but not particularly to aid the police, since he hated them also.

Danny Blaney had been on the Force. He had been an honest and conscientious officer. He had been framed by crooks, and his shield taken from him. Though he had not been tried for crime, the world had judged him guilty. Crooks had wrecked his career, because he had been too active in giving testimony against some of their leaders. And his comrades had believed!

So, Danny Blaney became the Green Ghost. It was a perilous role he played. Once he was suspected, it would become more perilous. He pretended that he had inherited some money. He owned a corner cigar store, and ran it with the assistance of three clerks. That was good cover.

Now he heard a burst of laughter, and opened the closet door a crack. The front door of Max Ganler's apartment had been opened, and Max stood framed in it—a short, squat, swarthy man with a twisted smile and the eyes of a killer.

Max Ganler was sending another man on an errand.

"Get those cigarettes! Be sure to mention I'm howling because I'm out, and that we've been having a party here since nine last night. Make it thick. And hurry back!" The other hurried toward the elevator. Max Ganler closed the door of the apartment. Blaney closed the door of the closet.

But he opened it a crack again not more than ten minutes later, when he heard somebody hurrying along the hall. Snoopy Carns and Bill Sorsten were there. They had got free of their bonds, as Blaney had expected they would.

They rang, and were admitted immediately. Inside the Max Ganler apartment, the sounds of merriment ceased suddenly. Blaney could visualize the scene—Carns and Sorsten telling what had happened to them in the alley, and Max Ganler at the point of murdering them.

In the near distance, an elevator door clanged. Blaney glanced through the door again. The man Ganler had sent for cigarettes was coming back.

As he passed the door of the closet, Blaney jerked it open and struck once with the blackjack. He caught the slumping form and pulled it inside. Working swiftly, he affixed a gag, and used the thin, tough cords to bind the man's wrists and ankles.

Breathing heavily, he stood against the door, listening. Nobody was in the hall. Blaney slipped out, and to the door of Max Ganler's apartment. He had stowed the blackjack away. Now he held an automatic pistol.

It was the Green Ghost who touched the bell button and then stood with his weight against the door. It was Max Ganler himself who opened it, expecting the friend he had sent to strengthen his alibi.

"Wh-what—?" Ganler began.

He caught sight of the incongruous headgear. But, before he could say more, before he could give a cry of warning, the muzzle of an automatic was jabbed into his belly. Suddenly white of face, Max Ganler put up his hands and stood back against the wall.

They were in the little entryway of the apartment, and could not be seen from the big living room unless somebody came to the doorway, which was shrouded with portieres. Through the slits in the hood he wore, the eyes of the Green Ghost gleamed malevolently.

"Wh—at—?" Max Ganler mouthed again.

"Quiet!" the Green Ghost hissed at him. "This is the night the cops get you, Max. They couldn't do it themselves, so I thought I'd help."

Ganler collected his nerve. He was trembling a bit, but managed to speak in whispers.

"What have you got against me?"

"Nothing any more than I have against all big crooks, Max."

"Why play the cops' game, Green Ghost? Maybe we can make a deal."

"I've got almost all the Carstairs swag now, Max, so why should I?"

"That's only one job. I might let you in on—"

"I don't make deals with a thing like you! I work alone. There's a reason for it."

"You've got a nerve, coming right here to my apartment."

"Surprises you, does it? Here I stay, till I'm sure the cops are on their way for you."

"I don't know anything about that Carstairs job."

"You were there and bossed it," the Green Ghost said.

"You're crazy. I've been here since early in the evening. I've been giving a party to Lily Ratch, my girl. It's her birthday."

"Swell alibi, Max. The dumb cops probably will fall for it."

"It's the true goods," Max Ganler declared. "The superintendent of the building has been in and out half a dozen times. There have been twenty or thirty persons here since nine o'clock last night, coming and going. I've been seen almost every minute—"

"And yet I'm saying that you were at the Carstairs

house, two miles away, between twelve and one this morning, and engineered a jewel robbery."

"You're crazy! I don't know anything about it. If some of the other boys—"

"Carns and Sorsten are in there now—they've told you their yarn, about how I knocked 'em out and took the jewels from them. They were bringing you the swag. You didn't have the guts to pack it yourself."

"The boys came here to ask my advice about a fence."

"**So** that's your story! You'd throw down your pals and make them take the rap. Not even a decent crook!"

"How could you know anything about it—if it was true?" Max Ganler asked.

"Listen, you! I'm the Green Ghost, out to get crooks. I had you on my list. I've been watching you and your men for weeks. I know more about you than the whole police department could learn in five years!"

"What do you want here?"

Before the Green Ghost could reply to that, one of Ganler's male guests lurched through the portieres. He caught sight of the pair, and gave a squawk of terror when he saw the green hood. "He's here!" he howled, as he lurched back into the living room. "Snoopy! Sorsten! The Green Ghost—he's got Max out in the hall!"

Chapter Four

Now the Green Ghost was in a position to jerk the door open and get out into the hall, dodge into the supply closet again, or make a run for it. But he did not. He jabbed Max Ganler with the muzzle of the automatic again, grabbed his arm with his left hand and whirled him around. He compelled Ganler to step through the portieres and face those in the room.

"Careful, everybody!" the Green Ghost called. "I've got a gun muzzle jammed against Max's spine. Make a bad move at me, and I'll let him have it!"

They recognized the situation instantly. Where they were sitting or standing, they seemed suddenly like statues. The Green Ghost saw Carns and Sorsten at one side of the room. There were half a dozen others, including three girls.

A glance sufficed to show the Green Ghost that there had, indeed, been an all-night party. Ample evidence of that in the ash trays filled with cigarette ends, the empty bottles and stained glasses. The appearance of those in the room showed it, too. Only Max Ganler looked fairly fresh. But it was common report that Max Ganler seldom drank to excess.

Ganler was still holding up his hands. Urged by the Green Ghost, he stepped along the wall a short distance. Those in the room seemed to be waiting for Ganler to indicate what he wished them to do.

Bill Sorsten lurched forward. He ran more to brutality than brains. Here was the man who had knocked him out and tied him up, and taken the stolen jewels he had been carrying.

"Why, you—!" Sorsten began.

One of the girls gave a scream of fear and sprang forward, threw wide her arms as she faced Sorsten.

"Back, you fool! He'll kill Max!" she cried.

That was Lily Ratch. She was violently in love with Max Ganler, said those who knew. She had courage enough to attempt anything to save him, and brains enough to know that this was not the time to make a move.

"Everybody sit down!" the Green Ghost ordered. "Be careful how you move! Don't give me an excuse for bumping off Max."

They obeyed him in silence. Every man there was looking at Ganler, wondering what to do. Ganler gave no sign. He was trying to think of a way out of the predicament. The Green Ghost commanded the situation at the instant. But here, in Ganler's apartment, and with half a dozen of Ganler's desperate friends in the room, he was at a disadvantage.

That did not seem to worry the Green Ghost. He compelled Ganler to sit down also, on a chair not far from the door.

"Looks like you've been having quite a party," he said.

"It's like I told you. I've been here all night," Max Ganler replied.

"I suppose everybody here would swear to it?"

Lily Ratch stepped forward. "You—whoever you are!" she cried. "I don't know what you're up to, but you've got Max wrong tonight. He's been right here since nine o'clock, when I came. He's giving me this party."

"Didn't lose sight of him a moment since nine?" the Green Ghost asked.

"Oh, he went back into one of the other rooms a few times, but he wasn't gone for more than five minutes. He hasn't been out of the apartment. You've got your dope mixed."

"You believe," the Green Ghost said, "that you're speaking the truth."

"I know it! Are you crazy?" the girl asked.

"You're due for a big surprise," the Green Ghost replied. "Tell me, Max, did I get all the Carstairs jewels off Snoopy and Sorsten?"

"I don't know anything about 'em, I tell you. It's none of my business what jewels Snoopy and Sorsten have. None of yours, either!"

"What the hell?" Snoopy Carns cried. "Are we goin' to let this guy walk in here and boss us around? He's the guy who tapped us for the sparklers, Max. We must be gettin' soft!"

"Let's get him!" Sorsten barked.

The automatic of the Green Ghost barked also at that instant. Sorsten's right hand had made a dive beneath his coat, in the direction of his armpit. But his gun was not there. The Green Ghost had removed it in the alley and tossed it away. And now the Green Ghost merely put a bullet past Sorsten's head for moral effect.

It thudded into the wall.

One of the female guests screamed.

"Quiet, you fool!" Max Ganler cried. "Want the cops to pay us a visit? That shot of yours might bring 'em, Green Ghost."

"What of it?"

"They might be interested in seeing you with that green hood off your head."

"You're afraid to have them drop in, aren't you?"

"Not particularly," Ganler said. "Just don't want to attract their attention. Might think I was giving a wild party, instead of a quiet, classy one for Lily."

"They might ask about the Carstairs business."

"Let 'em ask!" Ganler said. "I've been here all night. Got plenty of witnesses to that."

"**Matter** of fact, I was just going to call the cops," the Green Ghost declared. "May I use your phone, Max?" He bowed.

"There it is on the table."

"Walk over and stand beside me, Max. Just now, I crave your close companionship. And your friends better stay put. You're too young to die, Max."

He forced Ganler to go to the telephone with him. Watching carefully, automatic held ready, the Green Ghost dialed the operator.

"Police Headquarters—quick!" he said.

"You're sure crazy!" Ganler told him. "Let the cops come! I'm clean. How about yourself?"

"An alibi is something I never bother about," the Green Ghost declared.

A raucous voice growled at him over the wire.

"Tell the jewel squad to come to Max Ganler's apartment, quick, if they want the lowdown on that Carstairs job," the Green Ghost growled back.

"Who's talkin'?" the desk sergeant asked.

"The gentleman known as the Green Ghost. I sent a note a couple of days ago, and said I'd turn in Max Ganler. Tell them to hurry. I want to get home and to bed."

He slapped the receiver back into place and motioned for Ganler to resume his seat.

Ganler was smiling whimsically now, as though this situation amused him. He acted like a man not afraid of the consequences.

But Snoopy Carns and Bill Sorsten had no adequate alibis. They had no wish to remain there until the police walked in on them. The police might ask questions.

"Get 'im!" Sorsten barked.

Snoopy Carns had been standing at the end of a davenport table, upon which there was a small statuette. With a sweeping motion, he had the statuette off the table and had thrown it at the Green Ghost. At the same instant, Bill Sorsten sprang forward.

The automatic of the Green Ghost cracked twice. Sorsten, the nearest menace, dropped to the floor, his right leg sagging beneath his weight ominously. Snoopy Carns reeled back against the wall, clutching a wounded right shoulder.

"Max, get 'em out of here!" Lily Ratch cried. "You're all right, but these nuts may get us all in wrong. Give 'em the rush!"

But there was not time. Somebody pounded on the hall door. A stentorian voice commanded,

"Open up! It's the police!"

The Green Ghost knew that voice. It belonged to Sergeant Tim O'Ryan, in charge of the jewel squad—a police officer with whom no man trifled without being sorry for it.

Chapter Five

Danny's telephone call had been superfluous. The Carstairs robbery having been reported a few minutes after it had occurred, the jewel squad had got busy immediately. It looked like a Max Ganler job, so Sergeant Tim O'Ryan took two men and hurried to Max Ganler's apartment.

Max Ganler had been flaunting himself in the faces of the police too long. Sure of his guilt in many nefarious enterprises, they had been unable to pin it on him. They could connect no suspects with Ganler's guiding hand. And Ganler himself always had a perfect alibi—not one of the ordinary crook variety, but an ironclad one. Ganler's alibis were always based on the axiom that a man can't be in two places at the same time.

"Open up!" Sergeant Tim O'Ryan pounded on the door again.

"We'll let 'em in," the Green Ghost said.

He prodded Ganler with the muzzle of the automatic and urged him into the entryway. He stood to one side as Ganler opened the door. Sergeant Tim O'Ryan and his men made the usual police entrance—striding into the room in determined fashion, slightly arrogant.

By doing this, they swept past the Green Ghost, and he slammed the door shut and stepped up behind them.

"Get your hands up!" he barked.

O'Ryan and his men turned, their hands groping for weapons. But they did not draw. The muzzle of the automatic menaced them. The sight of the Green Ghost startled them. They put up their hands.

"What's all this?" O'Ryan demanded. "Why the

trick costume?"

"I'm the Green Ghost."

"Oh, yeah? Cap'n got a letter of some sort. Thought it was a joke."

"I'm going to turn in Max Ganler, as I promised."

"Do that, and I'll shake hands with you," Sergeant Tim O'Ryan declared, "though I may be tearin' off that green hood afterward."

"I'm holding this gun on you because I don't want you to interfere with me," the Green Ghost said. "You might spoil the party."

O'Ryan motioned his two men to places against the wall. The Green Ghost stood at the end of the davenport, where all in the room were under his eyes. "**I suppose** the Carstairs job brought you here, O'Ryan?" the Green Ghost asked.

"You're right. I thought Max might know something about it."

"Don't even know what you're talking about," Ganler said.

"O'Ryan, here's Snoopy Carns and Bill Sorsten. I had to stop 'em, but they're not hurt bad. Better send 'em in and have 'em patched up, though. A little judicious questioning—"

"I don't know nothin' about nothin'," Sorsten put in. "This guy comes in here and starts shootin' for no reason at all. Max has been givin' a party, 'cause it's his girl's birthday, and I dropped in with Snoopy to snatch a drink. What's wrong in that?"

"Yes, I've been giving a party," Max Ganler said. "If there's been a job pulled off, O'Ryan, I don't know anything about it. I've been right here since nine last night. Ask these folks. Ask the building superintendent, who's been in a dozen times to get a drink and see how we were gettin' along."

"Oh, he's got an alibi, O'Ryan!" the Green Ghost said.

O'Ryan snarled. "Yeah? We're goin' to bust this one wide open. This time, Max, you were seen!"

"How's that?" Ganler asked.

"You were seen not two blocks from the Carstairs house. That's a couple of miles from here. And you were seen between twelve and one o'clock. Laugh that off!"

"Between twelve and one tonight?" Max Ganler did laugh. "Wasn't I right here, Lily? Wasn't I, folks?" he appealed to the others.

A chorus assured him that he had been. "Of course, O'Ryan, these are my friends," Ganler went on. "You might not believe them on that account. But the building superintendent and his wife came up about midnight, and stuck around for an hour or more. A boy from the drug store at the corner brought up some cigarettes. I had sandwiches sent in at midnight from the café below—ask the man who brought them. They'll all say I was here. I couldn't have had time to get to the Carstairs place and back."

"**Same** old alibi," O'Ryan said. "How about Carns and Bill Sorsten?"

"You'd better ask them," Max Ganler said. "They dropped in a few minutes ago. Old friends of mine—did some work for me once. It's Lily's birthday, and—"

"Here!" O'Ryan barked. He had seen Bill Sorsten make a move at the end of the davenport. Disregarding the Green Ghost for the moment, O'Ryan made a quick dive forward. Bill Sorsten was trying to ditch a couple of pieces of jewelry beneath the couch.

"Some of the swag!" O'Ryan barked. "This funny brooch, especially—the old Carstairs lady mentioned that. Got you, Sorsten!"

"I don't know nothin' about that; I saw it on the rug and kicked at it to turn it over."

"Trying to plant something on me?" Ganler snarled. "Why, you rat! Take 'em away, O'Ryan!"

"And you're tryin' to make us take the rap, huh?" Bill Sorsten snarled back. "Through with us, are you? Goin' to have us put away, so it'll be safer for you. You'll go along with us!"

"Talk, Sorsten!" O'Ryan said.

"'**Course** we did that Carstairs job. Max planned the thing. And he was there with us tonight, bossin' the works. His alibi's a fake!"

Max Ganler's laughter filled the room.

"You see, O'Ryan?" he asked. "Sorsten and Carns may have pulled off something, but it'll do them no good to try to drag me in. Saying I planned the thing—you might have believed that. But Sorsten queers himself when he says I was with them. If he lied about that, he probably lied about everything. Any jury would say as much."

"You were with us, damn you! O'Ryan says somebody saw you in the neighborhood."

"Somebody was mistaken. I've been right here all night."

Max Ganler's tone was one of confidence.

Lily Ratch suddenly confronted O'Ryan. "Can't you see that somebody's trying to frame Max?" she demanded. "Use your brains! Look up his alibi. If these two cheap crooks—" She withered Snoopy Carns and Bill Sorsten with her flashing glances.

"He was there with us!" Sorsten cried.

"Yeah, he was!" Snoopy Carns added. "He opened the trick safe in the library wall. You know damned well, O'Ryan, that neither me or Bill is a box man."

"Let's stop this damned nonsense, and get on with the party!" Max Ganler said. "What are you going to do, O'Ryan? These two bums are trying to hang something on me. I've got twenty or more who'll swear I was right here all night. All that against the words of two bums."

Sergeant Tim O'Ryan dropped into the nearest chair. He extracted a cigar from his waistcoat pocket and ignited the smoke.

"I'm going to see what this Green Ghost chap does about it," O'Ryan said. "I don't know him or anything about him. But he says he can deliver the goods."

"With pleasure!" the Green Ghost said. "O'Ryan, I happen to know you cops have been after Max Ganler for a long time. A dozen times, you thought you had him. And you always ran up against a stonewall alibi."

"Right!" O'Ryan admitted.

"Max was always somewhere else when a crib was cracked and had reputable witnesses to prove it. He has tonight, O'Ryan. If you get to work, you'll find that a score or more are ready to swear Max was right here between nine and two tonight. And the joke of it is that they'll believe they're telling the truth. They are not just helping him out."

"What's the answer to that?" O'Ryan asked.

"**The** answer is that Max has a new sort of alibi. It's a pip. Not every crook can work it. You're due to be startled, O'Ryan. Tell me this—if you can prove that Max could have been out of this apartment an hour or so during the night, would you have him?"

"I would that, along with other evidence and the confessions of these two."

"Then, you've got him, O'Ryan! I started in after Max Ganler a couple of months ago. I've been studying him and his methods. I learned a lot about him. I camped around this building for hours at a time, always on the dodge. That ironclad alibi of his had me worried, too. I knew there was a trick, and I decided I'd get to the bottom of it."

"I'm still waitin' for the answer," O'Ryan complained.

"Promise you won't interfere for a few minutes and watch Max closely. He might get violent, when he understands that his game is up."

"It's a go!"

"**Max** took a long lease on this apartment and spent a lot of coin having it done over," the Green Ghost explained. "This closet in the corner has a trick panel door in the back. You can go into a small passage which leads to the cross hall, and you can get to the basement by the service stairs or out to a fire-escape."

"What of it? A lot of places have getaways in them," O'Ryan said.

"This is going to be interesting," the Green Ghost went on. "I was watching tonight. I saw Max leave the building and I saw him return. He left about midnight and he was back at a quarter after one."

"Give that testimony and I've got him!" O'Ryan

cried. "That is, if you're a good witness. Take off that green hood and let's see."

"Wait," the Green Ghost begged. "When Max came back, I did what I'd planned—fixed the door at the end of the passage so it couldn't be opened from this side. Fixed it, O'Ryan, so nobody could leave this room through the closet and get out of the place."

"What damned nonsense!" Max Ganler cried. "O'Ryan, I'm sick of this. That big closet—why, it's where we hang coats and hats and I keep some liquor in there. I went into that closet several times during the night to get a bottle—"

"Take a look, O'Ryan," the Green Ghost said. "Better have your boys back you up and have your guns ready. Open the closet."

O'Ryan sprang up and motioned to his men. The closet door was opened. The police stood there, guns ready. They saw coats, women's wraps and two cases of liquor partially empty.

"Press along the wall in the right-hand corner," the Green Ghost instructed. "And be careful!"

O'Ryan and one of his men entered the big closet. O'Ryan fumbled at the wall. There was a click and a panel slid back.

"Come out of that!" O'Ryan barked. "Get your hands up!"

A man was crouching in the darkness behind that panel door. O'Ryan's companion reached in and grasped him by the shoulder and hauled him forth.

"Get into the room!" O'Ryan commanded.

He thrust the prisoner out into the bright light, where he reeled back against the wall.

There came a chorus of cries from those in the living room. Their astonishment was genuine, most of all that of Miss Lily Ratch.

Max Ganler, his face white and his eyes bulging as he saw a vision of the big stone house up the river, sat against the wall. But Max Ganler also stood there, his arms gripped by Sergeant Tim O'Ryan. The same in features, size, even to every detail of clothing.

"The ironclad alibi," the Green Ghost said. "A twin brother comes in handy some times, O'Ryan. There is your answer. Max slips into the closet and his brother comes out and goes right on with whatever Max was doing, and Max hurries away, does his job and comes back, signals, and the brothers change places again. Only, tonight, I fixed the door at the end of the passage, so this twin brother couldn't get out when the work was done."

"Got you, Ganler!" Sergeant Tim O'Ryan roared. "And now, Green Ghost suppose you tell me—"

But the Green Ghost had darted toward the entryway. As O'Ryan called to him to halt, as O'Ryan and his companions sought to stop him, the Green Ghost fired one shot over their heads as warning, jerked open the hall door and sprang out into the corridor.

Two bullets splintered the door a split second afterward. The Green Ghost darted along the hall and to the rear stairs. Down them he rushed, making little noise. Above, he heard the stentorian commands of Sergeant Tim O'Ryan.

To the basement the Green Ghost fled, and through the little door and out into the night. In the dark alley, he stripped off hood and gloves and stowed them away. He sped across a street and plunged into the darkness of the alley beyond.

A few minutes later, three blocks away, Danny Blaney engaged a cruising taxicab. He relaxed in the seat and yawned, like a man who had been keeping late hours. At a certain corner he dismissed the cab and entered a cigar store, where the night clerk was reading an early edition of a morning paper.

"Howdy, Boss! You're up late," the clerk said.

"Been paying a little visit uptown," Danny Blaney replied. "How's business?"

"Not so good, Boss. A few chauffeurs after cigs—that's all. Maybe it doesn't pay you to keep open all night."

"Oh, yes; it pays! It pays," Danny Blaney said. ♦

The Red Sword

By John Drummond

Into a Nazi trap deep in the heart of enemy territory ventures a fearless british agent who braves a mysterious castle dungeon to rescue two captured friends and smash a sinister plot!

Chapter One
The Spy at the End

Wind howled in from the sea, carrying white puffs of frozen spray over the shore as the sea crashed against the rocks at the foot of the cliffs, foamed into white whirlpools and receded again suddenly.

Low clouds raced through the sky, broken occasionally by the winter moon, picking out the ragged chalk shore in silver light, and showing the twisted little inn that stood alone on the cliff top. Its small-paned windows peered out from the shadow of deep, overhanging eaves, like the eyes of a frowning man. About it were gathered a few smaller buildings, old stables and coach-houses, almost crumbling from disuse.

Upon the hard, broken road, a man was walking, the sound of his heels and his cheerful whistling snatched away by the racing wind almost before they could be heard.

He was tall, muffled up in a black coat and hat. He carried a walking stick, but nothing else, and walked through the gale like a man taking a stroll, stopping sometimes to admire the view over the angry sea.

He strolled on towards the lonely inn, and once outside it, stopped. Above him the hanging sign of the inn swung in the wind, like a beckoning hand, and groaned regularly as the wind clawed it.

The stranger glanced up at the sign, then went towards the inn door and opened it. He came into the taproom, a small place of oak beams and shadows dancing from the flames of a blazing fire.

By the gaping brick fireplace a man was sitting in an oak pew, a small table in front of him. A meat pie, bread and butter, fruit and brown ale were on the table, but as the stranger came in, the man stopped eating and looked up with a start.

The stranger smiled and bolted the door behind him. He went to the middle of the room and hesitated a moment, as if in thought. Then he crossed the room, and bolted the only other door.

The man in the pew sat quite still, watching the stranger with narrowed eyes, the food before him forgotten.

The stranger took off his hat and a head of flaming red hair glinted in the firelight. His gray eyes twinkled with humor as he picked up a chair and carried it towards the pew.

He placed the chair and sat down before the fire, holding out his hands to the blaze. His thick walking stick rested between his knees, as if he did not care to lay it down anywhere.

"Well, my little German sausage, you've selected a cold, rough night for a sea trip," he said.

"Who are you?" asked the man in the pew.

The stranger frowned at the fire.

"Now, whom should we say?" he asked the fire. "I think we had better say the Sword. The Red Sword, my friend."

He turned and smiled at the man in the pew.

"Yes. I call myself Red Sword, since the sword is my favorite weapon," he went on. "And it grows red with the—er—with the blood from German sausages. Muller."

"Miller is my name," answered the man.

"In this country," agreed the Sword, nodding and smiling, "That is because if you called yourself Muller, people would all begin to think you must be a German spy or something. Wouldn't they?"

Muller shrugged.

"I don't find your conversation amusing he said in angry tones.

"Alas, I never was amusing," said the Sword sadly. "That was why I failed as an actor. They used to boo whenever I came on, Muller. It was really heartbreaking."

He looked at his wristwatch.

"We have just an hour before the submarine comes," he said reflectively. "That gives me plenty of time. The question is, what to do with you?"

There was a faint click as he drew the handle of his stick from the main body of it. A long, thin blade of steel flashed in the firelight. The Sword regarded it thoughtfully. Muller sat rigid as a dummy,

"If I killed you, it would be safer for me," said the Sword, and suddenly lunged across the table with the blade.

Muller jumped up quickly, but the thin blade merely speared an apple on a dish and lifted it away, The Sword took a bite at the apple and spun it around on the blade.

"On the other hand, murder is a messy business, and I do not care for it unless it is absolutely necessary. Have a bite?"

He thrust the apple towards Muller's face. The man started violently and pressed himself hard against the back of the pew. His face was white. He was too frightened to speak.

"You won't? Never mind." The Sword flicked the apple up off the blade, and as it fell he sliced it in two, and caught the two parts on the point of the blade again.

"I had to learn fencing to play one of the Three Musketeers," he said cheerfully. "I was terrible as a musketeer, but pretty good as a blade."

"What do you want with me?" Muller said in a hoarse voice.

"I want your identity," the Sword said sharply. "Tonight, at eleven o'clock, the submarine, U-Thirty-seven will surface off Noll's Head, and its boat will put ashore in the cove here to collect you and take you to Germany together with vital information which you have in your pocket there. Information concerning the invasion,"

He pressed the point of his blade against Muller's breast pocket and held it poised, while the threatened man stood stiff and still, his eyes bulging. .

The Sword lifted the blade and laughed, "Now it is urgent that I should make the voyage instead of you, my friend," he said. "I have a special need to get into Germany within the next four days."

"It would be suicide," Muller said in a whisper.

"Perhaps and perhaps not," the Sword said in German. "I am not yet dead, I might have a chance to live—even in Nazi Germany. Give me your wallet, please."

He flicked the blade lightly across the man's throat. Muller fumbled in his pocket and brought out the wallet, which he threw on the table.

The Sword picked it up and pulled out the contents. There were six one-pound notes in it, and nothing else.

"Six," murmured the Sword. "That would represent the six main points of invasion,"

He held one of the notes up to the light, and saw faint pinholes in the paper.

"Why, this is most ingenious, my friend," he said,

stowing the notes back into the wallet. "If we had a map of Europe, drawn to the size of six notes, we could lay these notes over it, two wide and three deep, and the pin-pricks would show the possible beachheads selected by Eisenhower's army. Am I right?"

Muller said nothing, but glanced balefully.

There came a sudden interruption. Someone was knocking on the door from the other side.

"Hey—open the door, there!" roared an angry voice.

"This must be the good landlord come to clear away your dinner," smiled the Sword. "Open the door, my friend."

Muller hesitated, then crossed to the door and unbolted it. The door opened, and a large, burly fellow in his shirtsleeves came in. He glared from one man to the other, then closed the door behind him.

"I hope you listened carefully at the keyhole, Tom?" smiled the Sword.

"Aye, sir." The landlord nodded and looked suspiciously at Muller. "You was right. He's a spy. Let's get the police."

"I told you last night we cannot have the police," snapped the Sword. "If he is arrested, the news cannot be kept a secret, and the information might reach Germany before I get there. Which would make it awkward for me, if I were to arrive, posing as Herr Muller, while the real Muller was imprisoned in the Tower of London."

"That's true," said Tom, rubbing his chin thoughtfully.

"You have a very fine cellar, Tom," the Sword said carelessly. "Surely you can allow Herr Muller to use it for a week?"

The landlord hesitated. He considered the danger, but patriotism and a sense of duty finally conquered his reluctance.

"You sure you'll be back in a week?" he asked doubtfully. .

"I hope to be out of Germany in a week," replied the Sword. "And that's all that matters."

"I'll risk it then," said Tom.

Muller had been standing silent, watching them. Now he suddenly darted a hand into his breast pocket. As his hand drew out a revolver, he felt the point of the rapier suddenly prick through the trigger guard and pierce the cloth of his coat.

"Leave the gun alone," the Sword said mockingly.

He pressed the blade in a quarter of an inch. Muller shuddered, and nodded weakly. The sword was withdrawn, and the revolver thudded to the floor.

The landlord swung round suddenly with a fist like a leg of mutton and knocked the spy against the wall Muller hung there, as if he had been prepped for a second. Then his knees collapsed and he fell in a heap to the floor.

"I thought we'd better get it over," the landlord explained. "There's some rope in the corner."

Muller was quickly tied up, and carried down, still unconscious, into the cellar below the old house.

The cellar had a stout door, which was padlocked. He and the Sword went up the sloping wooden stairs to the house again, where the landlord took charge of Muller's gun.

"You're sure you can take care of him?" The Sword asked, slipping the sword back into the stick, and putting on his belt. "Remember that if he gets away I shall be sent back from Germany F.O.B."

"Free on Board?" inquired Tom.

"No, Full of Bullets," said the redheaded man, and glanced quickly at his wristwatch. "Ten to eleven," he murmured. "Time for my rendezvous with U-Thirty-seven. Good-by, Tom!"

"Good-by, sir," answered the landlord, clutching the gun. "And good luck!"

The Sword opened the door, and the chill sea wind blew in. He turned, "I shall need a lot of luck," he said grimly.

The fire flared more brightly in the draught. The landlord saw the coat flutter, then the door shut. Tom crossed over and bolted it, then went out of the room and upstairs, where his wife stood in the darkened bedroom, staring out towards the cliff top. He joined her there. A sudden break in the clouds allowed the moon to shine through, and showed the black figure going down the cliff steps.

"Aye, he's got pluck," the landlord said, shaking his head. "If I had to rescue a couple of pals what were prisoners in Germany, I reckon I'd leave 'em there."

"Is—is that other man in the cellar?" asked his wife impatiently.

"Yes! And there he's got to stay for a week!"

In the meantime the small cockleshell boat, which the Sword had entered, rose and plunged on the angry swell as it swung towards the gray phantom shape of the U-boat, standing silently a quarter of a mile away.

The Nazi sailor who rowed the small boat said nothing. The Sword sat in the stern, his collar up and his hat pulled down, taking no notice of the heavy gusts of spray that swept over the boat like rain. His mind was fixed upon one thing only. He was memorizing every little gesture of Muller's, recalling every intonation of the man's voice. For a week past he had been following Muller, watching every move the man made, and he must forget nothing that he had learned.

A shout came across the water as the Sword stood up and gave the Nazi salute. A rope was thrown, and in a few seconds the rowboat was heaving against the steel side of the submarine,

The Sword leaped from the boat on to the wet steel plates. A sailor saluted as he climbed the ladder to the conning tower, He reached the top where a lieutenant awaited him.

The lieutenant led him down the inside of the tower into the shining, yellow-lighted interior of the ship, He was shown into the commander's tiny cabin, and left alone with the captain.

"Commander Heinz," he snapped, and clicked his heels.

"So," said the captain with a slight nod. "Your appearance is somewhat different from what I had been given to expect, Herr Muller."

"In my profession, appearance must often be changed as quickly as coats," the Sword replied. "And

THE RED SWORD 255

I have not seen the Fatherland, nor it me, for three years."

He dropped wearily on to a bunk and threw down his hat.

"I have almost forgotten my native tongue," he said with a faint smile. "But it is a good thing to forget in England."

The commander nodded grimly. Bells were clanging in the ship, a siren blared, and orders were being barked and repeated. The whine of the motors began, and the wash and thunder of the sea echoed dully through the steel as the ship plunged down beneath the surface.

"When do we reach port?" the Sword asked.

"Ten tomorrow night, at Brennerhaven."

"Good," said the Sword, and turning, he curled himself up on the tiny bunk, still clutching at his walking stick.

The captain watched him for a while, then seated himself at his table and began to study his charts. After a time, a lieutenant came in with a brief message. He glanced curiously at the man on the bunk, who was now fast asleep and snoring loudly.

"The greatest of our secret agents has the right, I suppose, to snore in a commander's cabin," said the scowling captain.

"It's a habit they catch from the English," answered the lieutenant. "The walking stick, too, is another of their habits. Look, he hugs it like a doll"

"One never knows what sticks may contain," retorted the captain. "And Herr Muller is bringing important information."

He bent to his charts again, and the lieutenant went out. Throughout the night hours the motors whined continuously, and the redheaded man snored…

Chapter Two
Into Nazi-land

After some hours the whine of electric motors gave place to the throb of Diesel engines. Out of the danger zone, the submarine was cruising on the surface.

The captain left the cabin for long stretches, and the redheaded gentleman was free to replace the six one-pound notes he had taken from Muller, with six of his own, and these he pricked with a pin to his own design.

He whistled softly as he pricked the notes, and actually the tiny holes made a design somewhat like the originals. Except that if the notes were all set out together, and then looked at from the back, the holes spelled "Rats!"

The Sword regarded them thoughtfully. Before the Nazi Secret Service detected the hoax he would either be gone—or dead.

Several times he stroked the growing bristles on his jaw. He had shaved the night before, but his beard grew quickly, and it would be twenty-four hours' growth by the time they made port.

All day the submarine thudded on through the sea until it was dark again, and the engines beat more slowly. The captain came back into the cabin and sat down.

"We are through the mine-fields, mein Herr," he said. "In another hour we shall reach port."

"Mine-fields!" exclaimed the Sword, and shuddered. "I'm glad I didn't know. I have always had a strong objection to things that go off with loud bangs. It's bad for my nerves."

"You seem to have developed an English sense of humor," said the captain dryly. "It would be best to forget that now, for who knows which side a spy may be on?"

"True, true," admitted the Sword, and rubbed his jaw. "Do you happen to have a razor?"

"There will be time to be shaved in Berlin," answered the captain.

"Berlin, eh? I shall have a four-inch beard by then."

"I think not, Herr Muller. No time will be wasted."

The Sword looked cheerful at this news. Half his traveling problems were to be solved for him by the German Government, which was a great convenience.

At last the beat of the motors grew slower, and

finally stopped. There were shouts from the deck above, and the captain rose.

"If you will follow me," he said curtly.

They climbed up the steel ladder on to the deck. On the black swell beside U-37 a fast motorboat rolled slowly with its engine burbling impatiently. The Sword jumped aboard it, and at once the craft shot away towards the docks.

The boat moored at the dockside, and the Sword was led up the steps to the cobbled quay, where a car waited. An army officer saluted him, and showed him into the car. Without a second's pause the car slid away and raced through the black streets of the town.

The Sword could see nothing of the town, but he could see that his reception committee was efficient—dangerously efficient. Everything had been arranged to the second, and no time at all was wasted.

"Baron von Stuck must be anxious to see me," he remarked as the car sped on. He was holding the walking stick between his knees.

The officer stared at him woodenly. "You bring important information. Herr Muller," he said. "And it will be used at once. We shall be at the airfield in a few minutes."

Ten minutes later the car ran into an airfield. The night was filled with the roar of powerful airplane motors as the car fled between lines of bombers, poised like crouching black eagles across the field. Many men were working beneath the shadows of the outstretched wings.

The car stopped beside a plane that stood in the center of the concrete runway. Its twin motors sputtered, and its propellers spun in silver arcs, reflecting the glare of a brilliant landing light.

The Sword was shown straight from the car into the waiting plane. A young officer came with him. The cabin door was locked, and immediately the motors opened up into a howling roar. The machine rumbled over the field, gathering speed and swaying. Then it ceased to sway, and swept up over the field on its spread wings.

"An English squadron would be glad to know about that field," said the Sword. "They don't know about this field?"

"It is still secret," admitted the officer.

"Thank you," said the redheaded man, with a grateful grin for the information. "Four hundred planes! Yes, it would be a nice target."

He looked down through the window, where only a few tiny lights glowed as the country fell farther and farther away below them.

An hour passed as the plane roared on. The Sword sat back in his seat, deep in thought. His heart beat faster as he thought of the coming interview with Baron van Stuck, of the Nazi Secret Service.

He had learned a good deal from Muller about the baron, but he did not yet know whether the baron had ever seen Muller. If he had, then the Sword's trip would come to a sudden end.

"But the chances are that they've never met face to face," thought the Sword. "Anyhow, it's a chance that must be taken."

He hummed a tune, and the young officer smiled.

"You are glad to be back?" he said cheerfully.

"I shall be happier when I'm really home again," answered the Sword, and laughed,

The officer laughed, too.

"You could do with a shave," he said, glancing toward the shut door of the pilot's compartment. The Sword rubbed his jaw and clutched his walking stick more tightly. The lieutenant glanced at him keenly and went on: "The real Herr Muller had coal black hair and a beard. I never heard of a dye that would make a beard grow out red!"

With a lightning movement the Sword bent forward, snatched open the officer's holster and whipped out his automatic.

"I didn't like your remark," explained the Sword coolly. "People have been hanged because of their beards before now."

Despite the leveled gun, the lieutenant continued to grin.

"Give me back the gun," he said, holding out his hand. "It was meant for the real Herr Muller—who has a black beard,"

The Sword hesitated. "I don't understand you, Lieutenant."

"I don't know who you are," said the lieutenant, "but I suspect you are the gentleman known to the Nazis as the Red Sword. If you are, I'm glad to meet you. The recognition words are—three little pigs!"

"Ah, another British agent," said the Sword, lowering the weapon.

"Right. I only hope you can use a parachute because we are not going to land in Berlin. I have urgent information for the British Royal Air Force, and an appointment with a bombing squadron, which cannot wait. My only disappointment is to find that having risked my neck for weeks to prevent Muller from reporting to von Stuck, you have forestalled me. However, We are now over Bavaria and time is up." He rose to his feet and faced the Sword. "My gun, please! The pilot is armed and I'm taking over this plane."

He held out his hand, and the Sword gave back the pistol. The lieutenant went to the pilot's door and opened it. The pilot looked round curiously, then started as he saw the pistol.

"No tricks, and do as you're told. Stand up!"

The plane swayed slightly as the pilot clambered to his feet and out of the forward compartment, his head bent against the low roof of the cabin. The lieutenant went behind him and unlocked the cabin door.

Suddenly be gripped the back of the Nazi pilot's jacket and bent him staggering back against the unlocked door. The man's weight forced the door open against the pressure of the screaming wind.

He fell through the door, slithered over the swoop of the wing and rolled off into the darkness below. The door slammed again.

The plane began to dive until the lieutenant took his seat at the controls and pulled it into level flight.

The Sword looked down through the cabin window.

For a moment he could see nothing, then there was a flutter of white in the darkness a thousand feet below the plane. It spread, then took shape, like a monstrous, ghostly jellyfish.

The Sword turned from the window and went to the lieutenant's side. At the controls, the second British agent had swung the plane around and was now flying due eastward.

"Where are you going?" asked the Sword. "I thought you said we were over Bavaria?"

The lieutenant glanced at him in the rear view mirror with an expression of surprise.

"This is Bavaria," he answered. "Baron van Stuck, one of the heads of the Nazi spy bureau has an estate near Landsberg, where we are now. I have a passenger to deliver—someone whose business it will be to watch him."

"Phew!" The redheaded agent made a gesture of annoyance. "Then Herr Muller must have lied to me. He said von Stuck would meet me in Berlin. I, likewise, have business with the Baron."

The Sword had vaguely been puzzled by the lieutenant's reference to a "passenger." But he had no time now to bother with puzzles. Reaching out, he lifted a parachute rigging from the rack on the cabin side, and fastened the straps over his shoulders and about his body. His sword cane he concealed by thrusting it through the belt, in back.

"When we reach Landsberg, tell me," he said. "I'll be leaving you there."

"But I thought I could take you back to England with me?" objected the lieutenant. "Your responsibilities are over. You have prevented Herr Muller from reporting to his superiors. There is nothing more you can do."

"Ah, but there is," answered the Sword. "Two dear friends of mine, the Count and Countess de Salle, are being held prisoners by Baron von Stuck. They were leaders of the French Underground movement. Unless they are rescued within forty-eight hours, they will be shot. Herr Muller told me that, and this time I am sure he told the truth. I cannot leave them to die, my friend, especially since they got into trouble through helping the Red Sword smuggle prisoners out of France, out of reach of the German beasts."

The lieutenant shook his head. "You are mad even to think of trying to rescue them under such circumstances. You are one man the German Gestapo would like, above all things, to capture. You are the Red Sword."

The Sword scratched his Stubbly chin, cautiously.

"I am afraid so," he said. "Yes, I am sure it will be a difficult job. First I must find out where the de Salles are being held prisoner, then I must get them out of prison and back to England."

"It's insane!" snapped the lieutenant. "You don't stand a chance. Every Nazi in the country is on the lookout for you."

"That does make it difficult," admitted the Sword. "Have we reached Landsberg yet?"

"Not yet." Despite his protests the lieutenant was staring at the cool-eyed, redheaded man in admiration. "Then—I'll try to help you. Tomorrow night I'm coming back with a British bombing squadron to raid that airfield you saw tonight. If I get a chance, I'll try to pick you and the de Salles up and take you home. If you can get to a radio, broadcast a message giving your position on any wavelength you choose. It will be picked up."

"Sounds easy," said the Sword with an ironical laugh.

"Use any code you like," said the lieutenant earnestly. "Only—before you say anything, say, 'The third little pig used bricks': After that, your message will be decoded no matter what it is. And now—here's Landsberg, and time to jump." The lieutenant raised his voice and called out, "Ada!"

As the lieutenant spoke there was a noise from the rear part of the plane. It was not easy to surprise the Sword, but now he swung around in astonishment. The door of the bomb stowage compartment in the rear swung open and from it into the dimly lighted cabin emerged a young, dark-haired, slender girl. Her pretty face was glowing with excitement. Under one arm she carried a small satchel. She was dressed like a German girl of the working class.

"I'm ready," she said in clear tones.

"Who's this?" asked the Sword, eyeing the girl.

"Another one of our agents," explained the lieutenant. "Her task will be to spy on Baron von Stuck and to keep us informed." He glanced at the girl. "Put on a parachute, Ada, and get ready to jump."

Before the girl could comply, in the darkness outside of the plane, there came the sudden screech and strain of wings, the howl of diving planes, the roar of racing engines and the staccato thunder of machine guns.

"British Spitfires," yelled the lieutenant at the top of his voice. "They've spotted us!" He tilted the plane and went into an abrupt dive. "Hold tight! We're in for it!"

Close by, a shell exploded, jarring the three occupants of the plane like kernels in a nut. Abruptly the lieutenant swung into an Immelmann turn. This violent maneuver threw both the Sword and the girl, Ada, off their balance. The girl had been reaching for a parachute, but her hand missed the rig, and she went whirling toward the unlocked door, which was sagging open.

The Sword leaped toward her, reeling as he went, and grabbing frantically to stop her from falling into space. The racing wind slammed the door shut, but her full weight against it tore it open again and she went spinning through. Just as she disappeared, the Sword made another frantic clutch and got her by the wrist.

But he was already off balance and the weight of her body and the bouncing plane wrenched him through after her, before he had time even to think.

Next moment they were twisting and turning through the air like helpless dolls, with the Sword still gripping the girl's wrist,

The plane roared on into the distance, feeling its way between the forest of searchlights which sprang out from various points of the city below.

The Sword pulled the ring of the parachute, then waited anxiously. The girl's weight on his left arm almost jerked the arm from its socket with the shock of the opening chute, but he held on.

They drifted downward through the bitter wind, and below him the Sword saw a few dim lights moving to and fro. They were sinking down towards a broad street, and soon he could make out the shadowy shapes of a few cars moving along it.

He seemed to fall faster, and the shadows of traffic below swelled at an alarming rate. Then suddenly they dropped in amongst it, and the squeal of brakes rose up as they struck the hard surface of a roadway, and the falling parachute covered himself and the girl in its silken folds.

"And here we are," he muttered grimly trying to scramble into a kneeling position on the road. "Are you hurt?"

There was a moment of hesitation, then she answered.

"No, and I must thank you for saving my life," she said hurriedly. "And now, though it may sound heartless and brutal, I'm going to desert you. I have my own duties to perform and I can't jeopardize them by staying around here with you. Good-by!"

And before he could answer, the cool-headed girl agent managed to free herself from the blinding folds of silk, and at once vanished in the midst of the confused and stumbling crowd which was gathering in the darkness round the parachute.

The Sword knelt beneath the silk, unfastening the buckles and trying to get free in order that he, too, could escape. Before he accomplished this, however, the parachute was pulled off him, and he was roughly jerked to his feet. He found himself surrounded by burly men in uniform. They studied him intently by the light of shielded torches.

"A spy!" snapped one. "Bring him to the car."

The Sword said nothing as they dragged him to a powerful car standing by the pavement. His heart was beating fast, but outwardly he was as calm and serene as ever.

They got into the car and sped away through the dark streets of the city.

"English spy dropped by parachute!" snarled one of his captors.

"That's correct," agreed the Sword cheerfully. "A very good guess of yours. But don't waste time. Take me to Baron von Stuck at once!"

"You'll see him soon enough'" answered the man.

The car sped on, then swerved into the roadside before a high gray stone building. The car door was flung open and the Sword forced out on to the pavement. Then unceremoniously he was hustled in through the doorway of the building. But he still managed to keep a hold on his inoffensive-looking walking stick.

Chapter Three
Fortunate Air Raid

Silence reigned in the huge room. A dozen guards stood about, covering each door from the room, motionless as waxworks. The Sword sat in a chair, covered by two armed men, and regarded the room with a benevolent gaze. A glint of anxiety showed in his eyes as he glanced toward the high gilt doors on his left.

They opened suddenly, and an order was barked out from the man who appeared in the opening. The Sword got up, two guards fell in behind him, and the trio marched through the open doors.

This room was even larger than the antechamber, and sumptuously fitted out. Behind a huge desk in the center of the floor was seated a large, bull-necked man in the uniform of a high Nazi officer. His cropped hair seemed to shine in the light, and his thin cruel lips were clamped tightly shut as he watched the prisoner.

The Sword strode towards the desk and stopped.

"Baron van Stuck," he snapped, and the voice was a perfect imitation of Muller's. "I shell be glad if you will clear this riff-raff out of the room. My business is with you alone."

The baron frowned.

"Who are you?" he sneered.

The Sword flew into a well-assumed rage.

"You'll soon find out who I am!" he shrieked. "Adolf, himself, shall hear about this! I should have been carried here carefully in a plane. Instead I was made to jump for my life in a parachute, and it was all your fault, you dumb calf head!" The redheaded man began to dance up and down, wave his fists, ranting just like Hitler. "You stupid pig in a gilt uniform! You promise me safe passage from England, then let me fall into the hands of an English spy in the very plane you send to bring me here! It's monstrous! You pig-pig-pig!"

"What is this?" The baron rose to his feet, white with dismay. It struck him this man was too insolent to be anything but genuine. "What nonsense are you talking now?"

"Nonsense?" bawled the Sword. "You talk of nonsense? Your plane stolen, your pilot thrown out of it, and me—me—my reward is to he brought here like a yellow dog, under guard? Ach! This is more than I can bear!"

The baron became silent. He reached out suddenly and snatched up a telephone. He kept his eyes on the redheaded man while he barked into the phone. Then he became calm and ironic.

"So the machine did not arrive, and the pilot was picked up at Mindelheim," he said clearly. "And why did you forget to tell me? Why did you forget? Thunder in heaven! I'll see that you don't forget again!"

He slammed the phone down as if he would break it, then signaled to the guards in the room to go out. They went, and the baron clasped his hands behind him.

"You must forgive us. Herr Muller," he said apologetically. "I knew nothing of this adventure, due, as you so truly said, to the inefficiency of the men at the airport." The baron was sweating profusely.

The Sword pretended to be placated.

"I lost my temper, I am afraid," he said coldly. "But you must understand that I have been through a rather unpleasant twenty-four hours. The sea trip, and now—this."

He pointed his stick at the ceiling, then shrugged.

"It is most regrettable," said the baron, seating himself at the desk and mopping his brow. "But first, let us see what you have brought for us." He held out his hand.

The Sword hesitated, then pulled Muller's wallet from his pocket and tossed it on the desk. The baron opened it carefully and brought out the pinpricked notes. He studied them in silence for some time.

"That should he interesting, Herr Muller," said the baron at last. "I will have it pieced together over the map and photographed while you refresh yourself with sleep at the Hotel Adlon. Suitable quarters have been arranged there for you."

"Thank you," said the Sword, and half turned towards the door.

"Just a minute, please," the baron called out deferentially.

The Sword stopped and turned back in haughty disdain.

"Yes?"

"Have you succeeded in finding out the identity of the Red Sword?"

"Believe me, baron, if I had found that out there would be no Red Sword," replied the Englishman sharply.

"Well spoken, my friend." The baron nodded with satisfaction. "But we have been having more trouble with him. Two weeks ago he came in an airplane and stole three people out of the country. But he will pay for it."

The baron scowled suddenly and banged his fist on the desk. The Sword swung his stick.

"Do you think he will come back again?" he asked

curiously.

"Ja, he will come back," said the baron. "We have set a trap, with two of his best friends as bait."

"It will have to be a strong trap," said the Sword. "And cunning, too. How do you propose to work it?"

The baron waved his hand and laughed.

"No, No! That is a secret even from you. You shall know in good time. Meanwhile—good-night, Herr Muller…."

The Hotel Adlon was filled with officers. Uniforms of every description filled the corridors and rooms on the ground floor. With the exception of the hotel staff, the Sword was the only civilian in the place. He walked through the throngs jauntily, swinging his stick, as if he had nothing at all to worry him. Seeking out the grillroom he sat down and ordered a drink. With that beside him, he began to think hard, for his mind was treading like a cat on a hot stove. Since leaving von Stuck, his uneasiness had increased. The baron had seemed certain his plan to capture the Sword would succeed, and the Sword did not care for the echoing memory of the baron's throaty laugh.

While he was thinking, an army captain came up to his stall.

"It seems that the baron gave you something to think about, Herr Muller," he said, with a quizzical look.

The Sword glanced up and recognized the captain. He had been in the baron's anteroom when the Sword had first gone in.

"You're right," be agreed. "He puzzled me a good deal."

"Ah, he's a wily one, von Stuck," said the captain, and sat down beside the Sword. "And I think I know what he was speaking to you about. The Sword, eh?" he added, dropping his voice.

"Yes, that was the subject of the discussion," the Sword said idly. "That fellow has been giving us trouble."

"Trouble!" The captain laughed. "It is nothing to what the impudent dog will get when he comes back again."

"Everyone seems so certain that the Sword will come back," said the redheaded man, frowning at his stick, which rested between his knees. "It sounds to me like nonsense. I hear the Sword's two friends helped the English devil get those refugees out."

The captain smiled. "True. Now they will help to get the Englishman in."

"If the Sword can find where they are," corrected the redheaded man.

"That will be easy enough for him," the captain said. "The baron pretends it is a deep secret but everyone has guessed where he has them hidden." He glanced quickly round the crowded room, as if anxious to see who might be watching him.

"They are at the baron's schloss in Bavaria, " he said in a whisper. "But, of course, we must keep pretending we do not know. The baron wants to keep it a deep secret."

Such an idea the captain regarded as a supreme joke and laughed very noisily. The Sword laughed too, for the talkative fellow was giving him the very information he wanted.

Von Stuck's chateau would be easy enough to find, for the Sword had seen photographs of it many times. It stood on a small, high island in the middle of a lake.

The quarter of a mile of unbroken water on all sides of the island would take some crossing without being detected. Secondly the rocky island itself would have its own defenses, with spies watching night and day for the approach of a stranger.

And no stranger would get to the island and get away again quickly.

After a while the Sword allowed his face to grow solemn as he looked at the captain.

"But supposing the Sword does not come back?" he said. "You know there is a rumor he is dead!"

"Dead!" The captain started. "Himmel. Did you tell the baron?"

The Sword shook his head.

"I said it was a rumor. The baron deals only in certainties."

"That's true," agreed the captain gravely. "But where did you get this?"

"They say the Messerschmitt in which he escaped a fortnight ago was shot down by English fighters near Dover. Here is a photograph from the English papers, though it does not say who was in the machine."

The Sword brought a clipping from his pocket and showed it to the captain. The man stared greedily at it.

"Himmell," breathed the captain. "Then they killed their own man. This is rich!"

The Sword grinned. He remembered too that furious dive a fortnight ago to get away from the guns of the fighters, and the rip and crash of the bullets as they had torn through the metal structure of the machine.

He put the cutting back in his pocket. The talkative captain was a perfect bearer of such a story. Within an hour or two it would be spread throughout his regiment, and soon all Bavaria would know it.

Rumor spreads as quickly as floodwater released from a dam.

It would have been no good telling such a story to von Stuck. That bull-headed man would have believed nothing had he been told the story direct. But delivered to him in such a way, von Stuck might be fooled by it.

The captain would be sure to spread the story broadcast. He was an incurable gossip—that was easy to surmise—and a lulling of suspicion for a brief time was what the Sword needed.

Just a few extra hours of time!

Meeting the talkative captain was a stroke of astounding luck, and the Sword had been quick to take advantage of it. He sat back in his chair, idly watching the revolving door as officers passed in and out of the hotel. He watched their faces as new ones came in.

Then suddenly he stiffened.

The door revolved violently, and a man in civilian dress appeared, his face white and angry. He came to a standstill, and glared quickly round the crowded grillroom, his eyes glinting viciously.

They halted, finally, on the face of the Sword, and lighted up with unholy joy.

The Sword recognized the face of Franz Muller, the spy who should have been still captive in the cellar of the lonely Kent inn.

Perhaps the landlord's wife had not been proof against Muller's blandishments, and the offer of several crisp bank notes. At any rate, now he was here—in Bavaria!

There was a strained look on the Sword's face as Muller headed toward him, a triumphant smile on his face.

Then suddenly everyone in the room stopped talking, and there was utter silence inside the hotel.

From the streets outside came the moaning wail of sirens, rising louder and higher into a frenzy of warning. And mixed with the rising and falling of the air-raid sirens came the distant thunder of anti-aircraft guns.

The lights in the hotel went out!

Chapter Four
Raid of Liberators

Confused shouts and sounds of movement in the vestibule mixed with the howling wail of the warning sirens. Shadows stumbled everywhere in the blackness.

"To the cellars '" came a cry above the noise of confusion. "This way quickly. The English planes are coming!"

Cursing men bumped each other in an effort to obey.

Far a second, the Red Sword remained still, standing by the table at which he had been sitting. He never shifted his eyes from the place he had seen Muller when the lights had gone out.

Then he moved forward and grabbed his man by

the arm.

"No shelter for you, Muller," whispered the Sword, jabbing him with his walking stick. "If you don't obey me, I'll shoot! Do you think they could find a murderer in all this hubbub?"

He forced Muller, who thought he had been jabbed with a gun, forward towards the broad stairs of the hotel vestibule. The shadowy shape of the marble steps could just be made out in the darkness.

The German complied without making a sound. He could feel the tip of a walking stick prodding his side; together they mounted the stairs to the broad landing above.

The wailing sirens had stopped now. The city seemed paralyzed with fear. The boom of distant guns could be heard.

But the gunfire was growing louder, and nearer. Muller stopped several times, uneasily.

"Keep on moving," said the Sword mockingly. "They're not overhead yet."

Muller trembled and went on up a further flight of stairs. They turned into a narrow corridor and came to a door at the end.

"This leads out to the fire escape," the Sword told him. "Open the door."

Muller did as he was told and the bitter wind came in like a phantom blanket of ice. The roar of guns was plain now, but even above their crashing, came the steady drone of raiding aircraft, racing through the icy night towards the city.

The German stopped, and tried to turn back.

"The fire escape, I said! Can't you realize that I'm in a hurry?"

"But—" Muller's words were lost in the growing thunder of the raiding engines. Searchlights stabbed the sky like great white pillars, glittering through the thinly falling snowflakes.

The Sword pushed the terrified man out on to the iron platform.

Muller's knees seemed on the point of collapse as they went down the fire escape into the darkness of the hotel yard. The world was shaking now with the tumult of guns and engines.

Muller staggered and fell against a clothes pole in the yard.

"Let me go, you fool!" he gasped. "Do you want to be blown to pieces?"

The Sword had found some clothesline tied to a post close to the wall. He reached up and tore it down, then turned to the cringing man against the brick wall of the back yard. Then he ran his hands over the man's clothing.

"No gun," said the Sword. "Still I'll feel safer after I've tied you up."

He tripped the German spy and sent him face downward to a heap of rubbish. Kneeling, he quickly bound Muller, leaving his legs free. Then he forced his captive towards the yard door, which he opened.

There was a narrow alley outside, empty but for a powerful black touring car, which was unattended.

"Why, this is fortunate," The Sword's voice was exultant. "Come on, Muller. Let's go for a ride."

"No, no—not a ride!" Muller was terrified. His high-pitched voice sounded faint against the thunderous drone of the Liberators overhead.

Guns roared from all over the city, and the winter sky flashed with the bursting of shells.

The Sword pushed Muller into the car. He jumped into the driver's seat, and drove the car out into a broad, quiet street. No other living soul moved in the darkness as the car gathered speed and headed east.

The sound of its motor was faint against the uproar in the skies.

Abruptly above the explosions of the guns came a weird whistling sound as the released bombs came whizzing down from the planes overhead. Then the whistling was lost, as the giant blockbusters hit the streets of the helpless city. The explosions were deep, heavy and ear shattering, and they were accompanied by intense white flashes such as lightning makes when it hits. The ground rocked and trembled. Buildings collapsed, walls crashed, dust flew and fires started everywhere. The result was ghastly—almost beyond description.

And through all this uproar of bursting bombs, falling houses, spouting fire and flying debris, the Sword drove the car swiftly and easily—cool and smiling—skillfully avoiding the many heaps of fallen stones.

"Nice night for a ride," be told his terrified captive. "I notice you're shivering. I do hope you aren't cold."

Soon they were out of the city. By that time the raid was over and the noise behind them had died out. The Sword turned east along a broad white road, which fled under them monotonously, like an endless white tape unrolling beneath the wheels. In back, the burning city reddened the sky.

Sudden gusts of thin snow were carried on the icy wind, but they made no difference to the relentless pace of the big touring car as it raced eastward through the heart of Germany.

For a couple of hours it kept on steadily, then turned off the broad road into the narrower, winding roads of a forest. They then grew slower, as the Sword keenly watched the trees that lined both sides of the road.

When they bad traveled a few miles through the forest, the Sword suddenly swung the car off the road on to a narrow path, and stopped with the front wheels on the edge of a lake.

"Get out!" he ordered, shaking Muller's shoulder.

The German woke from his sleep, but he could scarcely move from cold. With an effort he clambered out of the machine and stood by it, stamping his feet.

The Sword descended also, and stretched himself, then gave the car a sudden push. It needed only that to get the machine rolling over the edge of the lake. There was a heavy washing sound of water, a crunching of gravel, and then the car had gone, leaving only the sullen whirlpool on the water where it had sunk.

"Thus, all evidence of our journey is removed," the Sword murmured. "By my calculation, we are within half a mile of the baron's chateau."

The British agent still held his precious walking stick, for he expected to use it soon.

Muller stood still, watching the red haired man in the first gray light of the dawn.

"What are you going to do?" he asked, his voice hoarse and dry.

"You'll soon see," smiled the Sword, and grabbed his arm. "Come on!"

They trudged on through the forest, until a woodman's hut appeared amongst the trees.

"We shall make this our camp for the day," he said cheerfully.

Muller said nothing. He was frozen with cold and fear of what was going to happen to him.

"After you," said the Sword, pushing open the door of the deserted hut.

Muller stumbled into the wooden shack and stopped. The Sword followed him, and closed the door.

The place had a rough table and three chairs. An old iron stove rusted in one corner, with a coil of thick rope near by.

"Just what I want," said the Sword, stooping and picking up a length of rope. "I must keep you out of mischief, Muller."

With a swift movement he had Muller on the floor, and in a minute had trussed his legs securely.

"Comfortable?" asked the grinning Sword straightening. "Now I must leave you for a while!"

He turned and went outside. There was nothing moving in the wintry forest. He hesitated a moment, then set off through the forest in the direction he knew the chateau lay. He had seen the place, once before, in peacetime.

The redheaded agent went cautiously, but the place seemed to be deserted. After about twenty minutes he passed another hut and came to the crest of a long slope, thick with fir trees, which ran down to the edge of the lake. The lake water was gray and sullen, reflecting the winter sky.

In the centre reared the rocky island, crowned two

hundred feet above the water by a gray stone chateau. The place, with all its turrets and piling walls looked as if it had been hewn out of the island itself.

All round it the lake stretched out towards the forested shores, and at its narrowest was over three hundred yards wide.

On the shore below where the Sword stood, he could see the brown woodwork of a landing stage, and a corresponding one on the island itself, where a motor-launch was tied up. Standing by the launch he could see the figure of a sentry.

High above him, on the terrace in front of the chateau, two other guards could be seen, slowly pacing the length of the terrace and back again.

A few minutes study convinced him it was useless to try and steal into the closely guarded chateau by daylight. Which was just as well, the Sword concluded, as he was worn out by his recent exertion. He remembered the second woodsman's hut he had passed, and decided to spend the rest of the day there, sleeping.

By sunset, however, he was back at the lake's edge, studying the chateau, refreshed and ready for action. He was about to turn away when, above the moaning of the wind, he heard the hum of a powerful motor engine.

He hesitated a moment, then scanned the edge of the dim forest near him. About a hundred yards away, he could make out the black surface of a winding forest road, which he knew must be the private road that led to the lake. Retreating into the trees, he ran forward to the edge of the road, then stopped in the shadow of a giant tree.

The roar grew louder and tires squealed as the car swerved round the bend into sight. Inside was the solitary figure of an army officer.

The Sword waited until it was no more than thirty yards away, and then ran out in front of it. The car howled, swerved to avoid him, and pulled up with a jerk. The driver flung open the door and jumped out angrily to approach the fool who had got in his way.

The Englishman withdrew the rapier from his stick, and the officer halted suddenly to find the sharp point of the sword at his throat.

"Thunder in heaven!" he cried. "What is this?"

"A matter of necessity," explained the Sword softly. He looked into the other's face and grinned. "Why! It's my gossiping friend from the hotel last night!"

The officer started, and his eyes bulged. "You!" he gasped. "So you are the Sword! And you are in the trap already!"

His laugh was cut short as the rapier pricked his skin.

"Not yet, my friend," smiled the Sword. "But tell me, what brings you down here in such a hurry? What business have you at the chateau?"

"Why, it's simple! When the so-called Herr Muller had vanished from the hotel, we began to wonder how he had dyed his hair so red."

"And is there only one redheaded man in Germany?" asked the Sword. As he spoke, he swung his left fist round in a lightning blow to the other's jaw.

The officer reeled, fell back against the car, then dropped in a heap to the ground.

The Sword picked him up, bundled him into the car, got in himself, and turned the car round.

He drove back along the road, then turned off it and ran in between the trees to the woodman's hut where be had left Muller.

He stopped the machine, lifted the officer out and carried him into the hut. He set him down on the floor, and lighted the remains of a candle, which stood on the broken down table.

By the faint light he went through the officer's pockets. He found a piece of stiff folded paper, which he opened quickly. There was a crest at the top of it, and beneath it a typewritten message:

To the Commandant: Take orders from bearer. It is believed that the Sword will make an attempt tonight.

Von Stuck.

The Sword whistled, then laid the message carefully on the table and grinned. He bent and rapidly stripped the officer of his entire uniform. This done, he bound the man securely and wrapped him round with his own black overcoat.

"Here is a companion for you. Muller," he said, as be undressed himself rapidly.

Muller watched with baleful eyes as the Englishman donned the officer's uniform, and stowed Von Stuck's message carefully in his pocket. Without further delay, the British agent blew out the candle, and hurried outside. He closed the door behind him and dashed across to the car. It was almost dark now, and the snow was falling more quickly. He regretted that he would have to leave his walking stick behind him, but a Nazi officer did not usually carry such things.

However, he had the captain's sword, which would do just as well, He examined the captain's pistol from his holster and found the magazine was full. Slipping the pistol back, he got into the car and drove back along the black road to where the silver of the lake water shone between the black shapes of the pines.

Stopping near the landing stage, he climbed out and gave a shout. In the darkness, from the direction of the chateau, a faint cry came in answer. At once, he heard the motor of the launch burst into life.

His heart was beating fast, later, when the launch swung round broadside into the wooden stage and stopped. The Sword jumped down into it. The pilot saluted.

"Quickly'" The Sword snapped. "Take me to the commandant!"

The soldier saluted again and sent the launch racing forward towards the island. The dark bulk of the gray castle loomed against the violet sky forebodingly.

The launch moored at the pier, and the Sword leaped up on to the heavy planks, and mounted the long stone stairway that led up to the chateau.

He reached the terrace before the great oak door of the chateau. The two sentries there presented arms as he passed. He came to the door and thundered impatiently on it.

It was opened almost immediately by a servant in military uniform.

"To the Commandant at once '"bawled the Sword.

A moment later he was being shown into a room furnished as a luxurious study, with a broad window overlooking the lake. The Sword halted before a stocky man with many medals, cropped hair and a monocle.

He saluted, and handed over Von Stuck's message. The commandant read it quickly, then looked up.

"So he comes tonight, does he, Captain?" murmured the commandant, and grinned comfortably. "At last, we shall catch the rat!"

"I do not see how we can fail," said the Sword, and frowned out of the broad window. "But tell me, Commandant, where are these French hostages being kept?"

"In the old dungeons '"

"So I thought. And the Sword knows it, too. He knows, too, that it will be no use trying to rescue them from such a place. Therefore, if we are to succeed in drawing him here tonight, the de Salles must be put in a place, which apparently will be easier for him to get at. Bring them up here. Commandant. They will do no good in the dungeon. If you bait a trap, you must allow the mouse to smell the cheese."

The commandant nodded sourly, and pressed a bell on his desk. It was answered by a young officer.

"Bring the French pigs up here!" snapped the Commandant.

Chapter Five
Out of the Trap

Quickly the officer retired and the Sword began to pace the thick carpet. The most dangerous part of the game would be played in a few minutes.

The de Salles knew him well, but always under a disguise. Would they recognize him now? If, involuntarily, they were to betray him, the jaws of this military trap would snap together like lightning.

The door opened suddenly, and the Sword swung round, his heart thudding like a hammer.

The young officer came in, followed by four soldiers. And in between the soldiers were Count Armand de Salle and his wife, the Countess Lucille. They looked haggard and pale, but their eyes glittered with defiance. The Sword stared at them fiercely and Count de Salle returned the stare. But into the eyes of his wife there came a sudden light—the light of recognition.

The Sword felt a cold hand squeezing his heart. He saw her halt a slight, involuntary gesture and breathed again. She had recognized him, but she had controlled herself. Now she turned away.

"Ach—a pretty bait!" sneered the Sword, swaggering towards them. "It should be good enough to catch the fox. Send these men away!"

The commandant made a signal, and the officer with his guard left the room.

The Sword lighted a cigarette and stared insolently at the two French prisoners.

"So your mad English friend hopes to rescue you tonight," he said ironically, in French. "Do you think you would know him if you saw him?"

The de Salles were silent. For a moment they glanced at each other. The girl must have made some sign with her eyes, for her husband suddenly looked sharply at the Sword. He stared hard.

"Yes, I certainly would know him again," he said slowly.

"That's good," snapped the Sword. "You are going to be very useful to us."

He turned and grinned at the commandant.

"But what is your plan, Captain?" the commandant asked gruffly.

"My plan is to take these hostages ashore," rapped out the Sword. "That will make the Sword so reckless he will run into a trap."

"Ashore?" roared the commandant, jumping to his feet. "That is too dangerous!"

"Himmel, have you no faith in your officers?" snarled the British agent. "Do you trust only walls of rock? Give me one good officer, and I'll promise you the Red Sword shall be in this chateau tonight!"

"No, no!" cried the stocky man. "I will not do it!"

The Sword pointed to von Stuck's message, still lying on the desk.

"You seem to have forgotten your orders, Herr Commandant," he said icily.

The commandant stopped, glared at the document, then at the Sword.

"Very well!" he said resignedly, and pressed the bell again. The young officer came in once more.

"Lieutenant, you will go with the captain here to guard the two prisoners. You will obey his orders."

The lieutenant clicked his heels and looked towards the Sword.

"We go at once!" said the British agent, and turned to the de Salles. "If you make any attempt to escape, you will be instantly shot!" He turned to the young officer. "Keep your pistol in your hand, Lieutenant."

The lieutenant pulled his pistol from its holster and held it ready. The Sword strode to the door and out into the hall.

Count de Salle and his wife followed, with the lieutenant behind them. They crossed the hall and came out on to the terrace.

They hurried down on to the landing stage where the launch was still moored, and the soldier standing in it started the motor. The Sword stood to one side to let the count and countess clamber into the boat, then suddenly he turned and grabbed at the lieutenant's pistol, at the same time smashing his free fist into the man's face. The officer staggered backwards into the sentry, and both men reeled on the slippery boards of the pier.

Like lightning the British agent leaped down into the boat, whipped out his sword, knocked the pilot senseless with one blow of the flat side, cut the mooring line with a single stroke of the keen edge and pushed the throttle wide open.

The boat shot forward, and tore ahead like a mad

thing, out of control.

The Sword grabbed the senseless pilot and half-lifted, half-pushed him over the side of the boat. At the same moment Count de Salle reached out for the wheel and kept the boat steady, as it dashed away toward shore.

Crack! Crack!

Rifle bullets screamed through the snowy darkness, but the white curtain of falling snow had cut off the sight of the island behind them.

"They're shooting at the sound of the motor," panted the Sword. "Phew! I didn't know I could get so hot on such a cold night!"

"We're certainly charmed to see you," said the Count in English.

"You'd better keep looking where you're going," said the Sword. "This lake's small, and—look out! Here it comes!"

The snowy shore of the lake suddenly appeared directly before the bows. It was too late to steer away from it.

The boat bounced into the air, and shuddered as if some giant rasp dragged along the keel from bow to stem. The passengers were thrown forward into a heap, and with a final crunch the keel came to rest. The Sword clambered ashore, and helped the others down to the carpet of snow.

"Couldn't have done better," he laughed. "They're stranded on the island, with only a little rowboat. That gives us the time we need, but I'm afraid we're going to have to walk all night."

They started south through the forest, the snowstorm increasing to a blizzard before they had gone many miles. But there must be no stopping if they were to elude their pursuers.

Back at the chateau the agitated Commandant was doing his utmost to explain away the escape of his two French prisoners and the Sword. His interrogator was the infuriated Baron von Stuck, who had traveled by car from Landsberg in the vain hope of gloating over the victim of the trap he had so cunningly laid!

Before daybreak, the three fugitives, tired and hungry, but with the forest far behind, came upon the banks of a broad river. Seeing the drawn, lined face of the girl at his side, the Sword was tempted to stop at some cottage, in the hope of getting some food and rest. But he knew that a minute's delay might prove fatal. They must push on.

From where they stood, they could see the wide curve of the river curling away into the distance. The Sword handed round a packet of cigarettes and leaned against a tree, his eyes on the broad stream.

A steamboat slowly ploughed along, drawing a string of ammunition barges behind it. Sentries could be seen posted along the riverbanks.

"Well, the three R's of the escape are these," said the Sword slowly. "River, railway and road. The river, as you see, is too closely guarded. The railway would be impossible as it is now entirely organized by the enemy."

"And the roads?" suggested Count de Salle.

"Will be watched at every inch by soldiers looking for us," said the Sword.

"Then what's to be done?" asked the Countess de Salle anxiously.

The redheaded man laughed and threw away his cigarette.

"But there's just one hope," he said. "I met a friend, by accident, who later dropped me out of a plane near Landsberg. He told me that if I wanted help, I should get a radio and broadcast a certain phrase, and if it was possible, he would come."

"Broadcast?" echoed the girl in astonishment. "How on earth can you do that?"

"With a radio transmitter." The Sword was grinning broadly. "And the best place to broadcast is from the nearest Nazi broadcasting station. And I happen to know there is one in a big industrial town about ten miles southeast of where we stand. We'll make for that town. Then I'll get the Nazis to lend me their transmitter for a few minutes." He burst into laughter.

"You're joking," said Count de Salle, dubiously. The Sword did not answer, but continued to laugh.

Once again they started off, but now there was no talking among them. The de Salles were silent. They knew the fate awaiting the Sword if he were caught. Yet he did not hesitate.

They could not imagine how the Sword could venture into a broadcasting station without being instantly detected.

"I do not comprehend," said the puzzled Count de Salle, at last. "The idea is mad. Ah, monsieur—you are like the French—so debonair!"

The Sword halted suddenly and peered through the trees where part of a road could be seen. Three soldiers, with rifles slung across their backs, were pedaling laboriously through the snow on bicycles.

From time to time the riders raised their heads and looked around them, but they did not stop.

"A road patrol," muttered the Sword. "So they know we're in this area. Yes, we are in great danger!"

Picking their way cautiously after this, they came at last to the straggling outskirts of the town. It was almost dark now. Rows of houses in the streets stood silent and empty, for the place had obviously been bombed and evacuated by most of its residents.

"One of these empty homes will suit us for the time being;" said the Sword cheerfully.

He selected a residence on a dark corner of the street, and broke open a side door without much difficulty. They entered the silent house. Its furniture was still standing about in the rooms, covered with dustsheets.

"This'll do fine." Again the Sword was grinning. "Now just make yourself at home and have a snooze while I'm gone."

"Are you going?" the girl gasped anxiously, then broke off.

"I'm intending to make my first appearance on the Nazi radio," said the Sword, laughing. "Look, there's a receiving set in the corner. Turn it on in ten minutes, if you want some fun."

"But—" began de Salle. He never finished for already the Sword was gone.

Once clear of the house, the British agent walked slowly through the dark, deserted streets of the town. He was tired, and his very weariness brought a feeling of fear, unusual in him. But he shook it off with a shrug.

"No good my getting the jitters now," he muttered. "This is where I really must look the part."

Then from somewhere down the street he heard the tramp of army boots marching towards him. He looked round, and in the darkness made out a party of six soldiers, with a sergeant in command.

The Sword marched towards them, his step brisk. The sergeant saw him, halted his men and saluted stiffly.

"You are to come with me," said the Sword sharply. "Escort to the broadcasting station. I have an urgent message which must be sent out at once!"

"Yes, captain," answered the sergeant. "Apparently this fellow, the Red Sword, is somewhere in the vicinity," went on the British agent briskly. "The townspeople must be warned. Quickly, now!"

The sergeant barked an order to his men, and a moment later the Red Sword was marching away into the center of the town, with an escort of six men and a sergeant.

"Just what happens next," he thought, "I leave to Fate!"

They marched in silence, until they came to a large concrete building in the town square, where the sergeant halted his men.

"Wait here for me, Sergeant," the Sword said loudly.

The Sword saluted again, and the Sword went in through the narrow entrance. The brightly-lighted hall of the building was crowded with people.

A man with a sheaf of papers in his hand appeared and bowed to the travel-stained officer.

"I have an urgent message to be broadcast at the

command of Baron von Stuck," the Sword said. "I have come a long way, and facilities must be made at once."

"Yes, Herr Captain," said the man diffidently. "But have you the order? The Baron von Stuck's order?"

"What, you civilian pig!" roared the Sword. "Do you doubt my word, then? By thunder-lightning! If you wish to keep out of the concentration camp, you had better do as you are told!"

"Ja, ja, at once!" the man said, turning ashy pale. "Certainly! This way, please, captain."

Hurrying along the passage, with the Sword following, he stopped before a plain door. Opening it, he went in.

The room was a studio, and three men were standing around a microphone, with manuscripts in their hands. They looked up curiously as the official and the Sword came in.

The official made a signal, and the three men stepped back

The Sword put a hand into his pocket and brought out a piece of thick folded paper. Caught up in its folds was a monocle. Chuckling inwardly, the Sword twisted the round piece against his eye. It added to his disguise. He looked the complete German officer now.

He unfolded the paper, holding it in such a way that none of the four men in the room could see anything but the baron's crest at the top.

The message upon it was addressed to the officer whom the Sword had left in the woodman's hut with Muller. It commanded him at once to order a new supply of notepaper and envelopes for use at headquarters.

The Sword almost laughed outright as the radio official went to the microphone.

"We are interrupting the program for an important announcement," he said in cultured tones. "Stand by, please!"

He signaled to the Sword, and the actor came forward, frowning.

"Attention'" he said sharply. "Here is a warning from the High Command to all people within range of this station.

"The English spy, known as the Red Sword, is at large somewhere to the north of this town. It is believed that he will try to make an escape tonight, disguised in the uniform of an army officer. He will try to get in touch with other spies in the district, from whom he will expect to get help. For this purpose he will use a trick sentence, which is: 'The third little pig used bricks.'

"I will repeat that. 'The third little pig used bricks.'"

The Sword paused, then went on speaking again.

"If any person should hear him trying to give directions, such as east something or north something, they should notify the police at once, by telephone.

"The numbers are One-one-oh-two, and Forty-eight-oh-one. The Red Sword is believed to be in the company of two others, a man and a woman, both French. The woman is about twenty-two years of age and the man thirty. Heil Hitler!"

The Sword stepped back from the microphone and stuck the paper into his pocket. Casually he took the monocle from his eye, at the same time motioning to the three silent men to carry on with their broadcast.

The Sword went out of the room with the official, left him without a word, and rejoined his escort outside the building. He felt a desperate longing to mop his brow, but he dared not.

"Sergeant, you will return to headquarters at once," he said. "You will find orders waiting you there."

The sergeant saluted and led his men back across the square. The Sword walked away in the direction of the house where he had left the de Salles. Once inside, he threw himself on a sofa and flung his cap across the room.

"Well, we heard it," said the Count slowly. "But it sounded like gibberish to me. Do you really want to have the whole city looking for you?"

"My dear fellow, it was the only thing to do," sighed

the Sword wearily. "I hope the message got through, anyhow."

"But what was the message?" asked the Countess, a puzzled frown on her pretty face. "You merely told people how to catch us."

"Perhaps I am dull witted, too," grunted de Salle. "I hope your friends in England understood it."

"I have reason to believe they will," answered the Sword confidently. "But whether they can act on it is another matter. Y'see the two telephone numbers were fakes. One-one-oh-two means eleven degrees two minutes East longitude, and Four-eight-oh-one is forty-eight degrees one minute North latitude. Do you understand now?"

"Latitude and longitude, old fellow, and it gives the position of that broad plain we saw north of the town. An aeroplane could land there. I mentioned there were three of us, and by giving fake ages for you, gave the time we shall be there—twenty-two hours, thirty minutes—or to put it in simple language—half-past ten."

The Frenchman could not mask his astonishment.

"And now all we have to do is to wait," said the Sword calmly. "Gosh, I'm sleepy!"

A few minutes later he began to snore.

Count de Salle paced up and down the room, impatient and uneasy. His wife sat still in a chair, listening to the silence of the house, as if expecting it to be suddenly broken by a thunderous knocking on the outer door.

But no sound came to disturb the rhythm of the Sword's breathing!

Chapter Six
The Net Tightens

While the car sped through the darkness, above the noise of its progress came the powerful voice of a radio. Three men in the back seat of the car craned their necks forward, as if by staring at the loudspeaker they would see the face of the broadcaster.

Von Stuck sat still as a statue, the muscles of his neck swelling with rage. Muller stared as if he could not believe what he heard. The army officer, huddled up in the Sword's black overcoat, glared until his eyes stood out from his head.

The voice from the loudspeaker ended, and Von Stuck sat back.

"So!" he thundered. "Who authorized that warning?"

"Authorized it?" snarled Muller. "No one! That, I'm certain, is the Red Sword. I know his voice well enough by now."

"But it came from our station in Munich," cried the baron angrily. "Are you suggesting that this rogue has had the impudence to force his way in?"

"He forced his way into your headquarters without difficulty," Muller reminded him sourly. "And into the chateau, too. That was his voice, I tell you. There is no mistake."

There was silence between them for a minute or more.

"One-one-oh-two," Von Stuck muttered. "And four-eight-oh-one. That is a code of some sort. What can it be?"

"It sounds like foolery to me," grunted the officer. "Why should he risk his neck to talk about little pigs?"

The baron ignored him and bent forward to bellow to the driver.

"Faster, man! Faster!"

For another hour the car raced on, and nothing was said among the three men. But Von Stuck kept muttering the numbers he had heard broadcast, as if by repetition he could find the secret of them.

As they came into the outskirts of the city, the baron barked again.

"The broadcasting studios!"

The story he heard at the radio station increased his fury. He stamped out of the place and was driven to the military headquarters in the town. Quickly he called a conference of officers, who were as eager as he to get the Red Sword in their hands.

"You heard the broadcast?" he demanded. "What did you make of it?"

"Gibberish," answered a major. "It is the type of cipher which is arranged beforehand. Only the man he arranged it with can understand the meaning."

"That's possible," agreed Von Stuck, departing the room, "Yes, I think that is likely. You are having the town searched?"

"Yes. Since soon after we heard the broadcast. We suspected something wrong when the officer failed to report here after coming from the radio station."

"Why was the message sent?" Stuck snapped. "Was he appealing for help?"

"What help could he expect to get behind our lines?" asked the major, shrugging. "Remember, this is Germany,"

"That's true," agreed the baron. "Very well. All roads and the stations are being watched. Every train must be searched, and every car stopped. Issue an order at once for all civilians to stay indoors until dawn. Every house must be ransacked."

"That will be done, Herr Baron," said the major.

"Good!" Von Stuck grunted. "I think this time we have him."

He walked away, and the major hurried out to give his orders.

Within a few minutes, the townsfolk who had not evacuated felt the heavy hand of the military over them.

Cafes and shops were cleared, and the customers sent home. Within a half hour, no civilian was to be seen in the streets. Only the ceaseless beat of army boots patrolling the streets could be heard, and the noise of the Gestapo making a house-to-house search in every quarter of the town.

While in the house to the north of the town square, the Red Sword was still fast asleep.

He awoke some time later, to find Count de Salle shaking his shoulder. He sat up on the sofa and looked around. The whisper of a voice was coming from the radio set in the corner.

"What's happened?" he asked, and yawned

"They've given an order for all civilians to stay in till dawn," de Salle said. "It just came over the air."

"Drat them'" exclaimed the Red Sword. "Just what I'd expect of Nazis."

He got up, crossed to the window, and peered out. The snowy roofs of the houses made it light enough to see that the street was empty.

He looked at his watch.

"Twenty past nine," he muttered. "That plain is four miles away, too!"

"It's you they're after," Countess de Salle broke in, her pretty face showing the anxiety she felt for him. "Leave us now! In that uniform you could get through easily. Never mind about us. We'll manage somehow."

"Pardon me, Madame the Countess," replied the British agent with a smile. "But we go together, or not at all. As for this uniform, it's no longer any use as a disguise. I wear it because it's all I've got to keep me warm. They've seen it too often now."

He sat down on the sofa again and began to think. He knew the methods of the Gestapo too well to imagine that they would leave anything to chance. The city by now would be surrounded, and every exit double guarded.

"Listen!" Countess de Salle's terrified voice hissed in the dark room.

Both men turned their heads towards the curtained windows overlooking the street. The sound of marching feet could be heard.

The Sword darted to the window and peered beneath the blind. Carefully he raised the window au inch or two. In the street were three men in the uniforms of the S.S. guards. They stopped to argue.

"All these houses were evacuated," said one.

"Well, that's the sort of place he would choose to hide in," argued the second. "See if any of them have been broken into."

The Sword turned back from the window and grinned in the darkness.

"My friends, we're in luck," he said, drawing his

sword from his scabbard. "Here come three gentlemen bringing some very fine uniforms. Count, take this pistol! Use the butt only, if possible."

De Salle nodded, and took the pistol "Countess, you must keep still in a corner commanded the Sword. "There might be a little nasty Nazi horse-play in a minute or two."

"But can't I help somehow?" she asked eagerly. "I could—"

She stopped suddenly.

"Here—look!" cried a muffled voice. "This door has been forced!" Then voices whispered.

"Behind the door!" breathed the Sword. "And remember, no mercy!"

De Salle crept across the room and stood ready. The Sword remained facing the open door, testing the keenness of the blade he held.

Footsteps came into the house along the passage. A faint gleam of light darted through the open doorway, then vanished.

The men outside were creeping up on tip toe. If the Red Sword was in this house, they intended to take him by surprise.

The British agent glanced aside at the French girl, poised like a statue in a corner. He could just see her pale, pretty face in the shadows.

He looked back at de Salle behind the door, and grinned.

The cautious footsteps outside drew nearer and in the yawning doorway a dark form showed.

"Walk right in, gentlemen!" called the Sword loudly.

There was a muttered oath then the flashlight's beam sent its glare through the doorway. One man rushed in, lifting a pistol as be came.

Crack!

De Salle's weapon thudded on the man's skull. The fellow went headlong, half-way across the room, crashed into a chair and lay still.

The other two men hesitated. The foremost leveled his gun. The hesitation was fatal, for the Englishman's sword flashed in an arc like a lightning strike, and the gunman found his pistol snatched from his hand and sent spinning through the air towards the corner where Countess de Salle stood.

"Look after that!" cried the Sword, and sprang for the doorway.

Startled by the loss of his gun, the S.S. man staggered, but he whirled and grabbed the French girl, one hand against her throat as she screamed, the other clutching the automatic in her hand. The gun roared—the bullet plowing harmlessly into the floor.

De Salle drew a short length of rope from his pocket, whipped it around the Nazi's neck and drew it tight. The soldier released the girl—his fingers clawing at the rope that was pressing into the flesh of his throat.

Swiftly de Salle dropped the rope and an instant later his gun chopped down and the Nazi fell flat. The French girl's gun covered him.

Out in the hall the third S.S. man had snatched a heavy police club from his belt. He hit out fiercely at de Salle as the Frenchman came through the doorway into the hall.

But the Sword's blade was quicker. Before the blow could fall, it darted forward like a flashing sunbeam and transfixed the storm trooper like a fly. The man crumpled up as the blade was withdrawn, and then collapsed to the floor, dead.

"Nice work, Count," said the Sword. "You deserve a marble clock. But there's no time to waste. We must have these uniforms. Just the overcoats and caps. They'll be enough!"

The two men quickly got what they wanted from the Nazi troopers. Then they hurried back into the room where Countess de Salle was guarding the third man, who was beginning to recover consciousness. Although the Sword did not mention it, both of the men in the hall were dead.

"Bravo, Madame," cried the Sword. "Keep him covered. We want his overcoat and trousers."

The man had no choice. In a minute he was

stripped of the clothing, which the fugitives needed. That done, the Sword tore up one of the dustsheets from the furniture, and securely bound the man.

"Now then, get yourself into these leggings and coats," ordered the British agent. "And Countess, tuck your hair up into the cap—all of it! You've got to look the complete Nazi soldier!"

The transformation was made with all haste, as it was a quarter to ten.

The Sword turned to the captive storm trooper.

"I need a car quickly," he snapped. "Where's the best place to get one?"

The man laughed mirthlessly.

"Car! What chance do you think you stand of getting out of this town tonight? You stubborn pig! You'd be caught before you get a yard!"

"I need a car, my friend," repeated the Sword, lightly touching the man's throat with the point of his blade as he spoke.

The trooper hesitated, until he felt the full weight of the weapon resting by its point on his throat. He swallowed, and sweat broke out on his brow.

"We left one on the corner of the street," he croaked.

"Very thoughtful of you," smiled the Sword. "Come on, Count. I hope those boots aren't too uncomfortable, Countess, because you've got to step it out like a man!"

"I'll do my best!" She smiled, despite her fear.

All three reached the door.

"Good-night," the Sword said to the struggling trooper on the floor as they departed. "Pleasant dreams!"

Chapter Seven
Dash for Freedom

The street was still deserted when the fugitives left the house, but at the corner, about two hundred yards away, the black shadow of a waiting car could be seen.

They walked along to it, the graceful French girl stepping out as well as she could in the boots she wore.

"Get in—quick!" snapped the Sword suddenly, just as another car of the same type came crunching through the broken snow towards them. The second car slowed, and a storm trooper looked out. "Any luck?" bawled the Sword.

"Nothing yet," came the answer. "Have you seen anything?"

"No, but we've just broken into every house in this street," answered the Sword. "That'll cost something for new locks'"

There was laughter from the other car, which moved on again.

"Pardieu!" gasped Count de Salle with a strained laugh. "You have the nerves of steel!"

The Sword smiled as be clambered into the driving seat.

"We're not out of the woods yet," he said quietly. "Wait a while."

"Wait for what?" demanded de Salle.

"For an air raid," replied the Sword. "And woe to us if there isn't one at half-past ten precisely. For that would mean my message didn't get through."

He started the engine and sent the car crunching slowly over the rutted snow.

The Sword tapped impatiently on the rim of the wheel. It would be a bitter blow if they failed now.

Yet the odds were heavily against them, in this last half hour. There remained only one last rush to escape. After that all would be over with them, or they would be free.

"If he got the message, he will come," muttered the Sword. "I'm sure of that. But we mustn't hang around here."

He accelerated suddenly and swept round a corner, flinging a great wave of snow out as he turned. They passed a squad of soldiers on patrol. The Count leaned toward the British agent.

"Better not get too far away from the north end of the town," he warned the Sword.

"I'm going to keep within handy distance of it,

don't worry," retorted the Sword. "The road I'm going to take is right ahead of us now."

He pointed to a junction some distance away, and as he did so, two large cars sped across it, heading north. They were followed by two motorcycle combinations.

"That looks like my friend Van Stuck, taking his circus for a ride," said the Sword, slowing down again. "But I wonder why he's left headquarters?"

"You don't suppose he could have deciphered your message, do you?" Countess de Salle said anxiously. "That would be a very good reason for him to leave his headquarters."

"It would be an excellent reason." Agreed the Englishman grimly. "But I doubt it!"

The car slowed down almost to a stop.

"Ten-past," said the Count tonelessly.

The sound of crushing snow from behind caused the Sword to glance into the rearview mirror. The masked lights of a car were approaching from the rear, and he saw the pursuer skid as the driver applied the brakes suddenly.

"I'm afraid we're detected," breathed the Sword. "Hold tight and keep your heads down. I'm going to throw a party!"

The other car slewed alongside them, plowing up the slushy snow as it headed over to cut off the fugitive car. Even before it had stopped, the doors were opened to let out its passengers.

The Sword accelerated suddenly and steered over towards the still skidding pursuer. The cars met with a crash that echoed in the street.

Giving a sudden wrench to the wheel, the Englishman pulled out again quickly, leaving the other car to spin round in a wild circle, knocked completely out of control by the crash. It crashed into the wall of a house.

A Nazi lay sprawling in the snow, and another was hurled off the running board by the shock of the crash. With a grim smile on his face, the Sword kept his foot down on the accelerator and headed towards the junction.

He glanced quickly into the mirror, his lips tightening as the man lying in the snow scrambled up and put a whistle to his lips.

"We're done, I'm afraid," the Sword said calmly.

But the thin shriek of the warning whistle was submerged in sudden clamor. Almost it seemed as if the man in the snow had started some mighty organ going, for there was the loud howl of warning sirens.

"The raid!" yelled de Salle. "They got your message! They're coming."

"And we're going!" snapped the Sword. "Hold tight, because we're going to break a few things now—our necks, perhaps!"

He skidded round into the junction, then, straightening up, raced north along the road, flinging up sprays of snow from the wheels like the wash from a speedboat.

"Nice weather for skating," said the Sword happily.

The sirens booted in a frenzy now, and from the south of the city came the first crash of anti-aircraft guns. The streets were deserted, but the Sword leaned forward to peer ahead.

Two motorcycle combinations could be seen at the right of the road, with a large black car in front of them. Several men in uniform were standing by the machines. On the opposite side, fifty yards farther on, was the second staff car.

"My old friend the baron, as I live!" cried the Sword, laughing recklessly. "Here's where I sideswipe the swastika!"

He increased the speed. As they rushed forward, Von Stuck's car on the right began to move outwards to block the road.

"Just what I wanted," shouted the Sword. He drove straight at the moving car. Then, when it seemed they must smash bead on into the side of the stationary car, the Sword swung the wheel.

The car went into a skid, crashed into the other one, and bounced away again across the snow like a skater changing direction. Von Stuck's car heeled over and crashed over to its side, with its wheels still spinning.

The fugitive car continued its wild skid to the other side of the road. There it smashed into the front wheel of the second car. As it slid away, the Sword righted it and sent it racing on again, toward the plain in the north.

Behind them rifles and pistols were flashing, but the furious shooting did not keep de Salle from looking back through the rear window.

"Superb!" the Count chuckled. "Overturned one, and knocked the other one's wheels cross-eyed!"

The powerful car was roaring forward under the Sword's skillful guidance. But the two motorcycles had taken off in pursuit.

"We're about a mile from the plain," the British agent said quietly. "If my friend has had the same luck we have, he should be somewhere overhead by now. Unfasten the hood from the windshield, Count."

De Salle unfastened the clips that held the hood down. He pushed upwards. A sudden gale swept it up like the sail of a ship. The canvas bellied, then there was a cracking of wood and metal, and the whole hood was torn completely off. .

It flew backwards, turning over and over in the air, then bumped on the road and rolled away, straight for the leader of the oncoming motorcyclists.

The rider swerved, but he could not avoid the strange obstacle. He skidded into the torn canvas and bent metal stays, and crashed amid a cloud of snow. The rear motorcycle had to stop to avoid hitting him.

The Sword sped on until they reached the broad plain. Then the Count gave a shout and pointed above them.

"There he is. Right above us! And he's coming down!"

The Sword looked too. A hundred feet above them a huge bomber was screaming downward to land.

The huge landing wheels were dropping slowly out of their nests. From the wing came the brilliant glare of a landing light striking a great broad path across the white plain.

Lower and lower the bomber came. The Sword turned the car off the road and rocked over the rough field, almost directly beneath the landing plane.

He braked slightly, and the giant aircraft settled just ahead of them like some monstrous bird. It came to a standstill on the plain. The car swerved round to the side of it, as a door in the fuselage opened and a man looked out.

"Make it snappy!" shouted the Sword to his passengers.

Crack! Crack!

The sound of firing came from a squad of pursuing soldiers, who had now turned off the road to try to stop the fugitives.

Countess de Salle scrambled out of the car and dropped down into the deep snow. Her husband and the Sword followed her.

Crack! Crack!

The Sword felt something tear at his sleeve, and looked back over the plain.

A Nazi soldier was firing a rifle. The bullet hole in the Englishman's sleeve proved him to be a good shot.

The Sword ducked, but as he did so, the machine-gun in the tail of the plane began to roar. An arc of snow sprayed up from the ground immediately in front of the pursuing soldiers, who fled for their lives.

"Run for the plane!" yelled the Sword. "It's now or never!"

As the three fugitives clambered into it the engines roared, and the giant machine trundled over the snow, towards the sky and freedom.

Faster and faster it went, with waves of snow shooting out from its wheels. Then the bomber rose high over the fringe of tree at the edge of the field.

The de Salles sat together in the mail body of the plane, laughing from relief. The Sword made his way forward to the pilot's compartment.

The pilot looked round and grinned at him. Other crew members were smiling, too.

"So you made it," the pilot said to the Sword, cheerfully.

"Hello, old man, I hardly recognize you now," said the Sword airily. "You looked different in that Nazi uniform."

"I had a moustache then, and it was very dark that night," replied the pilot. "If it hadn't been for that little shaded light we had in the plane, I'd never have noticed your beard wasn't black, as it should have been."

"Lucky for me," laughed the Sword. "By the way, was there only one plane in this raid, old man?"

"Only one, around here. Your taxi, as I promised." Then the pilot looked glum. "And I'm afraid we're in a mess. I persuaded my crew to risk the trip. We—er—borrowed this kite!"

The Sword laughed.

"Then I'm afraid there's going to be trouble all right!"

The plane roared on for nearly thirty minutes. Then the observer made a signal from the front. The British channel lay behind them. They were again over England.

"The field's three miles exactly straight ahead," the observer called.

The engines died and the machine planed down towards the snowy airstrips below. The Sword left the pilot and went back to where the de Salles were seated.

The girl was in her husband's arms, both of them fast asleep. The Sword smiled and stood ready by the cabin door.

The plane came down, mushed through the snow and came to a standstill near the hangars. The Sword opened the cabin door, and jumped down to the snow.

The machine had stopped close to the trees, which ringed the field. The British agent ran in amongst the trees and in a moment was lost to sight. He kept running fast, threading his way round towards a block of low structures housing the Operations Command. Coming to the wall of the nearest building, he reached for a window.

He pushed up the sash, scrambled through the opening into the room beyond, crossed the room, and locked the door silently. Then he returned, fastened the window, and switched on the light.

He was in an officer's bedroom. For a moment he stood looking at his reflection in the glass above the washstand.

Inside a small locker he found a safety razor, brush and soap. In three minutes he had given himself a good shave.

He next took various bottles from a case standing by the bed, and crossing to the washstand, rapidly washed his hair. The red dye came out, and left a head of hair that was as yellow as straw.

"When the hair is red, the whiskers look red," he said, staring at the result in the mirror. "And when the hair is fair, the whiskers look fair. But woe betide if the whiskers are fair when they should be black!"

The Sword rubbed his head vigorously with a towel. When it was dry, he dressed himself in a uniform of the Royal Air Force, and half an hour later he left the room. He made his way to the staff room, where two officers were talking together.

"Hello, Daunton!" said one of the officers. "When did you get back?"

"Oh, about half an hour ago," the Sword answered leisurely.

"Have a good leave?" asked the officer.

"Pretty quiet, you know," replied the Sword, and sat down. "What's the news here?"

"Well, there's a bit of a business happening tonight," admitted the first officer. "Young Raleigh borrowed a kite to fetch a couple of French agents from somewhere, and the agents, Count and Countess de Salle are hollering about a chap called the Red Sword."

"I think you'd better deal with them," said the second officer.

"All right, send 'em in," said the Sword. He slipped on a pair of horn-rimmed glasses, and stared blankly at the de Salles when they were shown into the room. The Count explained what he wanted.

"Well, this fellow appears to have disappeared," the Sword said shortly. "I'd help you if I could, but—well, this is the Royal Air Force, you know, and we don't have much to do with—er—international adventurers."

"But the Red Sword saved our lives!" protested Countess de Salle.

The Sword shrugged.

"I'm very glad, for your sake," he said casually. "But your man seems to have vanished. Perhaps he didn't want to be thanked."

The de Salles looked doubtfully at each other.

"Well, thanks a lot, Monsieur—?" said the Count with a bow.

"Daunton—Squadron-Leader Daunton," said the Sword.

"Thanks, anyhow," said de Salle. "But I wish we could have found him."

They went out and the Sword sighed. He glanced at some papers on the desk, then looked up again, as Flying Officer Raleigh came in, looking rather flushed.

"You wanted to see me, sir?" he said.

"Well, I should think so, too, wouldn't you?" asked the Sword mildly. "I mean, we hardly expect men of your rank to 'borrow' Government machines for joy-rides!"

"No, sir."

The Sword rubbed his jaw.

"I really don't know what to do about it," he said thoughtfully. "I should punish you severely, but I've no doubt you're a hero, and it's wrong to punish heroes. You rescued a man and woman from Nazi Germany. Also a British agent?"

Raleigh said nothing.

"Also, I know that you're frequently allowed to do unusual jobs on behalf of the Secret Service," went on the Sword.

"Yes, sir—sometimes," admitted Raleigh.

"By the way, how did you know you were wanted tonight?" queried the Sword. "How did you get a message from this mysterious fellow the Red Sword?"

"We arranged that he should broadcast if be could," Raleigh grinned widely. "And be did—from the radio station in Munich. That fellow's got a nerve, sir!"

"Sounds like it," said the Sword, nodding. "But we're wandering from the point. You broke King's Regulations by taking this plane without permission."

"Yes, sir," agreed Raleigh, with rather a curious look. "You were once a famous actor, sir. Do you remember that play you were in before the war started—where you managed to give your position away by saying the longitude and latitude in the form of telephone numbers?"

The Sword frowned.

"What play was that?" he muttered. "Oh, yes. I think I remember."

"Well, this chap the Red Sword—he did the same thing tonight," said Raleigh, looking hard at his superior officer.

"Then I suppose he must have seen the same play," said the Sword with a smile.

"Yes, I suppose he did," said Raleigh slowly, still keenly observing his Squadron Leader. "You know, sir, I could have sworn that you were -"

"We will have no swearing here," interrupted the Sword finally. "You'll report to me in the morning. By that time I'll have decided what shall be done with you."

"Yes, sir!" Raleigh marched to the door, and stopped to look back. "The third little pig used bricks," he said suddenly.

"I beg your pardon?" said the Sword blankly. "What on earth are you gabbing about?"

"Sorry, sir," sighed Raleigh. "I must have been wrong, after all."

He went out and the Sword sat down again. He yawned at the clock then settled himself comfortably. In a few moments, he was asleep. ♦

Dorus Noel

By Tom Johnson

All Detective was an odd magazine in its time. For example, just look at the Nibs Holloway adventures by Edward P. Norris that ran from July 1934 to January 1935. Nibs fought the notorious Doctor Death, who died in each story only to appear again in the next one. For all intent and purposes, the readers must have thought Doctor Death truly died. It must have been a tremendous surprise when he returned from the dead. Whether this was the idea of Norris or the editors is not known, but it was an interesting series.

Earlier, from April 1933 through December 1934, Arthur J. Burks had a series running in *All Detective* with some similarities to Nibs Holloway and Doctor Death. Eleven stories appeared featuring Dorus Noel, a man who had spent many years in China, and now has settled in New York's Chinatown. A mysterious police official has made Noel an undercover detective for the police force. His station is Chinatown. However, he only reports to his unknown supervisor by telephone.

A sinister Chinaman that reminded me of the evil Doctor Death faces Dorus Noel, and this is where the series takes on some semblance to Nibs Holloway and Doctor Death. In the first story we are introduced to the Chinaman, Chu Chul, also known as The Cricket. Chu Chul had almost conquered Northern China before he was stopped. He had known Dorus Noel in China, and they were bitter enemies. Perhaps it was Noel who had ended his plans as emperor of China.

In the first story, "Death of the Flute" (April 1933), Chu Chul supposedly dies in a fire, but there is always a question mark. In "The White Wasp" (May 1933), Chu Chul's daughter shows up with plans to kill Noel, but in the end does not. Nor does Noel capture her, and she escapes. Then in "Bells of Pell Street" (June 1933), Chu Chul appears to be back. Again, he dies at the end of the story, but Noel discovers he's an actor disguised as the evil Chinese genius.

I don't know if the editors were trying to get Burks to actually bring the evil Cricket back issue after issue or not, but though Chu Chul is often mentioned in the later stories, he never returns. Dorus Noel does find more Chinese masterminds to thwart, however.

Sadly, after the final story, the series seemed to be left open, and needed an ending. In order to end the series, I wanted to bring Chu Chul and his daughter back for a final encounter with Dorus Noel. After all, there were still a few unanswered questions. Escaping the death by fire, The Cricket had gone through months of surgery and recuperation, but now wants to continue his quest for a throne in China. However, before he can begin his plans, he vows to kill his mortal enemy, Dorus Noel.

I hope you like the story…. ♦

The Black Shadow

By Tom Johnson

When a Korean assassin comes to New York's Chinatown in search of stolen vases from the Korya Dynasty, the trail leads to the lair of a man believed long dead. But Chu Chul was very much alive, and was even now plotting the death of Dorus Noel.

Prologue

In a small house somewhere near Mott Street in Chinatown, a curtained room was emblazoned with the imperial yellow of a reigning emperor, the drapes decorated with the five-toed dragon emblem. Columns upheld the roof, and around them wound the folds of five-toed dragons also done in gold. Chu Chul had once almost held all of North China in his hands. Small enough to be Cantonese, his skin was yellow and pitted with smallpox scars. His black eyes seemed to have no pupils. His hands were long, like claws. His face was beardless. He walked to a throne-like edifice in a stoop, a twisted caricature of what once was a man, where he placed a white mask over his burned and scarred face.

The Cricket remembered that time, not so long ago, when he had nearly died in a fire at the hands of his mortal enemy, Dorus Noel. His own words came back to his mind now as he glanced about the little chamber that had held him these long days while he heeled from the severe injuries. Chu Chul is never beaten, he had said. If the cat has nine lives, Chu Chul has nine times nine… and all of them shall be dedicated to the destruction of Dorus Noel and the working out of the mighty schemes of The Cricket.

His doctors had removed the dead scar tissue from his body, and though a lesser man might have died from the terrible torment, opium deadened the pain until he could again move among his subjects.

With the mask covering his dead face, he reached with a claw-like hand for a silk cord, which he pulled once and waited. Coolies erupted from rooms beyond the golden curtains, men enslaved to their leader, to see to his needs. Speaking in Cantonese, Chu Chul ordered his opium pipe, and then gave them their orders for the day.

The eyes of the Coolies never looked up to meet his, remaining always in supplication, nor did they turn their back to him when he ordered them from the chamber. Bowing, they backed to the curtains, and disappeared within their voluminous folds.

Inhaling deep from the long stem pipe for several minutes, The Cricket finally relaxed and again reached up to a second cord and pulled twice this time. Faraway, a musical chime tinkled in odd notes, as if in a French lullaby.

Five minutes later the curtains parted again, and a beautiful girl entered the presence of the would-be emperor. Unlike the coolies, she did not bow her head in supplication.

"I was bathing, father," she said. "What do you desire of me this morning?"

"Perhaps merely to look upon the daughter of my wife," he said from behind the mask. "Every day, you look more like your mother, Ghi."

"My mother was French, father. Her eyes were not slanted like mine," she said. "I shall never look like my mother."

"But you have her beauty, daughter—and my eyes." He chuckled.

"My mother wasted away while you tried to conquer China, Father. She was not much older than me when she died. Perhaps, if you had remained with us in France…?"

"That wasn't to be, daughter," Chu Chul shrugged. "Your mother knew I was destined for China's throne when she married me. What has happened has happened. There is no need to speak of it any more."

"Then why have you disturbed my bath, father?"

"It is time, my daughter. It is time for me to have my revenge on Dorus Noel."

"You say, 'what has happened has happened,' Father. Why not also put Dorus Noel behind us like you have my mother?"

"Enough of your arguing, child," he admonished. "It is time for us to make plans, and I will need the help of The White Wasp…."

Chapter One
A New Houseboy

Finishing a vigorous morning workout, Dorus Noel was relaxing in the China Room of his house, located just off the intersection of Pell and Mott Streets. The room was filled with Chinese bric-a-brac, which he himself had collected over the years. Clocks of strange design, tapestries beyond price, feather screens, jade ornaments, cloisonné, and porcelain. These were rare items brought back from his five years of adventures in China.

Bare from the waist up, Noel had a white towel, embroidered with red and green dragons, wrapped over his shoulders to absorb the sweat from his recent workout on a heavy bag. Clocks suddenly sounded off the hour as golden sand of China dribbled through an hourglass in Noel's Chinese Room of ancient artifacts. Over a dozen clocks, each of Chinese design, were sounding the eleventh hour. His favorite clock rolled a golden ball out of a notch in a winding stairway, visible only because the casing was of clear glass.

The sudden tinkling of tiny chimes brought him alert to the new sound, then he smiled. A Chinese gang had murdered his last houseboy, and the chimes had been set up to warn of visitors. With a sigh, Dorus wondered whom it could be calling upon him in the middle of the day. He threaded his way through the many treasures, passing a red lacquer screen with its decorations of tiny bird feathers. He passed a wall mirror, and then circled a screen just inside the door, which kept out evil spirits because they could only travel in a straight line.

He had lived three lifetimes in his 26 years, and though handsome, there were times he felt very old. His wavy brown hair was almost a deep red when seen in certain light, and his six-foot frame was solid muscle from daily exercise.

At the little door bordering on the sidewalk, he was surprised to see a small oriental boy he first took to be Cantonese, standing at the portal.

"A thousand pardons, Heavenborn," the lad smiled easily, "the wind whispers that you have need of a houseboy?"

The boy had spoke in fluent English, with very little accent, but Dorus answered in Cantonese, "More than likely, it was the whispering of Chinese merchants. Come in."

He was again surprised when the boy replied in kind, though he seemed not as familiar with the tongue.

Leading him to the China Room, Dorus removed the towel from his shoulders, and the lad gasped when he saw the burned scars on his chest. It was a strange mark, three parallel, horizontal bars, perhaps an inch in length, crossed by a diagonal transversal.

Bowing, his visitor muttered something in an odd prayer, and then spoke again in English, "I have heard that Dorus Noel was a master of men, and now I see it is true. You bare the mark of a ruler, or king, Heavenborn."

"You are familiar with this mark, then?" Dorus asked, a warning tingling the back of his neck.

"Yes, Heavenborn, they represent the Chinese character "wong" which means "ruler" or "master of men." Yet this one is different," he said, pointing to a tiny spot below the bars. "It is like a signature, the signature of Cricket."

"What is your name?" Dorus asked his visitor. "Why have you come to my house? You don't appear to be Cantonese, and I don't think you are wholly Chinese, either."

"I am Korean, Heavenborn. My name is Kim Young Ju. It is true. I am not Chinese. I seek merely to be your houseboy."

"As you can see, Kim, I am in need of a house boy," Dorus said. "But be warned, I have lost eleven boys already. There are plotters in Chinatown who would sacrifice your life in order to get to me. And these men are very dangerous."

Smiling broadly, Kim said, "A wise man once said, 'Tread not on a snake, least it be a venomous viper and deadlier than you!' I shall guide my steps well, Heavenborn."

"Very well, Kim. Chinatown has been quiet lately, so maybe I am in for a rest from the Tongs. The Society of The White Lily and the Red Spears are a particularly mean bunch, and occasionally the Hung Hu Tze sticks their nose into my business. You must always be on the alert for anything suspicious."

Two days went by without incident, and Kim Young Ju proved to be a well-trained houseboy, which seemed odd to Noel. There weren't many Koreans in New York's Chinatown, though they weren't uncommon. However, most Koreans tended to settle in California and Chicago. Noel could not shake the feeling that something wasn't right, and this persisted to bother him.

On the third day his curiosity was eating at him, so he left Kim with a few chores and walked down to the corner of Canal and Laffayette Streets to a small cigar store where a row of telephone booths were a distance from the counter. There he called his unknown and mysterious superior on Park Avenue.

When the phone was answered on the other end, he recognized his police contact instantly. "It's me, Noel."

"Is anything going on, Dorus?" the official asked. Oddly, Noel had never met his contact. When he returned from China, and settled in New York's Chinatown, a mysterious caller contacted him one night, and because of his China experience he was made an undercover detective in the district for the police department. The Chinese may have suspected that he was there to keep his eyes open for mysterious activity, but the Chinatown police squad was not aware of his true status.

"No sir, just curious if you've heard any rumors. It's too quiet in Chinatown to suit me. When it's this quiet, it usually means something is stewing beneath the surface somewhere."

"I haven't heard of anything, Noel. At least nothing concerning us."

Again, Noel felt a prickling on the back of his neck. "Nothing concerning us, sir? Is there something else that you are concerned with, maybe?"

"There have been a number of strange killings in San Francisco's Chinatown, but nothing that indicates it involves us in any way."

"What do you have on the killings?" Noel asked.

"The San Francisco Chinatown squad reported several key figures in Tongs were assassinated. That part isn't so strange, as Chinese are always fighting among each other. However, the Tong leaders were beaten to death, and evidently tortured for some kind of information they possessed. The police haven't been able to make heads or tails of anything. You know how the Chinese are closed mouth when it comes to their community!"

"But most of them are good people, sir," Noel said.

"The gangs cause the problems. I would guess it's merely a Tong war."

"Well, you're probably right. But be on the look out for strangers. If someone has it in for the Chinese, we don't want them coming to New York and starting a war."

Dorus was preparing to hang up, and then he thought of something else. "Has there been any activity in the Korean sector in San Francisco? Now or in the past?"

"Koreans?" his superior asked. "They are all Chinese to the police. There's nothing I've heard recently, but about five years ago we were notified of a Korean temple being looted, and valuable religious antiquities were removed. It was thought they might be heading for America. In fact, your old friend was implicated, as I recall."

"My old friend, sir?" Noel asked.

"The Cricket!"

Chapter Two
Korya Vases

At noon the next day, Kim was serving tea and rice cakes when the clocks again sounded the hour. Dorus Noel watched a beautiful gem encrusted clock that had once been given to Emperor Ch'ien Lung by Louis Fifteenth of France, and when it struck the hour, eight tiny human figures in blue came out on its top and danced a tinkling minuet.

"These are beautiful treasures, Heavenborn," Kim acknowledged, as he observed the many clocks. "Do you keep all of your treasures in the open, none are hidden perhaps?"

"No, Kim," Noel told him. "I bought each item legally, so there is no need to hide them. What good would they be if I could not view them daily?"

"Speaking of treasures, Kim, I heard that a Korean temple was looted about five years ago. Do you know anything about it?"

"Yes, Heavenborn, all of my people know of the incident. The mark on your chest is the signature of the robber. There could only be one Cricket," he said, "and the man that put the mark on you would be the robber of the temple."

"The Cricket's name is Chu Chul," Noel said, watching the Korean's face for any sign of recognition. "It was The Cricket who burned the mark on my chest. He wanted me to remember that he was the master of men, and my master as well."

"The wind has whispered this too," admitted the houseboy. "I believe he is here, in New York."

"He's dead, Kim, I saw him die," Noel said sternly.

"Perhaps, Heavenborn. But I've heard otherwise."

"Where did you learn to speak English so well, Kim? You do not strike me as a servant, but someone highly educated."

"The Kukkiway temple monks sent me to missionaries, Heavenborn, to see to my education. It was a duty I had to fulfill. If I seem educated, it is their teaching that should be honored, not my humble ignorance."

"How long have you been in New York, Kim?" Noel asked, a suspicion nagging at his mind.

"A while, Heavenborn. Do I not please you? The missionaries also taught me to serve, as did my temple."

Noel waved his question off. He was still concerned, considering the news his superior gave him about the killings in San Francisco. If Kim had been in New York's Chinatown for any length of time, why hadn't they crossed paths before now? Something else that worried him even more, though, was Kim's assertion that The Cricket was alive. If Chu Chul didn't die in their last encounter, he must have been badly injured. That could well account for his long absence. But if he had recovered….

Kim was not only an excellent houseboy, but also a marvelous cook, and prepared a breakfast the next morning fit for an emperor.

"Later this morning, you will accompany me shopping, Kim. I'm afraid that after such a meal I just had, we surely need more kitchen supplies."

"As you wish Heavenborn," Kim smiled at the compliment.

Hearing a tinkling at the door, Kim turned to leave, but Noel stopped him with another warning. "Be alert, Kim. I am not expecting anyone, and Death often comes to my door under the guise of visitors."

There was a smile on the Korean's face, but Dorus didn't miss the sudden fire flash from his eyes also. Again, that strange feeling ran through his body, and he recalled Kim's saying when they first met: "Tread not on a snake, least it be a venomous viper and deadlier than you!" There was more to the Korean than met the eye.

A few minutes later, Kim returned alone, but there was something in his hand.

"Who was it, Kim?" Noel asked.

"I do not know, Heavenborn," the houseboy said. "There was no one at the door. Only this little envelope penned to the portal."

"Give it to me, Kim, but be careful. Deadly poisons can be administered in many ways."

Finding a long, slim blade, Noel held the envelope away from his face, then slit it open and removed the rice paper folded inside. It was written in Mandarin.

"What does it say, Heavenborn?" Kim asked.

"You do not read or write Mandarin, Kim?" Noel asked.

"No, Heavenborn, though I understand a small amount."

"It is a simple message, Kim, it says that I should kill you before my own life is forfeit. Why would someone want me to kill you?"

Nodding, the Korean said, "Perhaps it is time I revealed my true purpose for coming to New York, Heavenborn."

"That would be a splendid idea, Kim. There is no better time than the present!"

"What I have told you is true, Heavenborn," he began. "However, I have not revealed it all. Five years ago I was a young man in my temple when a beggar came to our gate. He was small, and looked ill. I was guarding the entrance from bandits, but he looked hungry and helpless. I went inside to get a bowl of rice for him, and when I returned to the gate he was still waiting. However, I failed to see the one hiding in the shadows, who must have arrived in my absence, and something heavy struck me over the head. When I came to, our temple had been robbed, and I was blamed. Oh, not totally, but if I had been more alert, I would have called another to get the bowl of rice, and remained on my post.

"Of the treasures that were taken, only a set of vases was without price. Have you ever heard of the Korya Dynasty, Heavenborn?"

"Yes, of course," Noel told him. "I believe the Korya Dynasty was from the 11th century to the 13th century, is that not correct?"

Nodding his head in the affirmative, Kim continued. "The most rare of all antiquities that our temple possessed was the Korya Dynasty vases!"

"Whew!" whistled Noel. "I remember now. They were a set, two vases green in color and decorated with birds in flight. They were part of the treasure taken?"

"Yes, and the only thing we have not recovered. Chu Chul used the rest to finance his grab for rule of Northern China. The vases were never sold, and we believe he still has them. They would be worth a kingdom, and we think he is planning to return soon to try and regain his power in China."

"Since they blame you for losing the vases, you have been ordered to get them back, is that right?" Noel asked.

"Yes," Kim admitted. "But I volunteered for the assignment."

"You're just a lad, barely in your twenties," Noel snapped. "What do you think you can do against The Cricket, if he does still live? He would be surrounded by ta chuen warriors, men trained in killer jujitsu."

"Ta chuen, bah!" Kim waved the thought aside.

"When I arrived in New York, I heard about you, Heavenborn, and how Dorus Noel fought against

THE BLACK SHADOW

The Cricket and his evil minions. It was said that a Chinese Tong killed your last houseboy, so I decided to enter your home as a servant, and eventually enlist your aide in locating Chu Chul. I would have spoken to you soon about my mission."

Chapter Three
The White Wasp

Noel locked the door as they departed, but he knew it was merely an act of false security. The Chinese had ways of entering locked houses, and if a killer was interested in gaining his chambers the locked door would not bar his entrance.

They passed slow moving figures shuffling along the streets. Though the Orientals no longer wore pigtails and straw sandals, they had retained their homeland customs of rice and chopsticks. Nor had they given up their singsong language totally for English. The district was almost like a foreign country with Chinese shops and fish markets. Small cafes dotted the main avenue with hidden rooms behind them for mysterious purposes that Noel knew were probably Opium Dens.

There would be an atmosphere of the Orient, with silk draperies and flowered fans and paper lanterns. Most Chinese people were harmless, peaceful, and busied themselves with industrial activities. But occasionally a crafty, slant-eyed, malevolent Chinaman would rise to prominence, and take to the dark byways of crime. Chu Chul had ruled Chinatown for the last five years, and if was still alive, he would be at the core of what evil was growing now in those curtained rooms.

Passing a restaurant with large gilt letters proclaiming it to be the American equivalent of mother's home cooking, it was owned by a fat Chinaman named Ho Ling, and Noel knew the food served was as close to real China as anyone would ever find. On the other side of Ho Ling's was the old Chinese clock maker, a man who had repaired Noel's clocks many times in the past. His parchment like skin indicated his great age, yet his long, tapering fingers were gentle and sure, and he was a master of the clocks.

Kim walked briskly at his side, and his eyes never seemed to miss anything. Noel noticed a look of fear flash from eyes as Chinese scurried from their path, but the Korean had done nothing to incite the atmosphere that permeated the streets today.

Before they had gone more than two blocks, Dorus spotted a tiny figure ahead of them that looked familiar, though at first he couldn't view the woman in white's features. Then of a sudden he had it, and a gasp escaped his lips as he placed a restraining hand to Kim's chest.

"The White Wasp!" he warned, and then the Korean saw the girl too. As the girl turned into a shop, they got a clear view of her beauty. She had black eyes, and a wealth of black hair that formed a ruff for her shoulders. She had thin, white hands. From this distance she looked no more than eighteen or nineteen, her face was like peaches and cream. Her eyes were only slightly slanted, her lips like cherries, and teeth like little white pearls.

"She is the Cricket's helper," Kim said, "though I have not been able to find her identity. It is said that she is more deadly than Chu Chul. Be cautious, Heavenborn, but we must follow her. Perhaps she will lead us to Chu Chul."

"I've met her, Kim," Dorus said, as he tried to stay up with the running houseboy. "She said her name was Ghi."

"Ah!" Kim exclaimed, looking back. "Then we do know her, Heavenborn. Ghi is the daughter of Chu Chul. I should have known."

"Yes, she admitted it when we first met. She tried to poison me after I killed her father—or, thought I did, at least."

The Korean went through the door first, with Noel fast on his heels. They were just in time to see Ghi's white dress disappear through a back door.

"An alley!" Noel cautioned. But Kim did not slow down. An elderly Chinese woman was staring at them in surprise from behind a counter containing Oriental trinkets.

An avalanche of bodies met them in the narrow alley. A dozen men of the Hung Hu Tze Tong were standing just outside the shop's door, and the Korean was in their midst before anyone knew of their presence. Whether protecting Ghi's escape, or by accident, Noel didn't know. But the Tong was in no mood to discuss the situation. Jabbering in Tientsinese, hatchets appeared from the folds of their baggy shirts, and they attacked en mass.

Noel swung a solid uppercut as the first man reached him, just as he heard Kim laugh. He was too busy to see what the Korean was doing, but felt a thrill when the uppercut slammed the hatchet man backwards, striking the wall of another building with his head. But he had no time to admire his handy work, hatchets were swinging for his head, and hard muscles powered the arms behind them.

Using a savate kick, Noel caught a second hatchet man under the chin with the toe of his shoe, and then side-kicked a third. He was suddenly alone, and looked around to see the Korean standing about the remainder of the hatchet men; a few were moaning, but some were still and looked lifeless.

A musical voice came from the end of the alley, "I will be waiting, Dorus Noel," then there was silence. Neither saw which way the girl had gone.

Shrugging, Kim said, "We have lost her trail, Heavenborn. Maybe another day we will have better luck."

Noel started to suggest they question one of the Tong hatchet men, but then he heard a siren approaching, and said, "We had better get out of the alley before the police arrive, Kim. I have a suspicion they may want to talk to us about this."

"You are wise, Heavenborn," he smiled. "I think the police approach from this end, perhaps we should leave by the opposite end?"

They were gone by the time the Chinatown police squad found the bodies in the alley.

After replenishing the kitchen supply, they returned to Noel's house on Pell Street. They found the house undisturbed. Noel retired to his China Room while Kim prepared tea and rice cakes.

As they relaxed and watched the clocks again sound the hour, Noel said, "You fought well today, Kim. Unfortunately, I was too busy to see you in action." Grinning, he continued, "You must tell me how you were able to defeat nine hatchet men. I was hard pressed with three!"

"It was nothing, Heavenborn," Kim shrugged. "Chinese Tongs rely on their weapons of choice. One merely takes away their weapon, and they are defenseless."

"They are also trained in ta chuen, Kim," Noel told him. "I've had occasion to fight them in hand-to-hand combat, and they are darn tough."

Shrugging, the Korean merely smiled. "I must let nothing stand in my way in retrieving the Korya vases."

Noel nodded, "Count on me, Kim. If I can be of help, I will stand by you."

"You are a good man, Dorus Noel." Noel did not notice the Korean had called him by name, instead of Heavenborn.

The ringing of the telephone interrupted their discourse. Kim looked at Noel questioningly, and he nodded for the Korean to answer the instrument.

A moment later....

"A young lady, Heavenborn," Kim said. "She speaks English, but I believe she is Chinese."

A curious expression crossed Noel's face for a second, and then he reached for the phone:

"Dorus Noel," he said over the instrument.

"Listen closely, Dorus Noel, there is a little park at the end of Mott Street. At the statue of the Eternal Dragon, meet me there after dark. Do not bring the Korean assassin."

"Wait!" Noel started, but the phone clicked on the other end before he could say more.

"You look perplexed, Heavenborn," Kim told him.

"Was the call important?"

"It was our elusive lady in white, Kim. The White Wasp wishes to meet with me tonight. Alone," he said. "I wonder what this could mean?"

"A bit of cheese, perhaps?" the Korean warned. "It would be foolish for you to do as she bids, Heavenborn. I will accompany you!"

"No, Kim," he shook his head. "If she sees you, the lovely lady will disappear again. This may be our chance to discover the whereabouts of Chu Chul."

"I will not be seen, Heavenborn," Kim insisted. "I am oriental, and we have ways of becoming invisible when necessary."

"I won't permit it, Kim. You must remain here, but be alert," he warned, "this may simply be a ruse to leave you alone and vulnerable. I am tired of losing my houseboys!"

"As you wish, Heavenborn," the Korean shrugged. But there was something in his eyes that bothered Noel.

Chapter Three
The Black Shadow

As darkness descended on Chinatown like an ebony blanket, Dorus Noel departed his house on Pell Street, traveling alone. He looked deeply into the dark shadows along the storefronts and alleys, but saw no hidden lurkers. However, he knew that Kim was correct the oriental could become invisible when they desired. He walked up Mott Street at a brisk pace, but always on the alert for a knife or hatchet from a darkened recess along the street. There were few Chinese about tonight, and those who approached quickly crossed the street, as if to avoid some unknown menace. White men were not uncommon in Chinatown at this hour, for there were many pleasures awaiting them behind curtained portals, but only shopkeepers preparing to lock their doors paid any attention to him as he passed.

He felt eyes on his back, but was unable to detect any followers, or see furtive movements in the shadows. He put the odd feeling down as a case of nerves. Nevertheless, he kept a weary eye out for attack. Too many years in village back streets of China had taught him well the craftiness of the Chinese.

He stood in the shadows of a shop entrance for several minutes, trying to penetrate the ebony darkness of the tree-lined park with his eyes, but the flickering of gaslights along the street prevented his vision from discerning objects clearly. Finally, with a fatalistic sigh he crossed the street and entered the park, there he strolled along a narrow walkway that meandered through brush and small trees, and knew that this was an ideal place for assassination. Yet, he was not accosted, and soon came upon the stone statue.

Stopping as if to admire the statue, Dorus Noel read the Chinese writing easily. It was the history of the Eternal Dragon for which the park had been built. Although he appeared to be staring at the moonlit writing on the stone, his eyes were really darting about the area, watching for the slightest hint of betrayal. What could be Ghi's motive behind this meeting in the park at night? He couldn't help but be suspicious, yet something within him wanted this clandestine rendezvous, no matter the danger.

A flash of white caught his attention as it came from behind the stone statue, and a tiny voice began, "Doris Noel, it was not my...."

It was The White Wasp, and before she could finish her words, the darkness around him erupted with bodies. Evidently, men had been lying on the ground until now, and the appearance of Ghi was the order to attack. Noel knew the girl was extremely dangerous, but his immediate threat was the rushing forms that were almost upon him. That they were Chinese, there was no doubt. He recognized the Mandarin words spoken in low whispers.

Then it was almost as it they had struck an impregnable wall, as bodies began to fall and bounce about like crazy puppets on a string. Something as dark as the night itself appeared to be moving among the mass of attackers, but Noel could only see the blur of a black shadow that moved like a living cyclone, toppling trees in its path; in this case, the trees were living men, and they could not stand against the whirlwind that had come from nowhere to topple them.

His confusion passing quickly, Noel turned once more to confront the girl, but all he saw was a white wraith disappearing in the distance. Ghi had departed with the sudden destruction of the attackers from the darkness.

Peering back at the weird scene of battle, Dorus Noel no longer saw movement, and the black shadow was gone like the evaporation of a fog. What ever the shadow had been, it was fast and deadly. Nor had Noel heard the thing speak a word. It was merely a silent wraith that came from nowhere, struck swiftly, and then departed again with the night breeze. He went forward cautiously, and kneeled by the first prone figure he came to. Shining an electric torch at the face staring up from the ground with sightless eyes, Noel saw the white flower in a buttonhole, and nodded.

"The Society of The White Lily," he surmised. "Another Tong, and their appearance here tonight was not by accident. They were expecting me—or someone!"

The man was dead; his head twisted at an odd angle, and Noel quickly examined several others, finding that some unseen hand had killed each of them. But if the black shadow had been after the Tong, who had they been after? He couldn't be sure if he was the target of the Tong, or perhaps they were after The White Wasp. True, they had not attacked until the girl appeared. But how had they known of the rendezvous in the park, unless she revealed the information to them?

And had the black shadow been there to protect Ghi or himself? Was there only one killer, or several? It was dark, and the shadow had been a blur. There might have been more, but he wasn't sure.

"Kim?" he thought aloud. With the Korean in mind, Noel left the park. He had to get back to his house. If killers were about, they might also have targeted his new houseboy while he was away.

Noel's running footsteps pounded the sidewalks as he rushed home, and he didn't bother glancing into dark alleys or crannies this time, but sped past darkened shops and hidden entryways with little thought of danger to himself.

Arriving at his house, he burst through the door, expecting to find the worst, but was surprised to meet Kim coming from the kitchen with tea and rice cakes.

"Ah, Heavenborn returns early," Kim bowed. "Perhaps the lady did not show up, is that so?"

Sinking into his comfortable chair, Noel only now began to relax. His nerves were on edge, and his breath coming in quick gasps. When he caught his breath once more, he said, "It was a trap, Kim. The lady did show up, but so did a dozen Tong members. I don't know if they were waiting for me, or following Ghi. I was there ahead of her, but the attack started after she arrived. I don't know what to think,"

"It must have been a glorious battle, Heavenborn," Kim smiled. "You are hardly scratched. You must have killed many of the heathens!"

"They are all dead." Noel acknowledged. "But none by my hand, Kim. They were killed by a black shadow that came out of the darkness like a wraith."

"This is true, Heavenborn?" Kim asked in awe. "Then it is indeed a mystery. Perhaps, the wraith was Ghi's protector. Did you not speak with her about this?"

"No, she was gone by the time it was over. And so was the black shadow. The park was empty except for me, and I rushed home to see about your safety."

"For me, Heavenborn?" the Korean raised his eyebrows. "You should not concern yourself for me, I am merely a houseboy who prepares tea and rice cakes for his master."

The clocks again sounded the hour, and Noel was distracted while Kim disappeared back into the kitchen. There were too many mysteries in this mess, and Dorus wanted to get to the bottom of them before he or his houseboy met with an untimely death. Kim was sure that The Cricket still lived, and the appearance of The White Wasp seemed to confirm it. Why else would Chu Chul's daughter be back in Chinatown, if her father were not alive? The last he had heard from Ghi, she was on a ship, sailing for Paris. What had brought her back to New York, if it wasn't her father?

And what about the Korya Dynasty vases that Kim was searching for, did Chu Chul really have them, and was he planning another attempt at conquering Northern China? Were the vases that powerful? Perhaps their return to Korea could buy The Cricket an army. If that was the case, it had world political stakes, and the would-be emperor would kill all in his path to reach his goal.

The ringing of his telephone brought him out of his reverie. Kim reached it before him, then looked curios as he handed the instrument to his master, "It is her again, Heavenborn."

"Hello," he said over the instrument.

"Dorus Noel," came the soft voice in mandarin that he knew belonged to Ghi. "Beware, my father lives!"

Chapter Four
A Visit From the Police

Later the next afternoon the tinkling of the doorbell announced another visitor. Noel heard the houseboy speaking with someone in English, then a few minutes passed before Kim escorted a white man into the China Room where Dorus was admiring his antiquities from the orient.

Looking up, he was not surprised to see Lt. Marquiss of New York's homicide department following the Korean into the room.

"You don't look too pleased to see me, Noel," the lieutenant said. "I suppose you know why I'm here, then?"

"I'm never surprised to see an officer of the law in Chinatown," Noel grinned, not offering his hand to the detective. "What does bring you to my humble home, may I ask?"

"Can we speak in front of the Chink?" the detective nodded towards Kim.

"My houseboy is not a Chink, officer, and yes, whatever you have to say, you can say in front of him."

"You seem to know everything that goes on in Chinatown, Noel, and it seems we have a little mystery on our hands. Recently, there have been a lot of funny killings, and our Chinatown Squad doesn't know what's going on. They thought maybe you could shed some light on the matter, that's why I'm here."

"Probably nothing for you to be concerned with, Lieutenant," Noel told him. "From what I hear there may be a Tong war. Those things usually work themselves out in a few days, and the problems will cease. Just have the patrols keep an eye on large gatherings."

"Well, I would agree with you, Noel, except for one peculiarity about this mess," he stared at the houseboy intensely for a minute. Then: "In each case so far, just the members of a single Tong were killed."

"All from the same Tong, eh? That is curious, Lieutenant," Noel nodded.

"Well, actually there are two Tongs involved," the lieutenant corrected. "In one, it was the Society of The White Lily. In the second, it was the Hung Hu Tze. In each case, though, the killings only involved one particular Tong."

"Ah, I see," Noel nodded. "That is easily explained, Marquiss. The Hung Hu Tze ambushed the Society of The White Lily, and later The White Lily Tong ambushed their enemy in retaliation. That will probably end the whole affair."

"Humph," Marquiss growled. "You make it sound simple, Noel, but nothing is ever simple in Chinatown and you know it.

"By the way, my boys are hearing another rumor on the streets, something that should interest you. Word on the street is that Chu Chul is back, and he's gunning for you. Have you heard these rumors perhaps?"

"I don't pay attention to rumors, Lieutenant. I've been threatened before, and as you can see, I'm still here.

"Will that be all, Marquiss? I am a bit tired you know," Noel smiled. "Maybe we can continue this discussion another time." Nodding to Kim, he continued, "Show the gentleman out, please."

Lieutenant Marquiss growled something under his breath, but turned with Kim and left the room. Noel hated to treat the officer that way, he was sure the lieutenant suspected him of actually being an undercover cop. But he also figured there must have been orders come down from above that Dorus Noel was to be left alone.

He was considering a quick call to his mysterious boss to complain about the homicide detective when Kim returned.

"Police man suspicious, Heavenborn?" he asked.

"Perhaps, Kim," he said. "But we needn't worry. The officer will not interfere with us. However, we must discover the hidden lair of The Cricket if we are going to get your precious vases back. And that might not be so easy for a white man in Chinatown."

"But not for Kim?" the Korean smiled. "When darkness settles over Chinatown, I will seek out the abode of Chu Chul."

"Yes," Noel nodded, "I was thinking the same thing, Kim. But if you do this, I must demand that you return here with the information, and we will go together. Do not attempt to invade The Cricket's den alone. I know him better than you."

"As you wish, Heavenborn," Kim bowed.

"It will be a while yet before darkness, Kim, how about some bird's nest soup and rice cakes. At least we can die on a full stomach tonight."

Kim rushed off to the kitchen to prepare the Chinese soup and rice cakes. Soon he returned with two bowls and a platter filled with cakes. Setting them on a small table before Noel, he returned to the kitchen for tea. Then, without asking, he sat in a wicker chair opposite his employee.

"Those who are about to die should at least die as friends, isn't that true, Heavenborn?"

Smiling at the houseboy, Noel said, "The Chinese people have always been my friends, Kim. Whether Cantonese, Mandarin, or Korean, I consider you not only a friend, but also a brother. If we should die tonight, I could ask for no better companion at my side fighting against Chu Chul."

After their meal, Kim was returning the dishes to the kitchen when the tinkling of the doorbell again sounded.

"I'll get it, Kim," Noel called to the houseboy. At the door he noticed an odd black bundle on a small table near the entrance, but did not stop to examine the object.

Opening the door, he gasped as he peered into the almond-shaped eyes of the beautiful girl in white. He must have been staring for a full moment, as his eyes took in her lovely figure and white face.

"Why do you stare, Dorus Noel?" she asked in a musical voice.

"I was arrested momentarily by your beauty," Noel whispered.

"Please let me enter before I'm seen by my father's spies," she pleaded.

"Chu Chul did not send you to kill me?" he asked. "I suppose not, least you had done the deed while I stood transfixed just now."

Standing aside for her, the girl stepped through the portal to encounter the Korean face to face. For a moment they looked deep into each other's eyes, then Kim smiled. "Shall I prepare more tea for the lady, Heavenborn?"

"No!" Ghi shook her head. "I cannot stay long. I would speak to your master. Alone."

Looking up at Noel, Kim questioned silently, but received a negative shake of the head. He was not to interfere.

"We are not to be disturbed, Kim," he told the

houseboy.

"Very well, Heavenborn," the Korean bowed.

Leading the girl into the China Room, he seated her in his comfortable chair, and then sat in the wicker chair recently occupied by his houseboy.

"We must talk," Ghi began.

"I agree." Noel said. "Where is your father?"

"I cannot tell you that, Dorus Noel. It would mean your death this time."

"Would my death bother you?" he asked.

She did not answer. Instead Ghi glanced around the room for a moment. "Where is the Korean?"

"Kim is busy in the kitchen," he told her. "We told him we wanted to be alone, remember?'

Nodding as she faced him again, she said, "My father fears the Korean. He is an assassin, sent here to kill him."

"Understand me, Ghi," he said. "As much as I care for you, I would kill your father if the chance presents itself. Why do you serve him?"

"He is my father," she said matter-of-factly.

"Would you kill me also, Dorus Noel?"

"At one time, yes," he admitted. "Now I could not, even if you were to be my assassin."

She seemed to be waiting for more, and then a tear glistened in her eye. Standing, she nodded, "We know each other well, Dorus Noel. In the end, we will do what has to be done. That is our fate. My father waits for you, as do I. Now, if you will excuse me, I must leave before I am spotted at darkness."

Noel escorted the girl to the door. As they reached the portal he noticed the black bundle was now missing, and wondered about it. Ghi was preparing to leave when he caught her by the shoulder gently, turning her around to face him.

"Let me look upon your beauty one more time, Ghi," he told her. "I am told that my death is in the cards tonight. If that is true, I want to remember your face for eternity."

Her hands came up to his face then, and she lightly caressed his cheeks. "Then do not come to my father tonight, Dorus Noel."

Chapter Five
A Death in Chinatown

He watched the girl as she melted into a throng of Chinese merchants on the sidewalk, and then disappeared down the street.

"Kim!" he called, but there was no answer. "Dammit, where did he get off to now, it's too early to search for Chu Chul's lair."

Returning to the China Room, he dialed the number of his boss on Park Avenue. He didn't like using his phone to call the police official, in case someone was listening somewhere along the line. But in this instant, he knew he had to remain close to the house. The phone was answered immediately, "This is Noel," he said.

"Noel, my gosh man I've been on pens and needles. Lieutenant Marquiss tells me Chinatown has become another San Francisco. You're supposed to be preventing this kind of wholesale murder. What's going on?"

"I think I know, sir, but I've got to play the game through. It should be finished tonight, and either I will succeed, or I'll be dead. Double—triple the Chinatown Squad, and have them cover Mott Street and the immediate side streets. Let the people see that your police are covering Chinatown in force. That should keep them off the streets."

"What will you be doing during this time, Noel?"

"I believe I'm working with the San Francisco Chinatown assassin, sir. He's after Chu Chul and the Korya vases that were stolen from his temple. Either we will destroy The Cricket and his minions tonight, or he will kill us. The Tongs are following his orders, and will be guarding him. His daughter warned me that he knows I'm coming, so my invasion will be expected."

"Find his hidden den and phone it in, Noel. I'll have every police unit there in minutes to raid the place."

"That wouldn't work, sir. Chu Chul would disappear again, and we would have to start all over once more. No," Noel said. "I must do it my way. At least maybe I can kill the monster before I die."

Noel hung up the receiver before his boss could order him off the case. He knew police would cover Chinatown within the hour. He hoped they would be close to The Cricket's lair when this went down. But even if they weren't, he would not hesitate in the task ahead of him.

Thirty minutes later, Kim came into the China Room. He was removing strange black garments; a long black cape was swung over his shoulders, and a wide brim black satgat, a conical coolie hat—this latter was kept on his head by a black silk chinstrap.

"I figured as much, Kim," Noel admitted. "You are the black shadow that rescued me from the Tong. But why the disguise?"

"I am a Buddhist Monk, Heavenborn. It is true what I told you. Five years ago I was a young initiate guarding the temple when Chu Chul took advantage of my youth. As I grew older, I adopted the guise of The Black Shadow and trained extensively for my mission in tracking The Cricket to his lair. When we learned that Chu Chul was offering the Korya vases returned to our government for the price of one hundred thousand men to provide soldiers to wage his war for North China, I felt it my duty to take back the antiquities stolen from my temple, and to save my fellow men from a war to gain an empire for the thief. After all, if any must die, it should be me for my failure five years ago."

"Our chances will be slim, Kim," Noel told him. "I've seen you fight, so I know your ability. But so far we have merely been up against a few Tong members. The Cricket will have his best trained ta chuen warriors closely guarding him. I expect to die tonight, but if I can help you retrieve the ancient vases for your temple, you must take them and leave without me. Don't worry about Chu Chul, I'll kill him myself if I can."

"Ah, what are mere objects when real men stand together as friends prepared to die, Heavenborn? If I do not succeed, then another will surely come for Chu Chul. I, too, have prepared to die tonight, should it be my destiny."

"We must first find the lair of Chu Chul, Kim," Noel reminded him.

"I followed The White Wasp when she left, Heavenborn, and the girl led me to the evil one's den. We have but to retrace my footsteps, and rendezvous with our destiny."

"Ghi told me that her father would be waiting for me tonight, Kim, so she likely led you knowingly to her father's house of death."

Shrugging, the Korean said, "So be it. The house is a short ways from Mott Street. It appears empty, but that is deceiving. Curtains covered the windows, but I smelled smoke from an opium pipe within the house."

Picking up his fedora, Noel nodded, then: "We are already late, Kim. I suppose we should oblige them, and walk into whatever trap they have planned for us."

Grinning, the Korean slipped the black garments back on and they headed for the door. "You know, Kim," Noel said. "You made a damn good houseboy!"

"Thank you, Heavenborn. That is a great compliment for one who has dedicated his life as a servant. My temple would be pleased to know this."

The Black Shadow led the way, but the streets were dark and deserted tonight. Noel did not see any sign of police patrols, nor did he see lurkers watching for their approach. Chu Chul knew they were coming already, and did not need spies to watch for them. Their path would be clear until the trap was sprung.

Turning off Mott Street, Kim cautioned, "I have seen no lurkers, Heavenborn, but I think we are seen, nevertheless."

"I am sure of it, Kim," Noel agreed. "Proceed."

The portal was not locked, and Noel softly entered through thick curtains. Within there was a tiny flame of light. A single candle flickered in the center of a large chamber devoid of furniture. Hidden eyes must have only seen the tall white man, for Kim was a mere black shadow among many other dark shadows inside the room.

There were sudden yells as men erupted from behind curtains on every wall, and they were tightening a circle around Noel. They must have been expecting a quick victory, for there was an evil grin on their faces as they closed in for the kill.

A blur of shadow, and out of the corner of his eye Noel saw the Korean leap into the air and his feet shot out, one to right one to the left, and heels crashed into the faces of two of the advancing men while Kim was still airborne. Chu Chul's guards still had not seen the Korean in their midst, and when the shadow landed his arms wrapped around two necks and twisted. There was an audible crack, and two more attackers dropped to the floor, lifeless.

Then The Black Shadow whirled, his cape flaring outwards like the wings of some giant bat, deflecting knife thrusts and hatchet blades now that the ta chuen warriors saw their deadly enemy amongst them.

That was all Dorus Noel had time to see. The first attacker was almost upon him. A quick frontal savate kick, and the toe of Noel's shoe collided with the man's chin, sending him back against another. The American's six-foot frame also had a long arm advantage over the smaller Chinese fighters, and quick hard blows from his fist sent two more reeling away.

But there were fully two-dozen ta chuen guards in the room, and only a half dozen were out of the fight. A larger brute was reaching for him when he saw the girl in white standing by a curtained doorway, and heard Kim say, "Follow her, Heavenborn. I will hold Chu Chul's warriors as long as I can."

Dorus Noel threw a hard right and left combination and the Chinese brute walked into a solid fist that sent him crashing to the floor. Noel leapt over his prostate form and rushed after the girl who was disappearing through the curtains.

As soon as the drapes closed behind him, Noel knew he had made a fatal mistake. Here was the trap awaiting him. This was what The Cricket had planned all along should he evade his ta chuen guards and reach this chamber.

A thick fish net dropped over him from above, and weights at the bottom whirled about his legs in a way as to trap him securely. Unable to move, it would take precious minutes to extricate himself from the contraption.

Ghi approached from the side and reached a hand up to his face behind the netting, "I knew you would insist on coming, even after my warning. My French family have a saying, 'What will be will be'. So I knew what must be must be, Dorus Noel."

Nodding his head in a fatalistic motion, Noel said, "Then let me look upon your loveliness as I die, Ghi, so I will remember your beauty throughout eternity. I have loved you from the first time I laid eyes on you, even then knowing you were the daughter of Chu Chul."

A tear sparkled in Ghi's eyes, then a voice sounded from the other side of the room, "Very touching, Dorus Noel. Your declaration of love for my daughter is the height of arrogance. I will choose a husband for her. As for you, well look at the vat at my feet, it holds acid that will eat your body like the fire did mine. But for you there will be no return from the grave!"

The man standing before him was wearing an emperor's robe, emblazoned with the imperial yellow of a king. The material was decorated with the five-toed dragon emblem. Columns upheld the roof, and around them wound the folds of five-toed dragons done in gold. He knew it was Chu Chul, even covered by the white facemask. Small enough to be Cantonese, his skin was yellow and pitted with smallpox scars. His black eyes behind the mask seemed to have no pupils. His hands were long, like claws. He walked in a stoop, a twisted caricature of a man. Noel remembered him from the past.

The ugly vat at The Cricket's feet emitted a sickly

odor that Noel recognized as a virulent acid and shuddered.

Noel heard a scream of pain in the outer room, and wondered if it had been that of Kim finally succumbing to a superior force. Well, we expected death! He thought.

The Cricket reached up and removed the white mask, and Noel was shocked at the damage the fire had done to his face so long ago. Great surgeons must have attempted to reconstruct his face, but it had been a failure in the end. He might rule China as a king, but it would be from behind a mask.

From within the folds of his royal robes, Chu Chul withdrew an American revolver of small caliber and aimed it at Noel. "I wanted you to see my face as you died, Dorus Noel, so you will remember it for eternity, not that of my daughter's.

"I have been in contact with the Koreans, and they have offered me a hundred thousand fighting men for the return of the Korya vases. My plans are ready. I only delayed them until I could kill the man responsible for my infirmary—Dorus Noel!"

Raising the pistol he took careful aim, but there was a swift movement from Noel's side, and a tiny white object fluttered in the air for a second, then Chu Chul exclaimed in pain as the gun dropped from his hand. As the would-be emperor pulled something from his wrist, Noel saw that it was a tiny dart with fluffy white feathers.

Shock appeared in Chu Chul's eyes as he stared at Ghi. "The White Wasp death!" he gasped. "My own daughter would betray me?"

"I have honored you all my life, Father, as I was taught. Even as I watched you kill my mother so slowly over the years. No, you didn't kill her with your hands, but with your lack of love. The same lack of love you have shown me all my life. And now you threaten to take someone else I love, and who has just now told me he loves me. My honor has ended Father. I prefer to die with Dorus Noel, if that be our fate."

Noel watched the agony on the face of Chu Chul as Ghi removed the net from him, and saw his eyes bulge outwards while his tongue began to swell in his mouth. The evil genius was beginning to convulse. It was then he saw the evil old man fall face forward into the vat of acid.

The girl never looked back to see what was happening with her father.

With the net removed, Noel took her in his arms, and their lips met in a sweet embrace both had longed for since first meeting.

"I am a priest, Heavenborn," came a familiar voice from behind them. "Perhaps I might perform a wedding before leaving New York? But perhaps, this is neither the place or the time."

"Kim!" Noel shouted as he turned. "I was afraid you were dead."

Shrugging, The Black Shadow said, "They were merely ta chuen, Heavenborn. I am a Buddhist Monk."

"Then our return path is safe, Kim?" he asked.

Nodding, the Korean led the way into the outer passage. In the chamber were many bodies scattered about, lying lifeless.

"But you haven't found the Korya vases, Kim," Noel ejaculated. "We must search for them before we leave!"

"No need, Heavenborn," Kim said. After I see you and Ghi safely to the street, I will return for them. That one," and he pointed to a man who looked to have died in great pain, "told me where they were hidden before he died."

Noel remembered the cry of pain he had heard from this room a few minutes ago, and shivered at the thought of what Kim had done to the man to make him reveal the secret.

Once outside, Noel told the Korean, "We will wait for you at the house Kim, and I will serve tea and rice cakes to both my guests tonight!'

Epilogue

When Kim returned to the house at the intersection

of Pell and Mott Streets, he found Ghi and Noel sitting beside each other in the China Room, and as Dorus had promised, tea and rice cakes were on a tray. Apparently, they had been awaiting his arrival.

The Korean was carrying something wrapped in the black cape, which he placed gently on a pillow. "The Korya vases," he smiled.

"Kim, I'm going to miss you," Noel said. "You are the first houseboy who has survived in my employ. I would ask you to stay, but as it happens I may be leaving soon myself."

"Yes," Ghi smiled. "I have assured Dorus Noel that I have a private villa on the outskirts of Paris with only Chinese servants."

"I will still be in my beloved China, with the only woman I have ever truly loved," Noel smiled. "But how will you return to your country, Kim?"

"I will return to San Francisco by train from New York, and then book passage on a ship to Korea. It is a long journey, and one filled with much danger for a poor temple monk. I understand there are many American gangsters between New York and San Francisco that may want these vases. And should I make it to San Francisco, there is still the trip by ship, where I may be faced by pirates. Who knows, the most dangerous part of my job may still be ahead of me!"

Laughing, Noel said, "Somehow I don't envision many problems on your journey home, Kim. After all, The Black Shadow accompanies you."

"What will you do with these clocks, and your antiquities, Heavenborn?" the Korean asked, as he pointed about the room at the many valuable items displayed for their pleasure.

"Tomorrow, I will speak with the old clock maker. I understand that he is also a collector of antiquities and is very rich. Perhaps I may interest him in these worthless trinkets. I have the only treasure I will ever need now.

"By the way, the first thing I'm going to buy you, Ghi," he said, "is a blue dress. I've never seen you in anything but white, and I think you will be just as beautiful in blue."

"But white is my favorite color, Dorus Noel. My servants in France know me as The White Wasp. Blue might go against my authority over them."

"Let's not mention The White Wasp, my dear," he grinned. "I do hope you've destroyed those little darts of yours?"

Seeing a sudden tear come to her eye, he changed the subject quickly afraid she was remembering it was she that killed her father.

"Kim, it might be a good idea for us to say goodbye now, before the police arrive. They are sure to come here once they discover the house of Chu Chul and the bodies of the ta chuen warriors. My boss will expect to see my body also."

"Heavenborn could always disappear as well," Kim suggested. "The vat of acid might as easily hold two bodies as one. The police might believe you and Chu Chul fought, and both fell into the vat. Nothing would be left of either of you."

"No, I think not, Kim," he shook his head in the negative. "I owe it to my boss to explain my plans. He can't keep me here, and I owe him nothing. I settled in Chinatown to be among my real people, the Chinese. Once China gets in a white man's blood, he can never get the orient out of his system. I may be going to Paris, but I will be living among my people."

Bowing, the Korean picked up the vases and with a final smile left the China Room, and the house of Dorus Noel.

The Black Shadow was gone. ♦

A Look Back

By Ginger Johnson

Tom retired from the military in 1979. We moved back to Texas and started looking for a way to supplement our retirement checks each month. In 1980, after working at several jobs that did not suit us, we applied for a job managing a liquor store in Knox City, TX. Although, this job was not what we wanted or liked, it paid well, and we had some free time to devote to our hobby of collecting and researching Pulps.

We worked out of the house putting *Echoes* together and did all the editing and what typing that needed to be done on a manual typewriter, plus the paste-ups, reduction, copying, collating, folding, stapling and packaging and mailing every magazine that was sold.

In 1983 we moved back to Seymour, TX, where we were both from, and devoted our full time to the magazine. At the time we had about 250 subscribers, plus we were selling distributing copies to Robert Weinberg and to a fellow in England.

In 1995 we started to try the fiction magazines and came out with *Classic Pulp Fiction Stories*. About this time, Tom advertised in a major publication seeking manuscripts of short stories that we might use in this mag. Then he had the nerve to have an attack of sugar diabetes and was hospitalized for ten days, so they could get his blood count down and under control. Meanwhile, I'm sitting at home being bombarded with stories from all over the world and had to type each one on a manual typewriter, not to mention reading them first.

I was to visit Tom one day (the hospital was 60 miles away) and I decided to get his help in reading the manuscripts, so I took him a little more than half of the ones I had gotten so far.

After he was in hospital for ten days, he was released and when I picked him up I made a suggestion to him. "I am going to stop at this store I noticed and order something before returning home."

He said, "What are you going to order?"

I replied, "I am going to order a computer!"

The evolution of our fiction mags was manual typewriter, electric typewriter, word processor, and finally a computer! Then we had to learn the thing. I hired a tutor to help me and then taught Tom some of the workings of the thing. But boy, did the thing help! I had to learn how to open floppy discs, and get the stories off them that our writers had started to use. This saved tons of typing though, but didn't help with the editing, except the spelling. The grammar and proper phrasing of the sentence was left to us.

We had a lot of mistakes even after the computer, though. It was a learning process throughout the life of all the mags. But looking back, it was a project of love. We enjoyed putting all the mags together until that day that we had to stop publishing, and mailed out the last issues.

We printed some stories from some well-known authors, like James Reasoner, Will Murray, Clayton and Patricia Matthews, and C.J. Henderson. Plus, many new authors who went on to professional writing like Michael A. Black, Barbara Custer, and others. There were too many to recall.

Also, we had many artists that were both professional and newcomers. Ron Wilber, Kevin Duncan, Jeff Fraker, David Burton, Francis St. Martin, Franklyn Hamilton, Bobb Cotter, David Transue, Ray Capella, and many others.

Anyway, here is the list of the mags and their dates of publications:

- *Echoes*, 176 issues (June 1982–December 2004)
- *Behind the Mask*, 71 issues (May 1989-Winter 2005)
- *Classic Pulp Fiction Tales*, 91 issues (June 1995-December 2002)
- *Weird Stories*, 26 issues (October 1996-November 1998)
- *Double Danger Tales*, 63 issues (February 1997-June 2003)
- *Startling Stories*, 32 issues (August 1997-March 2000)
- *Detective Mystery Stories*, 55 issues (December 1998-December 2004)
- *Exciting UFO Stories*, 6 issues (February 1999-December 1999)
- *Alien Worlds*, 39 issues (April 2000-June 2003)
- *Action Adventure Stories*, 145 issues (?-January 2005)

Fading Shadows Back Issues for Sale

The following back issues of *Echoes* are still available at $6.50 each, postage paid (US). If interested, contact Tom or Ginger Johnson at fadingshadows40@gmail.com

Echoes #1, 2, 3, 4, 5, 6, 7, 8, 9, 21, 22, 25, 27, 28, 29, 30, 31, 32, 33, 34, 35, 36, 37, 38, 39, 40, 41, 42, 43, 44, 45, 46, 47, 48, 49, 51, 53, 55, 76 & 99.

Following is a listing of reprints in *Action Adventure Stories* published by Fading Shadows. Issues are $6.50 each, postage paid (US). Those numbers that are out of stock are so indicated. For information on ordering contact Tom or Ginger Johnson at fadingshadows40@gmail.com

#1: "The Torch of Doom" (Phantom Detective, February 1937)

#2: Phantom Detective Comics & "Hot Money" (Dan Fowler, December 1935)

#3: "The Spectral Strangler" (Secret Agent "X," February 1934)

#4: "The Case of the Laughing Corpse" (The Ghost, Fall 1940)

#5: "Decks of Death" (Alias Mr. Death, Thrilling Detective, May 1939) & "Death Over Verdun" (The Lone Eagle, April 1934)

#6: "The Fifth Column Murders" (Masked Detective, Winter 1942)

#7: Mark Hazzard trilogy: "Coffins for Two" (Secret Agent "X," August 1935), "The Murder Crypt" (Secret Agent "X," November 1935), and "Terror Tribunal" (Secret Agent "X," December 1935)

#8: "Empire of Terror" (Phantom Detective, October 1936) *Out of Stock*

#9: "Big Shot" (Dan Fowler, February 1936) *Out of Stock*

#10: "Ambassador of Doom (Secret Agent "X," May 1934) *Out of Stock*

#11: "The Blue Ghost" (Detective Fiction Weekly, February 3-March 3, 1940) *Out of Stock*

#12: "Blue Ghost Beware (Detective Fiction Weekly, November 16-December 14, 1940)

#13: "The Case of the Flaming Fist" (The Green Ghost, Winter 1941)

#14: "The Laughing Death Patrol" (The Lone Eagle, November 1934) *Out of Stock*

#15: "The Crimes of Stilicho" (The Masked Detective, Spring 1942) *Out of Stock*

#16: "Harvest of Death" (Phantom Detective, May 1937) & "The Case of the Luckless Gambler" (Thrilling Comics) *Out of Stock*

#17: "The Crazy Indian" (Mammoth Adventure, November 1946) & "Sting of the Scorpion" (Secret Agent "X," May 1934) *Out of Stock*

#18: "American Menace" (Dan Fowler, August 1936) *Out of Stock*

#19: "Talons of Terror" (Secret Agent "X," April 1935 & "Coiffeured to Kill" (Popular Detective, April 1944)

#20: "The Case of the Black Magician" (The Green Ghost, Summer 1941)

#21: "The Lone Wolf Rides" (Texas Rangers, October 1936) *Out of Stock*

#22: "Frontier Guns" (The Rio Kid, December 1939)

#23: "Wings of Disaster" (The Lone Eagle, October 1939) & "The Squadron in Scarlet" (Sky Birds, November 1931) *Out of Stock*

#24: "Juggernaut Justice" (Secret Agent "X," September 1935) & "Homicide Heiress" (Jim Anthony, June 1943) *Out of Stock*

#25: "Death Rides the Blizzard" (Phantom Detective, November 1936) *Out of Stock*

#26: "Give 'Em Hell" (Dan Fowler, January 1937) & "The Blue Lotus" (Mr. Richard Wong, January 1937) *Out of Stock*

#27: "Monarch of Murder" (Secret Agent "X," August 1935) *Out of Stock*

#28: "Gold of the Gestapo" (The Eagle, December 1940), "The Silver Mask Murders" (Detective Novels Magazine, October 1939) & "Mr. Wong Travels East" (Mr. Wong, July 1939) *Out of Stock*

#29: "Wings of the Damned" (The Lone Eagle, February 1935)

#30: "The Days of Death" (Jim Anthony, November 1942) & "The Phantom Juggernaut" (Secret Agent "X," October 1936)

#31: "The Voice of Murder" (Lynn Vickers) Feb 1936

#32: "The Henchmen of Death" (Phantom Detective) Mar 1937 *Out of Stock*

#33: "Brand of the Black Bat" (The Black Bat) Jul 1939

#34: "Murder in Alaska" (Dan Fowler) Jul 1939 & "A Matter of English" (short from G-Men) Jul 1939

#35: "The Fortune Hunters of Chavo" (The Masked Rider) May 1936 *Out of Stock*

#36: "Horror's Handclasp" (Secret Agent "X") Oct 1936 & "Satan's Masquerade" (short from Secret Agent "X") Dec 1935 *Out of Stock*

#37: "Murder Makes News" (short from Detective Novels) Apr 1941 & "The Crimson Mask's Scorpion Trail" (Crimson Mask) Apr 1941

#38: "Murder Between Shifts" (short from Super-Detective) Jan 1943 & "Corpse Court" (short from Secret Agent "X") Oct 1935 *Out of Stock*

#39: "Death Flies High" (The Lone Eagle) Mar 1935 & "Flaming Dawn" (The Lone Eagle) Mar 1935 *Out of Stock*

#40: "Pirates of the Air Mail" (Lynn Vickers) Mar 1936

#41: "Murder at the Circus" (Phantom Detective) May 1939

#42: "King Crime!" (Dan Fowler) Mar 1936

#43: "Badmen of the Cayugas" (The Masked Rider) Feb 1935 *Out of Stock*

#44: "Horde of the Damned" (Secret Agent "X") Oct 1935 & "Publicity for the Corpse" (short from Thrilling Detective) Dec 1944 *Out of Stock*

#45: "Claws of Satan" (Don Diavolo) Oct 1940 & "The Assassin's Shroud" (short from Red Star Mystery) Oct 1940

#46: "Hawks of Doom" (The Lone Eagle) Jul 1935 & "Rider of the Skies" (The Lone Eagle) Jul 1935

#47: "The Key to Murder" (Lynn Vickers) Jun 1936 *Out of Stock*

#48: "Double Stamped Doom" (Phantom Detective) Oct 1937

#49: "Bring 'em Back Dead" (Dan Fowler) Nov 1935

#50: "The Murder Brain" (Secret Agent "X") Apr 1937 & "Design for Destruction" (short from G-Men) Spr 1945 *Out of Stock*

#51: "The White Savage" (Matalaa) Jun 1940 & "The Trail of the Snake" (short from The Masked Rider Western Magazine) Feb 1935

#52: "The Masked Detective's Manhunt" (The Masked Detective) Spr 1941 *Out of Stock*

#53: "Wings of the Beast" (The Lone Eagle) Apr 1939

#54: "Murder in Hollywood" (Lynn Vickers) May 1936

#55: "Murder at the Worlds Fair" (Phantom Detective) Jun 1939

#56: "The Snatch King" (Dan Fowler) Nov 1938

#57: "The Sky Beast of Berlin" (Captain Combat) Apr 1940

#58: "The Murder Brain" (Secret Agent "X") Apr 1937 *Out of Stock*

#59: "The Cruise of the Savage" (Matalaa) Aug 1940 & "The Wolf of Aragon" (short from Thrilling Adventures) Jul 1941

#60: "The League of the Iron Cross" (The Masked Detective) Sum 1941

#61: "War Hawk" (The Lone Eagle) Feb 1937, "Trinidad Pay-Off" (short from Flying Aces) Sep 1934 & "Son of a Gun-Curse" (short from Adventure) Apr 1936

#62: "The Death Skull Murders" (Phantom Detective) May 1936 *Out of Stock*

#63: "Ghost Killer" (Dan Fowler) Sep 1936

#64: "Low Ceiling for Nazi Hell-Hawks" (Captain Combat) Aug 1940

#65: "Satan's Syndicate" (Secret Agent "X") Aug 1937 & "Murder Montage" (short from Detective Novels Magazine) Feb 1943

#66: "Curse of the Living Corpse" (The Masked Detective) Win 1942 *Out of Stock*

#67: "Treasure of the Savage" (Matalaa) Jan 1941 & "Blind Tiger" (short from Red Star Adventures) Jan 1941 *Out of Stock*

#68: "On Wings of Disaster" (Tailspin Tommy) Jan 1937

#69: "No Man's Air" (The Lone Eagle) Sep 1933

#70: "Written in Blood" (Phantom Detective) May 1935 *Out of Stock*

#71: "The Tropic Terror" (Dan Fowler) Oct 1936

#72: "Murder Syndicate" (Jim Anthony) Apr 1941 *Out of Stock*

#73: "The Grim Shadow of Hate" (Phantom Detective) Jun 1941

#74: "Death Before Midnight" (Dan Dunn) Sep 1936

#75: "Murder for Cash" (Dan Fowler) Nov 1939

#76: "The Kiss-and-Kill Murders" (short from Popular Detective) May 1953 & "The Assassins' League" (Secret Agent "X") Oct 1937 *Out of Stock*

#77: "Wings of War" (The Lone Eagle) Oct 1933

#78: "The Man Who Wasn't There" (The Green Lama) Aug 1940 & "The Last Man" (short from Adventure) Jan 1938 *Out of Stock*

#79: "The Crime of Fu Kee Wong" (Phantom Detective) Apr 1933

#80: "Star Trail to Glory" (Captain Future) Spr 1941 *Out of Stock*

#81: "War Cry of Death" (Dan Fowler) Oct 1939

#82: "The Golden Ghoul" (Secret Agent "X") Jul 1935 & "The Murder Stalks the Big Top" (short from Black Book Detective) Spr 1951 *Out of Stock*

#83: "Hell Bent for Glory" (The Lone Eagle) Dec 1933 & "The Voice of War" (short from The Lone Eagle) Dec 1933

#84: "The Case of the Clown Who Laughed" (The Green Lama) Oct 1940 *Out of Stock*

#85: "The Sabotage Murders" (Phantom Detective) Jul 1941

#86: "The Purple Shirts" (Dan Fowler) May 1936

#87: "The Lost World of Time" (Captain Future) Fall 1941

#88: "The Purple Death" (The Lone Eagle) May 1935

#89: "The Case of the Invisible Enemy" (The Green Lama) Dec 1940 & "The Case of the Broken Broom" (The Green Ghost) Fall 1943

#90: "Spawn of Death" (Phantom Detective) Sep 1934 & "Death Polls a Vote" (short from Detective Fiction Weekly) Sep 2 1939

#91: "Bullet Justice" (Dan Fowler) May 1937

#92: "Savage Jeopardy" (Matalaa) Oct 1940

#93: "Face of the Deep" (Captain Future) Win 1943

#94: "The Sky Crusader" (The Lone Eagle) Apr 1935 *Out of Stock*

#95: "The Case of the Fugitive Fingerprints" (The Green Lama) Jun 1941 & "Death Stops the Coal" (Dan Fowler) Win 1944 *Out of Stock*

#96: "The Phantom Comes Through" (Phantom Detective) Jan 1940

#97: "School for Murder" (Dan Fowler) Apr 1936

#98: "The Devil's Drome" (The Lone Eagle) Aug 1939, "The Return of Captain Future" (Captain Future) Jan 1950 & "X, the Phantom Fed" (Sure-Fire Comics) Sep 1940

#99: "X, the Phantom Fed" (Sure-Fire Comics) Jun 1940 & "The Case of the Hollywood Ghost" (The Green Lama) Oct 1941 *Out of Stock*

#100: "The Chain of Death" (Phantom Detective) Mar 1939

#101: "Black Magic" (Dan Fowler) Jul 1936

#102: "Patrol of the Silent Death" (The Lone Eagle) Aug 1940

#103: "The Case of the Vanishing Ships" (The Green Lama) Apr 1941

#104: "The Murder Syndicate" (Phantom Detective) Dec 1938

#105: "The Crimson Crusade" (Dan Fowler) Apr 1939 *Out of Stock*

#106: "Shadow of the Swastika" (The Lone Eagle) Feb 1941

#107: "Death's Head Face" (The Green Lama) Sep 1940

#108: "Cavalcade of Death" (Phantom Detective) Aug 1937

#109: "Master of Madness" (Lynn Vickers) Apr 1936

#110: "The Poison of Power" (Dan Fowler) Feb 1938 & "Chinese Puzzle" (Mr. Richard Wong) Mar 1937

#111: "Anzac Wings" (The Lone Eagle) Sum 1942 & "Ranger Wings" (The Lone Eagle) Spr 1943

#112: "The Case of the Crooked Cane" (The Green Lama) Aug 1941, "Mr. Wong Goes Fishing" (Mr. Richard Wong) Mar 1940 & "Treason in Oil" (Mr. Richard Wong) Mar 1941

#113: "The Crime Castle" (Phantom Detective) Dec 1934

#114: "Death Rampant" (Dan Fowler) Mar 1938 & "Mr. Wong in Panama" (Mr. Richard Wong) Mar 1939

#115: "The Ferrying Command" (The Lone Eagle) Win 1943 & "Exiled Wings" (The Lone Eagle) Feb 1942

#116: "Red Wings for the Blood Battalion" (Captain Combat) Aug 1940

#117: "The Magic Moon" (Captain Future) Win 1944

#118: "The Green Lama" (The Green Lama) Apr 1940 & "The Devil's Ambassador" (short from World Adventurer) Feb 1934

#119: "The Island of Death" (Phantom Detective) Jun 1933

#120: "The Black Caballero" (The Masked Rider) Apr 1934 & "Killer's Canon" (short from The Masked Rider Western Magazine) Apr 1934

#121: "Doom Over Paris" (The Lone Eagle) Jun 1938

#122: "Babies for Sale" (The Green Lama) Jun 1940 & "When England Vanished" (Philip Strange) Nov 1939

#123: "The Staring Killer" (Phantom Detective) Win 1953

#124: "Sapphire Mesa" (The Masked Rider) Aug 1934 & "Ranger's Reckoning" (short from The Masked Rider Western Magazine) Aug 1934

#125: "Wings of Treason" (The Lone Eagle) Aug 1941 & "Six Dead Men" (short from Sky Fighters) Sep 1937

#126: "Warrior's Wings" (The Lone Eagle) Aug 1936 & "Sky-Gun Scorn" (The Griffin) Nov 1939

#127: "Murder Cracks Down" (Phantom Detective) Nov 1935

#128: "High Ramparts" (The Lone Eagle) Dec 1941 & "North Sea Nightmare" (short from Sky Fighters) Jul 1937

#129: "Murder Rides the Skies" (Phantom Detective) Dec 1939

#130: "Champion of Destiny" (The Lone Eagle) Sep 1935, "Zeppelins Vanish" (short from Flying Aces) Sep 1936 & "Flight to Reality" by Robert C. Van Aken (new fiction story)

#131: "Curse of the Crimson Horde" (Secret Agent "X") Sep 1938, "The House of Kaa" (The Cobra) Feb 1934 & "Candidate for Death" (Scarlet Ace) Mar 1933

#132: "Outlaws of the Moccasins" (The Masked Rider) Feb 1936

#133: "Winged Peril" (The Lone Eagle) Oct 1935 & "The Phantom Foe" by Robert C. Van Aken (new fiction story)

#134: "The Medieval Murders" (Phantom Detective) Jul 1942

#135: "Wide Open Town" (The Masked Rider) Jun 1936 & "Jungle Slave" (short from Jungle Stories) Sum 1940

#136: "Hell Over America" (The Lone Eagle) Dec 1940 & "Deadly Disadvantage" by Robert C. Van Aken (new fiction story)

#137: "The Case of the Poison Formula" (Secret Agent "X") Dec 1945 & "Trap of the Mongoose" (The Mongoose) May 27 1933

138: "Brand of the Quanahy Clan" (The Masked Rider) Mar 1936

#139: "Sky Patrol" (The Lone Eagle) Apr 1937 & "The Doom Club" (Captain Death) Win 1937

#140: "Death in the Desert" (Phantom Detective) Jun 1943

#141: "Hollywood Czar" (Dan Fowler) Jun 1936

#142: "The Front Page Murders" (Phantom Detective) Jun 1938

#143: "The Valley of the Crucifixion" (The Masked Rider) Jan 1936 & "Bad Brand" (short from The Masked Rider Western Magazine) Jan 1936

#144: "Merchant of Murder" (Phantom Detective) Oct 1934 *Out of Stock*

#145: "Death Rides the Winner" (Phantom Detective) Aug 1946

The following issues of *Behind the Mask* are available at $6.50 each, postage paid (U.S.) If interested, contact Tom or Ginger Johnson at fadingshadows40@gmail.com

#47, Winter 1999: "Murder Never Dies" (Candid Camera Kid) Detective Novels Magazine, Oct 1942 & "Many Men Die" (Thrilling Detective) Oct 1935

#48, Spring 1999: "The Hills of Gold" (Thunder Jim Wade) Thrilling Adventures, Jun 1941, "Kwa, King of Ophir" (Kwa) Thrilling Adventures, Feb 1933 & "Death in Cupid's Alley" (Big-Book Detective Magazine) Jun 1942 *Out of Stock*

#49, Summer 1999: "Picture of a Ghost" (Candid Camera Kid) Detective Novels Magazine, Jun 1942, "Storm Over the Americas" (The Eagle) Thrilling Spy Stories, Fall 1939

#50, Fall 1999: "Cauldron of Death" (Jim Anthony) Super-Detective, Feb 1943 & "The Death-Chair Challenge" (Mark Hazzard) Secret Agent "X." Jan 1936

#51, Winter 2000: "Phantom Evidence" (Candid Camera Kid) Detective Novels Magazine, Mar 1944, "The Poison People" (Thunder Jim Wade) Thrilling Adventures, Jul 1941 & "Murder Is Easy" G-Men Detective, Jul 1947

#52, Spring 2000: "The Doomed Five" (Candid Camera Kid) Detective Novels Magazine, Oct 1941, "The Crimson Mask's Ghost Trail" (The Crimson Mask) Detective Novels Magazine, Aug 1941 & "Bike Bull" Oct 15, 1934

#53, Summer 2000: "Murder in Pictures" (Candid Camera Kid) Detective Novels Magazine, Jun 1939, "Four Men of Murder" (The Crimson Mask) Detective Novels Magazine, Dec 1942, "Clown of Doom" (Ed Rice) Popular Detective, Jun 1945 & "Hooks McGuire Scores Again" (Hooks McGuire) Dec 15, 1937

#54, Fall 2000: "The Candid Camera Murders" (Candid Camera Kid) Detective Novels Magazine) Aug 1939, "The Red Sword" (Red Sword) Popular Detective, Feb 1945 & "Negatives of Guilt" (Johnny Wells) Thrilling Detective, Nov 1944

#55, Winter 2001: "The Phantom Murders" Thrilling Detective, Apr 1932 & "Camera Trap" (Candid Camera Kid) Detective Novels Magazine, Feb 1942

#56, Spring 2001: "The Murder Master" Thrilling Detective, Apr 1934 & "Appointment With Murder" (Candid Camera Kid) Detective Novels Magazine, Feb 1944

#57, Summer 2001: "Murder in the Sky" (Johnny Wells) Thrilling Detective, Mar 1945, "The Lady's Out for Blood" (Myro Catin) Triple Detective, Spr 1953 & "Motto for Murder" (Detective Rufe Reed) Popular Detective, Jun 1945 *Out of Stock*

#58, Fall 2001: "Death from Damascus" (Celluloid Burglar) Detective Novels Magazine, Apr 1938 & "Picture of a Killer" (Candid Camera Kid) Detective Novels Magazine, Apr 1940

#59, Winter 2002 : "The Crimson Mask's Murder Trial" (The Crimson Mask) Detective Novels Magazine, Oct 1940 & "Death at the Worlds Fair" (Candid Camera Kid) Detective Novels Magazine, Oct 1940

#60, Spring 2002: "Gems of Disaster" (Candid Camera Kid) Detective Novels Magazine, Oct 1943, "The Bat Strikes" (The Bat) Popular Detective, Nov 1934 & "Death Comes in Black" Detective Novels Magazine, Mar 1948

#61, Summer 2002: "Blood Cargo" (Dr. Zeng) Popular Detective, Jun 1942, "The Brass Brain" Ten Detective Aces, Apr 1936 & "The House on Gay Street" All Detective Magazine, Feb 1933

#62, Fall 2002: "Murder Bride" (Wade Hammond) Ten Detective Aces, Aug 1936, "Suicide Lottery" (Paul Kirk) Ten Detective Aces, Apr 1936, "Dragnet Dynamite" (Captain John Murdock) Ten Detective Aces, Aug 1936, "The Scarlet Ace" (Major Lacy) All Detective Magazine, Feb 1933 & "A Stir-Bug's Bite" Ten Detective Aces, Aug 1936

#63, Winter 2003: "Vengeance of Vindex" (Vindex) Detective Fiction Weekly, Dec 29, 1934, "The Voice from Nowhere" (The Mongoose) Detective Fiction Weekly, Apr 23, 1932 & "Killer's Club Car" (Marty Quade) Ten Detective Aces, Aug 1936

#64, Spring 2003: "Mask of Vindex" (Vindex) Detective Fiction Weekly, Aug 31, 1935, "The Creeps" Black Mask, May 1945 & "The Seventh Griffin" (The Griffin) Detective Fiction Weekly, Oct 5, 1935

#65, Summer 2003: "Kwa of the Jungle" (Kwa) Thrilling Adventures, Aug 1932 & "Fangs of the Jungle" World Adventurer, Feb 1934

#66, Fall 2003: "The Hornet and the Vulture" (The Hornet) World Adventurer, Feb 1934, "The Hawk and the Yellow Dragon" (The Hawk) Top-Notch, Mar 1, 1932, "The Hawk's Double" (The Hawk) Top-Notch, Apr 15 1930, "Dice of Death" (Captain John Murdock) Ten Detective Aces, Apr 1936 & "Fall Guy" Federal Agent, Aug 1936

#67, Winter 2004: "Sword of Gimshai" Jungle Stories, Spr 1954, "Madman's Trek" Jungle Stories, Spr 1954, "The Fangs of Umkulu" Jungle Stories, Spr 1950 & "The Crocodiles' Saint" (Commissioner Sanders) Jungle Stories, Spr 1954

#68, Spring 2004: "Focus on Murder" (Candid Camera Kid) Detective Novels Magazine, Jun 1940, "The Blue Ghost Patrol" Flying Aces, Oct 1932, "The Hour Appointed" (The Griffin) Detective Fiction Weekly, Jan 3 1931 & "Taxi to Trouble" Detective Fiction Weekly, Dec 22, 1934

#69, Summer 2004: "Ki-Gor and the Cannibal Kingdom" (Ki-Gor) Jungle Stories, Sum 1940, "Elephant Law" Short Stories, Jun 25, 1935 & "Tomorrow" Argosy, May 27 1939

#70, Fall 2004: "Day of Doom" (The Griffin) Detective Fiction Weekly, Nov 19 1932, "Guns of the Griffon" (The Griffon) Flying Aces, Jun 1935, "Death Has Its Fling" (The Griffin) Detective Fiction Weekly, Dec 16, 1933, "Cavalry of the Clouds" (The Griffon) Flying Aces, Mar 1935 & "The Dust of Destiny" (The Griffin) Detective Fiction Weekly, Jul 30, 1932

#71, Winter 2005: "The Necklace of the Empress" Detective Fiction Weekly, Nov 10, 1934, "Profit for the Mongoose" (The Mongoose) Detective Fiction Weekly, Feb 25, 1933, "The Mongoose Strikes Again" (The Mongoose) Detective Fiction Weekly, May 7, 1932 & "Smoke of Vengeance" (The Mongoose) Detective Fiction Weekly, Sep 3, 1932

13512764R00169

Printed in Great Britain
by Amazon.co.uk, Ltd.,
Marston Gate.